Organizational Listening for Strategic Communication

Embracing listening as a useful tool for strengthening organization-publics and organization-employee relationships, this book offers theoretical and practical insights into listening across myriad strategic communication contexts.

Chapters authored by a diverse global collective of communication scholars and professionals present original research and case examples of listening for strategic communication in corporate, government, and nonprofit environments. They explore topics such as utilizing artificial intelligence and social media; activism, social justice, and ethics; and fostering diversity, equity, and inclusion within and outside organizations. Each chapter concludes with recommendations for strategic communication practice.

This book will be of interest to researchers and advanced students in public relations and strategic communication, organizational communication, and listening.

Katie R. Place is Professor of Strategic Communication in the School of Communication at Quinnipiac University, USA. Her research examines power, ethics, and listening in public relations. She has authored more than 60 conference papers or publications in such peer-reviewed journals as the *Journal of Public Relations Research, Public Relations Review*, and *Journal of Media Ethics*.

Routledge Research in Public Relations

Bringing together theories and thought from a variety of perspectives, this series features cutting-edge research addressing all the major issues in public relations today, helping to define and advance the field.

5 **Public Relations and Religion in American History**
   Evangelism, Temperance, and Business
   Margot Opdycke Lamme

6 **Public Relations in the Nonprofit Sector**
   Theory and Practice
   Edited by Richard D. Waters

7 **Public Relations and the Public Interest**
   Jane Johnston

8 **The Moral Compass of Public Relations**
   Edited by Brigitta R. Brunner

9 **Relationship Building in Public Relations**
   Petra Theunissen and Helen Sissons

10 **Advancing Crisis Communication Effectiveness**
   Integrating Public Relations Scholarship with Practice
   Edited by Yan Jin, Bryan H. Reber, and Glen J. Nowak

11 **Internal Communication and Employer Brands**
   Ana Tkalac Verčič, Dejan Verčič, and Anja Špoljarić

12 **Organizational Listening for Strategic Communication: Building Theory and Practice**
   Katie R. Place

For more information about this series, please visit: https://www.routledge.com/Routledge-Research-in-Public-Relations/book-series/RRPR

Organizational Listening for Strategic Communication
Building Theory and Practice

**Edited by
Katie R. Place**

NEW YORK AND LONDON

First published 2023
by Routledge
605 Third Avenue, New York, NY 10158

and by Routledge
4 Park Square, Milton Park, Abingdon, Oxon, OX14 4RN

Routledge is an imprint of the Taylor & Francis Group, an informa business

© 2023 selection and editorial matter, Katie R. Place individual chapters, the contributors

The right of Katie R. Place to be identified as the author of the editorial material, and of the authors for their individual chapters, has been asserted in accordance with sections 77 and 78 of the Copyright, Designs and Patents Act 1988.

All rights reserved. No part of this book may be reprinted or reproduced or utilised in any form or by any electronic, mechanical, or other means, now known or hereafter invented, including photocopying and recording, or in any information storage or retrieval system, without permission in writing from the publishers.

Trademark notice: Product or corporate names may be trademarks or registered trademarks, and are used only for identification and explanation without intent to infringe.

ISBN: 978-1-032-22715-3 (hbk)
ISBN: 978-1-032-22716-0 (pbk)
ISBN: 978-1-003-27385-1 (ebk)

DOI: 10.4324/9781003273851

Typeset in Times New Roman
by KnowledgeWorks Global Ltd.

Contents

List of Contributors viii
Foreword: Setting the Scene xvii
Acknowledgments xxxi

Introduction 1
KATIE R. PLACE

UNIT 1
Organizational Listening Competencies and Technologies 7

1 External Stakeholders' Conceptualizations of Organizational Listening: A Conceptual Replication of the Revised Listening Concepts Inventory 9
DEBRA L. WORTHINGTON AND GRAHAM BODIE

2 Incorporating Competent Interpersonal Listening Practices in Social Media 24
CHRISTOPHER C. GEARHART AND SARAH K. MABEN

3 Developing *Organizational Employee Communication Competency Diagnostics*: Breaking Employee Silence via Organizational Climate of Listening for Dialogic Employee Communication 41
MINJEONG KANG AND BITT MOON

4 The Power of AI-Enabled Chatbots as an Organizational Social Listening Tool 63
ALVIN ZHOU, LINJUAN RITA MEN, AND WAN-HSIU SUNNY TSAI

5 Evaluating Organizational Listening: Models and Methods for Measuring the Value of Listening for Identifying Opportunities, Risks, and Crises   81
SOPHIA CHARLOTTE VOLK

UNIT 2
Organizational Listening for Ethics and Justice   101

6 The State of Ethical Listening to External Stakeholders in US Organizations   103
MARLENE S. NEILL AND SHANNON A. BOWEN

7 Why Are Organizations Criticized for Not Listening? Findings from Practitioners and Stakeholders   121
LISA TAM, SOOJIN KIM, AND HELEN HUTCHINGS

8 Improving Organizational Listening to Build Trust with Black Residents and Disrupt Racism in Local Government   140
ASHLEY E. ENGLISH, JULIE O'NEIL, AND JACQUELINE LAMBIASE

9 Organizational Social Listening and Corporate Climate Advocacy: Amazon and Amazon Employees for Climate Justice   157
IOANA A. COMAN AND ROSALYNN VASQUEZ

UNIT 3
Organizational Listening for Diversity, Equity, and Inclusion   179

10 Organizational Listening for Diversity, Equity, and Inclusion   181
KATIE R. PLACE

11 Listening in Polarized Times: Centering Presence in Arendt's Actualized Plurality for Organizational Listening   199
LUKE CAPIZZO

12 Listening to Historically Marginalized Publics: A Conceptualization of Perceived Organizational Listening in LGBTQ Advocacy   219
HAYOUNG SALLY LIM, E. CISZEK, AND WON-KI MOON

13 Organizational Listening and Empowered Women in the
    Workplace: A Cross-Cultural Comparison between the United
    States and South Korea   232
    YEUNJAI LEE, YO-JUN QUEENIE LI, AND ENZHU DONG

UNIT 4
Cultural and Global Considerations for Organizational
Listening   251

14 The Local and the Global in Organizational Listening Amid
    an Evolving Media Landscape   253
    INGRID BACHMAN AND CLAUDIA LABARCA

15 Listening across Borders: Global Considerations for Listening
    and Public Diplomacy   269
    LEYSAN STORIE AND SARAH MARSCHLICH

    Conclusion: Directions for Future Research of Organizational
    Listening and Strategic Communication   288
    KATIE R. PLACE AND DEBASHISH MUNSHI

    Index   293

Contributors

Ingrid Bachmann (Ph.D., University of Texas at Austin) is Associate Professor in the School of Communications at Pontificia Universidad Católica de Chile, where she served as chair of the Journalism Department between 2016 and 2020. A former reporter, her research focuses on the role of news media in the definition of identities and meanings within the public sphere, and she specializes in the intersections between news narratives, gender, and political communication. Her research appears in *Digital Journalism, Feminist Media Studies, Journalism & Mass Communication Quarterly,* and *International Journal of Public Opinion Research,* among other journals.

Graham D. Bodie (Ph.D., Purdue University) is Professor of Integrated Marketing Communications in the Meek School of Journalism and New Media at the University of Mississippi. His research on listening and the social cognitive underpinnings of human communicative behavior has been published in *Human Communication Research, Communication Monographs, Communication Research, Communication Yearbook,* and the *International Journal of Listening,* among other outlets. Graham's research has been funded by the Louisiana Board of Regents and the National Science Foundation, and he regularly appears in local and national media outlets on issues relevant to listening in close relationships.

Shannon A. Bowen (Ph.D., University of Maryland) is Professor at the University of South Carolina. She specializes in ethics, issues management, and decision models. She is a former editor of *Ethical Space: The International Journal of Communication Ethics* and published more than 100 journal articles, chapters, books, and encyclopedia entries, as well as the *Dictionary of Public Relations Measurement and Research* (3rd ed.). She has won numerous academic awards, such as the *JJ&W Behavioral Science Research Prize*. She served on the Board of Trustees of the Arthur W. Page Society and sits on the Commission on Public Relations Education.

Contributors ix

Luke Capizzo (APR, Ph.D., University of Maryland) is Assistant Professor of Strategic Communication at the Missouri School of Journalism. A public relations researcher, educator, and practitioner, his scholarly interests include social issues management, DEI, dialogue, organizational listening, and the evolution of the PR profession. Broadly, his research examines the potential societal and democratic contributions of organizations through the public relations function. His research has been funded through two Arthur W. Page Legacy Scholar grants (2020, 2022). He serves on the editorial boards of the *Journal of Public Relations Education, Journal of Public Relations Research,* and *Public Relations Review.*

E. Ciszek (Ph.D., University of Oregon) is Associate Professor of Public Relations at the Moody College of Communication at The University of Texas at Austin. Ciszek's research is closely tied to commitments of advocacy and social change. Through rigorous qualitative methods and development of critical theory, Ciszek's research examines the intersections of public relations and social change. Ciszek's research attends to identity and communication, with an attention to strategic communication and historically marginalized and underrepresented communities.

Ioana A. Coman (Ph.D., University of Tennessee) is Assistant Professor at Texas Tech University. Her research examines how audiences make sense of health, risk, crisis, and hot-button issues and messaging and how messages and strategies can become more effective and inclusive. Her research has received national and international recognition, including the *Page/Johnson Legacy Scholar grants* (2019, 2020, 2021, 2022). She coedited the Routledge 2021 book, *Political Communication and COVID-19 Governance and Rhetoric in Times of Crisis* and published in various journals such as *Health Communication, Mass Communication and Society, Vaccine,* and *The International Journal on Press and Politics.*

Enzhu Dong (M.A., New York University) is a doctoral student in the Department of Strategic Communication at the University of Miami. Her research interests focus on internal public relations, leadership communication, corporate social responsibility, and relationship management. She earned her master's degree in public relations and corporate communication at New York University. In addition to conducting research in public relations with quantitative approaches, Dong is also an instructor for the statistical analysis course at the University of Miami.

Ashley E. English (Ph.D., University of North Texas) is Assistant Professor of Strategic Communication at Texas Christian University.

x   *Contributors*

She committed her life to service, and community engagement is the common thread through her professional and personal experiences. Dr. English earned a Ph.D. in Public Administration and Management with specialization in nonprofit management from the University of North Texas. Her current research examines organizational listening in public organizations and the community engagement efforts of megachurches. She has published research in outlets such as *Journalism & Mass Communication Quarterly*, *Nonprofit Management & Leadership*, *Journal of Public Relations Research*, and *Journal of Contingencies and Crisis Management*.

Christopher Gearhart (Ph.D., Louisiana State University) is Associate Professor and Department Head in the Department of Communication Studies at Tarleton State University, where he teaches in the area of professional and relational communication. His research has led to more than 20 published articles and book chapters on a variety of topics including listening, sports, and teaching methods. His work can be found in academic journals such as *Communication Quarterly*, *Communication Reports*, and *International Journal of Listening*. Dr. Gearhart is a graduate of the University of North Texas, San Diego State University, and Louisiana State University. He shares three wonderful sons, Christian, Luke, and Asher, with his wife, Kimberly.

Minjeong Kang (Ph.D., Mass Communication, Syracuse University) is Associate Professor in The Media School at Indiana University, where she teaches public relations and internal communication management courses. Kang's primary research has been centered on understanding engagement in various organizational stakeholder contexts, such as volunteers, employees, consumers, etc. Kang's research has received several national and international recognitions, such as emerald publishing's Literati Award of Excellence for Highly Commended for her 2017 publication in *Journal of Communication Management*, Gallup Korea's Outstanding Research Award for her 2019 publication in *Journal of Public Relations Research*, and 2009 Ketchum Excellence in Public Relations Research Award by Institute of Public Relation for her research proposal on blog credibility.

Soojin Kim (Ph.D., Purdue University) is Senior Lecturer at University of Technology Sydney. Her research explores how publics' cognitive and affective mechanisms explain their behaviors in diverse contexts from consumer-brand relationship, organization-employee relationship, to citizen-government relationship. Before joining UTS, she worked for Singapore Management University as Assistant Professor. Dr. Kim's work has been published in journals such as *Communication Research*, *Public Relations Review*, *International Journal of Communication*, *Journalism and Mass Communication Quarterly*, and *International Journal* *of Strategic Communication*, among others. She received her Ph.D. in Communication from Purdue University in 2014.

Claudia Labarca (Ph.D., Durham University) is Associate Professor in the School of Communications at Pontificia Universidad Católica de Chile, where she teaches undergraduate and graduate courses. She is the author of several articles and book chapters on strategic communication, business trust, and related topics. She is also the author *Ni Hao Mr. Pérez, Buenos Días Mr. Li,* a book on intercultural business communication with China. Her research interests focus on trust building, strategic communication, public diplomacy, and advertising. Currently, she participates in several research groups to study different dimensions on trust formation in corporate and institutional environments.

Jacqueline Lambiase (Ph.D., University of Texas at Arlington) is Professor in the Department of Strategic Communication in the Bob Schieffer College of Communication at Texas Christian University (TCU), where she served as department chair for more than six years. Jacqueline collaborates with other scholars to examine public sector communication and listening, to interrogate the ways advertising uses stereotypes, and to understand the use of sexuality in advertising. Through her work with the public sector, she has consulted for the US Department of Labor and cities across the nation. In 2013, she cofounded and still directs a graduate-level certificate program called the Certified Public Communicator Program™ at TCU.

Yeunjae Lee (Ph.D., Purdue University) is Assistant Professor in the Department of Strategic Communication at University of Miami. She specializes in employee communication, internal issue/crisis management, and organizational diversity and justice. Using public relations theories, Dr. Lee has conducted extensive research on employee behaviors within and outside of work in response to organizational crisis and diversity-related issues. Her work has been published in more than 50 articles in leading refereed journals such as *Communication Monographs*, *Communication Research*, *Journal of Public Relations Research*, *Journalism and Mass Communication Quarterly*, *Journal of Business Research*, and *Public Relations Review*, among others.

Jo-Yun (Queenie) Li (Ph.D., University of South Carolina) is Assistant Professor in the Department of Strategic Communication at the University of Miami. As an interdisciplinary researcher, her work blends public relations and health communication research with a focus on the strategic planning, application, and evaluation of communication campaigns that mobilize publics and facilitate health education, promotion, and social equality. She has published in leading scholarly journals such as *Communication Research*, *Public Relations*

Review, Journal of Health Communication, International Journal of Advertising, and *Journal of Public Relations Research.*

Hayoung Sally Lim (Ph.D., University of Texas at Austin) is Assistant Professor of Cultural Diversity and Brand Responsibility in the School of Journalism and Communication at the University of Oregon. Her research areas include brand activism, brand crisis communication, and consumer behavior and psychology on social media. Lim studies the interaction between brands and consumers on social media in the context of brand activism by examining how brands can deliver their messages more effectively, how consumers would react to it, and how brands listen and respond to consumers in developing their brand responsibility communication.

Sarah Maben (Ph.D., University of North Texas) is Associate Professor in the Department of Communication Studies at Tarleton State University. She teaches graduate and undergraduate courses in social media, public relations, and journalism, on the university's Fort Worth, Texas, campus. She is the founding editor of *The Journal of Social Media in Society*, an open-source peer-reviewed publication. Her research interests include public relations, social media, and ethics, and her scholarship appears in numerous peer-reviewed journals and has garnered top paper awards. Before her academic career, she was the Director of Communication for various associations. @SarahMaben on Twitter

Sarah Marschlich (Ph.D., University of Fribourg) is Assistant Professor of Corporate Communication at the Amsterdam School of Communication Research (ASCoR), University of Amsterdam. Before that, she worked at the Department of Communication and Media Research (IKMZ) at the University of Zurich and the University of Fribourg (Switzerland), where she received her Ph.D. in Social Sciences. In her dissertation, she explored the role of corporate diplomacy communication in gaining corporate legitimacy. In addition, her research focus includes public relations, corporate social responsibility, and organizational reputation, particularly emphasizing the role of news, social media affordances, and gender issues.

Linjuan Rita Men (Ph.D., University of Miami, APR) is Professor of Public Relations in the College of Journalism and Communications at the University of Florida. Men's background is based primarily in corporate communication research and consulting. Her research interests include internal communication, leadership communication, emerging technologies, entrepreneurial communications, and measurement and evaluation. Men has published more than 80 articles in refereed journals and as book chapters. Accredited in public relations, she has worked internationally with Alibaba Group, Inc., Ketchum, Inc., and provided management communication consulting for various multinational corporations, startups, and nonprofit organizations.

Bitt Moon (Ph.D., Indiana University) is Visiting Professor of Integrated Marketing Communications at the School of Journalism and New Media at the University of Mississippi. She received her Ph.D. in Media Arts and Sciences from Indiana University in 2022. Her current research includes reputation management, crisis communication, and internal communication. She has published various peer-reviewed articles in journals, such as *Journalism & Mass Communication Quarterly*, *Journal of Public Relations Research*, and *Public Relations Review*. She worked as a strategic researcher at Fleishman Hillard Korea and served as a member of the communication advisory committee for governmental institutions in Korea.

Won-Ki Moon (Ph.D., University of Texas at Austin) is Assistant Professor of Advertising in the College of Journalism and Communications at the University of Florida. He studies public understanding of science and health by focusing on individuals' information processing and decision-making in the context of strategic communication and consumer behavior. His recent research investigated how communication technology will help organizations enhance the public interest. He leads projects on the application of new media (e.g., artificial intelligence, virtual human, and virtual reality) in developing better social marketing campaigns.

Debashish Munshi (Ph.D., University of Waikato) is Professor in the School of Management and Marketing at the University of Waikato, whose research agenda spans disciplinary boundaries as he seeks answers to difficult societal questions of communication, diversity, sustainability, and social change. Munshi is author or editor of 6 books and over 150 articles, chapters, and research papers. His most recent book Munshi, D. & Kurian, P. (2021) *Public Relations and Sustainable Citizenship: Representing the Unrepresented* (Routledge, London) won the International Communication Association (ICA) PR Division's "Outstanding Scholarly Book Award" in 2022.

Marlene Neill (Ph.D., University of Texas at Austin, APR, Fellow PRSA) is Associate Professor and Graduate Program Director at Baylor University. Her research interests include public relations leadership, internal communication, and ethics. She has published 30 journal articles and coauthored 2 scholarly books on public relations ethics and women in leadership. She received her Ph.D. in advertising from the University of Texas at Austin, her Master of Arts degree in journalism from the University of Missouri at Columbia, and her Bachelor of Science degree in journalism from the University of Kansas. She previously worked for almost 12 years in nonprofit and government public relations.

Julie O'Neil (APR, Ph.D., University of Utah) teaches, researches, and consults in the areas of public relations, measurement and evaluation, and internal communication. She has published and presented more than 90 peer-reviewed journal articles, proceedings, and conference papers on topics ranging from organization-public relationships, nonprofit communication, employee communication, and media source credibility. She is the Associate Dean for Graduate Studies and Administration for the Bob Schieffer College of Communication at Texas Christian University. O'Neil is the Senior Associate Editor of the *Public Relations Journal* and serves as chair of the Institute for Public Relations Measurement Commission.

Katie R. Place (APR, Ph.D., University of Maryland) is Professor in the Department of Strategic Communication at Quinnipiac University whose research examines the nexus of power, ethics, and listening in public relations. She has authored more than 60 conference papers or publications in such peer-reviewed journals as *Journal of Public Relations Research*, *Public Relations Review*, *Journal of Mass Media Ethics*, and *Journal of Communication Management*. She is Past Head of the Public Relations Division of AEJMC and resides on the editorial boards of *Journal of Public Relations Research*, *Journal of Media Ethics*, *Journal of Public Relations Education*, and *Journal of Public Interest Communications*.

Leysan Khakimova Storie (Ph.D., University of Maryland) is Assistant Professor in the Department of Strategic Communication at Lund University, Sweden. Storie's research interests relate to global strategic communication, the role of culture in communication, and women in public diplomacy. Her studies have been published in the *New Media and Society* journal, *International Journal of Press/Politics*, *Journal of Public Relations Research*, *Public Relations Review*, and *International Journal of Strategic Communication*.

Lisa Tam (Ph.D., Purdue University) is Senior Lecturer in Advertising and Public Relations at Queensland University of Technology, Australia. Her research explores the dynamics of power and influence between organizations and publics as well as the roles of public relations practitioners in facilitating such dynamics. As a mixed-methods researcher with expertise in both qualitative and quantitative methods, her research has been applied to multiple research contexts including corporate social responsibility, employee communication, health communication, government relations, hospitality and tourism, issues and crises, and public diplomacy.

Wan-Hsiu Sunny Tsai (Ph.D., University of Texas at Austin) is Professor of Strategic Communication at the University of Miami. Her research has examined minority consumers' relationship with targeted and multicultural advertising, consumer advocacy and political polarization on social media, the interplay between brand globalization and localization, and most recently, the sundry social and ethical issues surrounding artificial intelligence-powered brand communication. Her work has been published in top journals in advertising, public relations, marketing, and communication, and received top research paper awards at major academic conferences.

Rosalynn Vasquez (Ph.D., Texas Tech University) is Assistant Professor of Public Relations in the College of Communication at Boston University. She has 15 years of public relations industry experience in corporate, agency, and nonprofit leadership roles. As a researcher, she primarily focuses on sustainability communications, corporate social advocacy, and DE&I in public relations. She has a Ph.D. in Media and Communications from Texas Tech University, an M.B.A. from the University of Dallas, and a bachelor's degree in journalism from Texas A&M University.

Sophia Charlotte Volk (Ph.D., Leipzig University) is Senior Research and Teaching Associate at the Division of Science Communication at the University of Zurich (Switzerland). Previously, she was a research associate at Leipzig University (Germany). Her research interests are at the intersections of strategic communication, science communication, and digital media environments. Sophia Volk coedited a special issue of the *Journal of Communication Management* on new directions in evaluation and measurement research and coauthored the book *Toolbox Communication Management* (Springer Gabler). Her most recent book, *Comparative Communication Research* (Springer VS), examines the methodological and social challenges of conducting comparative studies in international teams.

Debra Worthington (Ph.D., University of Kansas) is Director of the School of Communication & Journalism at Auburn University and has been an active teacher and communication scholar for over 30 years. Worthington is the lead author of one of the principal textbooks in listening, *Listening: Processes, Functions, and Competency*, and lead editor of *The Sourcebook of Listening Research: Methodology and Measures*. Her research has received multiple top paper, top convention, and top panel awards, among them: the Ralph G. Nichols Listening Award, the Burton Award for Legal Achievement, and the ILA Researcher of the Year Award.

Alvin Zhou (Ph.D., University of Pennsylvania) is Assistant Professor at the Hubbard School of Journalism and Mass Communication at the

University of Minnesota. His research centers around computational social science and strategic communication (advertising, public relations, and organizations). His work has appeared in major academic and popular outlets such as *Journal of Communication, Computers in Human Behavior, Journal of Computer-Mediated Communication,* and *The Washington Post.* He obtained a Ph.D. in Communication from the UPenn Annenberg School, an M.A. in Statistics and Data Science from the Wharton School, and an M.A. in Strategic Public Relations from the USC Annenberg School.

Foreword: Setting the Scene

Jim Macnamara

The editor and chapter authors are to be congratulated for producing this handbook, which offers a seminal contribution to communication studies and applied communication disciplines including corporate, government, organizational, and marketing communication, and public relations.

Eminent philosopher and psychologist John Dewey stated that "society exists in communication" (1916, p. 5), a view echoed by Raymond Williams (1976, p. 10) and many other social scientists. "Chicago School" sociologist and founder of American cultural studies, James Carey (1989), also emphasized the role of communication as the enabler of civilized society and culture. In contemporary literature, CCO theory, variously expressed as *communication constitutes organization* and the *communicative constitution of organizations* (Schoeneborn et al., 2019; Vásquez & Schoeneborn, 2018), specifically recognizes the fundamental role of communication in human organizing generally, and in the establishment and operation of organizations.

However, the term communication is commonly conflated with *information*, being frequently used to denote the creation and distribution of facts and messages through speaking, publications, broadcast media, websites, videos, presentations, and social media. For example, a 2021 "Basics for business communication" website describes communication as "the transmission of information among people within an organization for the organization's commercial benefit" as well as distributing "information for the promotion of its services or products to their consumers." The site further states: "Communication is a process whereby a message is successfully conveyed to the receiver" (Basics, 2021, paras 1–2), and lists the steps of the information transmission model of Shannon and Weaver (1949) and the similar *source, message, channel, receiver* (SMCR) model of Berlo (1960). Another website, described as "the world's largest tech marketplace," lists the same models under the heading "Everything you need to know about communication theory" (Novak, 2019). In scholarly literature, public relations is critically described as "about giving voice" to organizations, and even as a "megaphone" (Moloney, 2005,

p. 551). Others note that public relations and corporate communication strategies such as corporate social responsibility (CSR) initiatives, commonly employ an information transmission approach (Schoeneborn & Trittin, 2013).

While recognizing philosophical and epistemological diversity in what is arguably the field, "science," or "art" of communication—or what Waisbord (2019) calls the *post-discipline* of communication—it is foundational to discussion in this handbook to have a well-founded understanding of what constitutes communication. The English term communication is derived from the Latin root *communis* meaning common or public and the related noun *commūnicātiō*, which denotes "sharing or imparting," and the corresponding verb *communicare*, which means to "share or make common" (Peters, 2015, p. 78). While imparting information is one element in the process of human communication, it is an incomplete, one-sided, and unfulfilling experience without sharing of views and perceptions. Contemporary scholars emphasize sharing meaning and meaning making as the essence of communication (Craig & Muller, 2007; Littlejohn et al., 2017). Dictionaries define communication as "exchange" ("Communication," 2021a) and refer to "discussing, debating," and "conferring" ("Communication," 2021b).

Communication is therefore a *two-way* process. Some describe this two-way process as dialogue. However, even dialogue is commonly misunderstood, with many assuming that the Greek term *dia* means two, thus suggesting two parties engaged in mutual interaction. In fact, *dia* means "through," with *logos* meaning speech, logic, and reasoning or argument. In reality, dialogue can be no more than two or more parties speaking, with each paying little attention or giving little consideration to others.

Despite the etymology of the term, the study and practice of communication have been skewed for centuries by an egocentric focus on speaking. In Book 1 of his *Politics*, Aristotle wrote that "Nature ... has endowed man[1] alone among the animals with the power of speech" and identified speaking as a key attribute that defines humans (as cited in Haworth, 2004, p. 43). Voice and speaking have been studied and celebrated since the early Western civilizations of ancient Greece and Rome, where rhetoric—the art of speaking persuasively—was recognized as one of the foundational liberal arts based on the writings of Plato, Aristotle, Cicero, and Quintilian (Atwill, 1998; Kennedy, 1994). Rhetoric also was developed as an "art" as early as 500 BCE in Islamic societies of north Africa (Bernal, 1987), and in China (Lu, 1998). Renaissance philosopher Thomas Hobbes echoed Aristotle's trope in *Leviathan*, saying, "the most noble and profitable invention of all others was that of speech" (Hobbes, 1946, p. 18). John Durham Peters refers to communication as "the natural history of our talkative species" (1999, p. 9).

As recently as the twentieth century, the field of communication studies "developed in the United States ... which gained influence around the world" (Waisbord, 2019, p. 4) was widely researched and taught under the rubric of *speech communication* (Cohen, 1994; Rogers & Chaffee, 2006).

However, as contemporary communication studies scholar Robert Craig (2006) succinctly reminds us, communication requires "talking and listening" (p. 39). In writing about the importance of voice, sociologist Nick Couldry (2009) describes voice as "the implicitly linked practices of speaking and listening" (p. 580). It is significant that Couldry notes that listening is implicit, not explicit. Despite attempts by some, such as Back (2007), to highlight the importance of listening, Fiumara (1995) noted that listening has long been "a secondary issue" (p. 6).

Underpinning the importance of this book is that organizations play a central role in contemporary industrial and post-industrial societies (Bimber et al., 2012), or what Couldry (2010) calls "complex societies" (p. 100). People work in and are represented by organizations, and they need to interact with an array of organizations on a daily basis, including government departments and agencies, corporations, non-government organizations (NGOs), institutions such as churches, police, hospitals, libraries, schools, universities, and museums, as well as councils, associations, clubs, foundations, local businesses, and so on. Organizations provide essential goods and services, impose legislation and regulations, purportedly represent the interests of their stakeholders, and support or constrain almost every aspect of people's lives.

Communication between people and organizations is therefore essential for communities, economies, and society to function. Particularly in democracies in which *vox populi*—the voice of the people—is meant to be able to influence the policies and decisions of government and the exercise of power and authority (the *krátos*), true communication involving speaking and listening by the organizations that form the political, regulatory, and economic infrastructure of society is paramount.

However, a study in 2013 noted that, despite extensive focus on interpersonal listening in psychology, leadership studies, and therapeutic fields (Brownell, 2016; Worthington & Bodie, 2017), how organizations listen, and the extent to which they listen, have been little discussed and sparsely studied (Macnamara, 2013). Follow-on studies in what became the six-year Organizational Listening Project confirmed a lack of attention to organizational listening and found that as little as 5% of the communication resources of organizations are devoted to listening to their stakeholders (Macnamara, 2014, 2015, 2016a, 2016b).

The term "organizational listening" is not a misguided attempt to anthropomorphize organizations. While recognizing that it is humans in organizations who listen—or don't listen—organizations face particular challenges as well as responsibilities in relation to listening. Understanding these is the first step in examining how organizations listen and how their listening can be enhanced to generate substantial benefits for stakeholders, society, and organizations themselves.

The Characteristics and Challenges of Organizational Listening

The first important characteristic and challenge for organizations in relation to listening is the issue of *scale*—what political theorist Andrew Dobson calls the problem of "scaling up" listening techniques and practices from one or a few to many (2014, pp. 75, 124). Organizations often need to communicate with, and therefore need to listen to, thousands, hundreds of thousands in the case of large corporations, or even millions of people in the case of governments. In many cases, the stakeholders or organizations, such as customers, employees, members, and voters, are distanciated in time and space, separated from the organization by geography and sometimes time zones. This leads to the second and third characteristics and challenges of organizational listening.

Because of scale, organizational listening is *delegated* to functional units such as customer relations, call centers, human resources (HR), stakeholder engagement and public consultation teams, and agencies such as market research and media monitoring and analysis firms.

Third, because of scale, distanciation, and delegation, organizational listening is largely *mediated*. Beyond the limited opportunities for direct interpersonal listening in meetings with employees and small groups of other stakeholders, organizational listening involves processing of e-mails, letters, submissions to consultations, complaints in writing or to telephone call centers, reports, and monitoring traditional media reports and social media comments. Furthermore, to reach senior decision makers, these mediated expressions of voice are further mediated through presentations and reports to boards and committees.

In summary, in contrast with interpersonal listening that is direct with individuals or small groups, synchronous, and processed aurally, organizational listening typically has to be conducted on a large scale and is therefore delegated, mediated, asynchronous, and requires a range of data analysis tools and techniques.

Hearing vs. listening

While interpersonal listening is typically based on information received aurally and is often referred to as hearing, it is important to note a clear distinction between hearing and listening. Hearing by humans involves sound waves striking the ear drum (*tympanic membrane*). Listening requires cognitive and/or affective processing of those signals by the human brain. The organizational equivalent of hearing is the receipt of correspondence, telephone calls, research data, and so on. It is well known that much of what people hear is ignored—and the same occurs in the case of information, requests, and reports received by organizations (Macnamara, 2017, pp. 26–27). Listening is much more than hearing.

This indicates that we need a clear definition of organizational listening in order to proceed productively in research and practice.

Definitions of Organizational Listening

Glenn (1989) identified 50 definitions of listening in a literature review in the *International Journal of Listening*, almost all of which focus on interpersonal listening. Drawing on this literature, as well as political science, psychology, psychotherapy, and ethics, "seven canons" of listening were identified in Macnamara (2016a, pp. 41–43) that can be applied to organizations as well as individuals. These "seven canons" identify that listening requires:

1 *Recognition* of others as having rights to speak and be treated with respect (Honneth, 2007; Husband, 2009). In the absence of recognition, a potential listener "tunes out";
2 *Acknowledgment* (Schmid, 2001), without which speakers assume that they have not been listened to and may disengage themselves;
3 Giving *attention* to what is said (Bickford, 1996; Honneth, 2007; Husband, 2009);
4 *Interpreting* what others say fairly and receptively, such as avoiding stereotyping;
5 Trying as far as possible to achieve *understanding* of others' views and context (Bodie & Crick, 2014; Husband, 1996, 2000);
6 Giving *consideration* to what others say (Honneth, 2007; Husband, 2009); and
7 *Responding* in an appropriate way (Lundsteen, 1979; Purdy & Borisoff, 1997).

It is important to note that the literature does not suggest that agreement or compliance is required as part of listening. In many cases, there are good reasons that people and organizations cannot agree or comply with requests or recommendations. In such cases, an explanation can be an appropriate response. Nevertheless, response is essential to close the "communication cycle." William James (1952), the founder of American pragmatism, stated that ignoring someone is the most "fiendish" way to deal with another.

Burnside-Lawry (2011) is one of the few who have attempted a definition of *organizational listening*. In her study of listening competency of employees, she drew on the research of Flynn et al. (2008) in relation to listening in business to say:

> Organizational listening is defined as a combination of an employee's listening skills and the environment in which listening occurs, which is shaped by the organization and is then one of the characteristics of the organizational image.
>
> (Burnside-Lawry, 2011, p. 149)

This definition is useful in noting that skills are required for listening and for drawing attention to the organizational environment, which includes culture, policies, structure, and other elements. Burnside-Lawry's observations, along with identification of the distinguishing characteristics and challenges of organizational listening discussed previously, led to development of the concept of an *architecture of listening* (Macnamara, 2013, 2015, 2016a) as a necessary framework for effective listening in organizations. The requirement for an architecture of listening, which is explained in the following section, informed a definition of organizational listening in the 2016 book, *Organizational Listening: The Missing Link in Public Communication* (Macnamara, 2016a), that reported a study of 36 corporate, government, and non-government organizations (NGOs) in Australia, the UK, and the USA. This stated:

> Organizational listening is comprised of the culture, policies, structure, processes, resources, skills, technologies, and practices applied by an organization to give recognition, acknowledgement, attention, interpretation, understanding, consideration, and response to its stakeholders and publics.
> (Macnamara, 2016a, p. 52)

Further study of organizational listening in 2018 and 2019 explored the expanding range of systems including advanced digital technologies available for large-scale, delegated, mediated listening. This led to the following expanded definition of organizational listening that is offered as a part of a framework for further exploration.

> Organizational listening comprises the creation and implementation of scaled processes and systems that enable decision makers and policy makers in organizations to actively and effectively access, acknowledge, understand, consider and appropriately respond to all those who wish to communicate with the organization or with whom the organization wishes to communicate interpersonally or through delegated, mediated means.
> (Macnamara, 2019, p. 5191)

An Architecture of Listening

The Organizational Listening Project began with a pilot study of three organizations and was then deployed in three main stages as summarized in Table 0.1. In total, the "seven canons of listening," the preceding definition of organizational listening, and the concept of an "architecture of listening" are based on intensive study of 60 organizations including 39 government departments and agencies, 15 corporations, and 6 major NGOs in Australia; western, eastern, and southern Europe; the UK; and the USA. The 6 years of research (2013–2019) involved 327 interviews;

content analysis of 635 documents such as communication strategies, plans, and evaluation reports; and 14 months of observation inside organizations including attendance at 82 senior management meetings and forums. (See Table 0.1.)

A common response of CEOs and corporate, marketing, and organizational communication and public relations practitioners to the initial finding of a lack of listening in organizations is to seek a "silver bullet" solution. In particular, most look for a technological solution, such as an online platform, a mobile app, or increasingly an artificial intelligence (AI) solution. However, the extensive observation, interviewing,

Table 0.1 Summary of the organizational listening project

Study	Description	No. of organizations	Interviews	Documents analyzed
Pilot study (2013)	Test of methodology in Australia	3	3	
Stage 1. (2014/15)	Multi-country study of the external and internal communication of large corporations, government departments and agencies, and NGOs in Australia, the UK, and the USA	36	104	412
Stage 2 (2016)	Six months full-time based in the UK Department of Health, 79 Whitehall, working with 14 other government agencies, coordinated through the UK Government Communication Service and the Cabinet Office, Whitehall	15	76	92
Stage 3 (2018/19)	Contract research funded by Achmea International in the Netherlands, studying four corporate subsidiaries in Australia, Greece, Slovakia, and the Netherlands	4	129	88
Cognate studies (2017)	Greater Sydney Commission community engagement study	2	15	25
	European Commission—The Europe Dialogues and evaluation research for the Directorate-General for Communication (DG COMM)			18
TOTALS		60	327	635

and content analysis of plans and reports conducting during The Organizational Listening Project concluded that an "add on" technology or tool will not result in open, effective listening. To the contrary, it concluded that the lack of listening in organizations is systemic and requires a holistic approach. Eight key elements were identified as necessary for open, effective listening in organizations, as follows:

1. An organizational *culture* that is open to listening as defined by Honneth (2007), Husband (1996, 2009), and others—that is, one that recognizes others' right to speak, pays attention to them, and tries to understand their views. Unless there is a culture of listening, no technology or method will be effective;
2. Addressing the *politics of listening*, such as selective listening to certain individuals or groups, while others are ignored and marginalized, as discussed by Dreher (2009, 2010) and Bassel (2017);
3. *Policies* that specify and require listening in an organization;
4. *Systems* that are open and interactive, such as websites that allow visitors to post comments and questions;
5. *Technologies* that aid listening, such as monitoring tools or services for tracking media and online comment, automated acknowledgment systems, and analysis tools for sense-making. Examples of technologies are discussed in the following section;
6. *Resources* including staff to operate listening systems and do the *work of listening* (Macnamara, 2013, 2015), such as establishing forums and consultations, inviting comments, and monitoring, analyzing, and responding to comments and questions;
7. *Skills/competencies* for large-scale organizational listening, such as conducting textual analysis and social media content analysis;
8. *Articulation* of what is said to an organization to policy-making and decision-making. Unless there is a link to policy-making and decision-making for consideration of what is said to an organization, voice has no value, as Couldry (2010) notes.

These elements are referred to as comprising an *architecture* of listening because they identify key principles and elements that are widely applicable and which are necessary to ensure coherence and integrity. Like architecture for the built environment, the specific design of listening processes and systems in organizations can include many forms, styles, and infinitely varying scales to suit circumstances and contexts.

Listening Systems

In addition to proposing that listening has to be designed into an organization as outlined in the "architecture of listening"– not simply "bolted on" to an existing structure, the third stage of The Organizational Listening

Project explored a range of specialist methods and systems including digital technologies. While organizations typically have sophisticated systems for speaking, such as website development teams, media production departments, and advertising and public relations units or agencies, they often lack specific methods and tools for listening.

Listening systems do not replace face-to-face and other forms of interpersonal communication, such as meetings, telephone calls, and video conferencing, which are emphasized by many researchers (e.g., Bassel, 2017; Bodie & Crick, 2014). But various listening systems are essential for delegated, mediated listening by organizations at scale.

In particular, organizational listening requires and depends on systematic *analysis* of data, not simply collection and receipt of data such as correspondence, research reports, submissions, and feedback. Too often, vast quantities of information from stakeholders remain unread and unused. For example, the second stage of The Organizational Listening Project focused on listening by government organizations in the UK found 127,400 public submissions on health topics had not been analyzed because the department had no natural language processing (NLP) textual analysis software with machine learning capabilities, or staff with the necessary training, to undertake such a task (Macnamara, 2017, pp. 26–27). This example illustrates that organizational listening requires tools, resources, and skills for analyzing unstructured as well as structured data. People speak and write in words, not numbers. Therefore, textual analysis and related analysis methods such as content analysis are essential skills for a listening organization.

In addition, as well as employing traditional quantitative and particularly qualitative research methods such interviews and focus groups, organizational listening can be implemented through a number of advanced research and engagement methods including *deliberative polling* (Fishkin, 2011); *participatory action research* (PAR); *sense making methodology* (Dervin & Foreman-Wernet, 2013) *appreciative inquiry* (Cooperrider et al., 2008); *behavioral insights* (Thaler & Sunstein, 2008); and *customer journey mapping* (Court et al., 2009).

The rapidly growing field of *data analytics* includes many systematic ways that the voices of stakeholders and citizens can be accessed and considered. Digital technologies such as voice to text (VTT) software enable recorded phone calls to call centers and complaints departments to be transferred to text for analysis that can identify common messages, themes, and patterns.

Organizations are also adopting artificial intelligence (AI) tools such as *chat bots* to "listen" to users of web pages and respond with relevant information, as well as learning algorithms based on NLP that responds to users' data entry, menu selections, and even spoken voice (Macnamara, 2019).

The Ethics of Listening

Concerns are rightly raised about some applications of organizational listening. Listening conducted by organizations for intelligence and spying is not the focus of this handbook. However, organizational listening applied in marketing and political campaigns to target consumers and voters with customized messages based on personal data collected also raises ethical concerns. Critical technosocial and technocultural scholars warn of the potential for *digital surveillance*, or what some call *dataveillance*, to undermine human rights and privacy (e.g., Gillespie, 2018; Landau, 2017; Napoli, 2014). They also are concerned about the negative effects of algorithms, such as *algorithmic filtering* (Caplan, 2018). As Caplan says, in many, if not most, online platforms, algorithms decide "the inclusion or exclusion of information" (2018, p. 564). Algorithms contribute to *filter bubbles*, also referred to as *echo chambers*, in which people receive only information that aligns with their pre-identified interests. Even more seriously, algorithms and their application in AI tools can lead to "baked-in bias" (Ayre & Craner, 2018) caused by what one author calls "toxic tech" (Wachter-Boettcher, 2017). This suggests that communication professionals need to take a measured approach rather than a headlong rush in adopting "commtech." The collection, analysis, and use of human data is an important area for continuing research.

The Benefits and Necessity of Listening

While recognizing risks, research indicates that active, ethical listening by organizations offers many benefits to individuals, organizations themselves, and society. Reports show that commercial organizations gain benefits such as increased customer loyalty; increased employee morale, motivation, and productivity; and increased insights into market needs through better listening (Jenkins et al., 2013; Leite, 2015). Responsive listening by governments and political institutions has the potential to redress the "democratic deficit" (Norris, 2011) and what some researchers identify as a "crisis of democracy" (Przeworski, 2019; van der Meer, 2017), as well as the decline of trust in governments, corporations, and many institutions (Edelman, 2021). NGOs and nonprofit organizations can achieve increased and more equitable representation of interests; better understanding of diversity; increased social and political engagement by citizens; and even improved health and well-being through increased understanding and reflection of community concerns, fears, anxieties, and needs. Organizational listening is essential for an organized society to be equitable and sustainable. Thus, this book offers an important contribution to communication studies literature and identifies an important direction for research and transformational practice in corporate, government, organizational, and marketing communication, and public relations.

Note

1 Gendered term in original text.

References

Atwill, J. (1998). *Rhetoric reclaimed: Aristotle and the liberal arts tradition.* Cornell University Press.

Ayre, L., & Craner, J. (2018). The baked-in bias of algorithms. *Collaborative Librarianship, 10*(2), Article 3. https://digitalcommons.du.edu/collaborativelibrarianship/vol10/iss2/3

Back, L. (2007). *The art of listening.* Berg.

Basics. (2021). *Basics of business communication.* https://www.basic-concept.com/c/basics-of-business-communication

Bassel, L. (2017). *The politics of listening: Possibilities and challenges for democratic life.* Palgrave Macmillan.

Berlo, D. (1960). *The process of communication: An introduction to theory and practice.* Harcourt/Holt, Rinehart & Winston.

Bernal, M. (1987). *Black Athena: The Afroasiatic roots of classical civilization.* Rutgers University Press.

Bickford, S. (1996). *The dissonance of democracy: Listening, conflict and citizenship.* Cornell University Press.

Bimber, B., Flanagin, A., & Stohl, C. (2012). *Collective action in organizations: Interaction and engagement in an era of technological change.* Cambridge University Press.

Bodie, G., & Crick, N. (2014). Listening, hearing sensing: Three modes of being and the phenomenology of Charles Sanders Peirce. *Communication Theory, 24*(2), 105–123. https://doi.org/10.1111/comt.1203

Brownell, J. (2016). *Listening: Attitudes, principles, and skills* (5th ed.). Routledge.

Burnside-Lawry, J. (2011). The dark side of stakeholder communication: Stakeholder perceptions of ineffective organizational listening. *Australian Journal of Communication, 38*(1), 147–173.

Caplan, R. (2018). Algorithmic filtering. In P. Napoli (Ed.), *Mediated communication* (pp. 561–583). De Gruyter.

Carey, J. (1989). *Communication as culture: Essays on media and culture.* Unwin Hyman.

Cohen, H. (1994). *The history of speech communication: The emergence of a discipline, 1914–1945.* Speech Communication Association. https://www.natcom.org/sites/default/files/pages/The_History_of_Speech_Communication_byCohen.pdf

Communication. (2021a). Merriam-Webster. *Merriam-Webster Dictionary.* https://www.merriam-webster.com/dictionary/communication

Communication. (2021b). *Online Etymology Dictionary.* https://www.etymonline.com/word/communication

Cooperrider, D., Whitney, D., & Stavros, J. (2008). *Appreciative inquiry handbook* (2nd ed.). Crown Custom.

Couldry, N. (2009). Commentary: Rethinking the politics of voice. *Continuum: Journal of Media & Cultural Studies, 23*(4), 579–582. https://doi.org/10.1080/10304310903026594

Couldry, N. (2010). *Why voice matters: Culture and politics after neoliberalism*. Sage.

Court, D., Elzinga, D., Mulder, S., & Vetvik, O. (2009, June). The consumer decision journey. *McKinsey Quarterly*. https://www.mckinsey.com/business-functions/marketing-and-sales/our-insights/the-consumer-decision-journey

Craig, R. (2006). Communication as a practice. In G. Shepherd, G. St John, & T. Striphas (Eds.), *Communication as … perspectives on theory* (pp. 38–49). Sage.

Craig, R., & Muller, H. (Eds.). (2007). *Theorizing communication: Readings across traditions*. Sage.

Dervin, B., & Foreman-Wernet, L. (2013). Sense-making methodology as an approach to understanding and designing for campaign audiences. In R. Rice, & C. Atkin (Eds.), *Public communication campaigns* (4th ed., pp. 147–162). Sage.

Dewey, J. (1916). *Democracy and education*. Macmillan.

Dobson, A. (2014). *Listening for democracy: Recognition, representation, reconciliation*. Oxford University Press.

Dreher, T. (2009). Listening across difference: Media and multiculturalism beyond the politics of voice. *Continuum: Journal of Media & Cultural Studies, 23*(4), 445–458. https://doi.org/10.1080/10304310903015712

Dreher, T. (2010). Speaking up or being heard? Community media interventions and the politics of listening. *Media, Culture and Society, 32*(1), 85–103. https://doi.org/10.1177/0163443709350099

Edelman. (2021). *2021 Edelman trust barometer*. https://www.edelman.com/trust/2021-trust-barometer

Fishkin, J. (2011). *When the people speak: Deliberative democracy and public consultation*. Oxford University Press.

Fiumara, G. (1995). *The other side of language: A philosophy of listening*. Routledge.

Flynn, J., Valikoski, T., & Grau, J. (2008). Listening in the business context: Reviewing the state of research. *International Journal of Listening, 22*(2), 141–151. https://doi.org/10.1080/10904010802174800

Gillespie, T. (2018). *Custodians of the internet: Platforms, content moderation, and the hidden decisions that shape social media*. Yale University Press.

Glenn, E. (1989). A content analysis of fifty definitions of listening. *The International Journal of Listening, 3*(1), 21–31. https://doi.org/10.1207/s1932586xijl0301_3

Haworth, A. (2004). *Understanding the political philosophers: From ancient to modern times*. Routledge.

Hobbes, T. (1946). *Leviathan*. Basil Blackwell. (Original work published 1651.)

Honneth, A. (2007). *Disrespect*. Polity.

Husband, C. (1996). The right to be understood: Conceiving the multi-ethnic public sphere. *Innovation: The European Journal of Social Sciences, 9*(2), 205–215. https://doi.org/10.1080/13511610.1996.9968484

Husband, C. (2000). Media and the public sphere in multi-ethnic societies. In S. Cottle (Ed.), *Ethnic minorities and the media* (pp. 199–214). Open University Press.

Husband, C. (2009). Commentary: Between listening and understanding. *Continuum: Journal of Media & Cultural Studies, 23*(4), 441–443. https://doi.org/10.1080/10304310903026602

Foreword: Setting the Scene   xxix

James, W. (1952). *The principles of psychology*. William Benton.
Jenkins, H., Ford, S., & Green, J. (2013). *Spreadable media: Crating value and meaning in a networked culture*. New York University Press.
Kennedy, G. (1994). *A new history of classical rhetoric*. Princeton University Press.
Landau, S. (2017). *Listening in*. Yale University Press.
Leite, E. (2015, January 19). Why trust matters in business. Address to the World Economic Forum, Davos-Klosters, Switzerland. https://agenda.weforum.org/2015/01/why-trust-matters-in-business
Littlejohn, S., Foss, K., & Oetzel, J. (2017). *Theories of human communication* (11th ed.). Waveland.
Lu, X. (1998). *Rhetoric in ancient China fifth to third century BCE: A comparison with classical Greek rhetoric*. University of South Carolina Press.
Lundsteen, S. (1979). *Listening: Its impact on language and the other language arts*. ERIC Clearing House on Reading and Communication Skills.
Macnamara, J. (2013). Beyond voice: Audience-making and the work and architecture of listening. *Continuum: Journal of Media and Cultural Studies, 27*(1), 160–175. https://doi.org/10.1080/10304312.2013.736950
Macnamara, J. (2014). Organizational listening: A vital missing element in public communication and the public sphere. *Asia Pacific Public Relations Journal, 15*(1), 90–108. https://novaojs.newcastle.edu.au/apprj/index.php/apprj/article/view/45
Macnamara, J. (2015). The work and "architecture of listening": Requisites for ethical organization-public communication. *Ethical Space: Journal of the Institute of Communication Ethics, 12*(2), 29–37. http://journals.communicationethics.net
Macnamara, J. (2016a). *Organizational listening: The missing essential in public communication*. Peter Lang.
Macnamara, J. (2016b). Organizational listening: Addressing a major gap in public relations theory and practice. *Journal of Public Relations Research, 28*(3–4), 146–169. https://doi.org/10.1080/1062726X.2016.1228064
Macnamara, J. (2017). *Creating a "democracy for everyone": Strategies for increasing listening and engagement by government*. The London School of Economics and Political Science. https://www.lse.ac.uk/media-and-communications/assets/documents/research/2017/MacnamaraReport2017.pdf
Macnamara, J. (2019). Explicating listening in organization-public communication: Theory, practices, technologies. *International Journal of Communication, 13*, 5183–5204. https://ijoc.org/index.php/ijoc/article/view/11996/2839
Moloney, K. (2005). Trust and public relations: Center and edge. *Public Relations Review, 31*(4), 550–555. https://doi.org/10.1016/j.pubrev.2005.08.015.
Napoli, P. (2014). Automated media: An institutional theory perspective on algorithmic media production and consumption. *Communication Theory, 24*(3), 340–360. https://doi.org/10.1111/comt.1203
Norris, P. (2011). *Democratic deficit: Critical citizens revisited*. Cambridge University Press.
Novak, M. (2019, April 8). Everything you need to know about communication theory. *G2*. https://www.g2.com/articles/communication-theory
Peters, J. (1999). *Speaking into the air*. University of Chicago Press.

Peters, J. (2015). Communication: History of the idea. In W. Donsbach (Ed.), *The concise encyclopedia of communication* (pp. 78–79). Wiley Blackwell. https://onlinelibrary.wiley.com/doi/abs/10.1002/9781405186407.wbiecc075

Przeworski, A. (2019). *Crisis of democracy*. Cambridge University Press.

Purdy, M., & Borisoff, D. (1997). *Listening in everyday life: A personal and professional approach* (2nd ed.). University of America Press.

Rogers, E., & Chaffee, S. (2006). The past and the future of communication study: Convergence or divergence? *Journal of Communication, 43*(4), 125–131. https://doi.org/10.1111/j.1460-2466.1993.tb01312.x

Schmid, P. (2001). Acknowledgement: The art of responding: Dialogical and ethical perspectives on the challenges of unconditional relationships in therapy and beyond. In J. Bozarth & P. Wilkins (Eds.), *Rogers' therapeutic conditions: Evolution, theory and practice* (Vol. 3; pp. 155–171). PCCS Books.

Schoeneborn, D., Kuhn, T., & Kärreman, D. (2019). The communicative constitution of organization: Organizing and organizationality. *Organization Studies, 40*(4), 475–496. https://doi.org/10.1177/0170840618782284

Schoeneborn, D., & Trittin, H. (2013). Transcending transmission: Towards a constitutive perspective on CSR communication. *Corporate Communications: An International Journal, 18*(2), 193–211. https://doi.org/10.1108/13563281311319481

Shannon, C., & Weaver, W. (1949). *The mathematical theory of communication*. University of Illinois.

Thaler, R., & Sunstein, C. (2008). *Nudge: Improving decisions about health, wealth, and happiness*. Yale University Press.

Van der Meer, T. (2017). Political trust and the "crisis of democracy." In Oxford research encyclopedia of politics. Oxford University Press.

Vásquez, C., & Schoeneborn, D. (2018). Communication as constitutive of organization. In R. Heath, & W. Johansen (Eds.), *The international encyclopedia of strategic communication* (pp. 1–12). Wiley & Sons.

Wachter-Boettcher, S. (2017). *Technically wrong: Sexist apps, biased algorithms, and other threats of toxic tech*. W.W. Norton & Company.

Waisbord, S. (2019). *Communication: A post-discipline*. Polity.

Williams, R. (1976). *Communications*. Penguin. (Original work published 1962.)

Worthington, D., & Bodie, G. (Eds.). (2017). *The sourcebook of listening research: Methodology and measures*. Wiley Blackwell.

Acknowledgments

Thank you to the tremendous community of international scholars who have contributed their research, insights, and feedback. This book would not have been possible without your expertise and diligence, particularly amidst the ongoing COVID-19 pandemic. Thank you, additionally, to Denise Bortree and the Arthur W. Page Center for Integrity in Public Communication for your generous support and guidance throughout the research and book development process. Lastly, thank you to the scholars who donated their time to conduct blind reviews of the chapters and offer feedback to the authors. Reviewers, in alphabetical order, included: Kati Berg, Nate Gilkerson, Jeong-Nam Kim, Nneka Logan, Jim Macnamara, Juan Meng, Geah Pressgrove, Adrienne Wallace, Antoaneta Vanc, Jennifer Vardeman, and Wen Zhao.

Introduction

Katie R. Place

Listening is the practice of receiving, constructing meaning from, and responding to spoken or nonverbal messages (International Listening Association, 2007). It involves respect of all partners engaged in dialogue, commitment to understanding shared messages, hearing diverse voices across contexts, and openness to multiple narratives (Parks, 2019). In organizations, listening necessitates structures, resources, skills, policies, and personnel for being responsive to the needs of organizational publics, particularly via two-way flows of communication (Macnamara, 2016a, 2016b; Worthington & Fitch-Hauser, 2018).

Unfortunately, an organizational listening crisis remains, as organizations have historically engaged in an 80:20 ratio of speaking versus listening, where listening is selectively done to promote marketing needs, provide competitive data, or identify methods to sell products (Macnamara, 2016a, 2016b). Similarly, scholars have found that communication professionals "value listening, but do not always make it the priority that it merits" (Neill & Bowen, 2021, p. 276). Listening in organizations still lacks adequate structures, resources, policies, and people to do the work of listening at the appropriate scale. Moreover, in the wake of COVID-19, #BlackLivesMatter, #DontSayGay, corporate greenwashing, social unrest, and strained global and diplomatic tensions, listening is needed to foster ethical, equitable, and respectful strategic communication among organizations and publics.

Purpose of the Book

The purpose of *Organizational Listening: Building Theory & Practice for Strategic Communication* is to expand upon the extant research regarding organizational listening and strategic communication, particularly regarding critical, ethical, cultural, and technological approaches. The chapters, authored by a diverse global collective of communication scholars and professionals, intend to lay the groundwork for next-generation organizational listening theory development and practical application.

DOI: 10.4324/9781003273851-1

From this book, new insights emerge to develop stronger organizational listening structures, policies, tools, and practices.

The book was also inspired by the Arthur W. Page Society principle #3: Listen to Stakeholders. This principle calls for public communicators to listen effectively and engage a diverse range of stakeholders through inclusive dialogue. Despite its status as a Page Principle, listening has received little explicit attention in public relations or strategic communications contexts. Listening is often perceived as essential to effective business and communication practice (Brunner, 2008), but it has traditionally been theorized as a function of interpersonal communication, human resources, education, or counseling (Macnamara, 2018).

Ultimately, *Organizational Listening: Building Theory & Practice for Strategic Communication* offers innovative models, theoretical approaches, critical provocations, and unique applications to build organizational listening theory and practice to enhance our ever-evolving public relations and strategic communication disciplines.

Organization of the Book

Unit 1: Organizational Listening Competencies and Technologies

The book is organized into four units highlighting new paths of growth for organizational listening theory and practice. *Unit 1: Organizational Listening Competencies and Technologies* builds upon extant organizational listening skill sets, approaches, and tools. In Chapter 1, Worthington and Bodie explore how external stakeholders conceptualize organizational listening, particularly regarding notions of listening as relationship building, information acquisition, learning, and critical engagement. Findings support extant organizational listening concepts (e.g., Burnside-Lawry, 2012; Macnamara, 2018), such as awareness and attention, recognition, understanding, supportiveness, and responding, but also draw heavily upon interpersonal listening concepts. In Chapter 2, Gearhart and Maben merge listening concepts from interpersonal communication research with mass communication and public relations practices to explore organizational listening competencies on social media. Whereas social media offers opportunities for two-way communication with stakeholders, the authors find that many organizations rely upon the one-way public information model. They suggest that organizations work more intentionally to create an architecture of listening and secure front-line teams to navigate the *masspersonal* landscape of social media. Kang and Moon explore effective frameworks and competencies for organizational employee listening, particularly to address employee silence in Chapter 3. Applying critical characteristics of a competent listener in the dialogic communication framework for participatory employee communication, they describe the cognitive, affective, and behavioral components of their Organizational Employee Listening Competency (OELC) model. Addressing considerations of scale and technological competencies for organizational listening, Chapter 4 authors Zhou et al. evaluate the potential of AI-enabled social chatbots as listening agents, emphasizing the increasingly important role of AI-powered and AI-mediated organizational listening. They theorize how organizations can effectively harness social chatbots for organizational listening, particularly by demonstrating social presence and conversational human voice. Lastly, in Chapter 5, Volk develops a framework for evaluation of organizational listening. She focuses on the evaluation of listening and provides an overview of how listening structures and processes and listening methods and tools can be evaluated. The chapter brings forth a new set of competencies to the public relations and strategic communications field for evaluation of organizational listening regarding inputs, outputs, outcomes, and impact.

Unit 2: Organizational Listening for Ethics and Justice

Unit 2: Organizational Listening for Ethics and Justice explores the roles of organizational listening to facilitate effective two-way communication and ethical, authentic, and responsible engagement and trust among publics. In Chapter 6, Neill and Bowen present findings from their mixed-method study regarding how organizations listen ethically to external stakeholders. They argue that listening is a critical component of effective and ethical issues management programs to guide strategic listening to external publics. By using a systems theory approach and environmental scanning, organizations can respond proactively and autonomously, building trust. In Chapter 7, Tam et al. argue that criticisms for the practice of organizational listening are caused by different expectations and experiences between practitioners and stakeholders. Findings from a survey of Australian citizens and findings from interviews with Australian practitioners showed that design of an organization's listening activities may be limited by an organization's goals and the discrepancy between organizations' and stakeholders' interests. English et al. in Chapter 8, share findings of their research regarding stakeholders and activists in Fort Worth, Texas before, during, and after the killing of a young Black woman, Atatiana Jefferson, by a White police officer in 2019. The authors center their recommendations to disrupt a system of listening that, in the past, has only included the most powerful residents. They recommend that cities must deliberately seek input and listen to underrepresented and minoritized communities, close listening loops, and facilitate listening led by underrepresented and minoritized communities themselves. Coman and Vasquez explore organizational and social listening for climate change advocacy in Chapter 9. They examine how Amazon addressed the call for climate change action spurred by the employee activist group, Amazon Employees for Climate Justice (AECJ). Their analysis reveals themes across company posts and publics' comments suggesting that Amazon positioned itself as a hero, while climate change takes a back seat to customer service, and activist engagement.

Unit 3: Organizational Listening for Diversity, Equity, and Inclusion (DE&I)

In *Unit 3: Organizational Listening for Diversity, Equity, and Inclusion (DE&I)*, these chapters build upon Macnamara's (2016a) call for further organizational listening research to examine how communicators can "listen across difference" particularly to those who are often "sidelined, ignored, and excluded" from public communication (pp. 314–315). Responding to this call, Place explores organizational listening for DE&I in public relations and strategic communication contexts in Chapter 10. Her findings suggest that organizational listening to support DE&I occurs via formal surveys and meetings, employee resource groups, designated organizational listeners, and invoking a grassroots approach. Listening in alignment with intersectional and corporate responsibility to race (CRR) approaches may provide particularly effective paths forward for developing authentic, equitable, and social-justice-oriented listening practices. Similarly, Capizzo, in Chapter 11, introduces additional critical and ethics-centered perspectives regarding organizational listening. Discussing the philosophy of Hannah Arendt, he shares how plurality-informed organizational listening has the potential to increase organizations' holistic and ecological knowledge of their communities and societies. Listening-informed public relations helps practitioners and others participate constructively in deliberative democratic society. In Chapter 12, Lim et al. explore what extant research on LGBTQ publics implies about organizational listening and the gaps that exist in research and practice. The authors argue that organizational listening is a significant practice for organizations wanting to move away from performative support to organizational allyship. They put forth an organizational listening scale and consider how sexual orientation, gender identity, race, and ethnicity affect perceptions of organizational listening.

Unit 4: Cultural and Global Considerations for Organizational Listening

Unit 4: Cultural and Global Considerations for Organizational Listening offers new paths for organizational listening in cross-cultural and global contexts. In Chapter 13, Lee et al. explore organizational listening efforts in South Korea to empower women to voice workplace discrimination concerns and address injustice issues. Findings highlighted the importance of organizational listening regarding diversity, inclusion, and gender equality in cultural settings with collectivistic value and high-power distance. Organizational listening efforts must equip employees with autonomy and power to cope with workplace gender discrimination proactively. Bachman and Labarca, in Chapter 14, argue that organizational listening formulations that may work in Global North settings may not be suitable in all international contexts. They propose that distinct features of other cultures need to be considered when trying to successfully establish relationships with different publics in other national or regional contexts, such as Latin America, where distrust stemming from a history of colonialism, political instability, human rights violations, and social inequalities have traditionally defined the configuration of publics and organizational communication practices. Practitioners must be mindful of cultural and sociopolitical systems that shape communication and listening processes. Finally, in Chapter 15, Storie and Marschlich explore how listening is a core function of diplomacy and how communicators use organizational listening to achieve public diplomacy goals. Relationship management and collaborative public diplomacy scholarship have opened new avenues for listening practice.

The book concludes with an overview of key research findings, examining how organizational listening research in the future may better foster mutually beneficial relationships, close listening loops, and advance more ethical, equitable, and sustainable listening practices.

References

Brunner, B. R. (2008). Listening, communication & trust: Practitioners' perspectives of business/organizational relationships. *The International Journal of Listening*, 22(1), 73–82. https://doi.org/10.1080/10904010701808482

Burnside-Lawry, J. (2012). Listening and participatory communication: A model to assess organization listening competency. *International Journal of Listening*, 26(2), 102–121. https://doi.org/10.1080/10904018.2012.678092

International Listening Association. (2007). https://listen.org/

Macnamara, J. (2016a). *Organizational listening: The missing essential in public communication*. Peter Lang.

Macnamara, J. (2016b). Organizational listening: Addressing a major gap in public relations theory and practice. *Journal of Public Relations Research*, 28(3–4), 146–169. https://doi.org/10.1080/1062726X.2016.1228064

Macnamara, J. (2018). Toward a theory and practice of organizational listening. *International Journal of Listening*, 32(1), 1–23. https://doi.org/10.1080/10904018.2017.1375076

Neill, M. S., & Bowen, S. A. (2021). Employee perceptions of ethical listening in US organizations. *Public Relations Review*, 47(5), 102123. https://doi.org/10.1016/j.pubrev.2021.102123

Parks, E. S. (2019). *The ethics of listening: Creating space for sustainable dialogue*. Lexington Books.

Worthington, D., & Fitch-Hauser, M. (2018). *Listening: Processes, functions, and competency* (2nd ed.). Routledge.

Unit 1
Organizational Listening Competencies and Technologies

1 External Stakeholders' Conceptualizations of Organizational Listening

A Conceptual Replication of the Revised Listening Concepts Inventory

Debra L. Worthington and Graham Bodie

Introduction

When individuals fail to listen, misunderstanding occurs, frustration ensues, and relationships can end (Bodie, 2012). When organizations fail to listen, the consequences are often even more sweeping. In her book, *The Power of Strategic Listening*, Laurie Lewis (2019) outlined contemporary cases such as the Boeing 737 Max 8 catastrophe and Facebook's role in the Cambridge Analytica scandal, which suggest that failures to take employee feedback seriously can cause damage to both inside and outside the organization. Indeed, poor organizational listening is linked to a number of cultural and social ills (e.g., democratic decline, falling public trust, and social inequity; Macnamara, 2016, 2018, 2020), a trend that could be reversed if governments and organizations would invest the necessary financial, technological, and human resources (e.g., social and market research, call centers, and social media engagement) required to build strong listening networks with their stakeholders (internal and external).

In general, organizations, like people, make choices whether (or not) to listen. And just like people seeking to improve their listening competence, organizations can improve their listening by first understanding what it is that their external stakeholders expect. Particularly relevant for this study is the degree to which organizational stakeholders evaluate organizational listening on a similar set of attributes that define listening in the interpersonal context. As we expand further, much of the research exploring implications for organizations who "listen well" frames competence in listening using terms and phrasing drawn directly from interpersonal communication literature. Thus, this study seeks to bring conceptual clarity to organizational listening, situating it alongside other, more established concepts and carving a unique space for its use in the larger organizational communication and public relations literatures.

DOI: 10.4324/9781003273851-3

Toward this aim, we first explore two approaches to defining organizational listening, making the case that understanding implicit theories of this concept is as important as crafting more formal theories. We then turn our attention to a study that provides evidence for what external organizational stakeholders mean when they claim an organization is (not) listening.

Literature

What Is Organizational Listening?

Like any contested term, defining listening has been the subject of deep scholarly debate. While there seems general agreement that "to listen" is distinct from "to hear," there remain dozens if not hundreds of definitions of what exactly comprises listening (for a review, see Worthington & Bodie, 2018). Indeed, while most agree that listening is a complex and multidimensional construct, there is much less agreement on the specific facets that comprise its core.

Particularly relevant for this study is the extent to which notions of what it means for one individual to listen to another individual (e.g., being attentive, friendly, and enabling meaningful conversations) are applicable to how organizations should listen to their multiple stakeholders. As Macnamara (2020, p. 387) noted, "While it is people inside organizations ... who ultimately listen (or don't listen) to stakeholders, listening in and by organizations needs to extend beyond interpersonal listening" because of three key characteristics: (1) it is largely delegated through organizational functions (e.g., customer relations, social media monitoring, and complaint handling); (2) it is generally mediated through practices such as emails, reports, social media posts, and survey responses; and (3) it is chiefly asynchronous. These characteristics mean that while interpersonal listening "is direct, face-to-face, and synchronous, organizational listening requires and depends on systems, structures, resources, and a range of processes, technologies, and specialist skills that can enable and facilitate delegated, mediated, large-scale listening" (p. 3). Thus, much of what Macnamara identified suggests that organizational listening is qualitatively different from its interpersonal counterpart.

At the same time, most descriptions of organizational listening mirror quite closely those descriptions of competent interpersonal listening. While recognizing that listening at the organizational level requires scaling, distance, and asynchronous timing not paradigmatically associated with listening interpersonally, Macnamara (2020) has defined organizational listening using attributes that readily describe quality interpersonal listening, namely attention, recognition, understanding, and responding (Bodie et al., 2012). Similarly, after interviewing stakeholders of two large organizations based in Australia, Burnside-Lawry (2012) defined "an effective listening organization" as "an organization that incorporated values and actions to listen accurately—the perception that the organization has accurately received and understood the message sent, and in a supportive manner—that enhanced the relationship between an organization and its stakeholders" (p. 113). She additionally noted qualities and behaviors of a competent organizational listing, including being open minded, asking and answering questions, attentiveness, willing to listen and address all issues, understands/comprehends appropriate corporate culture, eye contact, responds appropriately, appropriate staff involved, honesty, knowledgeable, responsible, good memory, respectful, and honesty. More recent work by Gearhart and Maben (2021) has shown that judgments of hypothetical, organizational social media responses (as indications that an organization "is listening") follow expectations from work on interpersonal listening competency, namely responses that were perceived as more active and empathic were also judged as more competent.

As seen above, many of the characteristics and behaviors of competent organizational listening identified by Macnamara, Burnside-Lawry, and others (e.g., Flynn et al., 2008; Place, 2019; Worthington & Fitch-Hauser, 2018) reflect those associated with competent interpersonal listening (e.g., asking questions, feedback, trust, sincerity, and eye contact; Bodie et al., 2012; Cooper, 1997; Halone et al., 1997). One potential explanation for this is that, like its interpersonal counterpart, organizational listening, as a competency, is defined by both attributes and behaviors. Attributes refer to the beliefs people hold regarding what an object is, whereas behaviors refer to the beliefs people hold regarding what an object does (Pavitt & Haight, 1985). Thus, listening attributes describe the essence of listening (e.g., attentiveness and understanding), which is then enacted by specific behaviors (e.g., eye contact and asking questions; see Bodie et al., 2012). This is, however, a largely untested assumption – one particularly relevant to external organizational stakeholders and one that can be tested using methods borrowed from work documenting implicit theories of listening in the interpersonal domain.

Why an Implicit Theory of Organizational Listening?

Implicit theories explore the mental representations individuals hold in their cognitive system and use to evaluate others (Plaks, 2017). Like other implicit theories (e.g., relationships; Knee, 1998), implicit theories of listening are knowledge structures that specify sets of interconnected listening-related attributes and their behavioral manifestations. The leading scale used to measure individual conceptualizations of listening, the Listening Concepts Inventory (LCI; Imhof & Janusik, 2006), asks respondents to indicate how similar a series of activities are to listening.

These activities cluster around four individual propensities to define listening as (a) *information acquisition* (listening is primarily an ability to organize and retain information); (b) *relationship building* (listening is about "bonding" and "caring" to maintain and establish close relationships); (c) *learning* (listening is the ability to interpret, analyze, and understand information); or (d) a *critical* endeavor (listening is a critical exercise useful when "arguing"). These individual concepts of listening form distinct belief systems about the roles and functions of this communicative activity (Bodie, 2010). If implicit theories of organizational listening are constituted similarly, we would expect responses to items on the LCI to similarly cluster around these four concepts.

H1: Items comprising the LCI will covary along four latent factors, equivalent to the measurement of listening concepts in the interpersonal domain.

In sum, this study begins the process of conceptually clarifying how organizational listening is construed in the minds of external organizational stakeholders, focusing on four primary attributes that define the purposes of listening. Findings from this study are discussed for their implications for organization-stakeholder relationship maintenance, as well as organization-public relationships at large. In the following, we describe the methods employed to test this prediction.

Methods

Participants

We collected a total of 521 usable surveys from individuals enrolled as Qualtrics panelists. Working with a panel provided the advantage of collecting data from a more diverse sample than typical college student samples (see Table 1.1). After a series of pilot tests that helped identify issues with survey design (e.g., length and broken branch chain coding), the full survey was launched on September 14, 2021. Between then and November 22, 2021, a total of 117 respondents failed one or more attention checks and were removed from the completed dataset. Within the items participants rated, there were four additional items that asked them to select a particular answer choice; participants selecting any other answer choice than the one mentioned thus failed that attention check.

Procedures

Our goal was to replicate past research on implicit theories of listening (Bodie, 2010; Imhof & Janusik, 2006). Although the original LCI)consisted of 33 items, in a series of studies, Bodie (2010) found that a 15-item revised version produced more stable results (for a review and critique of the LCI and LCI-R, see Worthington, 2018). As such, respondents were

Table 1.1 Demographic information for sample of 521 Qualtrics panel participants

Demographics	N	%
Sex		
Male	173	33.2
Female	343	65.8
Nonbinary/third gender	4	0.8
Prefer not to say	1	0.2
Income		
Less than $20,000	143	27.4
$20,000–$29,999	73	14.0
$30,000–$39,999	50	9.6
$40,000–$49,999	67	12.9
$50,000–$59,999	32	6.1
$60,000–$69,999	27	5.2
$70,000–$79,999	28	5.4
$80,000–$89,999	13	2.5
$90,000–$99,999	16	3.1
More than $100,000	48	9.2
Prefer not to say	24	4.6
Race		
Asian or Asian American	13	2.5
Black or African American	74	14.2
Latino or Hispanic	83	15.9
Native American or Alaska Native	6	1.2
White	332	63.7
Other	7	1.3
Prefer not to say	6	1.2
Education		
Less than high school	24	4.6
High school/GED	167	32.1
Some college	115	22.1
Trade school/associate degree	52	10.0
4-year degree (BA/BS)	102	19.6
Advanced degree	57	11.0
Prefer not to say	4	0.8
Age	*M*	*SD*
	48.8	17.6

provided with a list of these items (see Table 1.2) and asked to indicate how similar (or not) each reflected their perception of organizational listening using a scale ranging from 1 = not at all similar to 5 = identical.[1]

Results

After removing 16 univariate outliners (all on "Arguing" item) and 17 additional multivariate outliners (i.e., Mahalanobis distance > 34.5),

Table 1.2 LCI-R items used in conceptual replication of organizational listening

Factor	Item	Std. coeff.
Information acquisition (IA)		
M = 3.18	Storing information	.75
SD = .96	Drawing conclusions	.66
	Becoming aware	.67
	Retaining information	.74
Relationship building (RB)		
M = 2.94	Helping	.80
SD = 1.09	Comforting	.80
	Bonding	.67
Learning (L)		
M = 3.24	Learning	.70
SD = .96	Interpreting	.67
	Analyzing	.81
	Understanding	(Excluded)
Critical (C)		
M = 2.67	Arguing	.30*
SD = 1.03	Being critical	.54/.52
	Conceding	.59/.58
	Answering	.81

* Std. coeff. = Standardized coefficients, with the first number from initial 14-item mode; and the second number from model after removing "Arguing" (if only 1 number, estimate did not change).

the data submitted to confirmatory factor analysis included 488 total responses.

The 4-factor LCI-R model with 14 of the original 15 items was tested using the lavaan package in R (Rosseel, 2012) with estimates of reliability generated using semTools (Jorgensen et al., 2018). Although data conformed to the predicted model, CFI = .91, TLI = .88, RMSEA = .09 (90%CI = .08, .10), SRMR = .06, χ^2 (71) = 377.66, $p < .001$, the item "Arguing" returned a low parameter estimate that, upon removal, improved model fit, CFI = .93, TLI = .90, RMSEA = .09 (90%CI = .08, .10), SRMR = .052, χ^2 (59) = 306.58, $p < .001$. Reliability estimates for all four scales were also adequate: IA, ω = .80; RB, ω = .81; Learning, ω = .77; Critical, ω = .67. Descriptive data for these factors, computed from 13 total items (IA = 4 items, RB = 3 items, Learning = 3 items, and Critical = 3 items) are found in Table 1.2. Although small, differences between these mean values were all statistically significant, $p < .001$, suggesting that respondents view organizational listening an activity geared toward learning, followed by information acquisition and relationship building. The critical component of listening was not only the lowest value but it was also the only value statistically below the scale midpoint of 3, t (487) = 5.64, $p < .001$, $d = .34$.

Discussion

To date, research has largely worked from the assumption that organizational listening is conceptually similar to listening as it occurs in interpersonal contexts such as dating relationships or friendships. Even while acknowledging several essential differences (e.g., scale and timing) between organizational and interpersonal listening, Macnamara's descriptions of the fundamental nature of organizational listening still mirror attributes used to describe interpersonal listening. Moreover, research asking (Burnside-Lawry, 2012) or observing (Place, 2019) people inside of organizations often reports on behaviors indicative of competent listening found in studies that explore notions of competent relational (Halone & Pecchioni, 2001) or interpersonal (Bodie et al., 2012) listening. Thus, it stands to reason that everyday notions (implicit theories) of listening might be broad and include those attributes and/or behaviors enacted by a range of specific entities, from people they know well to people that work inside of organizations to those organizations themselves (and even "organizations like that one" in the more general case). This work exploring the structure and functions of implicit theories of organizational listening is much needed for our overall understanding of and to enable the better practice of a key part of organizational life.

We began our exploration into implicit theories of organizational listening by attempting a conceptual replication of the LCI (Bodie, 2010; Imhof & Janusik, 2006), the leading measure of beliefs regarding what listening is, organized around four primary conceptualizations: information acquisition, relationship building, learning, and critical. Our results suggest that external organizational stakeholders' beliefs about listening can be usefully organized around these same four constructs. We also found, however, that the extent to which each conceptualization "is similar" to organizational listening varied. As seen in Table 1.2, respondents viewed organizations who listen well, focusing mainly on learning and information acquisition, followed by relationship building; the notion that listening is a critical endeavor does not seem to align with "good" organizational listening.

That organizational listening appears to center around learning and information acquisition is mirrored by work that suggests organizations "listen effectively" when they employ highly scalable activities like social media listening. Organizations that monitor the conversations surfacing over Twitter, Facebook, Reddit, and other platforms, are thus engaged in important organizational listening. Of course, our results do not help us understand the specific behaviors associated with quality social media listening but there is other work that provides those insights; we also hope our study sparks additional research on this topic.

Organizations who listen well also likely do so in ways that help build relationships with external stakeholders, a finding supported by Gearhart and Maben (2021) who reported judgments of hypothetical, organizational social media responses reflected the expectations associated with interpersonal listening competency. In particular, responses worded to be more "active and empathic" were also judged as more competent. Essentially, quality organizational listening, like competent interpersonal listening, occurs when stakeholders feel they are engaging in a dialogue with the organization. When that dialogue is viewed as something more than just an exchange of information, it helps build bonds between stakeholders and the organization.

Of course, scanning the internet for how people are talking about a brand can also be an essential part of social listening. Stewart and Arnold (2017) defined social listening as the "active process of attending to, observing, interpreting, and responding to a variety of stimuli through mediated, electronic, and social channels" (pp. 12–13). Professionals also acknowledge the importance of social listening. For example, Newberry (2021), in a recent Hootsuite blog posting, described the goal of social listening as to better know and understand one's stakeholders by examining their social media postings and comments. She argued that central to this process is analyzing information and taking action (i.e., responding). Notably, she distinguished social listening from social media monitoring. Social monitoring emphasizes collecting data, while social listening considers the underlying "mood" (angry, confused, happy) behind the data – its social media sentiment. Closely listening allows organizations to adapt to changing social sentiments. As she wrote, "The defining feature of social listening is that it looks forward *and* backward. It's about analyzing the information you collect and using it to guide your strategy and day-to-day actions." Her description embraces the items composing each of the organizational listening factors (e.g., becoming aware, retaining information, bonding, and analyzing) and acknowledges the importance of relationship building.

Overall, our findings support previously presented perspectives of organizational listening (e.g., Burnside-Lawry, 2012; Macnamara, 2020), which identified organizational listening characteristics such as awareness and attention, recognition, understanding, supportiveness, and responding to describe organizational listening. These factors make sense as individuals' communications with organizations often focus not only on learning (i.e., the ability to interpret, analyze, and understand information) and information acquisition (i.e., awareness, retaining/storing information, and drawing conclusions) but also on relationship building (e.g., feeling heard and validated, and finding personal fulfillment in a brand). Notably, respondents' conceptualizations associated with organizational listening did not rate quality listening as a highly *critical* endeavor (listening is a critical exercise useful when "arguing"). As seen in Table 1.2, the Critical factor was below the scale midpoint, suggesting those sorts of activities are not as similar to listening as those found in the other three factors. That "arguing" was the source of all univariate outliners and had a problematic factor loading suggests this term does not fit the "critical" schema; rather, organizations that concede when they answer a stakeholder, perhaps in a way that addresses major arguments, might have an advantage.

While debates and conflict are a normal part of our everyday interpersonal interactions, "arguing" with an organization did not contribute to perceptions that an organization listens well. It is possible that the personalization of an organizational entity can only go so far. For example, when a customer complaint arises, that customer may be faced with a corporate representative who cannot address the issue or can only do so within specified constraints, may be shuttled among multiple individuals having to describe an issue multiple times, or, as is the case more and more, find themselves unable to directly speak with an individual and left to filling out a form, reducing the feeling of interpersonal contact and dialogues.

Recommendations for Practice

Organizations seeking to improve their listening competence must first understand what it is that their external stakeholders expect. First, results from this study suggest that stakeholders conceptualize organizational listening in many of the same ways as they do interpersonal listening, particularly in terms of information acquisition, learning, and relationship building. Thus, what external stakeholders expect from listening organizations is, in many ways, what they expect from listening individuals. Recognizing the underlying belief system stakeholders hold enables practitioners to work with, not against those beliefs. Certainly, social media provides a number of opportunities for dialogues between organizations and their stakeholders. At the same time, however, those platforms are often only used for strictly monitoring (rather than listening) purposes (Stewart & Arnold, 2017). Stakeholders prefer interactions that go beyond advice or a simple acknowledgment to increase feelings of being understood (see Weger et al., 2014; see also Tyler, 2011). While this does not mean that stakeholders are necessarily seeking deep discussions over a candle-lit dinner, they do expect a response, and preferably one keeping with the nature of their concerns, especially when interacting via social media (Gearhart & Maben, 2021. Unfortunately, organizations too often eschew dialogic communication when using social media (see, e.g., Kent & Taylor, 1998; 2002; Kim et al., 2014; Lee et al., 2014; Rybalko & Seltzer, 2010).

Second, the idea of relationship building is not new to public relations scholars. An important means of building relationships is engagement and the expectation of a response central to social presence (Lu et al., 2016). Moreover, social presence and its constructs are predictors of trust. Macnamara (2018) argued that a lack of listening has contributed to declining public trust in both public and private institutions. Thus, responding to stakeholders appropriately is essentially a trust building exercise – one that organizations cannot and should not ignore. Further, research has found that trust emerges from ongoing interactions (Canel & Luoma-aho, 2019) and dialogue (Hung-Baesecke & Chen, 2020; Yang et al., 2015), which suggests that a "one and done" approach to communicating with stakeholders may not be the best approach. Thus, for example, following up on customer communications may lead to feelings of an active interaction or dialogue between the organization and individual, which in turn may result in stronger relationships. Examples include following up on a customer complaint or ensuring that an order arrived safely. In another noteworthy example, when a client tried to return an unopened bag of food following her dog's death to Chewy, the pet company gave her a full refund, told her to donate the food to a shelter, and then followed up by sending her flowers and condolences (Dawn, 2022). While Chewy did this privately, once Anna Brose tweeted publicly about her experience, the tweet, and by extension Chewy, received over 744,000 likes.

There is a growing expectation that organizations will engage with their stakeholders (Reinikainen et al., 2020) and the best stakeholder engagement will include listening. Macnamara (2020) argued that organizations should have dedicated listeners whose job and role is to go beyond monitoring stakeholder communications (i.e., data collection) to understanding their wants, needs, and feelings and actively engaging with them (i.e., organizational and social listening). As those dedicated listeners engage in behaviors that signal underlying attributes of information acquisition, learning, and relationships building, the organization grows in its capacity to be judged as a listening organization. Likewise, as additional resources are allocated to the technologies, structures, policies, and practices that enable information acquisition, learning, and relationship building, organizations are more able to claim they are built on an architecture of listening (Macnamara, 2015).

Limitations and Directions for Future Research

In addition to our mishap of inadvertently excluding the term "understanding," this study is also limited to making claims about general features (attributes) of listening. And although much more work is needed on those fundamental building blocks of what listening is, so too is there a need to complement that focus with an equally in-depth look at specific ways in which organizations can enact "good" listening. With technology changing by the quarter, any research should avoid being platform or technology driven but rather look to general patterns and generalizable response typologies that can be adapted to multiple contemporary and future contexts. We also caution that this work should consider the global nature of organizational life. Because "good" listening likely differs in some important ways across cultures (e.g., Ala-Kortesmaa & Valikoski, 2011; Imhof, 2003; Roebuck et al., 2016), any work that focuses exclusively on organizations in Western, Educated, Industrialized, Rich, and Democratic (WEIRD) societies (Henrich et al., 2010) may not apply to those outside of these parameters. Although our Qualtrics sample goes beyond the typical college-student sample found in the majority of listening research (Keaton & Bodie, 2013), our participant pool is far from representing the entirety of the population who interact with organizations. Even so, we have provided a general framework for launching a rich research program on implicit theories of organization listening that should bear theoretical and practical fruit alike.

Potential areas of research include the relationship between the nature and type of organizational listening to building stakeholder relationships (Broom et al., 1997), perceptions of mutual benefit (Bruning et al., 2006), stakeholder satisfaction (Bruning & Ledingham, 1999, 2000), and other elements of stakeholder dialogue, management, and engagement (Bendell, 2003; Johnson-Cramer et al., 2003; Tsai & Men, 2013). Ultimately, researchers and practitioners alike seek a better understanding of the factors that aid in managing public relations (e.g., Grunig & Hunt, 1984; Hon & Grunig, 1999; Huang & Zhang, 2015; Ledingham, 2003; Ledingham & Bruning, 1998), and effective organizational listening is among those factors.

Note

1 The item "understanding" was inadvertently left off the survey, thus leaving us with a 14-item version of the LCI.

References

Ala-Kortesmaa, S., & Valikoski, T. (2011, May 25). *Professional communication and listening concepts of Finnish and American legal professionals*. Paper presented at the Annual Meeting of the International Communication Association, Boston, MA. Retrieved from http://citation.allacademic.com/meta/p488673_index.html

Bendell, J. (2003). Talking for change? Reflections on effective stakeholder dialogue. In J. Andriof, S. Waddock, B. Husted, & S. S. Rahman (Eds.), *Unfolding stakeholder thinking 2: Relationships, communication, reporting and performance* (pp. 53–69). https://doi.org/10.4324/9781351281843

Bodie, G. D. (2010). The revised Listening Concepts Inventory (LCI-R): Assessing individual and situational differences in the conceptualization of listening. *Imagination, Cognition and Personality*, 30, 301–339. https://doi.org/10.2190/IC.30.3.f

Bodie, G. D. (2012). Listening as positive communication. In T. Socha, & M. Pitts (Eds.), *The positive side of interpersonal communication* (pp. 109–125). Peter Lang.

Bodie, G. D., St. Cyr, K., Pence, M., Rold, M., & Honeycutt, J. (2012). Listening competence in initial interactions I: Distinguishing between what listening is and what listeners do. *International Journal of Listening, 26*, 1–28. https://doi.org/10.1080/10904018.2012.639645

Broom, G. M., Casey, S., & Ritchey, J. (1997). Toward a concept and theory of organization-public relationships. *Journal of Public Relations Research, 9*(2), 83–98. https://doi.org/10.1207/s1532754xjprr0902_01

Bruning, S. D., DeMiglio, P. A., & Embry, K. (2006). Mutual benefit as outcome indicator: Factors influencing perceptions of benefit in organization–public relationships. *Public Relations Review, 32*(1), 33–40. https://doi.org/10.1016/j.pubrev.2005.10.005

Bruning, S. D., & Ledingham, J. A. (1999). Relationships between organizations and publics: Development of a multi-dimensional organization-public relationship scale. *Public Relations Review, 25*(2), 157–170. https://doi.org/10.1016/S0363-8111(99)80160-X

Bruning, S. D., & Ledingham, J. A. (2000). Perceptions of relationships and evaluations of satisfaction: An exploration of interaction. *Public Relations Review, 26*(1), 85–95. https://doi.org/10.1016/S0363-8111(00)00032-1

Burnside-Lawry, J. (2012). Listening and participatory communication: A model to assess organization listening competency. *International Journal of Listening, 26*, 102–121. https://doi.org/10.1080/10904018.2012.678092

Canel, M., & Luoma-aho, V. (2019). *Public sector communication: Closing gaps between public sector organizations and citizens.* Wiley.

Cooper, L. O. 1997. Listening competency in the workplace: A model for training. *Business Communication Quarterly, 60*, 75–84. https://doi.org/10.1177/108056999706000405

Dawn, R. (2022, June 17). Woman whose dog died tries to return unused pet food – and gets a sweet surprise. *Today.* https://www.today.com/pets/pets/chewy-sends-flowers-woman-pet-food-dog-dies-rcna33956

Flynn, J., Valikoski, T.-R., & Grau, J. (2008). Listening in the business context: Reviewing the state of research. *International Journal of Listening, 22*, 141–151. https://doi.org/10.1080/10904010802174800

Gearhart, C. C., & Maben, S. K. (2021). Active and empathic listening in social media: What do stakeholders really expect? *International Journal of Listening, 35*(3), 166–187. https://doi.org/10.1080/10904018.2019.1602046

Grunig, J. E., & Hunt, T. (1984). *Managing public relations.* Holt, Rinehart and Winston.

Halone, K. K., Wolvin, A. D., & Coakley, C. G. 1997. Accounts of effective listening across the lifespan: Expectations and experiences associated with competent listening practices. *International Journal of Listening, 11*, 15–38. https://doi.org/10.1207/s1932586xijl1101_2

Halone, K. K., & Pecchioni, L. L. (2001). Relational listening: A grounded theoretical model. *Communication Reports, 14*(1), 59–71. https://doi.org/10.1080/08934210109367737

Henrich, J., Heine, S., & Norenzayan, A. (2010). The weirdest people in the world? *Behavioral and Brain Sciences, 33*(2–3), 61–83. https://doi.org/10.1017/S0140525X0999152X

Hon, L. C., & Grunig, J. E. (1999). *Guidelines for measuring relationships in public relations.* Institute for PR. http://www.Instituteforpr.Org/Research_single/Guidelines_measuring_relationships

Huang, Y.-H., & Zhang, Y. (2015). Revisiting organization-public relationships research for the past decade. In E.-J. Ki, J.-N. Kim, & J. A. Ledingham (Eds.), *Public relations as relationship management: A relational approach to the study and practice of public relations* (pp. 3–27). Routledge.

Hung-Baesecke, C.-J. F., & Chen, Y.-R. R. (2020). Explicating trust and its relation to dialogue at a time of divided societies. *Public Relations Review, 46*(1), 101890. https://doi.org/10.1016/j.pubrev.2020.101890

Imhof, M. (2003). The social construction of the listener: Listening behavior across situations, perceived listener status, and cultures. *Communication Research Reports, 20*, 357–366. https://doi.org/10.1080/08824090309388835

Imhof, M., & Janusik, L. (2006). Development and validation of the Imhof-Janusik listening concepts inventory to measure listening conceptualization differences between cultures. *Journal of Intercultural Communication Research, 35*, 79–98. https://doi.10.1080/17475750600909246

Johnson-Cramer, M. E., Berman, S. L., & Post, J. E. (2003). Re-examining the concept of "stakeholder management." In J. Andriof, S. Waddock, B. Husted, & S. S. Rahman (Eds.), *Unfolding stakeholder thinking 2: Relationships, communication, reporting and performance* (pp. 145–161). https://doi.org/10.4324/9781351281843

Jorgensen, T. D., Pornprasertmanit, S., Schoemann, A. M., & Rosseel, Y. (2018). semTools: Useful tools for structural equation modeling. R package version 0.5-1. Retrieved from https://CRAN.R-project.org/package=semTools

Keaton, S. A., & Bodie, G. D. (2013). The statistical and methodological acuity of scholarship appearing in the *International Journal of Listening* (1987–2011). *International Journal of Listening, 27*(2), 115–135. https://doi.10.1080/10904018.2013.813206

Kent, M. L., & Taylor, M. (1998). Building dialogic relationships through the world wide web. *Public Relations Review, 24*(3), 321–334. https://doi.org/10.1016/S0363-8111(99)80143-X

Kent, M. L., & Taylor, M. (2002). Toward a dialogic theory of public relations. *Public Relations Review, 28*(1), 21–37. https://doi.org/10.1016/S0363-8111(02)00108-X

Kim, D., Chun, H., Kwak, Y., & Nam, Y. (2014). The employment of dialogic principles in website, Facebook, and Twitter platforms of environmental nonprofit organizations. *Social Science Computer Review, 32*, 590–605. https://doi.org/10.1177

Knee, C. R. (1998). Implicit theories of relationships: Assessment and prediction of romantic relationship initiation, coping, and longevity. *Journal of Personality and Social Psychology, 74*, 360–370. https://doi.org/10.1037/0022-3514.74.2.360

Ledingham, J. A. (2003). Explicating relationship management as a general theory of public relations. *Journal of Public Relations Research, 15*(2), 181–198.

Ledingham, J. A., & Bruning, S. D. (1998). Relationship management in public relations: Dimensions of an organization-public relationship. *Public Relations Review, 24*(1), 55–65. https://doi.org/10.1016/S0363-8111(98)80020-9

Lee, A. M., Gil de Zúñiga, H., Coleman, R., & Johnson, T. J. (2014). The dialogic potential of social media: Assessing the ethical reasoning of companies' public relations on Facebook and Twitter. In M. W. DiStaso, & D. S. Bortree (Eds.), *Ethical practice of social media in public relations* (pp. 157–175). Routledge.

Lewis, L. (2019). *The power of strategic listening.* Rowman & Littlefield.

Lu, B., Fan, W., & Zhou, M. (2016). Social presence, trust, and social commerce purchase intention: An empirical research. *Computers in Human Behavior, 56*, 225–237. https://doi.org/10.1016

Macnamara, J. (2015, June). *Creating an "architecture of listening" in organizations: The basis of engagement, trust, healthy democracy, social equity, and business sustainability*. University of Technology Sydney. https://www.uts.edu.au/sites/default/files/fass-organizational-listening-report.pdf

Macnamara, J. (2016). *Organizational listening: The missing essential in public communication*. Peter Lang.

Macnamara, J. (2018). Toward a theory and practice of organizational listening. *International Journal of Listening, 32*, 1–23. http://dx.doi.org/10.1080/10904018.2017.1375076

Macnamara, J. (2020). Listening for health democracy. In D. L. Worthington and G. D. Bodie (Eds.), *The handbook of listening*. Wiley Blackwell.

Newberry, C. (2021, November 22). What is social listening, why it matters, and 10 tools to make it easier. Hootsuite. https://blog.hootsuite.com/social-listening-business/

Pavitt, C., & Haight, L. (1985). The "competent communicator" as a cognitive prototype. *Human Communication Research, 12*(2), 225–241. https://doi.org/10.1111/j.1468-2958.1985.tb00074.x

Place, K. R. (2019). Listening as the driver of public relations practice and communication strategy within a global public relations agency. *Public Relations Journal, 12*(3), 1–18. https://prjournal.instituteforpr.org/wp-content/uploads/katieplace_listening.pdf

Plaks, J. E. (2017). Implicit theories: Assumptions that shape social and moral cognition. *Advances in Experimental Social Psychology, 56*, 259–310. https://doi.org/10.1016/bs.aesp.2017.02.003

Reinikainen, H., Kari, J. T., & Luoma-aho, V. (2020). Generation Z and organizational listening on social media. *Media and Communication, 8*(2), 185–196. https://doi.org/10.17645/mac.v8i2.2772

Roebuck, D. B., Bell, R. L., Raina, R., & Lee, C. E. (2016). Comparing perceived listening behavior differences between managers and nonmanagers living in the United States, India, and Malaysia. *International Journal of Business Communication, 53*, 485–518. https://doi.org/10.1177/2329488415572789

Rosseel, Y. (2012). lavaan: An R package for structural equation modeling. *Journal of Statistical Software, 48*(2), 1–36. http://www.jstatsoft.org/v48/i02/

Rybalko, S., & Seltzer, T. (2010). Dialogic communication in 140 characters or less: How Fortune 500 companies engage stakeholders using Twitter. *Public Relations Review, 36*, 336–341. https://doi.org/10.1016/j.pubrev.2010.08.004

Stewart, M. C., & Arnold, C. L. (2017). Defining social listening: Recognizing an emerging dimension of listening. *International Journal of Listening, 32*, 85–100. https://doi.org/10.1080/10904018.2017.1330656

Tsai, W.-H. S., & Men, L. R. (2013). Motivations and antecedents of consumer engagement with brand pages on social networking sites. *Journal of Interactive Advertising, 13*(2), 76–87. https://doi.10.1080/15252019.2013.826549

Tyler, J. A. (2011). Reclaiming rare listening as a means of organizational re-enchantment. *Journal of Organizational Change Management, 24*, 143–157.

Weger, H., Castle Bell, G., Minei, E. M., & Robinson, M. C. (2014). The relative effectiveness of active listening in initial interactions. *International Journal of Listening, 28*, 13–31. https://doi.org/10.1007/s12525-011-0065-z

Worthington, D. L. (2018). Listening concepts inventory. In D. L. Worthington & G. D. Bodie (Eds.), *The listening sourcebook: Measures and methods.* Wiley-Blackwell.

Worthington, D. L., & Bodie, G. D. (Eds.). (2018). *The listening sourcebook: Measures and methods.* Wiley-Blackwell.

Worthington, D. L., & Fitch-Hauser, M. (2018). *Listening: Processes, functions and competency* (2nd ed.). Routledge.

Yang, S.-U., Kang, M., & Cha, H. (2015). A study on dialogic communication, trust, and distrust: Testing a scale for measuring organization–public dialogic communication (OPDC). *Journal of Public Relations Research, 27*(2), 175–192. https://doi.org/10.1080/1062726X.2015.1007998

2 Incorporating Competent Interpersonal Listening Practices in Social Media

Christopher C. Gearhart and Sarah K. Maben

Introduction

Public relations literature has long called for two-way communication and better dialogue between organizations and individuals, especially in the digital and social media landscape. Listening has rarely been the focus of such inquiries but has received attention in interpersonal communication research (e.g., Bodie, 2009; Worthington, 2005, 2008). In an analysis of current strategic communication evaluation models, Macnamara and Gregory (2018) found that one-way communication was still predominant with two-way communication and stakeholders secondary in organizational communication.

Recently, special calls for research like the ones from the Arthur W. Page Center for Integrity in Public Communication and the *International Journal of Listening* have asked scholars to further investigate the role of listening in digital organizational communication. In answering these calls, researchers have suggested that organizational listening expectations and strategies align with those for interpersonal listening, and current research has demonstrated that claim to be partially true (Gearhart & Maben, 2019; Maben & Gearhart, 2018). This chapter merges listening concepts from interpersonal communication research with mass communication and public relations practices in social media. Here we attempt to answer the question of what do stakeholders expect organizational listening to look like on social media.

Bridging the once-dominant view of a divide between mass communication and interpersonal communication, Cathcart and Gumpert (1983) proposed the idea of mediated interpersonal communication. They offered a communication typology that included media involvement in interpersonal communication. "The interposed medium determines the quantity and quality of information and also shapes the relationships of the participants" (p. 271). In 2018, O'Sullivan and Carr coined "masspersonal communication," which considers certain forms of mediated communication as both mass and interpersonal communication. The masspersonal communication model, or MPCM, theorizes two

DOI: 10.4324/9781003273851-4

dimensions of message qualities: message accessibility ("the *perceived accessibility* dimension involves the degree of perceived accessibility to a particular message at any particular time"; O'Sullivan & Carr, 2018, p. 1165) and message personalization ("*Personalization* involves the degree to which receivers perceive a message reflects their distinctiveness as individuals differentiated by their interests, history, [and] relationship network"; O'Sullivan & Carr, 2018, p. 1166). Masspersonal communication is, then, marked as communication activities high in personalization yet also highly accessible to a larger public audience—such as communication via social media. With this view in mind, an interpersonal communication activity such as listening can be performed and widely accessed (and, crucially, evaluated by others) in a mass communication context, thus masspersonal communication.

For organizations, social media channels created more potential for direct dialogue with stakeholders, which requires listening or evidence of listening. In particular, we have focused our efforts on understanding stakeholder perceptions of organizational listening behavior (Maben & Gearhart, 2018) and specifically the use of active-empathic listening (AEL) strategies by organizations on social media (Gearhart & Maben, 2019). Active-empathic listening, or AEL, is considered competent listening, where the listener is focused, attentive, and shows empathy for the speaker (Bodie, 2011; Drollinger et al., 2006). We have forwarded the argument that because past research has established that organizations should listen in the same manner that people do, they should employ interpersonal listening behaviors and strategies—namely AEL—in their communication with stakeholders.

The purpose of this chapter is to cover how active listening, a listening technique studied largely in the interpersonal communication context, is experienced by stakeholders in their social media communication with organizations. What follows is an overview of research on organizational listening competency.

Organizations Listening Interpersonally

Organizations have a long history of "listening" to their stakeholders in a passive fashion of surveillance and monitoring. Scanning the public sphere to learn what people are wanting or needing, sending out satisfaction surveys to garner data from individuals, and other market research activities are ways in which organizations typically "listen." These behaviors, however, are largely one-directional, whereby the organization collects the information from the consumer or stakeholder and there is no response back. How can an organization respond in accessible and personalized ways to an anonymous survey response? The purpose of the "listening" was to solicit feedback for improvement and, therefore, additional sales, donations, etc.,—for the organization's sake, not necessarily its stakeholders. For many organizations, this feedback solicitation disguised as listening was only window dressing and not an authentic attempt at relationship building and dialogue. In today's digital landscape, the use of social media to strategically collect a follower's personal information, all too often without their knowledge or consent, has become a huge industry. However, digital eavesdropping is far from listening.

But, when genuine and done well, listening fosters dialogue and keeps the communication flowing both ways, which is ideally how organizations would utilize networks such as social media platforms. Like a conversation between two individuals, true listening involves actions and responses by both parties. In social media, these actions could be simple, less personalized acknowledgments such as a heart on Twitter or Instagram or more elaborate like a specifically tailored comment, with or without graphics like emojis or GIFs, on YouTube or Facebook.

From the masspersonal communication view, listening can be accomplished by an organization and ideally results in a dialogue or conversation. This can take several forms: (a) an organization finds a particular person's social media post regarding their organization or industry and they publicly respond to the individual; or (b) an organization is tagged by an individual and they publicly respond accordingly; or (c) an organization posts on social media and an individual responds back to them. In all of these situations, the key elements are that the message is accessible to a public and the message is personalized. Blanket statements, boilerplate, or generic bot responses in any of these cases would fall into a more mass communication-centric realm that belies one-way communication attempts.

In our early work in organizational social media listening, we analyzed companies lauded for their social media conversations and high degrees of engagement with followers: Lowe's, Old Navy, Best Buy, Nordstrom, and Amazon.com (Maben & Gearhart, 2018). These companies used techniques from interpersonal listening to help connect with stakeholders. For example, a fashionista tagged Nordstrom on a Twitter post to let users know the origins of his ensemble. Nordstrom responded with a celebratory comment about his look, like you would say to a friend trying a new outfit (Nordstrom, 2017a). In another case, a customer of Best Buy explained his negative experience with returning a TV and his frustration at not being able to receive a full refund. He implored for help on the Best Buy Facebook page, to which an employee named Lee replied, "I'm sorry to hear the new TV didn't quite work out, especially if you were unexpectedly charged for something you weren't aware even came with the purchase" (Best Buy, 2017). These examples are indicative of effective listening and continue the conversation beyond mere monitoring or surveillance.

As we found examples of interpersonal listening in the organizational social media posts, we also identified missed opportunities and potential pitfalls special to the digital platforms. For instance, Nordstrom posted a question asking, "Who's pumped for the Big Game?" in a post promoting Jimmy Choo pumps (Nordstrom, 2017b). Several dozen responses came in but there was only one response back on the part of the organization, leaving the conversation unattended and a missed opportunity. Social media listening competency requires an understanding of interpersonal listening in a masspersonal communication world and requires at least some type of response from the organization.

Active-Empathic Listening in Social Media

Listening can be considered from perspectives of listening presage, process, and product (Bodie et al., 2008). In presage, listening is viewed as an individual difference whereby entities—either individuals or organizations—vary in their skillful behavior. Process reflects "covert mental behavior and ... overt behavior" (p. 113). Listening product is the varied outcomes that are associated with the listening process and often relate to relationship building, affect, or information acquisition. Conceivably, individuals who are "better" listeners will tend to have more skills, be more involved in the listening process, and achieve positive listening outcomes.

One study investigated what listening behaviors constituted "good" or competent listeners (Bodie et al., 2012). Interestingly enough, the category of behaviors that most closely aligned with competent listening were verbal behaviors, specifically actions such as asking/answering questions, making relevant remarks, and elaborating on previous statements made by speakers. This is important for social media listening because listening is accomplished largely through verbal messaging, such that there is some textual response on the part of the hearer (either the individual or the organization). While some responses may be nonverbal (such as emojis, GIFs, or likes), most are written responses that include the use of language.

It is assumed that entities that are competent listeners also have a variety of different listening strategies they are able to perform. One such particular listening strategy is AEL, which is the active and emotional involvement of a listener. Listening responses that are higher in AEL tend to be more responsive to the needs and feelings of the speaker, and they are generally original messages specifically tailored to the listening situation. Therefore, alignment with the message personalization dimension of masspersonal communication becomes clear. Additionally, AEL behaviors are similar to the verbal responding behaviors that are utilized by competent communicators including asking/answering questions, paraphrasing, and elaborating on previous statements made by the speaker. As such, it holds to reason that those entities, in this case, organizations, that utilize listening responses higher in AEL will be perceived as more effective and appropriate in their listening.

An example of an organizational response that is high in both activity and empathy would be one that acknowledges how the person could feel in that situation and provides clarity on how both parties can proceed next toward a solution. An example can be seen in another Best Buy exchange when a follower complained to the company on Facebook about how he felt he was not being listened to by a customer service representative. A Best Buy representative, in turn, responded how "I'd certainly be frustrated" too, expressing sympathy for the follower, and continued to press for further information to determine how the difficulty could be resolved (Best Buy, 2017). Messaging could fall into a quadrant of both high activity and empathy, low activity and empathy, or a mix of low and high (see Figure 2.1). A standard message you see from many companies on social media is "DM (direct message) us for more help," which would be low on

Original Post by Follower of a Hardware Store	
Hello. I am hoping to get some assistance from your company. My step dad was in a bad accident on Monday July 3. In Granbury, TX right outside your store. He was t boned while riding his motorcycle, and it amputated his left leg above the knee. He is in good spirits, but it will be a long road ahead. I am coming to you because I am needing assistance purchasing supplies to build a wheelchair ramp for his house. Any help would be greatly appreciated!	
High Activity-High Empathy	Low Activity-High Empathy
We're sorry to hear of your step father's accident-this must be a trying time for your family. In situations like this people need some aid. How can we help? Maybe through discounts or even free supplies. If you could please send a formal request for supplies to our Senior Management team at your local store we will assist you with your needs (for Granbury that's Name @ 817-555-1234 or granburystore@company.com). Again we are sorry for this terrible accident to your stepfather, we understand your concern about taking care of him.	*We apologize for just now contacting you. This sounds like it is a difficult time for you--it must be overwhelming. Again we are sorry for this terrible accident to your stepfather, you must be concerned.*
High Activity-Low Empathy	Low Activity-Low Empathy
We saw your post from earlier today. What exactly do you need? Likely a ramp for any stairs in the home. Contact our Sales team at (888)-555-1234 so that we might further assist you in finding the supplies you will need. Ask for Angela at extension 4567.	*Please reach out to our Sales team at (888)-555-1234 and a product specialist will be able to assist you with locating the supplies that you need.*

Figure 2.1 Example matrix of active-empathic response types

the AEL scale. It offers no acknowledgment of the stakeholder's feelings and the action is vague and another step. A sample response from an organization when a complaint was posted shows an acknowledgment of feelings and action: "We are sorry to hear about your recent experience. A mid-day meal mishap can ruin a day, and for that we are sorry. Let us treat you and your lunch friend next time. Message us a convenient time and Marcie will call with the deets."

Stakeholder Expectations for Organizational Listening

With the amount of traffic on social media daily, how can an organization listen to all of its stakeholders? Our research project aimed at helping to identify more clearly stakeholder expectations for organizational listening. Some stakeholders may not expect much, and others want action and to feel as if the organization really listened to their communique, whether a complaint, question, or kudos. If you were to post a "loved your new hair care product" on a company's Facebook page, do you expect a response or evidence of listening? When you complain about lost bags on an airline's Twitter feed, what kind of listening do you expect? The key is to identify the level of action and empathy expected, and what will build and maintain the stakeholder relationship with the organization.

In thinking about this question for an organization, it should be noted that AEL listening in interpersonal communication is contextual (Bodie et al., 2013). That is, not all listening situations are equal or many may not even necessitate a high AEL response. Individuals hold schemas for AEL that become activated when particular features of a message trigger or compel someone to use an active and empathic response. We believe that the same should hold true for organizations. They should develop such schemas as well to identify those types of situations and message characteristics that would elicit a high AEL response.

Indeed, in our research, we have found patterns that individuals rate some followers' posts as needing more or less activity or empathy from the organization than others (Gearhart & Maben, 2019). For example, on a scale of 1 (strongly disagree) to 7 (strongly agree), college students rated a situation where the poster expressed feelings of being discriminated against by the organization as having high levels of agreement for expected activity (4.94) and empathy (4.50). However, in a situation where a poster simply gave praise to an organization for great service, levels of expected activity (3.65) and empathy (3.72) were much lower. Thus, social media followers showed differing expectations regarding how much AEL a particular message might require, so it is important for organizations to understand what those situations might be. In a second study, we found the same pattern but among an older sample (average age 52 years old). We further analyzed the situations and again found that when the organizational follower was posting complaints or frustrations with the quality of service from the organization, expectations for activity and empathy were higher as compared to other contexts like praise or donation requests.

Organizational Response Competency

We have consistently found that stakeholders of all types hold different expectations for organizations to employ AEL strategies dependent upon the context of the conversation. After understanding the differences in expectations, we then asked the question if certain types of organizational responses were rated as more effective or appropriate (what we also call "competent") than others. What we found was that when responses from organizations are more active and empathic—regardless of the context of the situation—stakeholders rate them as more appropriate and effective (Gearhart & Maben, 2019).

In our study of college students (Gearhart & Maben, 2019), we tested four situations where a follower of an organization posted a hypothetical social media message directly to an organization's account. A social media emulator was used to make fake messages that resembled actual posts on Facebook, Twitter, and Instagram (see Figure 2.2). The organizations varied from a home improvement store to a police department and the messages contained both positive and negative content. Then, survey takers received a randomly assigned response from the organization. Respondents could have received one of four types of responses and they all varied with respect to the amount of activity and empathy in the response (see Figure 2.1). After reading the random response they received, the college student survey takers then rated how competent the

Figure 2.2 A sample scenario from the study

organization's response to the original poster's message was on a scale of 1 (strongly disagree) to 7 (strongly agree). In three of the four situations, it was found that the response high in both activity and empathy (high AEL response) was rated as being the most competent (average rating 5.9). Similarly, in three of the four situations, the opposite was found for the low AEL responses; those messages low in activity and empathy were rated the least competent (average rating 4.6).

To again test the effectiveness of high versus low AEL organizational responses, we replicated the study described above with an older adult sample. Survey takers were presented with a follower's hypothetical post to an organization's social media page, were then randomly presented either a high AEL response or a low AEL response from the organization, and were asked to rate how competent they perceived the response to be. We found that, across all four hypothetical situations, the high AEL responses showed competence scores equal to or greater than low AEL responses (interestingly, the situation in which ratings of competence were the same for high and low AEL responses was a message from a follower asking for a product donation). This indicates that, at the least, responses higher in AEL are as effective and appropriate as low AEL responses and, at best, higher AEL responses can garner higher perceptions of competence for the organization than lower AEL responses.

Taken together, the results of these two studies support the use of more active and empathic responses by organizations on their social media platforms, noting again that some situational contingencies can come into play. This type of response promotes listening, can spark dialogic, two-way communication, and offers a more personalized and immediate experience for the stakeholders. Some of the responding behaviors that organizations can employ are discussed later in the Recommendations for Practice section.

Just as our finding that not all situations activate or require AEL behaviors, not all posts or messages directed at an organization will be prime for true dialogue (Kent & Lane, 2021). Kent and Lane (2021) suggest that, over the years, public relations literature has compressed the definitions of two-way communication and dialogue. True dialogue may not be possible in all situations and may happen outside of orchestrated communication. "There are of course dozens of other possibilities, but for dialogue to occur, the focus has to be on interaction and understanding not on problem-solving, persuasion, or promotion/marketing" (Kent & Lane, 2021, p. 7). Many online interactions will be transactional in nature like Buber's description of technical dialogue (Kramer & Gawlick, 2003). In technical dialogue, communication is based on a need to exchange information for a purpose. We found this to be true in our research. Stakeholders were driven by a need to have an issue resolved, a question answered, or a compliment to be delivered. Whether true dialogue or technical dialogue, the respondents wanted to be heard—they wanted some acknowledgment that their message had been received and considered.

Although these studies provide data to support that stakeholders hold certain expectations for how organizations should listen and that organizations who respond in more active and empathic ways are perceived positively, we also collected qualitative responses and anecdotal evidence that show the practical ways in which organizational listening competence matters.

What Stakeholders Said

In our survey of older adults, we asked the respondents to think of a specific time they contacted an organization through social media and provided details about the exchange. Scenarios included asking about locating an advertised product, needing help or information related to a purchase or potential purchase, thanking a company or giving public "high fives," notifying a company of a hacked Facebook page, and complaints about service, products, and deliveries. Some used social media after not receiving responses through other options like phone calls or email. One respondent used Facebook as a way to contact a company because it was the "best way to reach them." Through past successful responses, the respondent anticipated future responses and evidence of listening.

For respondents using social media to connect with organizations regarding unsatisfactory products or services, they were looking for resolutions, whether a found delivery or free coupons to soften a bad experience. "It's nice to get a response and to feel heard. If I don't receive a response, I feel less heard and I'm less likely to use/order from that company in the future," said one respondent. Another respondent noted how social media provides a central spot for contacting the organization: "I valued having the option to write without having to find addresses, etc." When celebrating a company for its communication, respondents included the name of the company. For example, Imperfect Foods "acknowledged my reaching out and responded graciously." The Krusteaz's Facebook team even sent blueberry muffin mix to a respondent who contacted them about an inappropriate message on their site.

Social media outlets provide alternatives to stakeholders who do not get a response through other channels. If a phone call or general email account doesn't work, social media might, especially if the message is accessible to other stakeholders. One respondent resorted to a message to his bank on Twitter after trying to reach customer service "for days without any response." The bank's social media team resolved the problem, and the customer was satisfied with the response. Another tried calls and several emails to a local internet provider but turned to a public "scathing" message on Facebook. He said too many companies are removing emails or not monitoring those accounts and forcing stakeholders to "use chat bots or call them, and that is unacceptable."

One respondent notified a cemetery of the property's poor condition and was not satisfied with the automatic, generic response received. Another said, "I received a robot response and the issue was never officially resolved. The only benefit from contacting them on Twitter was you got an automated response." The automated message, whether machine or human, left respondents feeling that competent listening was missing. One respondent contacted a restaurant about breaches in COVID-19 protocols and the response was a form to fill out. The respondent said, "Actually listen/read rather than asking to fill out a standardized form after all the details were given in the original message."

Respondents really want acknowledgment that organizations received and understood their message. One said: "I wanted at least an acknowledgment." Another said a response itself is more important than the outcome of the issue, pointing to the listener's expectation to be heard and personally recognized. Respondents were very satisfied or most happy when organizations met this simple acknowledgment threshold and then added a small discount, concession, coupon, contest entry, or other nominal tokens.

Timing matters for some listening situations more than others. One respondent asked a bar its hours via Facebook and did not receive a timely answer, so his potential bar-hopping plans changed. Another contacted an organization via social media just to test it as a communication vehicle. He had a response from Autozone's Facebook team within 15 minutes. The immediacy was not as important as receiving evidence of listening, but organizational social media teams can identify potential messages that would merit a quicker response.

Respondents reported being satisfied even when their message was a compliment that did not require a remedy. "Whether or not the response is what I'm hoping to hear, at least someone takes the time to respond and that is most important." One respondent thanked a page for a virtual concert and received a satisfactory response: "They said they were glad I could attend and hope I will attend more. Good answer."

Mediated Listening Responses

We have begun investigating perceptions of the organizational use of media—emojis, GIFs, and memes—in their social media responses and evidence of listening. To investigate this, respondents were queried about their perceptions of the appropriateness of organizations using GIFs, emojis, and memes in their responses to stakeholders. Results indicated limited support for the use of some of these types of media in organizational responses. We found that GIFs and emojis were deemed acceptable in responses by about a third of respondents, leaving more room for investigation.

Table 2.1 Totals and percentages for appropriateness of organizational media use in responses

	GIFs	Emojis	Memes
Slightly inappropriate/inappropriate	99 (33%)	85 (28%)	106 (35%)
Neutral	101 (34%)	86 (29%)	97 (33%)
Slightly appropriate/appropriate	99 (33%)	128 (43%)	96 (32%)

Media richness theory states that users should match the richness of the medium and the equivocality of the communication task (see Daft & Lengel, 1984, 1986; Daft et al., 1987; Ishii et al., 2019). In other words, the more complicated the task, a richer medium would be used for more effective communication. Originally tied to organizational communication, the theory suggested a technical explanation might require a face-to-face meeting, while sharing data might only require a written memo. One part of media richness is the availability of additional cues. Emojis offer cues to a message, especially about the intended tone. An unhappy stakeholder might use the red mad face emotion 😡 to illustrate an extreme level of anger.

GIFs and Memes

Participants were approximately equal when reporting the appropriateness of the use of GIFs in an organization's social media response, with nearly a third of participants indicating either no support, neutrality, or support for GIF use (Table 2.1). Respondents were divided into thirds when rating the appropriateness of memes, with a few more participants indicating that it was slightly inappropriate or inappropriate. When asked their feelings about the appropriateness of an organization using GIFs or memes (1 not appropriate to 5 appropriate), respondents were neutral for GIFs ($M = 2.96$) and found memes to be only slightly appropriate ($M = 2.36$).

We asked respondents to give examples of times it would be acceptable for an organization to use GIFs or memes. They said using either would be appropriate if the original message used such graphics. Positive or friendly messaging makes the image-based responses more appropriate, according to respondents. They suggested that humorous messages could elicit a GIF or meme-based response. They cautioned though that GIFs were more acceptable than memes.

Emojis 🙂

Respondents were relatively more accepting of an organization's use of emojis in their responses ($M = 3.20$) with 43% ($n = 128$) reporting they were "slightly appropriate" or "appropriate." We asked survey respondents to give instances where they felt it would be acceptable for an organization to use an emoji in a response. They offered that organizations could use emojis in response to a good review, when content was friendly or positive, to respond to an emoji, and/or to convey meaning like a stronger indication of the message.

With respect to the use of media by organizations in their responses to followers, data indicate limited support for the appropriateness of emojis but offer no conclusive support for or against the use of GIFs and memes. The evidence suggests that organizations should temper their use of these types of richer media types despite the added benefits that accompany the availability of nonverbal cues in communication (Tang & Hew, 2019). Das et al. (2019) found that advertising communication including an emoji "lead to greater positive affect and more favorable purchase intentions than those that do not, at least for hedonic products;" findings were not as strong for utilitarian products (p. 154). Emoticons, emojis, and stickers supplement expressions and "influence interpersonal relationships" (Tang & Hew, 2019, p. 2468) and we suggest they could influence stakeholder-organization relations as well if implemented cautiously and based on the organization's social media analytics and stakeholder profile.

Recommendations for Practice

Moving toward a mindset of listening is a huge shift, even in a medium developed for multi-way communication. Social media outlets offer opportunities for direct lines of two-way communication with stakeholders. But for many organizations and communicators, the public information model, which is one-way and organization-centric, is entrenched and will be difficult to shed. Intentional listening will need to be incorporated into communication plans, policies, training, and the overall communication culture of the organization.

Listening Agents

Recast social media team members as dedicated listeners of the organization. Organizations can better incorporate active listening strategies through the use of "listening agents" or "listening trainers" to meet stakeholder expectations and improve two-way communication. For the organization to be perceived as one that listens, its frontline teams (whether social media or otherwise) should be trained as such. Understanding the role of the organizational listeners emphasizes the importance of the social media team in the dialogue of social media. If social media response teams see themselves as the listening agents or a bridge to stakeholders, they may approach responses in a different light. Seek social media team members with high AEL markers themselves. Their ability as competent listeners will likely transfer to an organization's digital communication platforms.

Listening Training

Train and educate listening agents in competent listening practices from interpersonal communication literature. AEL is a place to start. Using AEL techniques, organizations can bolster the listening piece in stakeholder dialogue. One strategy is to start thinking about the common messages your organization might receive from stakeholders and anticipate ways the organization could respond in higher active and empathic ways. Core messages could then be tailored to individuals using social media to communicate with the organization. Ways organizations can do this are by asking questions that continue the dialogue, following up with stakeholders, providing additional information to supplement what was requested, and acknowledging feelings expressed or implied by followers. Of the AEL strategies from interpersonal listening, these were the ones that translated to the online realm. Listening agents should be trained to craft high activity and high empathy responses, showing competent listening on behalf of the organization. They can also identify situations where higher AEL will be necessary, such as messages with complaints or dissatisfied stakeholders.

Policies

Organizations must review communication plans and social media policies for listening as an important part of the communication process. If it is not mentioned, consider updating the policy. Add objectives related to organizational listening and dialogue to communication plans. Call this your listening plan. For organizations with decision flow charts on when and how to respond on social media, those sample response flow charts will need an update to emphasize listening for dialogue, not just surveillance. Give listening agents latitude to converse in a tone consistent with your brand but also in the manner set by the stakeholder. If the stakeholder uses an emoji, allow your team to respond in kind. Listening agent guidelines should allow flexibility and make room for high AEL responses.

Responding

Respond. The volume of social media traffic makes this a large task, but responding in some form will go a long way toward building and maintaining stakeholder relationships. In the digital realm, a response, whether a like, a quick emoji, or a text response, is evidence that an organization is listening. "Response to customers is more important than the outcome of the issue," one survey participant said. This suggests people want to be heard, even if they do not have a resolution to the exact situation. This simple acknowledgment of your stakeholders shows that you are at least listening, and for many, that is enough. Organizations can use the stakeholder's original message as an indicator of a threshold for appropriateness of organization response with memes, GIFs, and emojis. If your stakeholder uses an emoji, especially in a positive message, it's likely acceptable for you to respond similarly.

Social Media Analytics

Social media managers can use analytics to inform an organization's listening plan. By looking at their platform reports, they can see which messages and responses resonate with their stakeholders. In our research, respondents were almost split into thirds about the appropriateness of using graphics like emojis and GIFs. Some of this may be because emojis and GIFs are associated with more interpersonal messages to friends for entertainment or humor. Using A/B testing for messages with additional media richness, like emojis and GIFs/memes, can compare effectiveness to text-only messages. Each organization should identify appropriateness for its stakeholders and platforms. A third of respondents were neutral on the use of the graphics, which leaves room for exploration for each organization. Given the ambiguous nature of some emojis, it might be wise to have a list of emojis that align with the organization's goal and a list of those with connotations inappropriate to the organization's mission. In the first half of 2021, there were more than 1 billion instances of the loudly crying face 😭, which is typically viewed as having a rather positive sentiment (Brandwatch, 2021).

Moving Forward

Listening in social media is more than surveillance. Listening is an investment of time and resources to build relationships with stakeholders. Evidence of listening is required and takes the form of responses, replies, likes, favorites, shares, mentions, GIFs, and even emojis. The rewards are more than what is garnered through surveillance for stakeholder preferences or purchasing intentions. Dialogue with stakeholders creates a more equitable and symmetrical model of communication, one deemed more ethical in public relations scholarship (Macnamara, 2019). In addition to ethics, listening and dialogue are beneficial in building trust. A recent study has shown that competent listening in social media helped organizations of various types build trust with Generation Z (Reinikainen et al., 2020). The newest generation of social media users and changing technology will continue to shape how organizations and stakeholders communicate.

Social media teams constantly adapt to changing technology. They will need to adapt listening methods as platforms enhance features and offerings. Where a text response may suffice today, a short tailored video with captions may be necessary in the near future. What does not change is the need to keep the channels open for competent listening. Organizations will need to work intentionally to create Macnamara's "architecture of listening" (2019) and social media platforms and their managers are the frontline team to listen. Structures and the latitude to listen and then craft an appropriate response will need to extend to the appointed listening agents as they translate interpersonal listening skills to the masspersonal landscape of social media.

Acknowledgments

This project was supported by a Page Legacy Scholar Grant from The Arthur W. Page Center at The Pennsylvania State University's College of Communications. Any opinions, findings, conclusions, or recommendations expressed in this material are those of the author(s) and do not necessarily reflect the views of The Pennsylvania State University.

Graduate students Amme O'Grady and Jessica Pounds contributed to this research project. We would like to acknowledge the help of doctoral students facilitated by Dr Graham Bodie for their assistance in reviewing the organizational responses.

References

Best Buy. (2017, March 26). *That feeling when the latest weekly deals arrive and you want them all*. [Status update]. Facebook. https://www.facebook.com/bestbuy/posts/10155256110587022\

Bodie, G. D. (2009). Evaluating listening theory: Development and illustration of five criteria. *International Journal of Listening*, *23*(2), 81–103. https://doi.org/10.1080/10904010903014434

Bodie, G. D. (2011). The Active-Empathic Listening Scale (AELS): Conceptualization and evidence of validity within the interpersonal domain. *Communication Quarterly*, *59*, 277–295. https://doi.org/10.1080/01463373.2011.583495

Bodie, G. D., Gearhart, C. C., Denham, J. P., & Vickery, A. J. (2013). The temporal stability and situational contingency of active-empathic listening. *Western Journal of Communication*, *77*(2), 113–138. https://doi.org/10.1080/10570314.2012.656216

Bodie, G. D., St. Cyr, K., Pence, M., Rold, M., & Honeycutt, J. (2012). Listening competence in initial interactions I: Distinguishing between what listening is and what listeners do. *International Journal of Listening*, *26*(1), 1–28. https://doi.org/10.1080/10904018.2012.639645

Bodie, G. D., Worthington, D., Imhof, M., & Cooper, L. O. (2008). What would a unified field of listening look like? A proposal linking past perspectives and future endeavors. *International Journal of Listening*, *22*(2), 103–122. https://doi.org/10.1080/10904010802174867

Brandwatch. (2021). *Emojis and emotions report*. https://www.brandwatch.com/reports/emoji-emotions/view/

Cathcart, R., & Gumpert, G. (1983). Mediated interpersonal communication: Toward a new typology. *Quarterly Journal of Speech*, *69*(3), 267. https://doi.org/10.1080/00335638309383654

Daft, R., & Lengel, R. (1984). Information richness: A new approach to managerial behavior and organization design. In B. M. Staw & L. L. Cummings (Eds.), *Research in organizational behavior* (Vol. 6, pp. 191–233). JAI Press.

Daft, R. L., & Lengel, R. H. (1986). Organizational information requirements, media richness, and structural design. *Management Science*, *32*, 554–571. https://doi.org/10.1287/mnsc.32.5.554

Daft, R. L., Lengel, R. H., & Trevino, L. K. (1987). Message equivocality, media selection and manager performance: Implications for information systems. *MIS Quarterly*, *11*, 355–366. https://doi.org/10.2307/248682

Das, G., Wiener, H. J. D., & Kareklas, I. (2019). To emoji or not to emoji? Examining the influence of emoji on consumer reactions to advertising. *Journal of Business Research*, *96*, 147–156. https://doi.org/10.1016/j.jbusres.2018.11.007

Drollinger, T., Comer, L. B., & Warrington, P. T. (2006). Development and validation of the active empathetic listening scale. *Psychology & Marketing*, *23*, 161–180. https://doi.org/10.1002/mar.20105

Gearhart, C. C., & Maben, S. K. (2019). Active and empathic listening in social media: What do stakeholders really expect. *International Journal of Listening*. https://doi.org/10.1080/10904018.2019.1602046

Ishii, K., Lyons, M. M., & Carr, S. A. (2019). Revisiting media richness theory for today and future. *Human Behavior & Emerging Technologies*, *1*, 124–131. https://doi.org/10.1002/hbe2.138

Kent, M. L., & Lane, A. (2021). Two-way communication, symmetry, negative spaces, and dialogue. *Public Relations Review*, *47*(2). https://doi.org/10.1016/j.pubrev.2021.102014

Kramer, K., & Gawlick, M. (2003). *Martin Buber's I and thou: Practicing living dialogue*. Paulist Press.

Maben, S. K., & Gearhart, C. C. (2018). Organizational social media accounts: Moving toward listening competency. *International Journal of Listening*, *32*(2), 101–114. https://doi.org/10.1080/10904018.2017.1330658

Macnamara, J. (2019). Explicating listening in organization-public communication: Theory, practices, technologies. *International Journal of Communication*, *13*, 5183–5204. https://ijoc.org/index.php/ijoc/article/view/11996

Macnamara, J., & Gregory, A. (2018). Expanding evaluation to progress strategic communication: Beyond message tracking to open listening. *International Journal of Strategic Communication*, *12*(4), 469–486. https://doi.org/10.1080/1553118X.2018.1450255

Nordstrom. (2017a, March 26). *Lookin' snazzy, Caleb! We're adoring your dapper ensemble*. [Tweet]. Twitter. https://twitter.com/Nordstrom/status/846212267788156928

Nordstrom. (2017b, February 5). *Who's pumped for the Big Game? #football #heels* [Tweet]. Twitter. https://twitter.com/nordstrom/status/828367281839230978?lang=en

O'Sullivan, P. B., & Carr, C. T. (2018). Masspersonal communication: A model bridging the mass-interpersonal divide. *New Media & Society*, *20*(3), 1161–1180. https://doi.org/10.1177/1461444816686104

Reinikainen, H., Kari, J. T., & Luoma-aho, V. (2020). Generation Z and organizational listening on social media. *Media and Communication*, *8*(2), 185–196. https://doi.org/10.17645/mac.v8i2.2772

Tang, Y., & Hew, K. (2019). Emoticon, emoji, and sticker use in computer-mediated communication: A review of theories and research findings. *International Journal of Communication*, *13*, 27. https://ijoc.org/index.php/ijoc/article/view/10966/2670

Worthington, D. L. (2005). Exploring the relationship between listening style preference and verbal aggressiveness. *International Journal of Listening*, *19*(1), 3–11. https://doi.org/10.1080/10904018.2005.10499069

Worthington, D. L. (2008). Exploring the relationship between listening style and need for cognition. *International Journal of Listening*, *22*(1), 46–58. https://doi.org/10.1080/10904010701802154

3 Developing *Organizational Employee Communication Competency Diagnostics*

Breaking Employee Silence via Organizational Climate of Listening for Dialogic Employee Communication

Minjeong Kang and Bitt Moon

Introduction

Organizations spend much effort and dedicate many resources to understanding their external environments because this understanding is imperative for organizational survival and success. However, when it comes to communicating with employees, organizations find it challenging to foster open and safe internal communication environments where employees can bring up work-related issues and/or ideas. Cultivating good relationships with talented, engaged, and loyal employees is important to organizations because employees can directly affect the organizational success (Park et al., 2014). How organizations communicate with employees generally affects employee-organization relationships (EORs) (Kang & Sung, 2017) because relationships are built on participatory communication and exchanges grounded in dialogues (Baxter, 2004).

Participatory employee communication can be realized when willingness and competency exist from both organizations and employees. Organizations, however, are ill-equipped for participatory employee communication despite installing channels and introducing policies to *listen* to employees. Pulse and regular employee surveys have become staple practices of the contemporary organizational management of human resources and employee communication. Nevertheless, organizational communication with employees has focused mainly on speaking to employees in a typical top-down manner (Macnamara, 2016).

Despite the recognition of listening as a critical management skill (Abrashoff, 2001; Flynn et al., 2008), the extant listening research at the organizational level has been grounded in a largely intuitive and anecdotal foundation that lacks the conceptualization and measurement of listening competency at the organizational level (Flynn et al., 2008). In this project, which is dubbed *Organizational Employee Listening Competency*

DOI: 10.4324/9781003273851-5

(OELC) Diagnostics, we explore critical organizational, supervisorial, and psychological characteristics of employee silence to improve effective and appropriate organizational listening; develop *OELC Diagnostics* by exploring and extracting concepts that reflect OELC; and examine how OELC may reduce employee silence.

To foster organizational conditions wherein members of an organization can honestly and safely voice their work-related issues and concerns and contribute to participatory communication, employee communication should be supported with organizational principles and characteristics that create psychological, interpersonal, and organizational conditions that reduce employee silence. The following section discusses what constitutes employee communication for participatory organizations. Additionally, we discuss how organizations can reduce factors that may induce employee silence from intra (psychological), supervisorial, and organizational levels. Finally, we explore, propose, and test *OELC Diagnostics* as a strategic assessment tool for appropriate and effective employee communication.

Participatory Employee Communication: Dialogic Employee Communication

Employee communication is "a process between an organization's strategic managers and its internal stakeholders, designed to promote commitment to the organization, a sense of belonging to it, awareness of its changing environment, and understanding of its evolving aims" (Welch & Jackson, 2007, p. 186). Unlike top-to-bottom internal communication, employee communication should focus not only on providing and sharing information from management to employees but also on enhancing employees' overall workplace interactions in which employees actively and voluntarily seek to engage with their organizations.

The value of employee communication goes beyond the operational and functional merits (e.g., informed and engaged employees). Excellent employee communication fosters organizational pluralism by increasing the diversity and inclusion of varying ideas and views and strengthening organizational culture by cultivating shared identities among employees (Morrison & Milliken, 2000). Further, effective employee communication can enhance organizational innovation and learning through the open and free exchange of ideas and views to and from employees. The foundational principles for participatory employee communication can be found in dialogic theories (Foss & Griffin, 1995; Taylor & Kent, 2014; Yang et al., 2015).

Dialogic Employee Communication

Dialogic principles of public relations reflect an organization's orientation to ethical communication that serves to mitigate unequal power between an organization and its publics (Kent & Taylor, 2002; Lane & Kent, 2018;

Taylor & Kent, 2014). Yang et al. (2015) noted that "due to power imbalances, organizations have often been ignorant of publics in communication, considering that publics are powerless" (p. 175). However, in recent years, increasing scholarly emphasis has shifted away from an organization-centric focus of strategic organizational communication to a co-orientation approach (Macnamara, 2016), which empathizes understanding the views and interests of publics and balancing the interests and views of the organization with those of its publics (Cornelissen, 2012). Among various stakeholders that organizations are intricately interdependent for success and survival, employees are one of the most important stakeholders that organizational communication can significantly influence (Park et al., 2014).

Dialogic communication principles are particularly relevant for fostering participatory employee communication for at least two reasons. First, dialogic communication alleviates the power imbalance that often causes employee silence. As Botan (1997) noted, "dialogue elevates publics to the status of [a] communication equal with the organization" (p. 196). Dialogic principles emphasize that "the exercise of power or superiority should be avoided" (Kent & Taylor, 2002, p. 25), and communicative participation should not be discouraged (Lane & Kent, 2018). As such, dialogic principles for employee communication can facilitate opportunities that are equal, open, and easily accessible to all interested employees.

Second, dialogic principles can foster psychological, interpersonal, and organizational conditions that reduce employee silence and increase organizational listening. Based on shared trust, dialogic communication fosters the rule and understanding that those individuals who disagree with an organization's decision should be respected and listened to (Kent & Taylor, 2002). As such, dialogic communication can help organizations form an internal climate where employees feel that any opinions, issues, and/or problems raised by them will be valued or, at least, not punished. But without deliberate organizational efforts to understand employees' perspectives via carefully implemented structures, policies, procedures, and cultures, the inherent power asymmetry between organizations and employees can create psychological, interpersonal, and organizational barriers that impede open and mutually oriented interactions between employees and organizations (Morrison & Milliken, 2000).

Yang et al.'s (2015) organization-public dialogic communication (OPDC) can provide a conceptual framework for developing employee communication principles that can result in mutually beneficial relationships to both employees and organizations via two dimensions (i.e., the orientation of mutuality and climate of openness). The first dimension of OPDC, the orientation of mutuality, involves "the mutual confirmation of unique values in different views" (Yang et al., 2015, p. 177) due to the mutual dependence or interrelatedness in relationships between an organization and its publics. Both an organization and the employees must recognize and pay attention to each other's needs with respect and empathy (Burleson & MacGeorge, 2002, as cited in Yang et al., 2015) for "the co-creation of shared understanding by the organization and stakeholders, involving interactive behaviors including active listening and constructive exchanges" (Burnside-Lawry, 2012, p. 102).

The second dimension of the OPDC, the climate of openness, involves a "willingness and opportunities for open and honest communication" (Yang et al., 2015, p. 179) between an organization and its publics. Yang et al. (2015) noted that an open and honest climate for communication is the foundation for communication to not become manipulative. Therefore, dialogic employee communication requires open access to information and communication channels by the organization, allowing employees to freely share their views and ideas and providing timely and relevant information to employees (Yang et al., 2015). On the other hand, Yang et al. (2015) noted that employees also need to be honest and forthcoming with differing points of view and opinions.

While dialogic principles can help organizations foster participatory employee communication, the reality of the internal organizational communication environment is embroiled with the general lack of organizational competency to truly listen to employees, along with pervasive employee silence.

Challenges for Participatory Organizational Employee Communication: A Lack of Organizational Listening Competency and Employee Silence

Burnside-Lawry (2012) noted that organizations' abilities to listen and negotiate are critical for building competitive advantages. The inevitable rise of conflicts and misunderstandings from engaging with various stakeholders prevents organizations from effectively learning and adapting to the environment. Notably, organizations' competencies to listen to employees can be crucial to building organizational effectiveness, quality EORs, and positive employee outcomes. Despite its central role in the success of the organization, organizational listening remains one of the most neglected aspects of organizational communication (Brownell, 1994; Flynn et al., 2008), and "listening as an organizational variable continues to be seen as a soft skill worthy of little attention in the scholarly business literature, in the business classroom, and in organizations" (Flynn et al., 2008, p. 143). Macnamara (2016) also criticized the primary focus of organizational communication on *speaking to* its stakeholders and not necessarily *communicating with* them and urged organizational communication scholars and professionals to seek an understanding of establishing *the architecture of listening*. Flynn et al. (2008) noted that the challenges associated with organizational employee listening practices and research might be attributed to the absence of conceptualization and the measurement of listening competency at the organizational level.

Understanding Listening

Listening has not been considered a legitimate scholarly field in communication research due to its limited conceptual clarity and operational difficulty (Janusik, 2004). Early listening research, which was influenced by linear models of psychological attention and memory in cognitive psychology (e.g., Broadbent, 1971; Shannon, 1948), focused on message recall as the measure of listening competency. Since extant listening research is still conducted primarily in interpersonal, educational, and counseling-oriented contexts, listening has been primarily conceptualized and understood from the theoretical framework of cognitive psychology (Purdy & Manning, 2015), which views listening primarily as comprehending and retaining the spoken contents between individuals. However, scholars and professionals in the past two decades have begun espousing listening as part of the transactional communication process involving shared meaning-making (Craig & Muller, 2007; Littlejohn & Foss, 2008; Yang et al., 2015). Influenced by Baddeley and Hitch's (1974, 2001) Working Memory model, the transactional or relational perspective model of listening has shifted a listener from a mere receiver of the message to an *interactive communicator* (Brownell, 2009) and has incorporated the concepts of a listening channel capacity and storage into the conceptualization of listening competency (e.g., Just et al., 1996).

According to Cooper (1997), listening is a *multidimensional* construct, a communication behavior that requires *cognitive* (listening knowledge), *affective* (a willingness to engage as a listener), and *behavioral* (appropriate acts of listening) components (Cooper, 1997; Wolvin & Coakley, 1994). Listening acts can be *verbal* or *nonverbal,* involving *overt* or *covert responses* (*ILA Definition of Listening,* 1994). Listening is also *nonlinear,* in that communicative behaviors involve interactions or exchanges designed to create meanings via shared symbolic and intentional acts (Cooper, 1997).

Listening in a conversational context is *dynamic* (Schiffrin, 1987) and *connected* (Grice, 1975), in that a conversation is a reactionary and responsive interaction, not a collection of separate actions (Nofsinger, 1991). Janusik (2004) argued that, as a collection of actions, a conversation is a learned and patterned behavior governed by exchange norms. For communicative interactions to function appropriately, speaking and listening behaviors must be governed by shared norms and rules of engagement. Thus, the role of the listener is as a *co-creator* of the meaning instead of as a passive repository for the message (Resnick & Klopfer, 1989).

Organizational Employee Listening Competency

Listening competency generally refers to appropriate and effective listening that involves understanding interactions that adhere to conversational norms and rules and achieving interaction goals, such as meeting the needs, desires, and intentions of the interactions (Cooper, 1997). For organizational listening competency, Cooper (1997) noted that listening research has not been able to elucidate much about which organizational characteristics significantly influence how competent organizational listening is perceived. For example, the Managerial Listening Survey (MLS, Cooper & Husband, 1993), the most widely used organizational listening scale, was designed to evaluate supervisors' perceptions of their listening competencies and focuses on transmission-centered listening competency at the individual level. Nearly 20 years later, since Cooper's (1997) criticism of the state of listening research, Macnamara (2016) called for conceptualizing listening for organizational communication at the organizational level instead of looking at interpersonal listening competency in the workplace. Among the few studies that have examined listening competency at the organizational level, Burnside-Lawry (2012) applied Wolvin and Coakley's (1994) and Cooper's (1997) descriptions of competent listening in the context of stakeholders' organizational listening characteristics and qualities. Burnside-Lawry's (2012) study found that the attributes and qualities that stakeholders expected from a *listening* organization largely corresponded with the qualities and characteristics of a good listener. Burnside-Lawry's (2012) findings revealed that external stakeholders perceived a higher listening competency when the organization demonstrated appropriate organizational behaviors, sincerity, knowledge, comprehension, and culture that showed commitment to listening and ideal speech conditions where participatory communication was offered.

According to Macnamara (2016), organizations, in contrast to humans, face particular and unique challenges and responsibilities when it comes to listening. Unlike interpersonal listening, organizational listening is primarily *delegated* to functions that involve *mediated* collection and understanding of various stakeholder insights/voices in an asynchronous manner (Macnamara, 2016). Also, the scale of organizational listening is enormous, involving listening to tens of thousands of voices from various stakeholder groups (Macnamara, 2016). These characteristics of organizational listening mean it "requires and depends on policies, systems, structures, resources, and a range of processes, technologies, and specialist skills that can enable and facilitate delegated, mediated, large-scale listening" (Macnamara, 2018, p. 3), which he calls *the architecture of listening*.

Creating organizational listening characteristics is complex and ill-defined as the construct refers to employees' perceptions of the organizational condition, rather than individual characteristics, that foster internal organizational listening (Brownell, 1994). Employees consider organizational listening as an organizational characteristic that is embedded in organizational terms, such as culture (Gilchrist & Van Hoeven, 1994), in which listening is viewed as an essential organizational value (Flynn et al., 2008), supported and facilitated by organizational infrastructure (Murray, 2004; Stine et al., 1995). Based on the previous review of listening conceptualization, we define OELC *as the clusters of organizational characteristics for cognitive, affective, and behavioral intentions and efforts by the organization, perceived to be effective and appropriate by employees to establish, achieve, and sustain shared interaction goals with employees, based on mutual needs, desires, and intentions, via participatory organizational norms, procedures, structures, and policies.*

In addition to the general lack of listening at the organizational level that can guide management to understand the current level of OELC, the pervasiveness of employee silence in an organization poses a significant impediment to a genuinely pluralistic organization that values multiple views and diverse ideas (Morrison & Milliken, 2000). When silence becomes a pressure mechanism in the organization, the organization cannot attain chances to fix problems promptly or may not even be aware that potential issues exist (Beheshtifar et al., 2012; Morrison et al., 2015).

As employees' expectations for participatory organizations increase, organizations should approach their communication as dialogic, where employee insights and opinions are legitimately valued, genuinely listened to, and appropriately reflected on in organizational decision-making (Yang et al., 2015). An organization's success and its employees are intricately intertwined. Severing the EORs comes at a high cost to both the organization and its employees. Despite the high level of interdependence, the power dynamic in the EOR is asymmetrical, in that individual employees do not have a compatible level of power/control over the organization. This power imbalance in a typical EOR context can create a workplace climate conducive to pervasive employee silence, detrimental to participatory employee communication (Morrison & Milliken, 2000).

Understanding Employee Silence

Employee silence has been conceptualized in various disciplines of organizational management, such as human resources, business ethics, and organizational psychology. As a discrete, multidimensional concept, employee silence differs from the absence of the employee voice (Milliken et al., 2003; Morrison, 2014; Morrison et al., 2015; Pinder & Harlos, 2001) and various motives may be attributed to employee silence (Brinsfield, 2012; Knoll & van Dick, 2013; Tangirala & Ramanujam, 2008; Van Dyne et al., 2003). Employee silence is commonly characterized as the intentional or purposeful withholding of meaningful information, including questions, concerns, and suggestions (Brinsfield, 2012; Morrison & Milliken, 2000; Milliken et al., 2003; Pinder & Harlos, 2001; Tangirala & Ramanujam, 2008; Van Dyne et al., 2003).

Employee silence reflects an individual behavior, while *organizational silence* describes "a collective phenomenon where employees withhold their opinions and concerns regarding work-related problems and issues"

(Morrison & Milliken, 2000, pp. 706–707), and can be reinforced and reproduced when most employees in an organization are reluctant to express their opinions. As employees tend to learn the rules and norms of avoiding talking through their experiences and observations of other colleagues (Morrison et al., 2003), employees' perceived climates of silence can lead to their individual decisions to remain silent.

Employee silence differs from employee voice (Brinsfield, 2012; Hao et al., 2022; Sherf et al., 2021; Van Dyne et al., 2003) with research suggesting that silence should be theorized and measured as a unique construct (e.g., Detert & Edmondson, 2011; Hao et al., 2022; Sherf et al., 2021). Employee silence is likely to stem from *behavioral inhibition systems* triggered by potential threats (e.g., punishments), whereas employee voice is likely to come through a *behavioral activation system* stimulated by desirable goals (e.g., rewards) (Sherf et al., 2021). Hence, the identified antecedents of voice do not always predict silence in opposite but similar ways (Hao et al., 2022).

Causes of Employee Silence

Employees can be motivated to remain silent for different reasons (Brinsfield, 2012; Knoll & van Dick, 2013; Pinder & Harlos, 2001; Van Dyne et al., 2003). While various motivational aspects may exist that lead to employee silence[1] (Brinsfield, 2012), we focus on two primary forms of employee silence, i.e., *quiescent silence and acquiescent silence*, which are detrimental to participatory employee communication for pluralistic organizations (Pinder & Harlos, 2001).

Quiescent silence is viewed as "a form of silence that represents deliberate omission" (Pinder & Harlos, 2001, p. 348), is defensive, and reflects self-protective withholding behaviors to avoid negative consequences (Van Dyne et al., 2003). Quiescent silence is likely to occur based on the fear of being punished or labeled a troublemaker (Van Dyne et al., 2003). Acquiescent silence represents negligence or a reluctance to make a difference (Pinder & Harlos, 2001) and is likely to occur based on an opinion that an employee perceives that speaking up is not helpful or does not make any changes (Pinder & Harlos, 2001; Van Dyne et al., 2003). Researchers have demonstrated that these two motives of employee silence are often triggered by psychological, interpersonal, and organizational factors.

Key Psychological Factors

According to Morrison (2014), an employee's decision about whether to remain silent is based on two fundamental psychological judgments regarding voicing: *efficacy* and *psychological safety* due to perceptions of unequal power relations in the workplace that are associated with organizational hierarchies and culture (Morrison & Milliken, 2000).

Key Interpersonal Factors

When it comes to interpersonal factors, researchers have suggested that supervisors/leaders' leadership characteristics and relational qualities between supervisors/leaders and employees may play a significant role in employee silence (Detert & Burris, 2007; Morrison & Rothman, 2009; Morrison et al., 2015; Song et al., 2017; Tangirala & Ramanujam, 2012). According to Detert and Burris (2007), supervisor behaviors influence employees' decisions to speak up or remain silent. Speaking up generally represents delivering information to someone with a higher position (Detert & Burris, 2007; Pinder & Harlos, 2001). Individuals in less powerful positions are likely to perceive a sense of powerlessness, which activates the behavioral inhibition mechanism that stimulates avoidance-related behaviors, such as employee silence (Morrison & Rothman, 2009; Morrison et al., 2015). When the perceived powerlessness is combined with abusive supervisor behaviors (Shaw et al., 2011), employee silence is likely to occur (Song et al., 2017) because supervisors' authorities to administrate rewards or punishments make employees highly sensitive to supervisors' behaviors (Detert & Burris, 2007).

A leader's openness also provides a cue to employees that the leader is approachable, values the employee voice, and is willing to consider employees' ideas and suggestions carefully (Detert & Burris, 2007; Morrison et al., 2015) by signaling employees that speaking up will not result in personal harm. A supervisor/leader must demonstrate *openness* to employees because the negative impact of an employee's perceived powerlessness on silence can be mitigated by a leader's openness (Morrison et al., 2015).

Additionally, trust between a leader and an employee is an essential relational factor in attenuating employee silence (Dedahanov & Rhee, 2015; Song et al., 2017). Trust entails one's expectations that the other party's actions "will be beneficial, favorable, or not detrimental to one's interests" (Robinson, 1996, p. 576). In this sense, employees' trust in their leaders can alleviate fear and cause an anticipation of harmless consequences of voice, encouraging employees to speak up.

Key Organizational Factors

Organizational factors, such as power structure, internal communication systems, organizational justice, and organizational ethical climate, can play a significant role in reducing employee silence (Morrison & Milliken, 2000; Morrison, 2014; Vakola & Bouradas, 2005; Wang & Hsieh, 2013; Whiteside & Barclay, 2013). According to Morrison and Milliken (2000), implicit managerial beliefs that "employees are self-interested; management knows best; unity is good and dissent is bad" (p. 709) generate a centralized decision-making process and lack of feedback mechanism. Such closed organizational structures and policies shape a *climate of silence* where employees share collective perceptions that "speaking up about problems is not worth the effort and voicing one's opinions and concerns is dangerous" (Morrison & Milliken, 2000, p. 714).

Critical considerations exist for organizational characteristics to reduce employee silence. Researchers have emphasized the importance of adequate and sufficient communication opportunities and channels (Dedahanov et al., 2015; Vakola & Bouradas, 2005). Vakola and Bouradas (2005) found that employees were less likely to remain silent when they were aware of "a systematic and organized exchange of knowledge and experiences among employees and adequate communication between employees and top managers" (p. 448).

Organizational justice can also alleviate employee silence (Huang & Huang, 2016; Whiteside & Barclay, 2013). This type of justice reflects employees' perceived fairness in terms of distributed outcomes (i.e., distributive justice), procedures applied to decide outcome distribution (i.e., procedural justice), and interactional ways in which individuals were treated with respect and dignity (i.e., interpersonal justice) and procedures and outcomes were explained clearly (Colquitt et al., 2001; Greenberg, 1993). According to Whiteside and Barclay (2013), overall organizational justice enables employees to lessen uncertainty related to voice because fairness signals that the organization is willing to care about employees' concerns and opinions and listen to employees. Organizational justice also gives employees a cue that they will not be punished for expressing their ideas or critical questions (Whiteside & Barclay, 2013). Accordingly, empirical research has found that organizational justice attenuates acquiescent and quiescent silence (Huang & Huang, 2016; Whiteside & Barclay, 2013).

Proposal of Components of the OELC

Based on the review of listening and employee silence literature, we propose that fostering participatory employee communication involves developing OELC as perceived by employees that the organization has intentions and is willing to put efforts and resources into establishing, achieving, and sustaining shared interaction goals with employees. Further, for OELC, the organization must attune to mutual needs, desires, and intentions with employees by creating participatory norms, procedures, structures, and policies that reduce employee silence.

Components of OELC

Applying critical characteristics of a competent listener in the dialogic communication framework for participatory employee communication, we describe the cognitive, affective, and behavioral components of OELC as follows:

- Cognitive (knowledge about what listening entails)
    - Giving consideration to employee voices
    - Acknowledging employees as legitimate partners
    - Being fair and receptive in interpreting employee voices
- Affective (willingness to engage as a listener)
    - Paying attention to employee voices
    - Valuing and respecting employee voices
    - Being open-minded
- Behavioral (appropriate acts of listening)
    - Inviting employees to voice
    - Investing in communication channels and resources to understand employee voices
    - Acknowledging, responding, and feedbacking to employee voices
    - Modifying organizational actions according to mutual interests and concerns

OELC Diagnostic Scale Development

A survey method was adopted to extract key OELC characteristics for participatory employee communication based on the concepts reviewed as relevant for OELC and employee silence.

Procedures

First, a pilot survey with 86 full-time US employees was conducted using an M-Turk panel. Based on the pilot survey data, we narrowed the initial 38 items for the OELC scale to 21 items. The original list of items was compiled from crucial concepts identified in the literature review (e.g., dialogic communication, listening, fair procedure, employee voice, voice culture, and voice opportunity). With the refined OELC scale of 21 items, the main survey with 660 full-time US employees in health care, government, education, high-tech, pharmaceutical, and finance/banking industries was conducted using a Prolific panel. After an attention check, a final sample of 570 participants was retained. The survey data was analyzed using SPSS Version 28 and Amos Version 28.

A monetary incentive was provided for the survey participants ($2 for the M-Turk panel; $8.50 for the Prolific panel). The Institutional Review Board (IRB) of the principal researcher's institution reviewed and approved the survey questionnaires for the ethical treatment of the study participants for research.

Participants

The participants in the main survey ranged from 18 to 70 years with a mean age of 34.6 (SD: 9.02). The genders of the participants were male (58.2%, $n = 332$), female (40.9%, $n = 233$), and other (.9%, $n = 5$). The ethnicities of the participants were White (69.5%, $n = 396$), Black or African American (18.4%, $n = 105$), Asian (8.8%, $n = 50$), and Native American or Pacific Islander and others (3.3%, $n = 19$). The levels of education were bachelor's degree (36.1%, $n = 206$), master's degree (33.9%, $n = 193$), some college (10.7%, $n = 61$), associate degree (8.9%, $n = 51$), doctorate or professional degree (6.5%, $n = 37$), and high school or less (3.9%, $n = 22$). The survey participants held entry-level (13.5%, $n = 77$) or intermediate or experienced, nonmanagerial positions (33.5%, $n = 191$), followed by mid-level management (26.1%, $n = 149$), first-level management (21.1%, $n = 120$), and others (5.8%, $n = 33$). The participants reported having held their current positions for less than three years (44.9%, $n = 256$), between three and six years (40.2%, $n = 229$), and longer than seven years (14.9%, $n = 85$). The tenure length of about 70% participants (67.7%, $n = 386$) at their current organizations was less than six years, while 184 participants (32.3%) had tenure durations more than seven years.

Dimensions of the OELC

Based on the insights from the literature review, we generated an initial pool of 38 items representing dialogic communication, voice opportunity, culture, and justice perceptions. This pool was then tested for construct validity, convergent reliability, item reliability, measurement reliability, and discriminant validity. The pilot test for the scale refinement yielded 21 items for the OELC scale. The exploratory factor analysis (EFA) of the refined 21-item OELC scale revealed five factors that reflected the characteristics of OELC from the perspective of employees. Using the selected items, we conducted a confirmatory factor analysis (CFA) to assess the fit of the proposed OELC model in terms of $\chi^2/df < 3$, root-mean-square error of approximation (RMSEA) $< .05$, normed fit index (NFI) $> .90$, and comparative fit index (CFI) $> .90$ (Hu & Bentler, 1999). The results of the CFA showed that the proposed five-factor model was statistically reliable and valid ($\chi^2 = 430.704$, $df = 179$, NFI $= .959$, CFI $= .975$, RMSEA $= .050$). Each item showed significant coefficients (see Table 3.1). The five dimensions of the OELC are as follows.

- *Transparent Communication Manner (TCM)* represents the extent to which the organization communicates with employees in a straightforward, easy, and timely manner.
- *Accessibility to Voice (AV)* reflects the extent to which the organization provides employees with easy, safe, and sufficient access to voice their opinions, concerns, and suggestions.

Table 3.1 OELC scale

Organizational Employee Listening Competency (OELC)		λ	SE	CR	p-value	r	AVE
Legitimacy of Employee Voice and Perspective (LEVP)						0.936	0.71
LEVP_1	Leaders of my organization accept employees' opinions as worthy of consideration	0.891	0.036	27.048	***		
LEVP_2	Leaders of my organization invite employees to communicate with	0.894	0.036	27.22	***		
LEVP_3	Leaders of my organization try to understand problems from employees' perspectives	0.776	0.041	21.808	***		
LEVP_4	Leaders of my organization are not arrogant in communicating with employees	0.871	0.038	26.043	***		
LEVP_5	Leaders of my organization pay attention to what employees say	0.76	0.038	21.153	***		
LEVP_6	Leaders of my organization recognize the unique value of employees' opinions	0.854	0.033	25.226	***		
Transparent Communication Manner (TCM)						0.895	0.739
TCM_1	Leaders of my organization are timely in providing information to employees	0.87	0.037	25.587	***		
TCM_2	Leaders of my organization are straightforward in communicating with employees	0.87	0.04	25.617	***		
TCM_3	Leaders of my organization are clear to understand when communicating with employees	0.839	0.041	24.197	***		
Explanation of Voice Procedures and Outcomes (EVPO)						0.913	0.723
EVPO_1	Leaders of my organization are candid in their communication with employees about the procedures and the outcomes	0.837	0.04	24.188	***		
EVPO_2	Leaders of my organization explain the procedures for voicing suggestions and concerns thoroughly	0.846	0.041	24.615	***		

(*Continued*)

Table 3.1 OELC scale (Continued)

Organizational Employee Listening Competency (OELC)	λ	SE	CR	p-value	r	AVE
EVPO_3 Leaders of my organization provide reasonable explanations regarding the procedures for voicing	0.868	0.038	25.648	***	0.878	0.59
EVPO_4 Leaders of my organization communicate details of the procedures and outcomes in a timely manner	0.851	0.038	24.827	***		
Fair Procedures to Listen (FPL)						
FPL_1 In my organization, there are procedures in place for employees to express views and feelings	0.755	0.039	20.521	***		
FPL_2 In my organization, employees can influence the decision arrived at by organizational procedures	0.766	0.046	20.981	***		
FPL_3 In my organization, the procedures used to listen to employee opinions are applied consistently	0.789	0.044	21.871	***		
FPL_4 In my organization, there are procedures in place that enable employees to appeal the decisions	0.756	0.051	20.589	***		
FPL_5 In my organization, employees like me have significant say in how things get to be done	0.774	0.048	21.287	***		
Accessibility to Voice (AV)						
AV_1 In my organization, employees like me freely voice out opinions and concerns	0.844	0.039	24.403	***	0.888	0.725
AV_2 In my organization, there are sufficient channels for employees like me to provide our voices and inputs	0.857	0.041	24.963	***		
AV_3 In my organization, employees like me can bring up different opinions to the management	0.854	0.039	24.829	***		

Note: *** indicates $p<.001$.

- *Explanation of Voice Procedure and Outcomes (EVPO)* reflects the extent to which the organization provides precise and thorough explanations of organizational procedures for employees to voice their opinions and valid explanations for the outcomes of employee voice.
- *The Legitimacy of Employee Voice and Perspective (LEVP)* reflects how much the organization values employee voice and perspectives as worthy of consideration and legitimate to organizational success.
- *Fair Procedure to Voice (FPV)* reflects the extent to which fair and consistent applications of voice procedures exist in the organization for employees to voice their opinions, concerns, and suggestions for organizational decision-making.

Assessment of the OELC Diagnostic Scale

We calculated the construct reliability (CR) and average variance extracted (AVE) of each construct to assess the construct validity of the OELC model. The results of the CFA showed that the proposed five-factor model fit the data well with acceptable fit indices (χ^2 = 430.704, df = 179, χ^2/df = 2.41, NFI = .959, CFI = .975, RMSEA = .050). The standardized loading estimate (λ) for each item was greater than .50 at a significant level (p < .001) by showing no weak associations between an indicator and a latent construct. The CR and AVE for the five organizational listening factors were acceptable as the CRs were above 0.7 and AVEs were above 0.5 (Fornell & Larcker, 1981). As a result, the construct validity of the proposed five-factor OELC model was statistically acceptable. Our findings suggest that organizational listening is a multidimensional construct (Macnamara, 2016) that encompasses communication policies, systems, structures, procedures, technologies, and specialized skills that "enable and facilitate delegated, mediated, large-scale listening" (Macnamara, 2018, p. 2).

OELC and Employee Silence Motives

As the results indicated that the five-factor OELC model was acceptable in terms of reliability and validity, we conducted a structural equation modeling (SEM) analysis to test whether employees' perceived OELC was significantly and negatively associated with two types of employee silence. The results showed that the expected model fit the data well (χ^2 = 807.805, df = 317, NFI = .941, CFI = .963, RMSEA = .052). The coefficients for all of the paths were significant at p < .001 (see Table 3.1). The OELC was negatively associated with employee quiescent silence (β = −0.64, p < .001). It showed that employees were unlikely to engage in fear-based silence when they perceived an organization of being capable of listening to employees' voices. The OELC was also negatively associated with employee acquiescent silence ($\beta = -0.86$, $p < .001$). It demonstrated that employees were unwilling to engage in disengaged silence when their organization was perceived as an active listener.

The results suggest that both acquiescent and quiescent silence can be alleviated by an organization's genuine listening efforts to value different voices; communicate with employees in straightforward and timely manners; provide employees with easy, safe, and sufficient access to voice out; offer clear and thorough explanations of organizational procedures; and establish consistent and fair applications of voice procedures.

Discussion

Our project aimed to explore factors that impede dialogic employee communication with two foci: employee silence and organizational listening competency. We started by asking how organizations could leverage employee suggestions, concerns, and opinions for organizational learning by creating participatory employee communication under the reality of pervasive employee silence and the general lack of listening competency at the organizational level. Dialogic employee communication can be characterized by mutuality orientation and the climate of openness for participatory communication. Hence, we focused on exploring the nature of OELC at psychological, interpersonal, and organizational levels, which encompasses the orientation, communication climate and manner, access and opportunities, and fair policies. We suggest that these multiple listening aspects serve as foundational components to foster OELC and reduce employee silence.

Based on empirical research on employees' evaluation of organizational listening competency via multistep scale development procedures, we identified five factors representing five conceptual dimensions reflecting the OELC with 21 items. These five dimensions are *TCM*, *AV*, *EVPO*, *LEVP*, and *FPV*. Taken together, these five OELC dimensions represent not only the importance of organizational listening structures and policies for safe, open, and fair transmission of employee voice from bottom to top but also, and more importantly, listening as part of transactional and relational communication, which recognizes employees as the legitimate partners for organizational success as well as interactive communicative partners (Brownell, 2009). The five OELC dimensions, in other words, represent tri-part dimensions of the listening competency of an organization, which comprises listening as cognitive, affective, and behavioral (Cooper, 1997) and dynamic and connected in the sense that listening is part of a conversation involving reactionary and responsive interactions between the organization and employees (Nofsinger, 1991).

Additionally, our results of the SEM to examine the effects of the OELC dimensions on reducing employee silence show that acquiescent silence and quiescent silence can significantly decrease when an organization's listening competency across the five dimensions is strong within the entire organization. It can be concluded that the OELC can contribute to breaking employee silence. Employees would be more likely to stop being silent based on improved psychological safety and sense of power when they perceive an organization's abilities and efforts that demonstrate openness, transparency, fairness, receptiveness, and genuineness in employee voice. We further note that organizational listening for breaking employee silence is not limited to having just upward communication channels. Instead, a listening organization builds multi-level listening orientation and capacities that range from interpersonal listening competency to organizational listening systems/procedures.

Recommendations for Practice

We believe that *The OELC Diagnostic Scale* can be useful as a tool to strategically plan, implement, and evaluate different aspects of organizational listening competency. The proposed *OELC Diagnostic Scale* is based on the individual-level assessment of the organizational listening competency, which allows organizations to examine group and sub-unit differences in terms of their members' perceptions of the OELC, such as differences by department, division, demographic group, or rank.

Specifically, we suggest the following steps for assessing the OELC.

1 Administer *The OELC Diagnostic Scale* to diagnose the state of employee communication properly
2 Examine the multi-dimensional OELC assessment to pinpoint areas of improvement and areas of excellence for comprehensive and comparative analysis and benchmarking across various levels of communication unit (team, division, company, and the entire organization)
3 Engage in exploratory research (interviews, meetings, town hall meetings, employee consultation, reflecting) of the weak OELC areas (dimensions) to gain follow-up insights and feedback to obtain a contextual and detailed understanding of the reasons for the poor OELC assessment
4 Identify problems and brainstorm solutions
5 Develop strategic plans to improve the weak OELC areas based on strategies and insights from benchmarking practices of units or departments with excellent OELC
6 Reassess the OELC with *The OELC Diagnostic Scale* as the evaluation tool to assess the success of the implemented plan

In summary, the OELC is not an absolute, static, and objective assessment. Indeed, it is not a one-stop and one-shot fix to employee silence. Instead, because listening competency is based on perceptions of employees that expect listening as an interactive and relational process for participatory organizational communication, organizations must be able to assess the current and accurate state of the OELC and invest for the OELC to be periodically assessed to be able to use the assessment results as the starting point for strategic planning, implementation, and modification for improving the OELC in regard to channels, policies, communication manner, and orientation that foster employee voice and break employee silence.

Note

1 Drawing from Pinder and Harlos' (2001) conceptualization, Van Dyne et al. (2003) proposed three forms of silence: *acquiescent silence, defensive (quiescent) silence,* and *prosocial silence*. Knoll and van Dick (2013) further identified an additional form of silence: *opportunistic silence.*

References

Abrashoff, D. M. (2001). Retention through redemption. *Harvard Business Review, 79*(2), 136–141. https://hbr.org/2001/02/retention-through-redemption

Baddeley, A. D., & Hitch, G. (1974). Working memory. In G. H. Bower (Ed.), *Psychology of learning and motivation* (Vol. 8, pp. 47–90). Academic Press.

Baddeley, A. D., & Hitch, G. (2001). *Working memory in perspective*. Psychology Press.

Baxter, L. A. (2004). A tale of two voices: Relational dialectics theory. *Journal of Family Communication, 4*(3–4), 181–192 https://doi.org/10.1080/15267431.2004.9670130

Beheshtifar, M., Borhani, H., & Moghadam, M. N. (2012). Destructive role of employee silence in organizational success. *International Journal of Academic Research in Business and Social Sciences, 2*(11), 275–282. Retrieved from https://hrmars.com/papers_submitted/9343/destructive-role-of-employee-silence-in-organizational-success.pdf

Botan, C. (1997). Ethics in strategic communication campaigns: The case for a new approach to public relations. *The Journal of Business Communication, 34*(2), 188–202. https://doi.org/10.1177/002194369703400205

Brinsfield, C. T. (2012). Employee silence motives: Investigation of dimensionality and development of measures. *Journal of Organizational Behavior, 34*(5), 671–697. https://doi.org/10.1002/job.1829

Broadbent, D. E. (1971). *Decision and stress*. Academic Press.

Brownell, J. (1994). Managerial listening and career development in the hospitality industry. *International Listening Association. Journal, 8*(1), 31–49. https://doi.org/10.1080/10904018.1994.10499130

Brownell, J. (2009). *Fostering service excellence through listening: What hospitality managers need to know*. https://ecommons.cornell.edu/handle/1813/71020

Burleson, B. R., & MacGeorge, E. L. (2002). Supportive communication. In M. L. Knapp & J. A. Daly (Eds.), *Handbook of interpersonal communication* (3rd ed., pp. 374–424). SAGE Publications.

Burnside-Lawry, J. (2012). Listening and participatory communication: A model to assess organization listening competency. *International Journal of Listening, 26*(2), 102–121. https://doi.org/10.1080/10904018.2012.678092

Colquitt, J. A., Conlon, D. E., Wesson, M. J., Porter, C. O., & Ng, K. Y. (2001). Justice at the millennium: A meta-analytic review of 25 years of organizational justice research. *Journal of Applied Psychology, 86*(3), 425–445. https://doi.org/10.1037/a0031757

Cooper, L. O. (1997). Listening competency in the workplace: A model for training. *Business Communication Quarterly, 60*(4), 75–84. https://doi.org/10.1177/108056999706000405

Cooper, L. O., & Husband, R. L. (1993). Developing a model of organizational listening competency. *International Listening Association. Journal, 7*(1), 6–34. https://doi.org/10.1080/10904018.1993.10499112

Cornelissen, J. P. (2012). Sensemaking under pressure: The influence of professional roles and social accountability on the creation of sense. *Organization Science, 23*(1), 118–137. https://doi.org/10.1287/orsc.1100.0640

Craig, R. T., & Muller, H. L. (2007). *Theorizing communication: Readings across traditions.* Sage.

Dedahanov, A. T., Kim, C., & Rhee, J. (2015). Centralization and communication opportunities as predictors of acquiescent or prosocial silence. *Social Behavior and Personality, 43*(3), 481–492. https://doi.org/10.2224/sbp.2015.43.3.481

Dedahanov, A. T., & Rhee, J. (2015). Examining the relationships among trust, silence, and organizational commitment. *Management Decision, 53*(8), 1843–1857. https://doi.org/10.1108/MD-02-2015-0041

Detert, J. R., & Burris, E. R. (2007). Leadership behavior and employee voice: Is the door really open? *Academy of Management Journal, 50*(4), 869–884. https://doi.org/10.5465/AMJ.2007.26279183

Detert, J. R., & Edmondson, A. C. (2011). Implicit voice theories: Taken-for-granted rules of self-censorship at work. *Academy of Management Journal, 54*(3), 461–488. https://doi.org/10.5465/AMJ.2011.61967925

Flynn, J., Valikoski, T. R., & Grau, J. (2008). Listening in the business context: Reviewing the state of research. *The International Journal of Listening, 22*(2), 141–151. https://doi.org/10.1080/10904010802174800

Fornell, C., & Larcker, D. F. (1981). Evaluating structural equation models with unobservable variables and measurement error. *Journal of Marketing Research, 18*(1), 39–50. https://doi.org/10.1177/002224378101800104

Foss, S. K., & Griffin, C. L. (1995). Beyond persuasion: A proposal for an invitational rhetoric. *Communications Monographs, 62*(1), 2–18. https://doi.org/10.1080/03637759509376345

Gilchrist, J. A., & Van Hoeven, S. A. (1994). Listening as an organizational construct. *International Listening Association. Journal, 8*(1), 6–30. https://doi.org/10.1080/10904018.1994.10499129

Greenberg, J. (1993). Stealing in the name of justice: Informational and interpersonal moderators of theft reactions to underpayment inequity. *Organizational Behavior and Human Decision Processes, 54*(1), 81–103. https://doi.org/10.1006/obhd.1993.1004

Grice, H. P. (1975). Logic and conversation. In P. Cole & J. L. Morgan. (Eds.), *Syntax and semantics, Vol. 3, Speech acts* (pp. 41–58). Academic Press.

Hao, L., Zhu, H., He, Y., Duan, J., Zhao, T., & Men, H. (2022). When is silence golden? A meta-analysis on antecedents and outcomes of employee silence. *Journal of Business and Psychology.* https://doi.org/10.1007/s10869-021-09788-7

Hu, L. T., & Bentler, P. M. (1999). Cutoff criteria for fit indexes in covariance structure analysis: Conventional criteria versus new alternatives. *Structural*

Equation Modeling: A Multidisciplinary Journal, 6(1), 1–55. https://doi.org/10.1080/10705519909540118

Huang, L., & Huang, W. (2016). Interactional justice and employee silence: The roles of procedural justice and affect. Social Behavior and Personality: An International Journal, 44(5), 837–852. https://doi.org/10.2224/sbp.2016.44.5.837

Janusik, L. A. (2004). Researching listening from the inside out: The relationship between conversational listening span and perceived communicative competence. University of Maryland.

Just, M. A., Carpenter, P. A., Keller, T. A., Eddy, W. F., & Thulborn, K. R. (1996). Brain activation modulated by sentence comprehension. Science, 274(5284), 114–116. https://doi.org/10.1126/science.274.5284.114

Kang, M., & Sung, M. (2017). How symmetrical employee communication leads to employee engagement and positive employee communication behaviors: The mediation of employee-organization relationships. Journal of Communication Management, 21(1), 82–102. https://doi.org/10.1108/JCOM-04-2016-0026

Kent, M., & Taylor, M. (2002). Toward a dialogic theory of public relations. Public Relations Review, 28, 21–37. https://doi.org/10.1016/S0363-8111(02)00108-X

Knoll, M., & van Dick, R. (2013). Do I hear the whistle? A first attempt to measure four forms of employee silence and their correlates. Journal of Business Ethics, 113(2), 349–362. https://doi.org/10.1007/s10551-012-1308-4

Lane, A., & Kent, M. L. (2018). Engagement as dialogue, dialogue as engagement. In K. Johnston & M. Taylor (Eds.), Handbook of communication engagement (pp. 61–72). Wiley-Blackwell.

Littlejohn, S., & Foss, K. (2008). Theories of communication (9th ed.). Wadsworth.

Macnamara, J. (2016). Organizational listening: Addressing a major gap in public relations theory and practice. Journal of Public Relations Research, 28(3–4), 146–169. https://doi.org/10.1080/1062726X.2016.1228064

Macnamara, J. (2018). Toward a theory and practice of organizational listening. International Journal of Listening, 32(1), 1–23. https://doi.org/10.1080/10904018.2017.1375076

Milliken, F. J., Morrison, E. W., & Hewlin, P. F. (2003). An exploratory study of employee silence: Issues that employees don't communicate upward and why. Journal of Management Studies, 40(6), 1453–1476. https://doi.org/10.1111/1467-6486.00387

Morrison, E. W. (2014). Employee voice and silence. Annual Review of Organizational Psychology and Organizational Behavior, 1(1), 173–197. https://doi.org/10.1146/annurev-orgpsych-031413-091328

Morrison, E. W., & Milliken, F. J. (2000). Organizational silence: A barrier to change and development in a pluralistic world. Academy of Management Review, 25(4), 706–725. https://doi.org/10.5465/amr.2000.3707697

Morrison, E. W., & Rothman, N. B. (2009). Silence and the dynamics of power. In J. Greenberg & M. S. Edwards (Eds.), Voice and silence in organizations (pp. 112–133). Emerald.

Morrison, E. W., See, K. E., & Pan, C. (2015). An approach-inhibition model of employee silence: The joint effects of personal sense of power and target openness. Personnel Psychology, 68(3), 547–580. https://doi.org/10.1111/peps.12087

Murray, K. (2004). Create a listening organization. Strategic Communication Management, 8(5), 5.

Nofsinger, R. E. (1991). *Everyday conversation*. Sage Publications.
Park, S. H., Kim, J. N., & Krishna, A. (2014). Bottom-up building of an innovative organization: Motivating employee intrapreneurship and scouting and their strategic value. *Management Communication Quarterly, 28*(4), 531–560. https://doi.org/10.1177/0893318914541667
Pinder, C. C., & Harlos, K. P. (2001). Employee silence: Quiescence and acquiescence as responses to perceived injustice. *Research in Personnel and Human Resources Management, 20*, 331–369. https://doi.org/10.1016/S0742-7301(01)20007-3
Purdy, M. W., & Manning, L. M. (2015). Listening in the multicultural workplace: A dialogue of theory and practice. *International Journal of Listening, 29*(1), 1–11. https://doi.org/10.1080/10904018.2014.942492
Resnick, L. B., & Klopfer, L. E. (1989). *Toward the thinking curriculum: Current cognitive research. 1989 ASCD Yearbook*. Association for Supervision and Curriculum Development Yearbook.
Robinson, S. L. (1996). Trust and breach of the psychological contract. *Administrative Science Quarterly, 41*(4), 574–599. https://doi.org/10.2307/2393868
Schiffrin, D. (1987). *Discourse markers*. Cambridge University Press.
Shannon, C. E. (1948). A mathematical theory of communication. *The Bell System Technical Journal, 27*(3), 379–423. https://doi.org/10.1002/j.1538-7305.1948.tb01338.x
Shaw, J. B., Erickson, A., & Harvey, M. (2011). A method for measuring destructive leadership and identifying types of destructive leaders in organizations. *The Leadership Quarterly, 22*, 575–590. https://doi.org/cqkvgb
Sherf, E. N., Parke, M. R., & Isaakyan, S. (2021). Distinguishing voice and silence at work: Unique relationships with perceived impact, psychological safety, and burnout. *Academy of Management Journal, 64*(1), 114–148. https://doi.org/10.5465/amj.2018.1428
Song, B., Qian, J., & Wang, B. (2017). Are you hiding from your boss? Leader's destructive personality and employee silence. *Social Behavior and Personality an International Journal, 45*(7), 1167–1174. https://doi.org/10.2224/sbp.6421
Stine, M., Thompson, T., & Cusella, L. (1995). The impact of organizational structure and supervisory listening indicators on subordinate support, trust, intrinsic motivation, and performance. *International Journal of Listening, 9*(1), 84–10. https://doi.org/10.1080/10904018.1995.10499143
Tangirala, S., & Ramanujam, R. (2008). Employee silence on critical work issues: The cross level effects of procedural justice climate. *Personnel Psychology, 61*(1), 37–68. https://doi.org/10.1111/j.1744-6570.2008.00105.x
Tangirala, S., & Ramanujam, R. (2012). Ask and you shall hear (but not always): Examining the relationship between manager consultation and employee voice. *Personnel Psychology, 65*(2), 251–282. https://doi.org/10.1111/j.1744-6570.2012.01248.x
Taylor, M., & Kent, M. L. (2014). Dialogic engagement: Clarifying foundational concepts. *Journal of Public Relations Research, 26*(5), 384–398. https://doi.org/10.1080/1062726X.2014.956106
Vakola, M., & Bouradas, D. (2005). Antecedents and consequences of organisational silence: An empirical investigation. *Employee Relations, 27*(5), 441–458. https://doi.org/10.1108/01425450510611997

Van Dyne, L., Ang, S., & Botero, I. C. (2003). Conceptualizing employee silence and employee voice as multidimensional constructs. *Journal of Management Studies*, *40*(6), 1359–1392. https://doi.org/10.1111/1467-6486.00384

Wang, Y.-D., & Hsieh, H.-H. (2013). Organizational ethical climate, perceived organizational support, and employee silence: A cross-level investigation. *Human Relations*, *66*(6), 783–802. https://doi.org/10.1177/0018726712460706

Welch, M., & Jackson, P. R. (2007). Rethinking internal communication: A stakeholder approach. *Corporate Communications: An International Journal*, *12*(2), 177–198. https://doi.org/10.1108/13563280710744847

Whiteside, D. B., & Barclay, L. (2013). Echoes of silence: Employee silence as a mediator between overall justice and employee outcomes. *Journal of Business Ethics*, *116*(2), 251–266. https://doi.org/10.1007/s10551-012-1467-3

Wolvin, A. D., & Coakley, C. G. (1994). Listening competency. *International Listening Association. Journal*, *8*(1), 148–160. https://doi.org/10.1080/10904018.1994.10499135

Yang, S. U., Kang, M., & Cha, H. (2015). A study on dialogic communication, trust, and distrust: Testing a scale for measuring organization–public dialogic communication (OPDC). *Journal of Public Relations Research*, *27*(2), 175–192. https://doi.org/10.1080/1062726X.2015.1007998

4 The Power of AI-Enabled Chatbots as an Organizational Social Listening Tool

Alvin Zhou, Linjuan Rita Men, and Wan-Hsiu Sunny Tsai

Introduction

In the rapidly evolving digital media landscape, chatbots, a popular artificial intelligence (AI) application, have emerged as a new communication channel that may revolutionize publics' experience with organizations. Programmed to identify both intellectual and emotional signals, chatbots can be optimized for interactive and empathetic communication, where human feelings, intent, and needs can be recognized and responded to, making them an ideal tool for organizational digital listening (Men et al., 2022b). This chapter explores the potential of social chatbots as a listening agent for organizations. Informed by a comprehensive review of literature in public relations, computer-mediated communication, and human-machine communication, this chapter presents a holistic framework to theorize how organizations can effectively harness the power of social chatbots for organizational listening. We further discuss how listening via social chatbots may influence public relations effectiveness.

This chapter is structured to include the following sections: (1) The introduction of AI-powered social chatbots and the key features, with a focus on chatbot listening and the implications for organizational social listening; (2) the theoretical foundation based on social presence and conversational human voice (CHV) as the antecedents of chatbot-mediated organizational listening; (3) impact of organizational social listening via chatbots on public relations outcomes, including perceived organizational transparency, corporate character, and organization-public relationships (OPRs); and (4) implications for public relations practice.

Scaling Up Organizational Listening with Artificial Intelligence

Some might find listening—an interpersonal construct and an individual act—conceptually far away from what AI entails. Therefore, in this section, we first define listening and then connect the dots to lay out why

DOI: 10.4324/9781003273851-6

AI matters for organizational listening and how its practical applications can have profound implications for strategic communication.

It is undeniable that listening, as it relates to organizational processes, has been studied mostly in interpersonal settings where a human speaks and another human listens (Kluger & Itzchakov, 2022). Broadly defined as the process of receiving information, understanding and interpreting meanings, responding to speakers, and remembering what is heard (Cooper, 1997), listening is an integral component of communication (Lipari, 2010). Bodie and Crick (2014) defined listening as a "capacity to discern the underlying habitual character and attitudes of people with whom we communicate … (which) brings about a sense of shared experience and mutual understanding" (p. 106). Brownell (2017) described a skill-based model of listening, suggesting *hearing, understanding, remembering, interpreting, evaluating*, and *responding* as basic elements of effective listening. The concept of listening has been applied to various social contexts including inside the organizations. For example, supervisor listening has been found to induce a feeling of being heard among employees, which promotes citizenship behaviors and reduces turnover intentions (Lloyd et al., 2015). When listening is incorporated into the strategic communication literature, which brings forth the term "organizational listening" (Borner & Zerfass, 2018; Macnamara, 2016b), this concept serves to humanize organizations, indicating that organizations as a collective entity can listen. In this way, organizational listening shifts the focus from an interpersonal process involving conversational exchange and dialogic participation (Baxter, 2011; Heath et al., 2006) to an institutional function that incorporates internal and external stakeholders' feedback, builds and maintains relationships with them, and uses the acquired information to assist strategic decision-making (Barbour, 2017; Brunner, 2008).

Therefore, one key difference between interpersonal listening and organizational listening is their scale. When organizations listen, they have to listen to numerous stakeholders, including but not limited to employees, customers, suppliers, activists, and partners. As Macnamara (2019) contended, organizations have to deploy a "delegated, mediated, and large-scale listening" system in this digital age (p. 5190). This is where AI-powered communication technologies come into play. AI applications, such as social media monitoring services, effectively scale up organizations' listening capacities and enable organizations to gather multiple streams of external inputs at once.

AI further enables organizations to go beyond "gathering" information. With the advance of natural language processing (NLP), automatic speech recognition (ASR), and computer vision (CV), AI-powered listening systems allow organizations to analyze collected data (e.g., text, audio, and video) on stakeholders' multimodal engagement behaviors (e.g., social media posts and voice search) and then automatically

Power of AI-Enabled Chatbots   65

respond to them in real time. Organizations' prompt responses signal to concerned stakeholders that their inputs have been received and processed and that the organization strives to be a good listener.

As such, in Figure 4.1, we delineate how AI can help organizations listen to mass stakeholders on digital platforms. In particular, in this chapter, we focus on using AI-enabled social chatbots for organizational listening and consider how they can fulfill strategic communication purposes and achieve relational outcomes in this process.

AI-Enabled Social Chatbots

AI-powered communication technologies can be easily integrated into organizations' digital repertoires. One of such applications is AI-enabled social chatbots, commonly found on corporations' Facebook pages, mobile apps, and official websites. Once summoned by visitors for one-on-one conversations, these chatbots can listen to user input, search databases for potential answers, formulate responses to address inquiries, and direct them to external resources. These chatbots, as Men et al. (2022b) argued, embody organizational listening's key features of "scale, delegation, and mediation" (Macnamara, 2019, p. 5190).

Chatbots play an essential role in collecting user inputs when stakeholders initiate conversations and ask questions in the online interface (the *input* process in Figure 4.1). Less understood and carrying more potential for the management of strategic communication is social chatbots' *response* process, underlined in Figure 4.1. The response process is an essential component of organizational listening (Macnamara, 2019). Admittedly, organizations cannot control or predict what concerns or comments may arise from stakeholders, but they can program listening delegates' response strategies to improve perceptual and relational outcomes. In this chapter, we focus on the central perceptual outcomes of perceived chatbot listening and perceived organizational listening and

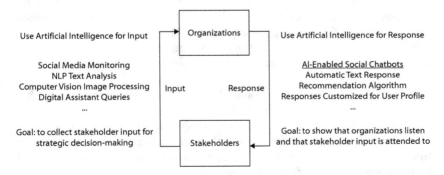

Figure 4.1 Using artificial intelligence for organizational listening

its consequences on public relations effectiveness indicated by perceived organizational transparency, corporate character, and OPRs.

While listening is what *organizations* do, equally important in the communication process is the perspective of *stakeholders* who evaluate the organization they are speaking to. Perceived organizational listening is different from organizations' actual listening behavior as defined by Macnamara (2016a). However, it is an instrumental component and perceptual outcome of organizations' listening efforts. Next, we draw from various theoretical frameworks and recent empirical research to discuss how organizations should design their AI-enabled social chatbots so that stakeholders will perceive the chatbot and its represented organization as *good listeners* and how such perception can lead to better public relations outcomes.

Chatbot Social Conversation

Listening is more than hearing. When stakeholders initiate conversations with social chatbots, they expect chatbots to not only receive their messages (i.e., hearing) but also be attentive. This distinction relates back to the rich literature on active listening (e.g., Bodie, 2011; Jones et al., 2019; Jonsdottir & Fridriksdottir, 2020). Active listening, in the interpersonal domain, requires the listener to not only pay attention to what is said but also sense the speaker's emotions, process relayed information, show body language, and follow up with questions (Bodie, 2011).

Chatbot-stakeholder communication is a form of human-machine communication that is mediated by computers and deprived of interpersonal social cues and physical presence. Chatbots cannot nod, frown, or emote. Therefore, it diverges from the original conceptualizations of active listening. However, we suggest that two communication strategies—social presence and CHV—can be utilized to compensate for the lack of interpersonal cues and help instill the perception that the chatbot and its represented organization are actively listening to stakeholders. Specifically, we follow Men et al. (2022b) and define chatbot social conversation as engaging conversations between chatbots and users which are characterized by social presence and CHV, through which chatbots can be designed to achieve strategic communication excellence. It serves as the antecedent driving publics' perception that the organization is a good listener.

Lee and Shin (2012) defined social presence as "the extent to which a person feels as if he/she were 'with' the communication partner, engaging in a direct, face-to-face conversation" (p. 516). In other words, social presence captures the degree to which computer-mediated communication resembles the physical and psychological closeness in interpersonal communication. Therefore, social presence is a perceptual variable that is oftentimes measured as the perceived warmth, sociability, and sensitivity conveyed by the messages (B. Lu et al., 2016; Men et al., 2018) or by the medium (Short et al., 1976; Zhou & Xu, 2022).

Social presence has long been studied as the antecedent of important strategic communication outcomes. For example, Chen et al. (2021) showed that start-up companies' social presence on social media drives organization-public dialogic communication and nurtures publics' trust and positive word of mouth toward companies. Establishing social presence on social media platforms through digital communication is an effective conduit for organizations to build their reputation. Men et al. (2018) examined social presence's effects on engagement metrics such as likes, shares, comments, and reactions, a series of outcomes that are less perceptual and more practical than organization-public dialogic communication. They showed that social presence trumps previous proposed strategies, such as generating return visits and creating dialogic loops, in driving those metrics that are used in many organizations to evaluate the success of digital campaigns. The positive effect of social presence on organization-level outcomes has also been shown in Han et al.'s (2016) study, which demonstrated that social presence induced by machine interactivity, person interactivity, and self-disclosure can lead to trust in the company and nurture positive relationships in the long run. Specifically for the context of chatbot-mediated communication, social presence has been shown to induce parasocial interactions and enhance consumer engagement when employed by brands (Tsai et al., 2021) and improve service encounter satisfaction when employed for business operations (Verhagen et al., 2014).

Various measurement items for social presence have been proposed. To operationalize chatbot social conversation, Men et al. (2022b) adapted wording from B. Lu et al. (2016) and prompted participants who interacted with AI-enabled social chatbots to evaluate their experiences on the following items: "There is a sense of human contact," "there is a sense of personness," "there is a sense of sociability," "there is a sense of human warmth," "there is a sense of human sensitivity," "I can make sense of the attitudes of the virtual agent," "there is a sense of human touch," and "communication is warm."

Compared to social presence, which stems from psychology literature, CHV is a concept that originated in the field of strategic communication. CHV is an informal, engaging, and natural style of mediated organizational communication that reflects attributes of interpersonal communication. In its original conceptualization (Kelleher, 2009; Kelleher & Miller, 2006), CHV is used to characterize how organizational communications on blogs deviated from the language patterns of official publications by resembling the communication styles of personal blogs. The concept is also used to conceptualize the humanness of organizations which has been shown to cultivate and maintain relationships between organizations and their strategic publics (L. Lu et al., 2022). In essence, organizational communication that is mundane, authoritative, and stiff can signal power imbalance between organizations and stakeholders and inhibit relational closeness that precedes quality OPRs. By contrast, CHV can make organizational communication interesting, relatable, and enjoyable. Subsequent studies have extended CHV's application beyond organizational blogs to areas such as social media communication.

Through an online experiment, van Noort and Willemsen (2012) demonstrated that CHV can attenuate the detrimental effect of negative electronic word of mouth on brand evaluations. Addressing consumer complaints through CHV, as the study showed, created a collaborative online environment where the company was perceived to be more apologetic and willing to make course corrections (van Noort & Willemsen, 2012). Later studies provided more nuanced analyses of these effects. For example, Gretry et al. (2017) focused on the effect of CHV on brand trust and showed that the informal communication style could backfire when consumers are not familiar with the brand. However, when stakeholders are actively engaging with organizational communications (e.g., evoking chatbots, following Facebook pages, and liking promotional tweets), CHV can serve as an important mechanism that mediates the effect of social media use on purchase intention (Beukeboom et al., 2015). More specifically, for the context of chatbot interactions, Liebrecht and van Hooijdonk (2020) advised developers to incorporate linguistic elements from CHV into chatbots' communication design in order to improve customer service automation and create positive perceptions of organizations.

Adapting this concept from organizational blogs to chatbot-stakeholder communication, Men et al. (2022b) used measurement items from Sweetser and Kelleher (2016) and prompted participants who interacted with AI-enabled social chatbots to evaluate chatbots' communication style with the following items: "the chatbot uses a sense of humor," "the chatbot makes our communication enjoyable," "the chatbot would admit mistakes," and "the chatbot positively addresses complaints or queries."

Conceptually, social presence and CHV are integrally related (Kelleher, 2009). However, they are also distinct in terms of theoretical origins, focal objects of evaluations, and potential variables that could influence them. For example, social presence evaluates the psychological perceptions of conversation interlocutors, while CHV evaluates the tone, style, and content of the sent messages. Social presence is psychological, while CHV is communicated through linguistics. Additionally, CHV is affected by organizations' communication strategies and, in our case, how they program chatbots for instant responses, while social presence can be established through design choices and media affordances (cf., Men et al., 2018; Short et al., 1976; Zhou & Xu, 2022). For example, the "someone is typing" indicator implemented by messaging apps contributes to social presence but not CHV, while a filler word "hmm" used by conversational agents contributes to CHV but not social presence, as it deviates from the serious tone used in official organizational reports but arguably does not reduce the psychological distance between the two communicators. We thus integrate these two theoretical frameworks into chatbot social conversation to capture vital elements in designing social chatbots and discuss how it serves as antecedents to various strategic outcomes at the perceptual and relational levels.

Strategic Outcomes of Chatbot Social Conversation

Perceived Listening

One strategic outcome that can be directly affected by chatbot social conversation is perceived chatbot listening (Men et al., 2022b). With chatbot social conversations implemented, where a chatbot addresses user inputs in a friendly, warm, and attentive way and signals that it is attentively listening to the user, stakeholders who engage the organizational delegate in one-on-one conversations should see the chatbot as a good listener.

To illustrate the point, we can imagine two counterfactual scenarios. First, if a user evokes a chatbot and provides a series of long comments about its organization but the chatbot keeps quiet no matter what follow-up messages the user sends, it is very unlikely that the stakeholder would feel that the chatbot is listening to their inputs. They might even question if the chatbot is functional and if their messages have been successfully delivered to the organization's social media team. Second, if the chatbot only returns automatic, mundane, and machine-like responses after user inputs such as "thank you for the message and it has been forwarded to our team," although stakeholders can be certain that there is no technical problem and their concerns have been *delivered*, they could hardly consider they have been attentively *listened to*.

Once perceived chatbot listening is established, it should also foster stakeholders' perception that the represented organization is a good listener. After all, chatbots are developed, programmed, and placed on organizations' official websites, social media pages, and mobile apps, where organizational affiliations are prominently shown. Perceived organizational listening, as we previously discussed, is a stakeholder's perception that the organization is a good listener, which is different from actual organizational listening. Organizational listening focuses on the agency of an organization that executes listening behavior, considers stakeholder needs, and changes its course of action accordingly. However, as argued by Men et al. (2022b) and Macnamara (2015), organizations should also put their listening programs on display, and making stakeholders feel they are heard is as important as organizations' actual listening efforts.

In summary, we define perceived chatbot listening as a stakeholder's perception that a chatbot attends to, understands, and appropriately responds to their inputs, while perceived organizational listening pertains to a stakeholder's perception of the listening efforts of the organization the chatbot represents. Chatbot social conversation can lead to perceived chatbot listening, which in turn leads to perceived organizational listening (Men et al., 2022b).

Perceived Organizational Transparency

Organizations are not usually transparent in their communication since transparency could invite imitation from competitors and create potential risks for their bottom lines (Bernstein, 2012). However, with stakeholders requesting more information disclosure from major businesses and interest groups demanding legislative changes to enforce larger-scale voluntary corporate reporting, the public is getting to know more about the organizations that they purchase products from, invest in, or work for. The interconnecting nature of Web 2.0 also accelerated this trend, with information becoming freely available and circulating through social networks (Ticoll & Tapscott, 2014).

The availability, disclosure, and accessibility of organizational information are critical components of organizational transparency, but organizational transparency is more than making internal information publicly accessible (Albu & Flyverbom, 2019). Transparency is communicative, and it begets public communication to establish a mutual understanding of what the organization is doing to stakeholders, communities, and society (Albu & Flyverbom, 2019; O'Neill, 2006). Conceptually, it follows that organizations are transparent only when they sincerely communicate and that the ways in which they communicate can affect outcomes such as perceived transparency. Rawlins (2008) suggests that perceived organizational transparency consists of at least two dimensions: perceived informational transparency and participatory transparency.

Chatbot interactions contribute to both of these transparency dimensions. First, by searching databases for correct answers, directing users to useful resources, and fulfilling its utilitarian purpose, chatbot communication should lead to perceived informational transparency since the organizational delegate satisfies stakeholders' information needs. Second, chatbot interactions are communicative give-and-takes that involve exchanges of information, ideas, and opinions between a stakeholder and an organization. Chatbots only respond when users have something to say, and chatbots ask questions that need users to reply back. Those who use the chatbot, therefore, should feel that they are participating in the organizational communication process, and they have control over where the conversation is going. Users' sense of "I am actively involved in the back-and-forths" is a great example of participatory transparency (Rawlins, 2008), which should lead to the positive perceptual outcome of perceived organizational transparency.

Moreover, the two elements of chatbot social conversation—social presence and CHV—can further enhance perceived organizational transparency. Organizations will not be perceived as transparent or trustworthy when they communicate in an opaque, ambiguous, and inaccessible way (Schnackenberg & Tomlinson, 2016), which is exactly the opposite of chatbot social conversation. Chatbot social conversation is fun, humanized, casual, and meaningful. Both social presence and CHV contribute to perceived organizational transparency in various ways. For instance, by projecting that the organization is actually there and presenting its true beliefs to stakeholders without anything to hide, social presence is associated with perceived organizational authenticity, which in turn improves perceived transparency (Cohen & Tyler, 2016; Jiang & Shen, 2020; Lee, 2020). CHV also enhances the sense of interactivity, further making stakeholders feel that they are *actively* (*participatory* transparency) acquiring *information* (*informational* transparency) from organizational representatives (Liebrecht & van Hooijdonk, 2020; Rawlins, 2008).

Perceived Corporate Character

Corporate character has long been suggested as a vital measure of public relations effectiveness (Leffingwell, 1980). Defined as "how a stakeholder distinguishes an organization, expressed in terms of human characteristics" (Davies et al., 2004, p. 127), corporate character is conceptualized as a humanized approach to understanding corporate reputation. It has been associated with various organizational outcomes such as customer-organizational identification, public engagement, and OPRs (Ji et al., 2022; Men & Sung, 2022; Men & Tsai, 2015). Chun (2006) defined five types of corporate character, namely, agreeableness, enterprise, competence, chic, and ruthlessness. An *agreeable* company communicates in a friendly, pleasant, and straightforward manner; they show empathy, concern, and support toward stakeholders. They also act as a sincere, honest, responsible, and trustworthy corporate citizen (Men & Sung, 2022). A company that is *enterprising* is perceived as innovative, trendy, up-to-date, cool, and exciting. The corporate character of *competence* pertains to conscientiousness, drive, and technocracy of the organization and can be described as reliable, hardworking, ambitious, leading, and technical. A company with a *chic* corporate character, especially for those in the retail industry, can be perceived as charming, stylish, elegant, refined, or elitist (Chun, 2006). Lastly, the corporate character of *ruthlessness* portrays the organization as controlling, totalitarian, arrogant, competitive, or aggressive (Chun, 2006; Men & Sung, 2022; Men & Tsai, 2015).

Previous research has established the connections between corporate communication and corporate character. For instance, Men and Sung (2022) and Ji et al. (2022) demonstrated that corporate symmetrical communication emphasizing two-way communication, feedback, reciprocity, and balance of power helps define positive corporate characters of agreeableness, enterprise, and competence in the eyes of employees and customers. Likewise, in the chatbot-mediated communication context, we argue that chatbot conversation that projects social presence and CHV sends a welcoming and sincere message to users and denotes friendliness, warmth, and sociability, which could lead to public perception of agreeableness of the organization. A responsive, enjoyable, and positive conversation via the novel tool of chatbots also indicates the organization's technocracy, competence, and innovative spirit. As chatbot social conversation invites active participation from publics, provides additional accessibility and visibility of the organization, and fosters dialogue via authentic and humanized messaging and active listening, publics are less likely to perceive the organization the chatbot represents as controlling, authoritarian, arrogant, or aggressive. In short, chatbot social conversation can not only enhance perceived organizational listening and transparency but also attenuate negative corporate characters and nurture positive corporate characters, which lead to other favorable outcomes such as OPR (Men et al., 2022a).

Organization-Public Relationships

One key relational outcome that comes from chatbot social conversation and perceived organizational listening is OPRs. OPRs are one of the focal goals of strategic communication, especially for the practice of public relations. OPRs denote "the patterns of interaction, transaction, exchange, and linkage between an organization and its publics" (Broom et al., 2000, p. 18) and consist of dimensions such as trust, commitment, satisfaction, and control mutuality (Hon & Grunig, 1999).

Trust refers to a party's confidence and willingness to open oneself to the other party (Hon & Grunig, 1999). It indicates that the public deem the organization credible, put faith in its integrity, and are open to potential future risks when engaging it. It is a concept transplanted from literature on interpersonal relationships but applicable for organizational context (Huang, 2012). Compared to trust, commitment characterizes a more longitudinal and cognitive process. Relationships need two parties' continuous investment. They need to spend time, energy, and sometimes monetary resources to maintain their relationship. Commitment taps into these dimensions and is related to concepts in marketing literature such as brand loyalty (Morgan & Hunt, 1994). By contrast, satisfaction is affective. It is created when positive expectations about the relationship are reinforced repeatedly (Hon & Grunig, 1999). Satisfaction is the hallmark of effective relational maintenance and exists when the two parties do not hold grudges and feel content with their relationship's current stage. Control mutuality comes from a critical assessment of the possibility of establishing true relationships with strategic publics. In a good relationship, two parties should be able to influence one another on equal footing; however, it is usually not the case in organization-public settings where the organization possesses much more power in influencing stakeholders than the other way around. This dimension is included to assess how much the publics perceive themselves to have the agency to stand up to the focal organization and how much they feel empowered to improve, maintain, disengage, or terminate their relationship with the organization (Huang, 2001).

OPRs have been widely studied as an outcome imperative to the excellence of strategic management (Grunig, 1992), while recent studies also take OPRs as an outcome to characterize relational implications of organizations' communication toward internal and external publics (Cheng, 2018). For example, Men et al. (2020) showed that organizations' two-way symmetrical communication and information dissemination in internal social media contribute to employees' relationships with their employers. These intangible relational assets, as some literature has shown, can translate to lower employee turnover and higher revenue generation down the line (Huang, 2012).

We argue that the way a chatbot responds to stakeholders during AI-mediated communication matters for relationships and that listening—the topic under investigation throughout this book—mediates the effect of chatbot social conversation on quality OPRs. In other words, perceived listening (including perceived chatbot listening and perceived organizational listening) should serve as the mechanism: relationships will only develop when stakeholders perceive the chatbot and its organization to be attentive to what they have to say.

Studies have empirically established such a connection. By instructing participants to converse with corporate chatbots on Facebook and report their perceptions of conversation quality, perceived listening, and organizational relationships, Men et al. (2022b) showed that the quality of chatbot conversations—a chatbot-level antecedent—did not directly contribute to OPRs—an organization-level outcome. It is only through perceived listening that the positive experience with a company's chatbot can translate to stakeholders' trust and satisfaction in the company (Men et al., 2022b). This "conversation-listening-relationship" chain of effect once again highlights the important role of listening in strategic communication, illustrated in Figure 4.2.

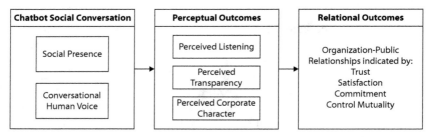

Figure 4.2 Theoretical framework of chatbot social conversation and perceived organizational listening

Recommendations for Practice

As AI-enabled technologies continue to revolutionize strategic communication practices, organizations that strive for communication excellence should be actively exploring the potential of new AI tools, such as chatbots, into their communication mix. In addition to ensuring the task performance of chatbots (e.g., providing accurate and complete answers to publics' inquiries) and fulfilling the publics' utilitarian needs such as information seeking or customer service, chatbots should be programmed in a way to have "emotional intelligence" and be equipped with a PR mindset. Focusing on organization listening, our chapter highlights that social chatbots can simulate the positive effects of interpersonal communication. Specifically, by infusing social presence and CHV in chatbot messaging using emojis, greetings with names, memes, or other design features ("… is typing"), chatbot messages can project humanness, warmth, sensitivity, and human touch. Through showing positivity and humor, chatbots can convey a relational orientation that fosters authentic interactions. In this last section, we connect our chapter with industry practices and specify recommendations for public relations professionals and communication management teams.

First, our model and conceptualization advocate for the necessity of including communication professionals in the development of AI technologies for strategic communication. The employment of AI in many industries is often considered a task mainly for computer scientists and engineers, which could create silos and blind spots that inadvertently limit the capabilities of these emerging technologies, such as using chatbots only for utilitarian Q&A purposes, and lead to unanticipated negative outcomes when applied to real-world situations (Piorkowski et al., 2021; Westerman et al., 2020). How AI communication agents are programmed matters for corporate image, OPRs, perceived listening, and other important strategic outcomes, as demonstrated by Men et al. (2022b). Therefore, teams developing AI communication systems should not only encompass user experience and user interface (UX/UI) specialists and front-end developers, but also include communication professionals who are content experts for crafting chatbot messages and responses that are engaging, friendly, and strategic. This call for action thus requires managerial stewardship to diversify organizations' AI development teams, and our chapter provides a strong rationale for leadership to execute those important human resources decisions.

Second, public relations professionals should take note of the increasingly important role of AI-powered and AI-mediated communication in their everyday practice (Hancock et al., 2020) and educate themselves to become more familiar with AI-assisted organizational listening. Listening has been considered a key public relations strategy in the industry, encompassing various processes ranging from social media monitoring to face-to-face public consultations to call center recordings (Macnamara, 2019). Many of these processes are becoming computer-mediated or AI-mediated. To strengthen the role of listening in public relations strategies as well as the role of public relations in corporate decision-making, strategic communication practitioners need to keep up with technological advancement and become well-versed in advising and collaborating with technology personnel. Companies should also provide training opportunities such as AI educational workshops or courses (e.g., "AI in Business" and "AI Decision Making") to employees, especially the communication team, to equip them with the emerging technology literacy, skills, and knowledge.

Third, our chapter demonstrates that, as social listening starts to embody new meanings with the evolution of AI, organizational listening repertoire should go beyond listening via Web 2.0 tools such as social networking sites or social messengers to include smarter, more efficient, and more automated chat agents. Admittedly, gathering information and feedback from publics and follow-ups are essential for actual organizational listening practices, and the 24-7 real-time humanized response from chatbots also shapes positive public perceptions that the organization is willing to listen and establishes a transparent organizational image and agreeable, competent, and innovative characters, which further contribute to relationship building with publics (Men et al., 2022b). It is important to note that *speaking* and *listening* are the two sides of effective communication which cannot be separated.

As organizations and brands continue to embrace the concept of "CommTech" (Samson & O'Leary, 2020), the future of strategic communication will be more intelligent, agile, and "social." While AI agents may never be able to replace human agents, it comes with enormous potential to transform the communication and listening practices and bring them to the next level. Eventually, AI-powered technologies such as chatbots can reshape publics' direct experiences with companies and brands through automated and humanized social conversations and listening. It is time for communication leaders to embrace AI technologies, think smart, and act AI-informed.

References

Albu, O. B., & Flyverbom, M. (2019). Organizational transparency: Conceptualizations, conditions, and consequences. *Business & Society, 58*(2), 268–297. https://doi.org/10.1177/0007650316659851

Barbour, J. B. (2017). Listening and organizing. In C. R. Scott, J. R. Barker, T. Kuhn, J. Keyton, P. K. Turner, & L. K. Lewis (Eds.), *The international encyclopedia of organizational communication*. Wiley. https://doi.org/10.1002/9781118955567.wbieoc126

Baxter, L. A. (2011). *Voicing relationships: A dialogic perspective*. SAGE Publications.

Bernstein, E. S. (2012). The transparency paradox: A role for privacy in organizational learning and operational control. *Administrative Science Quarterly, 57*(2), 181–216. https://doi.org/10.1177/0001839212453028

Beukeboom, C. J., Kerkhof, P., & de Vries, M. (2015). Does a virtual like cause actual liking? How following a brand's Facebook updates enhances brand evaluations and purchase intention. *Journal of Interactive Marketing, 32*, 26–36. https://doi.org/10.1016/j.intmar.2015.09.003

Bodie, G. D. (2011). The active-empathic listening scale (AELS): Conceptualization and evidence of validity within the interpersonal domain. *Communication Quarterly, 59*(3), 277–295. https://doi.org/10.1080/01463373.2011.583495

Bodie, G. D., & Crick, N. (2014). Listening, hearing, sensing: Three modes of being and the phenomenology of Charles Sanders Peirce. *Communication Theory, 24*(2), 105–123. https://doi.org/10.1111/comt.12032

Borner, M., & Zerfass, A. (2018). The power of listening in corporate communications: Theoretical foundations of corporate listening as a strategic mode of communication. In S. Bowman, A. Crookes, S. Romenti, & Ø Ihlen (Eds.), *Advances in public relations and communication management* (pp. 3–22). Emerald Publishing Limited.

Broom, G. M., Casey, S., & Ritchey, J. (2000). Concept and theory of organization-public relationships. In J. A. Ledingham & S. D. Bruning (Eds.), *Public relations as relationship management: A relational approach to the study and practice of public relations* (pp. 3–22). Routledge.

Brownell, J. (2017). *Listening: Attitudes, principles, and skills* (6th ed.). Routledge. https://doi.org/10.4324/9781315441764

Brunner, B. R. (2008). Listening, communication & trust: Practitioners' perspectives of business/organizational relationships. *International Journal of Listening, 22*(1), 73–82. https://doi.org/10.1080/10904010701808482

Chen, Z. F., Ji, Y. G., & Men, L. R. (2021). Effective social media communication for startups in China: Antecedents and outcomes of organization–public dialogic communication. *New Media & Society*. https://doi.org/10.1177/14614448211051984

Cheng, Y. (2018). Looking back, moving forward: A review and reflection of the organization-public relationship (OPR) research. *Public Relations Review, 44*(1), 120–130. https://doi.org/10.1016/j.pubrev.2017.10.003

Chun, R. (2006). The influence of corporate character on customers and employees: Exploring similarities and differences. *Journal of the Academy of Marketing Science, 34*(2), 138–146. https://doi.org/10.1177/0092070305284975

Cohen, E. L., & Tyler, W. J. (2016). Examining perceived distance and personal authenticity as mediators of the effects of ghost-tweeting on parasocial interaction. *Cyberpsychology, Behavior, and Social Networking, 19*(5), 342–346. https://doi.org/10.1089/cyber.2015.0657

Cooper, L. O. (1997). Listening competency in the workplace: A model for training. *Business Communication Quarterly, 60*(4), 75–84. https://doi.org/10.1177/108056999706000405

Davies, G., Chun, R., da Silva, R. V., & Roper, S. (2004). A corporate character scale to assess employee and customer views of organization reputation. *Corporate Reputation Review, 7*(2), 125–146. https://doi.org/10.1057/palgrave.crr.1540216

Gretry, A., Horváth, C., Belei, N., & van Riel, A. C. (2017). "Don't pretend to be my friend!" When an informal brand communication style backfires on social media. *Journal of Business Research, 74*, 77–89. https://doi.org/10.1016/j.jbusres.2017.01.012

Grunig, J. E. (Ed.). (1992). *Excellence in public relations and communications management*. Lawrence Erlbaum.

Han, S., Min, J., & Lee, H. (2016). Building relationships within corporate SNS accounts through social presence formation. *International Journal of Information Management, 36*(6), 945–962. https://doi.org/10.1016/j.ijinfomgt.2016.06.004

Hancock, J. T., Naaman, M., & Levy, K. (2020). AI-mediated communication: Definition, research agenda, and ethical considerations. *Journal of Computer-Mediated Communication, 25*(1), 89–100. https://doi.org/10.1093/jcmc/zmz022

Heath, R. L., Pearce, W. B., Shotter, J., Taylor, J. R., Kersten, A., Zorn, T., Roper, J., Motion, J., & Deetz, S. (2006). The processes of dialogue: Participation and legitimation. *Management Communication Quarterly, 19*(3), 341–375. https://doi.org/10.1177/0893318905282208

Hon, L. C., & Grunig, J. E. (1999). *Guidelines for measuring relationships in public relations*. Institute for Public Relations. https://www.instituteforpr.org/wp-content/uploads/Guidelines_Measuring_Relationships.pdf

Huang, Y.-H. (2001). OPRA: A cross-cultural, multiple-item scale for measuring organization-public relationships. *Journal of Public Relations Research, 13*(1), 61–90. https://doi.org/10.1207/S1532754XJPRR1301_4

Huang, Y.-H. (2012). Gauging an integrated model of public relations value assessment (PRVA): Scale development and cross-cultural studies. *Journal of Public Relations Research, 24*(3), 243–265. https://doi.org/10.1080/1062726X.2012.671987

Ji, Y. G., Chen, Z. F., & Men, L. R. (2022). Carving start-up character: Effects of symmetrical communication on start-up corporate character, customer-start-up identification, and customer advocacy. *International Journal of Strategic Communication, 16*(2), 239–254. https://doi.org/10.1080/1553118X.2021.2014502

Jiang, H., & Shen, H. (2020). Toward a relational theory of employee engagement: Understanding authenticity, transparency, and employee behaviors. *International Journal of Business Communication*. https://doi.org/10.1177/2329488420954236

Jones, S. M., Bodie, G. D., & Hughes, S. D. (2019). The impact of mindfulness on empathy, active listening, and perceived provisions of emotional support. *Communication Research, 46*(6), 838–865. https://doi.org/10.1177/0093650215626983

Jonsdottir, I. J., & Fridriksdottir, K. (2020). Active listening: Is it the forgotten dimension in managerial communication? *International Journal of Listening, 34*(3), 178–188. https://doi.org/10.1080/10904018.2019.1613156

Kelleher, T. (2009). Conversational voice, communicated commitment, and public relations outcomes in interactive online communication. *Journal of Communication, 59*(1), 172–188. https://doi.org/10.1111/j.1460-2466.2008.01410.x

Kelleher, T., & Miller, B. M. (2006). Organizational blogs and the human voice: Relational strategies and relational outcomes. *Journal of Computer-Mediated Communication, 11*(2), 395–414. https://doi.org/10.1111/j.1083-6101.2006.00019.x

Kluger, A. N., & Itzchakov, G. (2022). The power of listening at work. *Annual Review of Organizational Psychology and Organizational Behavior, 9*(1), 121–146. https://doi.org/10.1146/annurev-orgpsych-012420-091013

Lee, E.-J. (2020). Authenticity model of (mass-oriented) computer-mediated communication: Conceptual explorations and testable propositions. *Journal of Computer-Mediated Communication, 25*(1), 60–73. https://doi.org/10.1093/jcmc/zmz025

Lee, E.-J., & Shin, S. Y. (2012). Are they talking to me? Cognitive and affective effects of interactivity in politicians' Twitter communication. *Cyberpsychology, Behavior, and Social Networking, 15*(10), 515–520. https://doi.org/10.1089/cyber.2012.0228

Leffingwell, R. J. (1980). Social sciences commentary: Corporate personality, a measure of public relations effectiveness. *Public Relations Quarterly, 25*(3), 26.

Liebrecht, C., & van Hooijdonk, C. (2020). Creating humanlike chatbots: What chatbot developers could learn from webcare employees in adopting a conversational human voice. In A. Følstad, T. Araujo, S. Papadopoulos, E. L.-C. Law, O.-C. Granmo, E. Luger, & P. B. Brandtzaeg (Eds.), *Chatbot research and design* (pp. 51–64). Springer International Publishing. https://doi.org/10.1007/978-3-030-39540-7_4

Lipari, L. (2010). Listening, thinking, being. *Communication Theory, 20*(3), 348–362. https://doi.org/10.1111/j.1468-2885.2010.01366.x

Lloyd, K. J., Boer, D., Keller, J. W., & Voelpel, S. (2015). Is my boss really listening to me? The impact of perceived supervisor listening on emotional exhaustion, turnover intention, and organizational citizenship behavior. *Journal of Business Ethics, 130*(3), 509–524. https://doi.org/10.1007/s10551-014-2242-4

Lu, B., Fan, W., & Zhou, M. (2016). Social presence, trust, and social commerce purchase intention: An empirical research. *Computers in Human Behavior, 56*, 225–237. https://doi.org/10.1016/j.chb.2015.11.057

Lu, L., McDonald, C., Kelleher, T., Lee, S., Chung, Y. J., Mueller, S., Vielledent, M., & Yue, C. A. (2022). Measuring consumer-perceived humanness of online organizational agents. *Computers in Human Behavior, 128*, 107092. https://doi.org/10.1016/j.chb.2021.107092

Macnamara, J. (2015). Creating an "architecture of listening" in organizations: The basis of engagement, trust, healthy democracy, social equity, and business sustainability. https://www.uts.edu.au/sites/default/files/fass-organizational-listening-report.pdf

Macnamara, J. (2016a). Organizational listening: Addressing a major gap in public relations theory and practice. *Journal of Public Relations Research, 28*(3–4), 146–169. https://doi.org/10.1080/1062726X.2016.1228064

Macnamara, J. (2016b). *Organizational listening: The missing essential in public communication.* Peter Lang.

Macnamara, J. (2019). Explicating listening in organization-public communication: Theory, practices, technologies. *International Journal of Communication, 13*, 5183–5204. https://ijoc.org/index.php/ijoc/article/view/11996

Men, L. R., O'Neil, J., & Ewing, M. (2020). From the employee perspective: Organizations' administration of internal social media and the relationship between social media engagement and relationship cultivation. *International Journal of Business Communication.* https://doi.org/10.1177/2329488420949968

Men, L. R., & Sung, Y. (2022). Shaping corporate character through symmetrical communication: The effects on employee-organization relationships. *International Journal of Business Communication, 59*(3), 427–449. https://doi.org/10.1177/2329488418824989

Men, L. R., & Tsai, W.-H. S. (2015). Infusing social media with humanity: Corporate character, public engagement, and relational outcomes. *Public Relations Review, 41*(3), 395–403. https://doi.org/10.1016/j.pubrev.2015.02.005

Men, L. R., Tsai, W.-H. S., Chen, Z. F., & Ji, Y. G. (2018). Social presence and digital dialogic communication: Engagement lessons from top social CEOs. *Journal of Public Relations Research, 30*(3), 83–99. https://doi.org/10.1080/1062726X.2018.1498341

Men, L. R., Zhou, A., Jin, J., & Thelen, P. (2022a). Shaping corporate character via chatbot social conversation: Impact on organization-public relational outcomes. Paper presented at the Public Relations Society of America Educators Academy Summit, Grapevine, TX.

Men, L. R., Zhou, A., & Tsai, W.-H. S. (2022b). Harnessing the power of chatbot social conversation for organizational listening: The impact on perceived transparency and organization-public relationships. *Journal of Public Relations Research.* https://doi.org/10.1080/1062726X.2022.2068553

Morgan, R. M., & Hunt, S. D. (1994). The commitment-trust theory of relationship marketing. *Journal of Marketing, 58*(3), 20–38. https://doi.org/10.1177/002224299405800302

O'Neill, O. (2006). Transparency and the ethics of communication. In C. Hood & D. Heald (Eds.), *Transparency: The key to better governance?* (pp. 75–90). Oxford University Press.

Piorkowski, D., Park, S., Wang, A. Y., Wang, D., Muller, M., & Portnoy, F. (2021). How AI developers overcome communication challenges in a multidisciplinary team: A case study. *Proceedings of the ACM on Human-Computer Interaction, 5*(CSCW1), 1–25. https://doi.org/10.1145/3449205

Rawlins, B. (2008). Give the emperor a mirror: Toward developing a stakeholder measurement of organizational transparency. *Journal of Public Relations Research, 21*(1), 71–99. https://doi.org/10.1080/10627260802153421

Samson, D., & O'Leary, J. (2020). CommTech—the path to a modern communications function. PageTurner. https://page.org/blog/commtech-the-path-to-a-modern-communications-function

Schnackenberg, A. K., & Tomlinson, E. C. (2016). Organizational transparency: A new perspective on managing trust in organization-stakeholder relationships. *Journal of Management, 42*(7), 1784–1810. https://doi.org/10.1177/0149206314525202

Short, J., Williams, E., & Christie, B. (1976). *The social psychology of telecommunications*. Wiley.

Sweetser, K. D., & Kelleher, T. (2016). Communicated commitment and conversational voice: Abbreviated measures of communicative strategies for maintaining organization-public relationships. *Journal of Public Relations Research*, *28*(5–6), 217–231. https://doi.org/10.1080/1062726X.2016.1237359

Ticoll, D., & Tapscott, D. (2014). *The naked corporation: How the age of transparency will revolutionize business*. Free Press.

Tsai, W.-H. S., Liu, Y., & Chuan, C.-H. (2021). How chatbots' social presence communication enhances consumer engagement: The mediating role of parasocial interaction and dialogue. *Journal of Research in Interactive Marketing*, *15*(3), 460–482. https://doi.org/10.1108/JRIM-12-2019-0200

van Noort, G., & Willemsen, L. M. (2012). Online damage control: The effects of proactive versus reactive webcare interventions in consumer-generated and brand-generated platforms. *Journal of Interactive Marketing*, *26*(3), 131–140. https://doi.org/10.1016/j.intmar.2011.07.001

Verhagen, T., van Nes, J., Feldberg, F., & van Dolen, W. (2014). Virtual customer service agents: Using social presence and personalization to shape online service encounters. *Journal of Computer-Mediated Communication*, *19*(3), 529–545. https://doi.org/10.1111/jcc4.12066

Westerman, D., Edwards, A. P., Edwards, C., Luo, Z., & Spence, P. R. (2020). I-It, I-Thou, I-Robot: The perceived humanness of AI in human-machine communication. *Communication Studies*, *71*(3), 393–408. https://doi.org/10.1080/10510974.2020.1749683

Zhou, A., & Xu, S. (2022). Computer mediation vs. dialogic communication: How media affordances affect organization-public relationship building. *Public Relations Review*, *48*(2), 102176. https://doi.org/10.1016/j.pubrev.2022.102176

5 Evaluating Organizational Listening

Models and Methods for Measuring the Value of Listening for Identifying Opportunities, Risks, and Crises

Sophia Charlotte Volk

Introduction

It is undisputed that the age of digitalization brings new opportunities and challenges for strategic communication and its sub-areas public relations (PR), corporate communication, advertising, internal communication, etc. One of these challenges is to build not only an "architecture of speaking" but also an "architecture of listening" (Macnamara, 2016). In today's digital information environments, employees, customers, journalists, politicians, corporate activists, and other stakeholders make their opinions about and criticism toward organizations known on various online and offline channels. Rumors, misinformation, or conspiracies about organizations can be spread globally (e.g., Ali, 2022; Macnamara, 2020). The global COVID-19 health threat demonstrates once again how organizations are embedded in an uncertain, volatile, and ambiguous environment. This makes it more important for organizations to listen to both analog and virtual conversations of stakeholders and monitor their attitudes, emotions, needs, and opinions (Place, 2022). By doing so, organizations can identify potential opportunities, such as innovative ideas, or anticipate potential risks and challenges, such as the spreading of false information or the arousal of social media crisis.

Despite the importance of organizational listening, both research and practice have so far often focused on the "messaging function" and neglected the "listening function" of strategic communication (Borner & Zerfass, 2018; Macnamara, 2016). Empirical research shows that only 55 percent of around 1,500 communications departments surveyed in Europe have defined a strategy for listening (Zerfass et al., 2015, p. 54), while at least 85 percent have a communication strategy and 78 percent have a content strategy. Thus, only every second department can build on a strategy for listening that defines contact points to collect feedback from stakeholders, establishes different instruments for listening or monitoring discussions, or encompasses plans to initiate stakeholder dialogues. The surveyed practitioners strongly value face-to-face approaches for listening to stakeholders (p. 60) but also make use of a variety of listening tools, ranging from traditional media monitoring to social media monitoring or issues monitoring (p. 61).

There is now an abundance of methods, free and paid tools and technologies, as well as data collection vendors and commercial data brokers for listening to and monitoring stakeholders on a multitude of platforms (Fitzpatrick & Weissman, 2021; Volk & Buhmann, 2023; Weiner et al., 2021). A lot of resources can be put into the development of sophisticated, real-time listening structures – or they can be wasted (Zhang & Vos, 2014). From an organizational perspective, the question then is whether listening is done in a goal-oriented, efficient, and effective manner. From a normative perspective, on the other hand, the question arises as to whether listening promotes participation of and dialogue with stakeholders and thereby serves the social responsibility of the organization. Hence, organizations are naturally forced to listen *intentionally* and *selectively* rather than *inclusively*, in order to support leadership decision-making. When determining a listening strategy, communications departments must make informed and strategic decisions, given the plethora of stakeholders, conversations and topics, and methods and tools available, such as:

- Which stakeholders are listened to, and which are left out?
- Which conversations in which media and on which platforms are listened to, and are these the relevant conversations?
- What methods and tools are used for listening, and do they serve their purpose?
- Are results of listening used meaningfully for strategy adaptation, or are they ignored?
- Are efficient processes and the necessary competencies for systematic listening in place, or are they potential being wasted?

This chapter focuses on the evaluation of listening and answers the question of how the use of listening can be assessed from an organizational viewpoint. First, the chapter elaborates on the relevance of evaluating listening and explains how listening and evaluation are related. Then, the chapter introduces a framework for evaluating listening that includes different stages and different methods and measures. In doing so, a distinction is made between the evaluation of (1) the *listening processes and structures* and (2) the *listening methods and tools*. Lastly, recommendations for practice are derived and directions for future research are discussed.

The Relevance of Evaluating Organizational Listening

Organizational listening is neither a new theoretical concept nor a new communication tool but has arguably experienced a new surge of interest in both research and communication practice in the age of digitalization. According to Borner and Zerfass (2018), strategic communication entails both *outbound* activities, i.e., messaging (sending, speaking, or positioning), as well as *inbound* activities, i.e., listening (interpreting, understanding, sensemaking, or reflecting). Following this understanding, listening as an inbound activity (also: outside-in) is the antipole to the outbound (also: inside-out) activity of *messaging*. A common definitional approach defines organizational listening as:

> [...] the creation and implementation of scaled processes and systems that enable decision makers and policy makers in organizations to actively and effectively access, acknowledge, understand, consider, and appropriately respond to all those who wish to communicate with the organization or with whom the organization wishes to communicate interpersonally or through delegated, mediated means.
> (Macnamara, 2019, p. 5191)

The concept of listening is closely related to the concepts of issues management, social media monitoring (sometimes: social listening), big data analytics, or tracking (e.g., Ingenhoff, 2018; Wiencierz & Röttger, 2017). It is also based on a holistic idea that conceives the function of listening not primarily as detecting risky issues but as taking into account diverse stakeholders' opinions and behaviors and being sensitive toward the environment (Ingenhoff et al., 2020). Underlying much of the work is a normative argument for the need for listening as a means to foster two-way participatory, consensual, and dialogic relationships between organizations and their stakeholders (e.g., Botan, 2018; Brunner, 2008; Navarro et al., 2017; Place, 2022). An example of the normative demands made on organizational listening can be found, for instance, in the "seven canons of listening" proposed by Macnamara (2016, p. 41): This includes inclusive rather than selective listening, i.e., even to marginalized or inactive stakeholders. Further, it involves acknowledging others' views, interpreting what others say fairly, and responding appropriately. However, in practice, research has shown that organizations in fact often listen selectively to generate marketing or competitive data, or upsell products or services to customers, or even engage in forms of fake listening (Macnamara, 2019).

A prerequisite for systematic listening is an "architecture of listening" (Macnamara, 2016), which is aligned with organizational goals and builds on a strategy for listening. Establishing an architecture of listening is an original operational contribution of communications departments (Zerfass & Volk, 2018) since the monitoring of public opinion, media agendas, or stakeholder expectations requires communications expertise and knowledge of media ecosystems. Such an architecture consists of both (1) *listening structures and processes* and (2) *listening methods and tools*. Efficient processes and structures must be developed and competencies must be built in order to ensure not only real-time listening but also "right-time" responses. This often involves the use of a central platform for aggregating listening data collected throughout the organization. Moreover, flowcharts, swim lanes, or checklists can be used to assign responsibilities and define sequences of action (Volk & Zerfass, 2021; Zerfass & Volk, 2019). Embedded in such overarching listening processes and structures are individual listening methods and tools. They encompass a variety of social science research methods that can be used to identify stakeholders' perspectives and opinions, ranging from stakeholder dialogs to surveys, (social) media monitoring, sentiment or topic analyses, focus groups, feedback forms, touchpoint or customer journey analyses, and so forth. Communication departments can choose from a width of providers of digital tools and technologies for listening and crawling sites (for an overview, see Ardila, 2020, pp. 69–74; Brinker, 2022), such as LexisNexis Newsdesk as a media aggregator or Talkwalker for social media monitoring. Further, they can make use of different solutions for aggregating and visualizing data and insights gained from listening, such as listening reports or dashboards (Volk & Zerfass, 2021).

Despite normative claims related to the dialogic and societal benefit of listening, from an organizational perspective, it would be inefficient and a waste of resources for communication departments to try to listen to *everyone and everything* rather than selectively and intentionally listening to those stakeholders in the media, social media, offline, or corporate world that are deemed of strategic significance to the legitimacy or survival of an organization (Zerfass et al., 2018). These could include internal stakeholders such as organizational leaders or critical employees or external stakeholders such as unsatisfied customers, corporate activists, or brand enthusiasts. Otherwise, organizations risk listening to too many conversations that have little or no relevance for them. Therefore, they usually combine two approaches: *structured* listening, i.e., with predefined keywords, issues, brands/products, actors, and platforms that are often used in combination with the organization's name (or its brands, products, services, figureheads, etc.), and *unstructured or explorative* listening based on using random searches of topics or subsets of conversations, in which the organization is not necessarily mentioned and actors do not belong to predefined target groups (e.g., not followers, fans). This ensures that listening does not miss trending "hot" topics, new emerging actors, or the right tone in conversations (Stieglitz & Dang-Xuan, 2013). When trying to distinguish relevant conversations from general noise and data overload, several decisions must be made so that listening adds value and benefit for an organization. First, it is critical that the "right" stakeholders, platforms, and conversations are selected for listening. Second, the "right" listening methods and tools must be selected and correctly used. Third, it is crucial that the "right" insights and interpretations are derived from listening and transformed into listening intelligence that is fed back into the strategy cycle. The question of what the "right" approach is will be answered from the viewpoint of the respective organization and situation (Zerfass et al., 2018). From a societal viewpoint, it can moreover be asked what conversations or stakeholders should be listened to with regard to the normative question of inclusivity of diverse stakeholder perspectives (Macnamara, 2016). Clearly, there is no one-fits-all answer to how listening should be performed.

Yet, it is important to ask whether the stakeholders and conversations (keywords, topics, issues, etc.) listened to are of strategic relevance (or not), whether listening methods perform well in their goal of producing relevant insights (or not), and whether the resulting insights are actually used for strategic purposes (or not). If this is not the case, listening could result in efficiency losses and be more of an expense than an added value. Therefore, it is important to regularly *evaluate* if listening in the organization is achieving its goals or if listening structures and processes or single methods and tools need to be adjusted (Macnamara, 2019).

Foundations of Evaluation

Organizational listening is closely related to evaluation, which is a cornerstone of communication management (Stacks, 2017; Watson & Noble, 2014) and is used to assess to what extent the purposeful use of communication contributes to realizing the strategy and objectives of an organization. *Evaluation* is generally understood as the systematic assessment of the *value* (quality and cost) of an object. This means that every evaluation contains value judgments (Buhmann & Volk, 2022).

The question of the *value of communication* has been discussed many times in the literature in strategic communication research and contains rationales such as building trust, brands, or a favorable reputation, increasing employee motivation, or gaining legitimacy. According to Zerfass and Viertmann (2017), these different rationales can be systematized into four generic dimensions of value creation. Strategic communication contributes value to the organization through:

1 enabling operations by influencing publicity, customer preferences, and employee commitment, and thus ensuring short-term success
2 building intangible values by boosting the organization's reputation, brands, and culture, and thus creating the immaterial assets needed for sustainable long-term success

3 ensuring flexibility by building organization-public relationships, trust, and legitimacy, and thus securing the organization's license to operate
4 adjusting strategy by engaging in thought leadership, identifying innovation potential, and building crisis resilience, and thus increasing the organization's reflective capacities

While messaging especially contributes to the first two dimensions of the value creation process, organizational listening plays a crucial role in indirectly adding value to the third and fourth dimensions, i.e., ensuring flexibility and adjusting strategy (Volk, 2016). By monitoring or responding to employee conversations in the intranet, customer complaints, or by debunking false information about the organization, listening serves as a "boundary spanning" function between the organization and its environment and makes important contributions to the organization's license to operate and self-reflexivity (Zerfass & Volk, 2018).

A central element of any value assessment is *measurement*, i.e., the use of qualitative or quantitative research methods (Buhmann & Volk, 2022). To this end, research instruments such as discussion guides for stakeholder dialogs, standardized questionnaires for surveys, or dictionaries for automated content analyses are developed to generate data and insights. The quantitative or qualitative insights generated are then used as indicators to compare intended goals and actual results. Metrics that combine critical and strategically relevant information into a single result are called key performance indicators (KPIs) (Van Ruler & Körver, 2019).

Evaluation constitutes the last of four phases in an overarching *management cycle* consisting of situation analysis, planning, implementation, and evaluation (Volk & Buhmann, 2023; Volk & Zerfass, 2018). This sequence is also known in PR practice as the RACE formula (acronym for Research, Action, Communication and Evaluation) or the ROPE formula (acronym for Research, Objectives, Programming and Evaluation) (e.g., Broom & Sha, 2013; Smith, 2017). Figure 5.1 illustrates how listening forms part of a basic management cycle that typically includes the following procedures:

1 The situation analysis phase uses research to assess communication needs with regard to the organization and its stakeholders and environment.
2 The planning phase includes strategizing, goal or objective setting, and tactical planning for communication activities, products, campaigns, or programs.
3 The implementation phase involves the execution or programming of communication strategies and activities.
4 The evaluation phase assesses to what extent goals set in the planning phase have been met and identifies opportunities for improvement that can be incorporated into future planning.

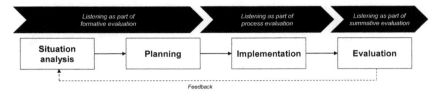

Figure 5.1 The basic management cycle

Organizational listening is considered a key component of evaluation and also plays an important part of situation analysis (Macnamara, 2022), indicating the interrelatedness and overlap of the management cycle. The literature distinguishes three basic types of evaluations (see, e.g., Buhmann & Likely, 2018; Watson & Noble, 2014), each of which builds partly on listening:

a *Formative evaluation* (also formative research) is intended to provide insights for strategy development and, therefore, often includes elements of situation analysis. Organizational listening is often described as an important basis for formative evaluation, besides other methods and approaches such as environmental scanning, risk, trend or landscape analyses, scenario techniques, and market or public opinion research (Macnamara, 2016; Macnamara & Gregory, 2018). Through careful listening to stakeholders, campaign messages can be pretested, and activities can be better aligned with stakeholder interests before implementation.
b *Process evaluation* (also monitoring) aims to observe ongoing activities during strategy implementation in order to intervene and adjust processes in case the activities do not achieve predefined goals (e.g., in terms of message reach, audience attention, or engagement). Listening is a foundational element in process evaluation, as it provides various methods and tools for continuous, real-time, and often automated monitoring, e.g., of social media or online media.
c *Summative evaluation* seeks to examine the extent to which communication activities, campaigns, or programs have achieved their goals and contributed to the achievement of a broader communication and organizational strategy. This is about accountability as well as learning and feedback for which careful listening to the evaluators, i.e., to communication staff responsible for listening, is a prerequisite.

When viewed through this lens, evaluating the results of listening could be conceived as a form of "meta-evaluation" since listening is already a component of evaluation as such. Such meta-evaluations of evaluations (and of its models, methods, metrics, etc.) are indeed important and should be conducted regularly, as they can reveal possible weaknesses in the evaluation that may lead to wrong strategic decisions.

Evaluation of Organizational Listening

While listening has often been emphasized as an important component of evaluation, the question of how organizational listening itself can be evaluated has not yet been explored in depth. This is little surprising, given that much attention has so far been devoted to evaluating the results of "messaging," e.g., campaigns or programs. In the following, the focus is directed toward the question of how the (1) structures and processes of listening, i.e., the overarching listening function, as well as (2) individual methods and tools of listening can be evaluated. This corresponds to what previous work has labeled as the evaluation of the "function" and the "individual" unit (Buhmann & Volk, 2022), both of which belong to the *management* level of strategic communication evaluation, whereas the *activity* level of evaluation comprises the "product," "campaign," and "program" unit:

- *Function:* aggregation of all individual units charged with managing communications across the organization
- *Individual:* individual units such as communication practitioners, methods, or tools
- *Products:* individual communication products such as a social media post or a press release
- *Campaigns:* series of communication products such as a branding or social media campaign
- *Programs:* whole "bundle" of campaigns such as a long-term cultural change program

When evaluating messaging, the focus can be on all five levels. In practice, however, evaluation is most likely to be of communication activities, i.e., the successes of communications products, campaigns, or programs, as empirical data from a survey among 1,601 communications practitioners from 40 European countries show (Zerfass et al., 2017). Evaluation of organizational listening, on the other hand, focuses on the function and the individual unit. It is carried out along different evaluation stages. These are typically laid out in *evaluation models*, which visualize different (often chronological) stages of evaluation and the presumed (causal) relationships between effects at each stage.

Evaluation models are often based on program theory (Frechtling, 2015; Rossi et al., 2004) and the theory of change (Clark & Taplin, 2012; Funnell & Rogers, 2011) and more or less resemble the structure of "logic models" (Kellogg Foundation, 2004; see also Macnamara, 2018). These logic models have as a common denominator that they distinguish between *inputs* (the resources that go into activities or programs), *outputs* (the activities that are produced and the immediate results from these activities), *outcomes* (the short- and medium-term effects that result from the activities), and *impacts* (the long-term changes or benefits). The idea of evaluation models has been adapted in strategic communication, e.g., in Cutlip et al.'s (1985) often-cited Planning, Implementation, Impact Model, Lindenmann's (1997) PR Effectiveness Yardstick, the German Deutsche Public Relations Gesellschaft/International Controller Association (DPRG/ICV) framework (DPRG & ICV, 2011; see also Buhmann et al., 2019), the British Government Communication Service (GCS) (2021), or International Association for the Measurement and Evaluation of Communication's (AMEC) Integrated Evaluation Framework (AMEC, 2016). The aim of these models is to provide a blueprint for evaluating the effects of communication – i.e., the messaging function. Detailed descriptions of different evaluation models and a historical overview can be found, e.g., in Macnamara and Gregory (2018).

In addition to the above-mentioned models for evaluation, models for assessing the *maturity* of evaluations have also emerged (Gilkerson et al., 2019). They provide an analytical framework to capture the maturity of evaluations (e.g., basic, advanced, or mature) and, importantly, identify potential constraining and facilitating factors that influence whether and how evaluations are conducted, pointing to the critical role of a supportive organizational culture (Romenti et al., 2019). The idea of assessing the maturity level of evaluation has been translated by AMEC into a survey-based diagnostic tool for practice, the so-called Measurement Maturity Mapper (M3).[1]

Buhmann and Likely (2018) have made a recent attempt to combine and synthesize varying evaluation models and terminologies, suggesting an integrated model for evaluation. Buhmann and Volk (2022) have further extended this model and introduced the evaluation of the management level of communication, which provides an important foundation for the following considerations.

The basic idea of evaluation models can be applied to evaluating listening. However, since evaluation models were primarily developed for the purpose of evaluating messaging, other questions have to be asked, and other methods and metrics need to be used when evaluating an architecture of listening. A particular difference lies in the fact that the evaluation of messaging typically draws attention to the intended effects of an organization's messaging on predefined target groups and often neglects to examine unintended or unexpected effects on audiences not defined as stakeholders (Macnamara & Gregory, 2018; Volk & Buhmann, 2019). In listening, this logic is reversed, as – at least theoretically – *any* topic, keyword, or target group could (or could not) become relevant, which is why listening must remain open and combine both structured and unstructured and exploratory approaches (Stieglitz & Dang-Xuan, 2013).

Evaluation of organizational listening must hence constantly check that the predefined topics, platforms, keywords, audiences, etc., are comprehensive and up-to-date and that unstructured approaches are detecting relevant conversations in which the organization is neither mentioned nor tagged. As introduced earlier, evaluation must furthermore make a distinction between the (1) overarching listening structures and processes (function) and the (2) listening methods and tools (individual unit), which are embedded in the former. Of course, the individuals in charge of listening can also be evaluated with regard to their performance or capabilities. While the target audience of messaging are typically internal and external target groups or the general public, insights from listening are usually summarized in a (daily, weekly, monthly, or quarterly) report specifically prepared for organizational decision-makers (e.g., communication team leaders, project managers, top managers, and business partners).

In the following, each phase of the evaluation model is first described in the original form for the messaging function and then the corresponding translation is made analogously for the listening function.

a *Inputs* include the human and financial resources needed to produce communication activities in evaluation models for messaging. When evaluating listening, inputs include the resources (e.g., budget, time, and service providers) that are invested in establishing or maintaining listening structures and processes or in purchasing and using listening methods and tools, as well as building competencies of those responsible for listening through workshops or trainings.

b *Outputs* include the communication activities that are produced, published, and received by the target audience in evaluation models for messaging. They can be distinguished into primary outputs (number of social media posts, stakeholder dialogs, press releases, etc.) and secondary outputs (reach of social media platforms, number of participating stakeholders, media coverage, website visits, etc.). In the case of evaluating listening, primary outputs comprise the listening activities established within an organization, e.g., the set-up of formalized structures and processes for coordinating listening and the number and type of methods and tools for listening. Secondary outputs include the quality, flawlessness, or efficiency of internal workflows and structures (e.g., the number of correctly identified false information), the usage intensity of listening methods and tools, and employees' level of satisfaction with them. Moreover, organizations can track the number of identified risks, issues, conversations, or target groups monitored; measure the decrease in negative comments or customer complaints; or count the number of listening reports prepared for decision-makers (Macnamara, 2022).

c *Outcomes* include the short- and medium-term effects of communication activities on the target audience in evaluation models for messaging. They can be distinguished into direct outcomes (likes, shares, engagement, etc.) and indirect outcomes (knowledge gain, attitude change, behavioral intentions, etc.). Since the target audience of listening evaluations are typically leadership decision-makers, outcomes comprise their level of awareness, knowledge, or satisfaction of listening insights (Macnamara, 2022), their ascribed relevance to the listening function, their readiness for taking advice, or their actual behavioral consequences for strategy execution made on the basis of listening intelligence (e.g., escalating an issue to the top management, convening the crisis team).

d *Impacts* include the long-term value created through communication for the organization (e.g., public trust, positive organization-public relationships, favorable reputation, and strong brand) or society (e.g., participation, inclusion, diversity, equity, and social justice) in evaluation models for messaging. When evaluating listening, impacts comprise the value created through listening structures, processes, methods, and tools. This can be indirectly assessed, e.g., by the added value of innovations that were identified through systematic listening or by the costs avoided and damage prevented through timely identification of risks and corresponding prevention or adequate preparation for crises through risk and crisis communication plans.

Building on previous work (Buhmann & Likely, 2018; Buhmann & Volk, 2022), the above reflections and assumptions can be visualized in a framework for evaluating organizational listening that relates the basic management cycle to (a) the three types of formative, process, and summative evaluation; (b) the four stages of evaluation during implementation (inputs, outputs, outcomes, and impact); and (c) the two units of assessment (individual and function).

Methods for the Evaluation of Organizational Listening

The evaluation of listening requires an orientation toward established methods originating in the field of business and management, which are typically used for assessing the inputs and impacts stages (e.g., Zerfass & Volk, 2020).

For evaluating the *inputs* going into an architecture of listening, budget analyses can be used in order to examine what resources are invested into listening and make-or-buy analyses can help to make a decision to either outsource certain listening activities or build up in-house architectures. A typical metric is budget and staff cost adherence. Competency or performance analyses, in turn, can be employed to verify whether communication staff have adequate knowledge, skills, and capabilities for engaging in listening and perform well (e.g., Burnside-Lawry, 2012).

For evaluating the *outputs* of listening structures and processes, communication departments can use methods such as performance measurement, productivity, or process analysis. These methods usually start by mapping existing internal structures or processes and then analyzing them to identify value-adding processes as well as bottlenecks (e.g., weak points in feedback loops, duplicate workflows or overlapping coordination processes, and unclear responsibilities), with the aim of building more efficient and effective listening structures and processes and thereby increasing performance (e.g., Zerfass & Volk, 2019). Typical metrics include error rates, lead times, response times, or productivity. Moreover, traditional social science methods such as surveys, observations, or interviews can be used to assess the frequency of use and level of satisfaction of communication staff with the processes, methods or tools used for listening, or the quality of cross-sectional client relationships (e.g., with internal partners or external agencies).

For evaluating *outcomes* of listening, i.e., effects on internal decision-makers, focus group discussions, observations, or informal feedback methods can be employed to assess whether listening is institutionalized as a "strategic attitude" in the mindset of decision-makers, whether they understand the listening results, and to what extent they make decisions regarding strategy implementation or planning based on listening insights. Given that presenting results from listening in a meaningful and easy-to-grasp manner is key to making quick decisions, especially when dealing with large amounts of data or crisis situations, evaluation can also focus on the perceived usability and comprehensibility of listening reports, dashboards, or cockpits (Volk & Zerfass, 2020).

At the *impact* stage, cost-benefit analyses can be utilized to assess whether the value created or the costs saved through listening actually legitimize the investment into an architecture of listening. Communications departments can use approximations to estimate how much avoided crises have saved costs or how much identified trending topics or product innovations have contributed value to the organization. Finally, to evaluate the overall architecture of listening, methods such as benchmarking or audits can be used to assess the overall performance of listening in comparison to other organizations (e.g., competitors or forerunners) or at earlier points in time (e.g., before restructuring of listening structures).

Recommendations for Practice

Organizational listening has become indispensable in today's hybrid media ecosystem, where different stakeholders can constantly express – often divergent and sometimes irrational – expectations toward organizations (Ingenhoff et al., 2020). For communication departments, therefore, the question is not whether but how the listening function and its evaluation should be designed.

- The first reference point in the process of establishing an architecture of listening – and its evaluation – should be the organization's overall strategy and the respective communication strategy, from which a strategy for listening should be derived that answers: Which goals and objectives are we pursuing with listening and how does it add value to the organization and to our communication? An important concern will involve how to build up a listening function under constraints of budgetary, workforce, and competency limitations (Place, 2022), so organizations need to weigh the benefits and costs of outsourcing listening (partly/fully) to external service providers versus building up an in-house listening competency.
- In the second step, decisions must be made as to the focus of listening, which should be systematically deduced from the listening strategy. Here, a series of questions need to be answered: Who are we listening to (e.g., employees, customers, communities, corporate activists, and thought leaders)? Which conversations or topics are we listening to (e.g., keywords, topics, issues, hashtags, competitors, and trending topics)? On which online or offline platforms and media are we listening (e.g., Twitter, LinkedIn, Facebook, TikTok, Instagram, Sina Weibo, etc.; news sites, alternative media, forums, blogs, and offline arenas)?
- Depending on these decisions, the third step is to select and implement suitable listening tools and methods from the plethora of technology providers or to hire external consultants to help with the implementation and training of communication staff. One of the important prerequisites is that tools are compatible with an organization's systems, culture, and workflows and that employees have or will acquire the necessary competencies to use them (Volk & Zerfass, 2018). Communication departments should hence ask: Which tools and methods fit our needs and are the requirements for their utilization given (e.g., Talkwalker, Hootsuite, Brandwatch, surveys, automated sentiment analyses, and trend analyses)?
- In the fourth step, communication departments need to establish efficient listening processes and structures for collecting listening data, analyzing and interpreting listening data, making sense of and visualizing listening insights, and transforming them into listening intelligence. Here, a challenge is to develop workflows that enable decision-makers to quickly comprehend whether listening insights have strategic or rather operational relevance and what implications can be derived for strategy execution or formulation.
- The fifth step involves the development of a sophisticated evaluation approach for assessing the efficiency and effectiveness of the listening

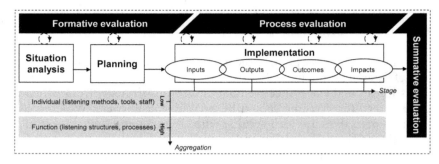

Figure 5.2 Framework for Evaluating Organizational Listening (based on Buhmann & Likely, 2018; Buhmann & Volk, 2022).

function as outlined in Figure 5.2. Communications departments should ask themselves at least once a year whether the listening function is achieving its goals and adding value to the organization and where adjustments to the listening strategy are necessary. In view of the rapid changes in the digital media landscape, it is necessary to check at short intervals whether the predefined platforms and media channels are still up-to-date.

Given the opportunities arising from technological innovations and the societal values of listening, the implementation of organizational listening as well as its evaluation brings many benefits. However, it also faces several challenges in the digital age (Volk & Buhmann, 2023). A fundamental problem already exists in the fact that, in practice, there are manifold barriers to conducting listening and evaluation as such, even for relatively simple ones such as media content analyses. For example, known barriers of evaluation and listening include (Austin et al., 2000; Macnamara, 2015; Nothhaft & Stensson, 2019; Zerfass et al. 2017): too little time or budget, lack of methodological competencies of the communicators, lack of standardized models and metrics, lack of client or management support or interest, or a strategic disinterest in (self-)evaluation. These barriers are now exacerbated by the fact that listening and its evaluation are undergoing a shift from a largely summative, retrospective approach to a real-time approach that makes use of large amounts of mostly unstructured data. The sheer volume and complexity of listening data available pose new challenges for the collection, storage, analysis, interpretation, and visualization of the data and come with increased costs for data processing and security.

At the methodological level, listening must inevitably rely on advances in artificial intelligence, machine learning, and natural language processing to collect and analyze listening data (Ardila, 2020). Since these methods are constantly evolving, it may be difficult for practitioners to track innovations. For example, automated text or sentiment analyses, e.g., based on dictionary or (un)supervised methods (e.g., Van der Meer, 2016), are still prone to errors (e.g., misinterpretation of sarcasm and irony), so the results must be manually validated and always be critically questioned as part of the evaluation.

At the organizational level, one of the greatest internal challenges is to establish a culture of listening and evaluation in organizations and to train and incentivize all employees' listening capabilities – not only those of communicators – accordingly (Ingenhoff et al., 2020).

Furthermore, at the societal level, the collection and utilization of listening data for strategic purposes such as microtargeting also raise important ethical, security, and legal issues for which organizations must be held accountable (White & Boatwright, 2020; Wiencierz & Röttger, 2017). Given the serious concern about dataveillance (Van Dijck, 2014) and surveillance capitalism (Zuboff, 2015), there is a pressing question about an ethical, morally responsible, and accountable approach to listening and evaluation (Volk & Buhmann, 2023). Such an approach must, at a minimum, preserve individuals' data protection and privacy (Gregory & Halff, 2020), be transparent about data collection and use, and avoid listening-based communication practices that contribute to further political polarization or fragmentation of society.

However, recent survey data indicates that communication practitioners around the world appear to find the exploitation of audiences' personal data only moderately problematic from an ethical perspective (Hagelstein et al., 2023). On a professional level, this raises the question of how ethical awareness can be heightened in practice and how practitioners can be trained in digital ethics (Bourne & Edwards, 2021).

Conclusion

While listening is considered an elementary part of evaluation, the evaluation of organizational listening has not yet been systematically researched, just as there is little empirical evidence about organizational listening itself. While studies based on in-depth interviews, document analyses, and field research offer valuable insights into how listening is practiced in organizations (e.g., Macnamara, 2016, 2019, 2022; Place, 2022), large-scale quantitative research would be valuable that compares listening practices and their evaluation both across countries and organizations (e.g., nonprofits, governmental organizations, public authorities, and agencies) and thereby identified generalizable patterns. Particular attention should be paid to critical research that sheds light on the driving motivations and uses of listening data in organizations. It would be interesting to explore whether listening – contrary to normative claims – is predominantly used for instrumental and persuasive goals or even as a legitimacy façade, i.e., without actually incorporating stakeholder perspectives into organizational decision-making processes (Ingenhoff et al., 2020; Macnamara, 2016). Given that contemporary evaluation practices in strategic communication are often based on easily measurable outputs such as clippings in the media or reach on social media channels (Zerfass et al., 2017), it is hardly plausible to assume that listening is evaluated as systematically in organizations as described here. This, however, does not change the meaningfulness of the question of whether listening is used efficiently and purposefully – and ethically. Future research should hence examine the barriers of evaluating organizational listening and the perceived benefits, as well as possible "pathologies" and ethical misconduct, such as whitewashing or misrepresentation of listening data (cf. Place, 2015; Volk & Buhmann, 2019).

Note

1 https://m3.amecorg.com

References

Ali, M. (2022). Fake-news network model: A conceptual framework for strategic communication to deal with fake news. *International Journal of Strategic Communication*, *16*(1), 1–17.

AMEC (2016). *AMEC Integrated Evaluation Framework*. Online: https://amecorg.com/amecframework/de/framework/interactive-framework/

Ardila, M. M. (2020). *The rise of intelligent machines: How artificial intelligence is transforming the public relations industry* [Doctoral dissertation, University of Southern California].

Austin, E. W., Pinkleton, B. E., & Dixon, A. (2000). Barriers to public relations program research. *Journal of Public Relations Research*, *12*(3), 235–253.

Borner, M., & Zerfass, A. (2018). The power of listening in corporate communications: Theoretical foundations of corporate listening as a strategic mode of communication. In S. Bowman, A. Crookes, Ø Ihlen, & S. Romenti (Eds.), *Public relations and the power of creativity: Strategic opportunities, innovation and critical challenges* (pp. 3–22). Emerald.

Botan, C. H. (2018). *Strategic communication theory and practice: The cocreational model*. Wiley-Blackwell.

Bourne, C., & Edwards, L. (2021). Critical reflections on the field. In C. Valentini (Ed.), *Public relations* (pp. 601–614). De Gruyter Mouton. https://doi.org/10.1515/9783110554250-031

Brinker, S. (2022). Marketing Technology Landscape 2022. https://chiefmartec.com/2022/05/marketing-technology-landscape-2022-search-9932-solutions-on-martechmap-com/

Broom, G. M., & Sha, B. L. (2013). *Cutlip and center's effective public relations* (11th ed.). Prentice Hall.

Brunner, B. R. (2008). Listening, communication & trust: Practitioners' perspectives of business/organizational relationships. *The International Journal of Listening*, *22*(1), 73–82. 10.1080/10904010701808482

Buhmann, A., & Likely, F. (2018). Evaluation and measurement in strategic communication. In R. L. Heath & W. Johansen (Eds.), *The international encyclopedia of strategic communication* (vol. 1, pp. 625–640). Wiley-Blackwell.

Buhmann, A., Macnamara, J., & Zerfass, A. (2019). Reviewing the "march to standards" in public relations: A comparative analysis of four seminal measurement and evaluation initiatives. *Public Relations Review, 45*(4), 101825.

Buhmann, A., & Volk, S. C. (2022). Measurement and evaluation: Framework, methods, and critique. In J. Falkheimer & M. Heide (Eds.), *Handbook of strategic communication*. Edward Elgar Publishing.

Burnside-Lawry, J. (2012). Listening and participatory communication: A model to assess organization listening competency. *International Journal of Listening, 26*(2), 102–121. 10.1080/10904018.2012.678092

Clark, H., & Taplin, D. (2012). *Theory of change basics: A primer on theory of change*. ActKnowledge.

Cutlip, S. M., Center, A. H., & Broom, G. M. (1985). *Effective public relations*. Prentice Hall.

Deutsche Public Relations Gesellschaft/International Controller Association. (2011). *Position paper communication controlling*. DPRG/ICV.

Fitzpatrick, K. R., & Weissman, P. L. (2021). Public relations in the age of data: Corporate perspectives on social media analytics (SMA). *Journal of Communication Management, 25*(4), 401–416.

Frechtling, J. A. (2015). *Logic modeling methods in program evaluation*. Wiley.

Funnell, S., & Rogers, P. (2011). *Purposeful program theory: Effective use of theory of change and logic models*. Jossey-Bass.

Gilkerson, N. D., Swenson, R., & Likely, F. (2019). Maturity as a way forward for improving organizations' communication evaluation and measurement practices: A definition and concept explication. *Journal of Communication Management, 23*(3), 246–264.

Government Communication Service. (2021). Evaluation Framework 2.0. https://gcs.civilservice.gov.uk/guidance/evaluation/tools-and-resources

Gregory, A., & Halff, G. (2020). The damage done by big data-driven public relations. *Public Relations Review, 46*(2), 101902.

Hagelstein, J., Volk, S. C., Zerfass, A., Athaydes, A., Macnamara, J., Meng, J., & Hung-Baesecke, F. (Under Review). Ethical challenges of digital communication: A comparative study of public relations practitioners in 52 countries. Manuscript under review.

Ingenhoff, D. (2018). Monitoring. In R. L. Heath & W. Johansen (eds.), *The international encyclopedia of strategic communication* (Vol. 2, pp. 962–968). Wiley Blackwell.

Ingenhoff, D., Borner, M., & Zerfaß, A. (2020). Corporate listening und issues management in der Unternehmenskommunikation. In A. Zerfaß, M. Piwinger, & U. Röttger (eds.), *Handbuch Unternehmenskommunikation*. Springer Gabler. https://doi.org/10.1007/978-3-658-03894-6_26-1

Kellogg Foundation. (2004). *Logic model development guide* [online]. (Original work published 1998). https://www.naccho.org/uploads/downloadable-resources/Programs/Public-Health-Infrastructure/KelloggLogicModelGuide_161122_162808.pdf

Lindenmann, W. (1997). *Guidelines for measuring the effectiveness of PR programs and activities*. Retrieved May 1, 2022, from www.instituteforpr.org/wp-content/uploads/2002_MeasuringPrograms.pdf

Macnamara, J. (2015). Breaking the measurement and evaluation deadlock: A new approach and model. *Journal of Communication Management, 19*(4), 371–387.

Macnamara, J. (2016). *Organizational listening: The missing essential in public communication*. Peter Lang.

Macnamara, J. (2018). *Evaluating public communication: Exploring new models, standards, and best practice*. Routledge.

Macnamara, J. (2019). Explicating listening in organization-public communication: Theory, practices, technologies. *International Journal of Communication, 13*, 5183–5204. https://ijoc.org/index.php/ijoc/article/view/11996/2839

Macnamara, J. (2020). *Beyond post-communication: Challenging disinformation, deception, and manipulation*. Peter Lang.

Macnamara, J. (2022). *Organizational listening in public communication: Emerging theory and practice*. University of Technology Sydney.

Macnamara, J., & Gregory, A. (2018). Expanding evaluation to progress strategic communication: Beyond message tracking to open listening. *International Journal of Strategic Communication, 12*(4), 469–486.

Navarro, C., Moreno, A., & Al-Sumait, F. (2017). Social media expectations between public relations professionals and their stakeholders: Results of the ComGap study in Spain. *Public Relations Review, 43*(4), 700–708.

Nothhaft, H., & Stensson, H. (2019). Explaining the measurement and evaluation stasis: A thought experiment and a note on functional stupidity. *Journal of Communication Management, 23*(3), 213–227.

Place, K. R. (2015). Exploring the role of ethics in public relations program evaluation. *Journal of Public Relations Research, 27*, 118–135.

Place, K. R. (2022). Toward a framework for listening with consideration for intersectionality: Insights from public relations professionals in borderland spaces. *Journal of Public Relations Research, 34*(1–2), 4–19. 10.1080/1062726X.2022.2057502

Romenti, S., Murtarelli, G., Miglietta, A., & Gregory, A. (2019). Investigating the role of contextual factors in effectively executing communication evaluation and measurement: A scoping review. *Journal of Communication Management, 23*(3), 228–245.

Rossi, P., Lipsey, M., & Freeman, H. (2004). *Evaluation: A systematic approach* (7th ed.). Sage.

Smith, R. D. (2017). *Strategic planning for public relations* (5th ed.). Routledge.

Stacks, D. (2017). *Primer of public relations research* (3rd ed.). The Guildford Press.

Stieglitz, S., & Dang-Xuan, L. (2013). Emotions and information diffusion in social media—Sentiment of microblogs and sharing behavior. *Journal of Management Information Systems, 29*, 217–248.

Van der Meer, T. G. L. A. (2016). Automated content analysis and crisis communication research. *Public Relations Review, 42*(5), 952–961.

Van Dijck, J. (2014). Datafication, dataism and dataveillance: Big data between scientific paradigm and ideology. *Surveillance & Society, 12*(2), 197–208.

Van Ruler, B., & Körver, F. (2019). *The communication strategy handbook: Toolkit for creating a winning strategy*. Peter Lang.

Volk, S. C. (2016). A systematic review of 40 years of public relations evaluation and measurement research: Looking into the past, the present, and future. *Public Relations Review, 42*(5), 962–977.

Volk, S. C., & Buhmann, A. (2019). New avenues in communication evaluation and measurement (E&M). Towards a research agenda for the 2020s. *Journal of Communication Management*, *23*(3), 162–178.

Volk, S. C., & Buhmann, A. (2023). Evaluation and measurement in the digital age: Challenges and opportunities for corporate communication. In V. Luoma-aho & M. Badham (Eds.), *Handbook of digital corporate communication*. Edward Elgar Publishing.

Volk, S. C., & Zerfass, A. (2018). Alignment: Revisiting a key concept in strategic communication. *International Journal of Strategic Communication*, *12*(4), 433–451.

Volk, S. C., & Zerfass, A. (2020). Management tools in corporate communications: A survey among practitioners and reflections about the relevance of academic knowledge for practice. *Journal of Communication Management*, *25*(1), 50–67.

Volk, S. C., & Zerfass, A. (2021). Management tools in corporate communication: a survey about tool use and reflections about the gap between theory and practice. *Journal of Communication Management*, *25*(1), 50–67. https://doi.org/10.1108/JCOM-02-2020-0011

Watson, T., & Noble, P. (2014). *Evaluating public relations* (3rd ed.). Kogan Page.

Weiner, M., DiStaso, M., Draper-Watts, P., Ehrhart, C., Fitzsimmons, A., Gilfeather, J., Hamid, M., Jekielek, R., Likely, F., Macnamara, J., McCorkindale, T., Mirkin, C., Monteiro, C., & Stacks, D. (2021). *The Communicator's Guide to Research, Analysis, and Evaluation*. Institute for Public Relations. Retrieved March 14, 2021, from https://instituteforpr.org/communicators-guide-research-2021/

White, C., & Boatwright, B. (2020). Social media ethics in the data economy: Issues of social responsibility for using Facebook for public relations. *Public Relations Review*, *46*(5). https://doi.org/10.1016/j.pubrev.2020.101980

Wiencierz, C., & Röttger, U. (2017). The use of big data in corporate communication. *Corporate Communications: An International Journal*, *22*(3), 258–272. https://doi.org/10.1108/CCIJ-02-2016-0015

Zerfass, A., Verčič, D., Nothhaft, H., & Werder, K. P. (2018). Strategic communication: Defining the field and its contribution to research and practice. *International Journal of Strategic Communication*, *12*(4), 487–505.

Zerfass, A., Verčič, D., Verhoeven, P., Moreno, A., & Tench, R. (2015). *European Communication Monitor 2015: Creating communication value through listening, messaging and measurement. Results of a survey in 41 countries*. EACD/EUPRERA, Helios Media.

Zerfass, A., Verčič, D., & Volk, S. C. (2017). Communication evaluation and measurement: Skills, practices and utilization in European organizations. *Corporate Communications: An International Journal*, *22*(1), 2–18.

Zerfass, A., & Viertmann, C. (2017). Creating business value through corporate communication: A theory-based framework and its practical application. *Journal of Communication Management*, *21*(1), 86–91.

Zerfass, A., & Volk, S. C. (2018). How communication departments contribute to corporate success: The communications contributions framework. *Journal of Communication Management*, *22*(4), 397–415.

Zerfass, A., & Volk, S. C. (2019). *Toolbox communication management. Thinking tools and methods for managing corporate communications*. Springer Gabler.

Zerfass, A., & Volk, S. C. (2020). Aligning and linking communication with organizational goals. In V. Luoma-aho and M.-J. Canel (Eds.), *The handbook of public sector communication* (pp. 417–434). Wiley.

Zhang, B., & Vos, M. (2014). Social media monitoring: Aims, methods, and challenges for international companies. *Corporate Communications: An International Journal, 19*(4), 371–383. https://doi.org/10.1108/CCIJ-07-2013-0044

Zuboff, S. (2015). Big other: Surveillance capitalism and the prospects of an information civilization. *Journal of Information Technology, 30*, 75–89.

Unit 2
Organizational Listening for Ethics and Justice

6 The State of Ethical Listening to External Stakeholders in US Organizations

Marlene S. Neill and Shannon A. Bowen

Introduction

Scholars have identified a "crisis of listening" in companies and organizations today with "an average speaking to listening ratio of 80:20" (Macnamara, 2016a, pp. 133,140). Similarly, recent studies have found that communication professionals "value listening, but do not always make it the priority that it merits" (Neill & Bowen, 2021, p. 276). As listening receives more attention in communication scholarship, researchers have stressed that organizational listening should be not only ethical but also strategic. As Lewis (2020) pointed out, collecting information does not result in strategic listening as "mere possession of information, no matter its relevance, quality, or uniqueness, cannot be strategically used until it is summarized, interpreted, and put into some context of decision making" (p. 79). Strategic listening also requires time for reflection and a response to the insights that have been gleaned (Lewis, 2020). This research reports findings along those themes and makes recommendations for practical improvement of listening efforts.

Ward and Wasserman (2015) pointed out that "the ethics of listening is not a polite conversation that papers over cracks and differences in an attempt to reach an easy but superficial consensus" (p. 838). They added that ethical listening involves respect for others and "to dialogue with another human being is more than to show toleration for the other person's right to express their views, no matter whether we think their views are incorrect or offensive" (Ward & Wasserman, 2015, p. 845).

The Theoretical Bases of Listening

Listening is comprised of many factors and is more complex than it may appear initially. Inspired by diverse literature focused on organizational listening, Macnamara (2016b) identified some ideal features associated with ethical listening such as offering recognition and respect to others, acknowledging their views in a timely fashion, paying attention, interpreting their feedback fairly, understanding their perspectives, giving consideration to their recommendations, and responding in an authentic manner.

Organizational listening also needs to be strategic in order to accomplish business objectives. Strategic listening requires "a set of methodologies and structures designed and utilized to ensure that an organization's attention is directed toward vital information and input to enable learning, questioning of key assumptions, interrogating decisions, and ensuring self-critical analysis" (Lewis, 2020, p. xvi). This definition is based on the assumption that members of senior leadership are genuine in their desire to learn and gather intelligence from listening, which can lead to increased trust and better relationships with key stakeholders. The goals of strategic listening "are to surface previous unknowns, question the taken-for-granteds, and challenge the long-held norms and preferences of powerful leaders and units to ensure quality decisions are made" (Lewis, 2020, p. 6).

Despite these ideals, Bieber (2018), the CEO of CDC Software, argued that businesses are falling short when it comes to acting on feedback from the voice of the consumer (VOC). VOC is considered a credible source for insights related to consumers' feedback on products and services, which is collected through various channels such as market research, customer satisfaction surveys, call centers, websites, and social media (Macnamara, 2020). Newer technologies can assist with data analysis to enable large-scale listening efforts such as computer-aided textual analysis and voice to text (VTT) software programs (Macnamara, 2020).

However, Bieber (2018) cited research by Gartner, a consulting firm, showing that "Only 29 percent of firms with VoC in place systematically incorporate insights about customer needs into their decision-making processes. And nearly three-fourths don't think that their VoC programs are effective at driving actions" (para. 3). More recently, some companies and organizations were criticized for trying to monetize Juneteenth, a holiday that commemorates the end of slavery in the United States, with products such as watermelon salad and a special flavor of ice cream (Ellis, 2022). If the companies had conducted research with African American consumers prior to making these decisions, they could have avoided the backlash.

The purpose of this study was to examine the channels and extent to which US organizations are listening to external stakeholders, such as customers, the media, government officials, and marginalized publics. The mixed method study involved 30 in-depth interviews with communication management professionals followed by an online survey with 300 US employees.

Defining Listening

Listening is comprised of at least three dimensions: cognitive, behavioral, and affective (Lipetz et al., 2020). The cognitive dimension involves activities such as understanding, receiving, and interpreting the message; the behavioral dimension refers to verbal and nonverbal responses including posing questions to clarify information and maintaining eye contact; and the affective dimension describes emotions such as empathy and respect (Lipetz et al., 2020).

Macnamara (2016b) identified 30 types of listening in the literature that included both positive and negative dimensions. For the purpose of this study, we focused on four types of listening: discriminative, comprehensive, critical, and appreciative (Barker, 1971; Wolvin & Coakley, 1996). First of all, discriminative listening allows leaders to differentiate the types of incoming stimuli, auditory but also visual, which enables them to understand, react to, and interact with the environment (Wolvin & Coakley, 1996). Comprehensive listening involves seeking to understand the message which is being conveyed (Wolvin & Coakley, 1996) and is beneficial when the message recipient interprets the meaning as closely as possible to the information which the sender intended to convey. Critical listening is focused on comprehension and evaluation of the message (Wolvin & Coakley, 1996) and focuses on the entire message – auditory, visual, and nonverbal cues, as well as attempts at persuasion, and includes the responsibility of one's personal response to the information that was conveyed. Finally, appreciative listening is undertaken to obtain stimulation or enjoyment (Wolvin & Coakley, 1996) and may often constitute the more creative side of public relations.

Listening and Systems Theory

Systems theory is based on the foundation of interdependency between an organization and its environment (Luhmann, 1984). Listening plays an essential and formative role in systems theory, often conceptualized as "Input" – a general term for incoming messages driven by formal and informal data collection from external publics. In systems theory, listening includes surveys and VoC research, as well as listening in community meetings, customer complaints, and informal means of data collection. In Luhmann's (1984) systems theory, these forms of input are used in strategy, transmuting it throughout. Throughput eventually enters the external environment through communication – called output – official public relations activities, most commonly. This output reaches external stakeholders who respond via input, creating an ongoing chain of dialogue.

Broom and Sha (2013) wrote that a systems perspective applies to public relations because the profession "deals with the mutually dependent relationships established and maintained between organizations and their publics" (p. 151). They added that "some organizations actively monitor their social environments and make adjustments based on what is learned" (Broom & Sha, 2013, p. 154). This process, often referred to as environmental scanning, involves listening by monitoring traditional and social media (Wilcox et al., 2015). Listening is essential to fulfill public relations' roles in the areas of issues management and ethics counseling (Lee et al., 2006), with the purpose of preventing crises by minimizing surprises and "serving as an early warning system for potential ... threats" (Wartick & Rude, 1986).

Issues Management: Theory and Strategy for External Listening

As mentioned above, issues management is the process for strategic organizational listening, highly based in systems theory but applying strategic management and public policy, as well (Heath & Nelson, 1986). The issues management process includes these steps: (1) identify public issues and trends, (2) evaluate impact, (3) conduct research and prioritize, (4) create strategy, (5) implement, and (6) evaluate (adapted from Buchholz et al., 1994). Bowen et al. (2019) adapted the issues management process to include a significant step of ethical analyses, including listening respectfully to the needs of the public and stakeholders.

Listening is crucial in issues management because it helps organizations to identify problems early before they become crises or lawsuits, and when they can be managed proactively and autonomously (Bowen, 2002). This type of external listening is also referred to as "Environmental scanning" in the issues management literature (Stoffels, 1994).

In modern relationship management, the demands on organizations for trust, accountability, and authenticity only heighten the importance of their issues management efforts. Ethical responsibility entails not only listening but listening with empathy and taking actions on the feedback to an organization from publics of all kinds, especially the government. The issues management function overlaps heavily with government and public affairs due to its incorporation of organizational policy alongside these efforts. Lerbinger (2006) explained that organizations must act quickly in issues management because "Should legislators become interested in an issue, it can escalate quickly to legislative action or a crisis" (p. 21). The importance of not listening to only customers but to all external stakeholder groups, and the government or public policy arena, will become apparent as we discuss the findings of our research later in this chapter.

Channels for External Listening

Macnamara (2016c) identified a number of organizational functions that are the most active sites for organizational listening, which included customer relations, research or insights departments, social media teams, government communication, marketing communication, corporate communication, and public relations. Companies, government agencies, and nonprofit organizations have a range of options to listen to external stakeholders. Some of the conventional approaches to receive feedback from external stakeholders include surveys and polls, focus groups, social media and media monitoring, town hall meetings, advisory boards, and analysis of calls to customer service representatives (Macnamara, 2018, 2019). One of the obstacles associated with analyzing this mixed data is that much of it is unstructured or "raw and unorganized," such as emails and social media posts (Weiner & Kochhar, 2016, p. 11), which can result in information overload (Lewis, 2020). Fortunately, new technology tools are being developed to assist with data collection, reduction, and analysis (Lewis, 2020; Macnamara, 2018).

In Macnamara's (2016c) study, even though he found evidence of listening occurring in areas such as customer relations and social media monitoring, he pointed out that listening was "mostly undertaken for instrumental organization-centric purposes" such as solving problems and serving the interest of the organization (p. 236). More specifically, he emphasized that customer relations were focused on resolving complaints rather than making substantial changes, while social media monitoring was focused on measuring the volume of the organization's own voice and gaining insights to promote their brands and services (Macnamara, 2016c). These practices are consistent with pseudolistening (Adler & Rodman, 2011) or offering faux voice (Lewis, 2020), which describes situations when stakeholders are allowed to vent and openly share their concerns, but it has no significant influence on decision-making, operations, or policy. When solicitation of stakeholder feedback is undertaken to merely "check a box," it will rarely result in new learning and perspectives or challenge leader assumptions (Lewis, 2020).

This review of the literature suggests several issues related to organizational listening that merit more attention. After narrowing down themes related to ethics, strategy, stakeholders, and issues management, our specific questions include:

RQ1: What primary methods are organizations using to listen to external stakeholders?
RQ2: How do US employees perceive the effectiveness of their organization's external listening efforts?
RQ3: What are some specific examples of effective ethical listening?
RQ4: What kinds of technology tools and analysis processes are organizations using to gain insights from ethical listening, particularly from large data sets such as social media listening and customer service calls?

Method

The study incorporated a mixed method design in two phases. To answer the research questions, we first conducted 30 interviews with communication management professionals working in the United States. The sample included 22 women and 8 men with an average 22 years of experience in public relations and communication. The participants represented employers in 13 states and the District of Columbia including Arkansas, California, Delaware, Massachusetts, New Hampshire, New York, North Dakota, Ohio, Oklahoma, Pennsylvania, Texas, Virginia, and Washington. The participants were recruited using purposive and snowball sampling (Wimmer & Dominick, 2006). The researchers recruited communication management or internal communication professionals from their personal network who were members of the Public Relations Society of America (PRSA) and the Arthur W. Page Society. After interviewing these initial professionals, the researchers asked them for referrals of other colleagues who work in the same profession. Due to the geographical distance between participants and physical distancing required by the global pandemic, interviews were conducted by phone between February and August 2020.

A primary interviewer was used for consistency across participants. The same interview protocol was used for all participants. The study followed IRB guidelines and approvals. All participants were provided consent forms detailing actions to preserve confidentiality. The interviews were audio-recorded and transcribed for analysis resulting in 320 pages of typed, single-spaced text and representing 22 hours of interviews averaging 44 minutes per interview.

For the second phase, a national online survey was conducted using a sample obtained by Qualtrics and its online survey platform to recruit participants for the study. We required study participants to be US employees with full-time employment. We also pre-specified two key demographic parameters, leadership position and gender, as part of our sampling strategy. The survey data were collected in July 2020 and after that data were cleaned; the survey sample consisted of 300 valid respondents (Table 6.1). Prior to beginning the study, the proposal was

Table 6.1 Survey sample characteristics

Rank of participants	60% nonmanagers
	40% managers, including:
	14.3% ($n = 43$) top/executive level
	18.3% ($n = 55$) mid-level management
	7.3% ($n = 22$) lower-level management
Gender	49.7% men
	50% women
	1 participant "other"
Age range	18–73, avg. 40
Length of employment	43.7% ($n = 131$) less than 5 years
	39.7% ($n = 119$) from 6 to 15 years16.7% ($n = 50$) 16 years or longer

reviewed by the IRB at the first author's institution and was determined to be exempt.

Measures

To assess organizational listening methods, a checklist was developed based on prior research on listening. Employees were then asked to assess the effectiveness of various external listening channels on seven-dimensional effectiveness questions using a Likert scale with 1 representing very ineffective to 5 very effective ($\alpha = .854$). To assess their organization's activities related to listening, gathering, and applying information, we used a scale with eight items created by Lewis (2020) also with a Likert measurement with 1 representing very ineffective to 5 very effective ($\alpha = .931$). To assess the use of various types of listening, we used a scale with four items created by Wolvin and Coakley (1996) with 1 representing never and 5 always ($\alpha = .931$).

Data Analysis

The data were analyzed using standard approaches for qualitative data analysis (Miles & Huberman, 1994), which involves three steps: data reduction, data display, conclusions, and verification. One investigator coded each interview individually under broad categories based on the conceptual framework and key variables under study such as methods of listening externally, specific examples of listening, and technology tools. Composite code sheets were then created electronically using QDA Miner software, which reflected all respondents' comments related to each category. To confirm reliability of the categories, a random sample of 20% of the transcripts was independently coded by a graduate assistant using a code book and QDA Miner software, which calculated inter-rater reliability as 96.3% agreement. After data reduction, each category was then qualitatively analyzed by both researchers, who wrote memos and analyzed the data further to identify additional insights, which were discussed and agreed upon prior to writing the findings. The data analysis also involved negative or discrepant case analysis to identify any examples that disconfirmed or challenged the emerging findings (Merriam, 2002).

Findings

Primary Channels for Listening (RQ 1)

The first research question examined the primary methods that organizations are using to listen to external stakeholders. Based on the online survey results, the most common forms of external listening were online forms (n = 132), calls to customer service (n = 124), online or telephone surveys (n = 108), social media listening (n = 99) and focus groups (n = 81).

In the interview phase of the study, the communication managers had a slightly different perspective. The most common forms of listening they described using were online surveys and polls (n = 11), followed by social media listening (n = 10), calls to customer service (n = 7), and monitoring news media coverage (n = 7).

A smaller number mentioned pulse (short and frequent surveys) on their customer service websites, letters of complaint, or the use of external customer service platforms, such as CSX, for new insights on customers. It was interesting to note that customers were the term of preference for participants when discussing external data collection, as they seemed to place far less emphasis on other types of external stakeholders, such as community or governmental publics, notably important groups from the issues management perspective. However, it is important to note that a communication and marketing manager working in the financial services industry did name legislators and government officials as the stakeholders that receive the most attention in her organization. On a related note, a communication manager working for a trade association named government affairs as the most influential internal stakeholder, which implies a high priority of organizational listening efforts are dedicated to government relations.

Employee Perceptions of Organizational Listening Effectiveness (RQ 2)

The second research question explored employees' perceptions regarding the effectiveness of their organization's listening efforts. When asked to evaluate the effectiveness of these listening efforts, US employees rated town halls the highest (M = 3.73), followed by media monitoring (M = 3.72) and focus groups (M = 3.69). They evaluated social media listening and calls to customer service equally (M = 3.64).

When evaluating the effectiveness of their external listening efforts (see Table 6.2), nonmanagers ranked media monitoring services the

Table 6.2 Ranking of external listening efforts by effectiveness

Form of listening	Manager ranking	Nonmanager ranking
Focus groups	1	4
Town hall meetings	2	2
Online/phone surveys	3	7
Media monitoring services	4	1
Online forms	5	6
Calls to customer service	6	5
Social media listening	7	3

Ethical Listening to External Stakeholders in US Organizations 111

highest (M = 3.69), followed by town hall meetings (M = 3.68), social media listening (M = 3.66) and focus groups (M = 3.61). In contrast, managers ranked focus groups (M = 3.82) as their most effective means of listening to external stakeholders, followed by town hall meetings (M = 3.80), online/phone surveys (M = 3.77), and media monitoring services (M = 3.76). When comparing the list of most common forms of listening to perceptions of effectiveness, it is important to note that while online forms and calls to customer service were the most common means for listening, neither managers nor nonmanagers perceived these as *effective* means for listening in their organizations.

However, a chief communications officer described his company's concerted efforts to specifically listen to customer service calls:

> I can give a practical example. We once a month, our team, and a number of teams that are like ours, so government relations, investor relations, we listen to customer calls, and we do it on a monthly basis. And we work with our customer service group, sort of the executive office portion of our customer service group, to listen to those sorts of calls. They're usually around different trends, and I think doing that once a month is good, but it would be even better if we were doing it once a week or even every day.

We also asked employees to evaluate the effectiveness of their organization's activities related to listening, gathering, and applying information. Both managers and nonmanagers rated their organizations highest for the use of technology for information needs (see Figure 6.1). Nonmanagers rated their employers lowest in the areas of collecting bad news (M = 2.97) and critiques, concerns, and dissent (M = 3.04). Managers' assessment was much more positive, particularly in the areas

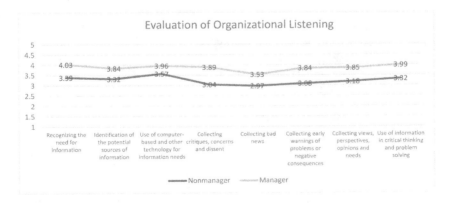

Figure 6.1 Employee evaluations of organizational listening by rank

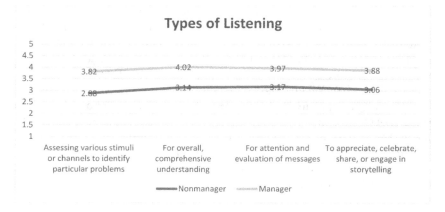

Figure 6.2 Employee evaluations of forms of listening

of recognizing a need for information (M = 4.03) and the use of information in critical thinking and problem-solving (M = 3.99).

Finally, we asked employees to evaluate various forms of listening based on the work of Wolvin and Coakley (1996). Nonmanagers rated their organizations unfavorably (M = 2.88; i.e., infrequently) on assessing channels to identify problems (i.e., discriminative listening) and in the range of neutral for the remaining items (see Figure 6.2). Managers rated their organization's highest (i.e., often) for comprehension and understanding (i.e., comprehensive listening) (M = 4.02) and similarly for attention and evaluation of messages (i.e., critical listening) (M = 3.97).

Specific Examples of Effective Organizational Listening (RQ 3)

The third research question identified specific examples of effective ethical listening. Participants were asked to think of a specific time when their organization engaged in ethical listening and describe that experience, beginning with what lead their organization to seek out the views of key stakeholders and how they went about gathering that information.

In the first example, a chief communications officer working in the financial services industry described how they identified issues with a website that was not user friendly:

> We were seeing people who were signing up for various payment programs through the federal government; it was very clunky. They would sort of have a conversation with one of our people, and then we would have to direct them to a website where they'd have to fill out the information, and then they'd have to actually sign it and send it in … we saw significant rates of people not ever following through and not getting on the payment program that they ultimately wanted.

He then described how they listened to customer concerns and ultimately resolved this issue:

> So, it took a great deal of work, but over the course of a couple of years, we were able to quickly get to a point where people didn't have to go to that website. We could send them the information, much of it was pre-populated, they could sign it electronically, and not have to put a physical signature on it. Again, at the core, it was filling a need for consumers, but at the same time, it was also eliminating a lot of steps and clunky process that we had that ultimately drove a higher operational cost. So that's where I think we operate best is when we see something like that that we can quickly act upon or somewhat quickly act upon. Everyone wins on those things.

In another example, a manager of measurement and analytics discussed how her organization conducts routine social media listening regarding social issues. As she explained:

> So, a lot of the social issues that our company has to respond to may not necessarily align with, or even impact our core business. And what I mean by that, a prime example is immigration. We were asked to weigh in on immigration, when there was a tweet I believe that got publicity because some of these children that were in immigration, their parents had been you know taken away ... They were traveling and so our industry was impacted by that. And so, what we had to do was we had to start listening for a social, you know, a topic that was very foreign to our company, because we really didn't get in on the immigration debate and it was very hot button topic. And so, we had to start listening for that and we provided insights to - we have a social topics committee. That's all they deal with everything from LGBT to immigration to racial tensions, I mean you name it.

These data are congruent with the issues management perspective of listening not only to individual stakeholders but monitoring social trends. This CCO then discussed the specific forms of listening that were used for this specific issue, immigration:

> So, I would say primarily through social media. We also do use news media when or if it's appropriate. So, when we need to go either get some background or secondary research to figure out what's been said in this situation. We also take a look at where's our company being mentioned, where are we not being mentioned, where should we be being mentioned?

We also asked participants to describe a specific time when their organization engaged in ethical listening connected to an ethical issue and describe that experience. A communication executive working in the energy industry talked about a neighboring business that was claiming some property damage. She described how they listened and responded to their concerns:

> We brought an individual from our lab out, tried to take a sample, so that we could understand. Certainly, we were looking at the times of when it was reported, looking at our operations, what had happened, and we got to this space - it was a bit of an impasse, it's like, well we don't know that it's us, I don't this it's us, certainly there's a thing here. They don't know who it is. And so, this escalated all the way up to our general manager ... We basically got to a spot where it was a bit of an impasse, what do we do?

She then discussed how her company responded to their neighboring business' concerns in an ethical manner:

> And our general manager said, "I don't know that we can say for 100 percent certainty that it's not us. And you know what we are the biggest player on the block here. We're just gonna make it right." And so, we paid. Let me tell you – talking to your lawyers about a settlement for something that you don't know if it's you or not was kind of an interesting conversation. And it was well below the threshold of a claim or something that would trigger an insurance claim. So, we just paid it outright. We drew up the paperwork and paid ... And it was a vote of confidence for me that our general manager said, you know what, we're just going to make it right and let's do it.

Another example discussed in the context of listening regarding an ethical issue involved allegations of discrimination involving a healthcare organization nearly a decade ago. A marketing communications director described the incident and eventual outcome:

> There was an investigation, so sort of a delving down into what happened and so that would involve interviews with employees and interviews with the people that had made the complaints, looking back to see if there were other similar concerns or complaints over a certain amount of time ... we really had to discipline some staff in order to adjust some policies to you know make sure ... that it was more inclusive and ... there was some education that needed to happen. So, other employees would know that this was not the way that certain people should be treated.

This participant added that the outcome of the listening and investigation that occurred resulted in changes in policies:

> The organization has gone on again under new administration to earn awards in certain areas that are related to the ethical treatment of people and human rights, so I do think that whatever was surfaced, you know, that long ago probably contributed to the fact that we have better policies and, you know, maybe better education and that certain behavior will not be tolerated.

In contrast, a chief communication officer of a financial service company described an example of a time that they did not seek consumer feedback before making a change to their online platform:

> And we made a system change that ultimately was going to result in an easier interface online, but it also took away some capabilities ... and on the new system, it was a little more clunky. And we went ahead, and we made the change, simply because we thought overall, the benefits were going to – it was a much smoother online platform. But at the same time, it was taking away one of the capabilities that a lot of people liked. That was a pretty vocal audience that responded very negatively to us and within about three months, we had to go back to the drawing board and figure out how to put this capability into that platform. It required a lot of rework, and ultimately it was more expensive than it probably would've been if we had built that in in the first place.

When asked how ethical listening likely would have made a difference in this situation, this CCO responded:

> I think we would have absolutely built in that capability. Because I think we would have realized how important it was to our customers and the users of the system. I think we chose not to simply because we – I don't know that there was an advocate in the room or a decision maker who was saying, "Hey, we should test this beforehand." I think they did a good job of looking at what were the tradeoffs, but I don't think the voice of the customer and the user was there, and I think it probably was more than anything else it was just not having an advocate for that voice in the room making the decision.

Technology Tools Utilized for Organizational Listening (RQ 4)

The final research question examined what types of technology tools and analysis processes organizations are using to gain insights from ethical listening, particularly large data sets from social media listening and customer service calls. Based on the personal interviews, organizations are engaging in social media listening and analyzing calls to customer service representatives. Some of the common technology tools they are using for external listening include survey platforms such as SurveyMonkey and Qualtrics, social media listening tools such as Sysomos, Spreadfast, Sprinklr, and Quid; media monitoring services such as Meltwater and Cision; and reputation management platforms such as Brandwatch.

When it comes to analyzing large data sets from social media and customer service calls, the communication managers discussed actually reading content line by line for insights and listening back to recorded calls on a monthly basis. As a manager of measurement and analytics expressed, a large amount of information coming from different platforms and channels is a barrier to effective listening:

> I think we listen, pretty well. I think one of the challenges we face is that with our company name being as broad as it is that sometimes we may miss some conversations. If somebody may be using an acronym, or somebody is not mentioning our whole company name, they're just mentioning part of it, because we've had to really narrow our focus on the tools that ... are keyword based. So, I do think that we face a challenge with just overall listening from an input perspective. I think that we also face a challenge with the volume, meaning we have thousands and thousands of mentions a day. And so sometimes that volume can be overwhelming.

It appeared, based on the interview responses, that communication managers are not taking advantage of newer technologies such as artificial intelligence (AI) when analyzing large volumes of data to gain insights.

Discussion

This study revealed that organizations are using a variety of communication channels to listen to external stakeholders. However, it was enlightening that both managers and nonmanagers perceived that some of the most frequently used channels were not effective means for listening, particularly online forms and calls to customer service. Nonmanagers also perceived that their organizations were not doing a good job of collecting critiques, concerns, dissent, and bad news, which are critical for effective issues management (Lee et al., 2006). Not surprisingly, managers were quite optimistic in their assessments of their organizations' listening efforts. Previous research conducted with US managers and their employees discovered that employees rated their supervisors as poor listeners while the supervisors rated own their listening behaviors more favorably (Lobdell et al., 1993).

Managers rated themselves most favorably in the areas of comprehensive and critical listening, while nonmanagers evaluated their organization's listening efforts unfavorably in the area of discriminative listening and neutral for other forms of listening. Based on the interview data, the types of listening we saw were primarily discriminative and comprehensive listening, and we recommend further emphasis on critical listening as a means of analysis and offering moral sensitivity to external stakeholders when appropriate.

This study provided examples of effective listening efforts as well as the consequences organizations faced when they did not listen to stakeholder concerns. A good example involved a financial services company that listened to customer concerns regarding an inefficient system for processing loan payments. While consumers were likely pleased their concerns were eventually addressed, they were probably frustrated that it took two years to identify a solution. In this example, government regulatory action was avoided, but the issues management perspective should have ranked this issue high enough for immediate response. There also were a couple of examples of listening related to marginalized publics. However, the social listening related to immigration issues was instrumentally focused or designed to help the organization achieve its own objectives (Macnamara, 2018). Another example involved a formal complaint filed with a regulatory agency that required listening to occur as part of an investigation into allegations of discrimination. Again, effective issues management would have ranked this issue high enough for priority resolution had listening happened faster. In contrast, it was admirable that an energy company listened to the concerns of a neighboring business and chose to pay for property damages despite concrete evidence that they were responsible.

Our research showed that relational damage can occur when organizations engage in pseudolistening (faux listening) or collecting data from stakeholders without implementing changes or authentic responses later. These decisions can result in costly damages in litigation and reputation. We recommend that critical listening analysis and earnest action should follow listening efforts and as a way to listen ethically and improve stakeholder relations.

Finally, we identified some technology tools that are being used for gathering and analyzing information as part of their listening efforts. Surprising, participants did not mention the use of newer AI technologies such as chatbots and tools for analyzing large volumes of social media data such as NVivo, Gephi, or NodeXL.

Recommendations for Practice

Based on our findings, we highlight the importance of ethical and effective issues management programs to listen strategically to external stakeholders. By using a systems theory understanding and environmental scanning, organizations can respond proactively and autonomously when they have not yet been forced to by government regulation. Vitally, a proactive and ethical response to issues as they arise will allow organizations to build trust with stakeholders.

Organizations should conduct a thorough audit of their listening channels to determine which ones they are using most frequently to listen to external stakeholders and include a more holistic systems theory approach to listening to multiple forms of audiences rather than only focusing on customers. Organizations should conduct survey research to determine which channels their external stakeholders prefer to use to share their concerns. Then they should do an assessment of their technology support as well as staff capabilities to analyze and interpret insights gained from listening and address any issues identified through new tools and training. Next, they should ensure the information is being shared with senior leaders and evaluate how often these insights are impacting organizational decision-making. Finally, in order to meet the standard of ethical listening, managers must examine if and how they are communicating with external stakeholders about how they are using their feedback to implement change as a means of closing the feedback loop. By doing so, they will be communicating to external stakeholders that their input matters, which will encourage future engagement.

Limitations and Recommendations for Future Research

While this study provided new insights regarding listening to external stakeholders, the data were collected during the beginning of the global pandemic, so it is unclear how those unique circumstances impacted our findings as organizations had to identify new ways of listening. The pandemic encouraged organizations to explore and adopt newer technologies, so perhaps a more recent study would discover wider adoption of technology tools for organizational listening, such as videoconference applications. Because our study was focused on the perspectives of communication managers and employees at all levels, future research could focus on senior leaders' perspectives or that of external stakeholders such as consumers or activist groups.

Conclusion

This study revealed that organizations need to place a higher priority on listening to external stakeholders as a routine part of their issues management activities and should assess the effectiveness of their listening efforts. Although it is tempting to focus only on customer relationships, we strongly urge organizations to think in terms of systems theory by revamping listening efforts to include all external stakeholders, as well as to include a public policy perspective as found in issues management. Issues management requires listening to identify issues before they become crises, and rapid action on newly identified issues can build trust and credibility with stakeholders. Not only is it an ethical responsibility, but there are significant financial and reputational consequences that occur when organizations are tone-deaf or not engaged in the type of proactive, organized, and ethical listening processes advised in this chapter.

References

Adler, R., & Rodman, G. (2011). *Understanding communication* (11th ed.). Oxford University Press.
Barker, L. L. (1971). *Listening behavior*. Prentice-Hall.
Bieber, M. (2018). Your customers are speaking: Are you listening? *CMSWire*. https://www.cmswire.com/customer-experience/your-customers-are-speaking-are-you-listening/
Bowen, S. A. (2002). Elite executives in issues management: The role of ethical paradigms in decision making. *Journal of Public Affairs*, *2*(4), 270–283. https://doi.org/10.1002/pa.119
Bowen, S. A., Rawlins, B. L., & Martin, T. M. (2019). *An overview of the public relations function* (2nd ed.). Business Expert Press.
Broom, G., & Sha, B. (2013). *Cutlip & center's effective public relations* (11th ed.). Pearson.
Buchholz, R. A., Evans, W. D., & Wagley, R. A. (1994). *Management responses to public issues: Concepts and cases in strategy formulation* (3rd ed.). Prentice Hall.
Ellis, N. T. (2022). "People were very offended": "Tone deaf" corporations facing backlash for Juneteenth themed products, *CNN*. https://www.cnn.com/2022/06/15/us/juneteenth-companies-tone-deaf/index.html
Heath, R. L., & Nelson, R. A. (1986). *Issues management: Corporate public policymaking in an information society*. Sage.
Lee, J., Heath, R., & Bowen, S. (2006). An International study of ethical roles and counsel in the public relations function. *Conference Papers – International Communication Association*, 1–37.
Lerbinger, O. (2006). *Corporate public affairs: Interacting with interest groups, media, and government*. Lawrence Erlbaum Associates.
Lewis, L. (2020). *The power of strategic listening*. Rowman & Littlefield.
Lipetz, L., Kluger, A. N., & Bodie, G. D. (2020). Listening is listening is listening: Employees' perception of listening as a holistic phenomenon. *International Journal of Listening*, *34*, 71–96. https://doi.org/10.1080/10904018.2018.1497489
Lobdell, C. L., Sonoda, K. T., & Arnold, W. E. (1993). The influence of perceived supervisor listening behavior on employee commitment. *International Listening Association Journal*, *7*(1), 92–110. https://doi.org/10.1080/10904018.1993.10499116
Luhmann, N. (1984). *Social systems*. J. Bednarz & D. Baecker (Trans.). Stanford University Press.

Macnamara, J. (2016a). The work and "Architecture of Listening": Addressing gaps in organization-public communication. *International Journal of Strategic Communication, 10*(2), 133–148. https://doi.org/10.1080/1553118X.2016.1147043

Macnamara, J. (2016b). Organizational listening: Addressing a major gap in public relations theory and practice. *Journal of Public Relations Research, 28*(3–4), 146–169. https://doi.org/10.1080/1062726X.2016.1228064

Macnamara, J. (2016c). *Organizational listening: The missing essential in public communication.* Peter Lang.

Macnamara, J. (2018). Toward a theory and practice of organizational listening. *International Journal of Listening, 32*(1), 1–23. https://doi.org/10.1080/10904018.2017.1375076

Macnamara, J. (2019). Explicating listening in organization–public communication: Theory, practices, technologies. *International Journal of Communication, 13,* 5183–5204.

Macnamara, J. (2020). Corporate listening: Unlocking insights from VOC, VOE and VOS for mutual benefits. *Corporate Communications: An International Journal, 25*(3), 377–393. https://doi.org/10.1108/CCIJ-08-2019-0102

Merriam, S. B. (2002). *Qualitative research in practice: Examples for discussion and analysis.* Jossey-Bass.

Miles, M. B., & Huberman, A. M. (1994). *Qualitative data analysis.* Sage.

Neill, M. S., & Bowen, S. A. (2021). Ethical listening to employees during a pandemic: New approaches, barriers and lessons. *Journal of Communication Management, 25*(3), 276–297. https://doi.org/10.1108/JCOM-09-2020-0103

Stoffels, J. D. (1994). *Strategic issues management: A comprehensive guide to environmental scanning.* Pergamon.

Ward, S. J. A., & Wasserman, H. (2015). Open ethics: Toward a global media ethics of listening. *Journalism Studies, 16*(6), 834–849. https://doi.org/10.1080/1461670X.2014.950882

Wartick, S. L., & Rude, R. E. (1986). Issues management: Corporate fad or corporate function? *California Management Review, 29*(1), 124–140. https://doi.org/10.2307/41165231

Weiner, M., & Kochhar, S. (2016). *Irreversible: The public relations big data revolution, institute for public relations.* https://instituteforpr.org/wp-content/uploads/IPR_PR-Big-Data-Revolution_3-29.pdf

Wilcox, D. L., Cameron, G. T., & Reber, B. H. (2015). *Public relations strategies and tactics* (11th ed.). Pearson Education Inc.

Wimmer, R. D., & Dominick, J. R. (2006). *Mass media research: An introduction.* Wadsworth.

Wolvin, A., & Coakley, C. G. (1996). *Listening* (5th ed.). McGraw Hill.

7 Why Are Organizations Criticized for Not Listening? Findings from Practitioners and Stakeholders

Lisa Tam, Soojin Kim, and Helen Hutchings

Introduction

Organizational listening is widely acknowledged as an essential component of public relations practice. It facilitates the co-adaption of cognitive, affective, and behavioral processes in *both* organizations and the multiple stakeholder groups involved ("strategic-behavioral paradigm," Kim & Ni, 2010). This co-adaption ensures shared decision-making and mutually beneficial outcomes (Brunner, 2008). It also highlights the roles of public relations professionals as *boundary spanners* who facilitate the listening process to generate intersubjective meanings between organizations and stakeholders and as the *organization's conscience* who advocate for *both* organizations and their stakeholders (Bowen, 2008; Grunig, 2006). Ideally, through the listening process, organizations "negotiate, balance, and satisfy the demands and interests of various internal and external stakeholders" (Saffer et al., 2018, p. 122). This allows organizations to learn from and adapt to the environments in which they operate (Fieseler et al., 2015; Jacobs & Coghlan, 2005). Moreover, the process provides stakeholders with some power to advocate for and balance their own interests with those of the organization and other stakeholders (Fitzpatrick, 2006).

Despite this premise, organizations have been criticized for their emphasis on building "an architecture of speaking" (Macnamara, 2016, p. 162) that focuses on organizations' efforts of communicating their perspectives to stakeholders to influence how stakeholders interpret organizations' actions and decisions (Grunig, 2009b; Kim & Kim, 2016). The listening that organizations undertake is "mostly instrumental, undertaken to serve the organization's interest such as gaining insights into consumer psychology to sell more products and services" (Macnamara, 2016, p. 157). Moreover, stakeholders criticize organizations for "hearing but not listening" and engaging in listening as "a mere gesture of taking note of public comments" (Conrad et al., 2011, p. 771). Organizational listening practices have been criticized for seeking to manage stakeholders' expectations and for privileging well-organized groups over

DOI: 10.4324/9781003273851-10

marginalized groups (Meesters et al., 2021). The public relations practice also has a tendency to pursue consensus, making it difficult to achieve the disagreements and differences embraced in the organizational listening process (Ciszek, 2016).

Despite the *ideal* outcomes of organizational listening in empowering stakeholders in getting their voices heard and incorporated into decision-making, the listening process is bounded by challenges. Macnamara (2016) notes: "listening is easier said than done because of the challenges of scale and diversity of views among stakeholders and publics that can lead to a cacophony rather than a consensus" (p. 163). Not only do different stakeholders have different viewpoints (and thus, expectations for the listening process), but the organization itself may also be bounded by factors such as the resources (e.g., time and workforce) needed for listening and having to accommodate feedback that may or may not be feasible to implement.

To explore the perspectives from both stakeholders and practitioners on how they evaluate the process of organizational listening and the factors that affect such evaluations, this chapter reports the findings from a survey conducted with a nationally representative sample of Australian citizens ($n = 400$) and from interviews conducted with public relations practitioners in Australia ($n = 26$). The findings will shed light on the factors that affect both the process and the outcomes of listening.

Literature Review

Organizational Listening from the Perspectives of Stakeholders

The strategic management of public relations begins with the identification of *stakeholders,* which refer to individuals and groups whose behaviors will influence the organization and who will be influenced by the organization's decisions and actions (Grunig & Repper, 1992). Due to the constraint of limited resources, organizations are advised to prioritize their resources to managing relationships with *publics* who affect or are affected by organizational decisions and create issues by engaging in communicative behaviors in order to resolve the issues (Kim et al., 2008). In the process of working with publics, public relations managers carry out *relational activities* by facilitating two-way communication with publics, both before and after organizational decisions are made (Grunig, 2018). By giving publics a voice in organizational decisions, they help organizations establish mutually beneficial relationships with publics, meet organizational objectives, and develop a favorable reputation (Grunig, 2018; Kim & Kim, 2016; Kim & Ni, 2010). Organizational listening is an essential part of these relational activities.

Macnamara (2015) defines organizational listening as being "comprised of the culture, policies, structure, processes, resources, skills, technologies, and practices applied by an organization to give recognition, acknowledgement, attention, interpretation, understanding, consideration and response to its stakeholders and publics" (p. 52). He later added that the processes should enable decision makers to "actively access, acknowledge, understand, consider and appropriately respond to all those who wish to communicate with the organization or with whom the organization wishes to communicate interpersonally or through delegated, mediated means" (Macnamara, 2019, p. 5191). This conceptualization highlights the two-way, relational activities between an organization and its stakeholders that ultimately benefit all parties involved (Macnamara, 2019). This concept of listening is also aligned with Taylor and Kent's (2014) dialogic engagement principles that "enables organizations and stakeholders to interact, fostering understanding, good will, and a shared view of reality" (p. 391). By improving understanding among organization-stakeholder interactions via organizational listening, decisions should be made to benefit all parties involved. Organization-stakeholder interactions are necessary for stakeholder counsel/advice on issues that affect both organization and stakeholders (Taylor & Kent, 2014).

Even though the ideal goal of listening is to create a more balanced partnership between an organization and its stakeholders by empowering the latter, listening activities could be criticized for being a "tokenistic, tick-box activity" (Tam et al., 2021, p. 116). Stakeholders' negative experiences with organizations can cause perceptions of inauthentic listening. For example, organizations might have predetermined decisions prior to the listening process, limiting the types and scope of changes allowed after considering stakeholders' feedback (Sahay, 2021). In addition, organizations' "product-focused and speaking-centered" approach to listening has been criticized for ignoring stakeholders' relational needs (Place, 2022, p. 4). There are many instances when publics are engaged in communicative behaviors in an attempt to resolve an issue, but organizational behaviors do not reciprocate (Kim, 2012). On the other hand, individuals may also have close-mindedness and reject any information that contradicts their preexisting beliefs (Kim & Grunig, 2021). Therefore, it is inevitable that there is a discrepancy between what an organization seeks to achieve and what its stakeholders wish to advocate for their interests (often arising from their different motivations and expectations for engaging in the listening process) (Tam et al., 2021). Individuals with predetermined issue motivations and preferred solutions to the issues could be advocating for their own stances while rejecting any counter-information from the organization or other publics (Kim & Grunig, 2021). These individuals find evidence to support their predetermined conclusions as opposed to finding evidence to make conclusions (Kim & Grunig, 2021). This is especially prominent when they do not trust the organization (Macnamara, 2018). Their issue involvement and perceptions toward an organization could also lead to motivated reasoning in responsibility attribution, that is, making attributions that are consistent with their prior beliefs (Zhao et al., 2022). Zhao et al. (2022) found in a US sample that individuals' issue involvement and perceived severity of the COVID-19 pandemic are positively related to their attribution of responsibility to China. Hence, this study makes the following propositions based on the above literature review:

Proposition 1: Individuals' situational perception about an issue (i.e., problem recognition) is positively associated with their attribution of responsibility to an organization for causing the issue.
Proposition 2: Individuals' trust in an organization is negatively associated with their attribution of responsibility to an organization for causing the issue.
Proposition 3: Individuals' attribution of responsibility to an organization for causing an issue affects their evaluations of the organization's listening efforts.

Organizational Listening from the Perspectives of Practitioners

The practice of listening is a critical condition to the pursuit of organizational learning (Jacobs & Coghlan, 2005). It involves scanning, interpreting, and understanding the environment in which an organization operates through which relationships are formed and intersubjective meanings are generated (Jacobs & Coghlan, 2005). It relates to the practice of environmental scanning in public relations (e.g., Dyer, 1996) and emphasizes the importance of acknowledging organizational stakeholders and their viewpoints in generating shared understanding (Jacobs & Coghlan, 2005). Instead of simply advocating for *listen more* or *listen better*, Jacobs and Coghlan (2005) stated: "future studies should investigate in more detail enabling and disabling aspects of the symbolic value of listening" (p. 134).

Listening is related to the practice of environmental scanning in public relations. Defined as "a method of gathering information from the external environment for use in issues management and the strategic decision-making process," environmental scanning is also known as "an early warning system," which helps management detect emerging issues to guide actions (Larsen, 2005, p. 341). Environmental scanning is an important diagnostic task for strategy formation; public relations practitioners' expertise in environmental scanning differentiates them from the marketing function and enhances the value of public relations to strategic management (Tam et al., 2022). Despite this, listening activities are lacking in organizations not only because of senior management but also public relations practitioners' focus on information transmission (Macnamara, 2016). In addition to having an architecture of listening within organizations, it is also important to note that listening "ultimately is a human undertaking" (Macnamara, 2018, p. 18).

In the practice of organizational listening, Place (2022) conducted interviews with 38 nonprofit and government public relations professionals in the United States and found that the participants develop listening activities with the consideration of intersectionality, defined as the interplay of social categories that shape human lives. Because multiple factors can come into play in shaping an individual's lived experience, the consideration of intersectionality will guide public relations practitioners in identifying alternative voices among marginalized publics (Place, 2022). Practitioners could be restricted by organizational constructs including the organizational culture for listening (Macnamara, 2016) and the organizational motivations for listening (Meesters et al., 2021) as well as professional constraints such as their positions' focus on speaking rather than listening (Macnamara, 2016).

In the context of engaging employees during organizational change, Sahay (2021) found that the lack of systems, processes, structures, resources, and skill sets had caused confusion, stress, and resistance among input providers. Brandt (2021) also found that organizational hierarchy could hinder information flow and knowledge transfer; even though frontline employees had more in-depth first-hand knowledge of customer problems and complaints, their insights were often ignored. Therefore, perceptions of the effectiveness of organizational listening could vary because of the roles that different parties play in the listening process (Brandt & Donohue, 2022). Organizational listening can be perceived as "a manifestation of hypocrisy" when stakeholders are invited to participate in a listening process that is framed as "an open dialogue" but did not have the "negotiation currency" to change organizational actions (Andersen & Høvring, 2020, p. 421). Oftentimes, organizations are perceived to be "better at capturing customer feedback than they are at analyzing, disseminating, or utilizing it to improve products, services and customer experiences" (Brandt, 2020, p. 156).

Therefore, this study makes the proposition that these factors, which enable and constrain how practitioners develop and implement an organization's listening efforts, can affect the outcomes of an organization's listening efforts.

Methodology

Survey

To test the extent to which individuals' issue motivations and their association of an organization with the issue affects their evaluations of the organization's listening efforts, a survey was conducted with a nationally representative sample (by age and gender) of 400 Australian

Table 7.1 Demographic characteristics of the respondents in the sample

Individual-level variables	N	Percent	Mean	Standard deviation
Age	400		45.34	17.90
Gender				
Male	192	48%		
Female	206	51.5%		
Nonbinary	1	0.3%		
Prefer not to answer	1	0.3%		
Education				
Less than high school	29	7.2%		
High school graduate	92	23%		
TAFE certificates	104	26%		
Bachelor's	118	29.5%		
Master's	46	11.5%		
Doctorate	6	1.5%		
Other	5	1.3%		
Annual pretax income				
Less than AUD$30,000	96	24%		
AUD$30,001–$60,000	100	25%		
AUD$60,001–$90,000	63	15.8%		
AUD$90,001–$120,000	48	12%		
More than AUD$120,000	60	15%		
Prefer not to disclose	33	8.3%		

citizens in December 2020 to January 2021. Upon receiving approval from the University's Ethics Committee, which is equivalent to the Institutional Review Board (IRB) in the United States, data were collected from research participants recruited through Qualtrics; they were compensated for their time based on their agreements with Qualtrics. Table 7.1 provides a summary of the key demographic characteristics of the sample.

Five variables were tested in the survey. To test individuals' motivation in an issue involving an organization, high-rise overdevelopment in Australia was used as an issue and the Australian government was used as an organization in the survey items. Respondents evaluated the statements on a Likert scale from 1 (strongly disagree) to 5 (strongly agree). First, to test an individual's issue motivation, problem recognition was conceptualized and tested as the extent to which an individual finds the issue of high-rise overdevelopment was problematic in Australia (Kim & Grunig, 2011). Five items were adapted from Kim and Grunig (2011), resulting in a reliability score of $\alpha = .948$. Second, to test the extent to which an individual's preexisting views about the organization influences evaluations of listening efforts, trust was tested with four survey items adapted from Moon and Yang (2015), resulting in a reliability score of α = .897. Third, because a combination of issue motivation and trust in the organization can affect how the organization is perceived in the issue, attribution of responsibility to the Australian government for the issue of high-rise overdevelopment was tested with five survey items adapted from Brown and Ki (2013), resulting in a reliability score of α = .904. Lastly, to test individuals' evaluations of the Australian government's listening efforts, two constructs were derived: selective listening and diverse listening. Selective listening was defined as the extent to which an organization is evaluated to be listening to only a selected group of stakeholders and was measured using seven items (α = .963). On the other hand, diverse listening was defined as the extent to which an organization is evaluated to be listening to its diverse stakeholders and was measured using seven items (α = .961). Table 7.2 shows the survey items used and the mean, standard deviation (SD), and standard error (SE) for each item.

Table 7.2 The survey items used and the mean (M), standard deviation (SD), and standard error (SE) for each item and for the weighted composite of each construct

Construct	Item	M	SD	SE
Problem recognition α = .948 M = 3.51 SD = 1.06 SE = .053	I consider the overdevelopment of high-rise apartment buildings in Australia to be a serious issue.	3.46	1.184	.059
	I am worried about the overdevelopment of high-rise apartment buildings in Australia.	3.48	1.17	.058
	Something needs to be done immediately to address the overdevelopment of high-rise apartment buildings in Australia.	3.54	1.196	.059
	People should pay more attention to the overdevelopment of high-rise apartment buildings in Australia because it is affecting us.	3.56	1.122	.056
	The government should take immediate action on the overdevelopment of high-rise apartment buildings in Australia.	3.55	1.147	.057
Trust α = .897 M = 2.95 SD = 1.07 SE = .053	Whenever the government makes important decisions, I know it will be concerned about its citizens like me.	3.23	1.161	.058
	The government can be relied on to keep its promises.	2.79	1.199	.06
	I believe the government takes opinions of people like me into account when making decisions.	2.85	1.216	.061
	I feel very confident about the government's policies and procedures.	3.03	1.204	.06

(*Continued*)

Table 7.2 The survey items used and the mean (M), standard deviation (SD), and standard error (SE) for each item and for the weighted composite of each construct (*Continued*)

Construct	Item	M	SD	SE
Attribution of responsibility α = .904 M = 3.48 SD = .951 SE = .048	The overdevelopment of high-rise apartment buildings in Australia is an issue caused by the government.	3.39	1.141	.057
	The government has knowingly contributed to the overdevelopment of high-rise apartment buildings in Australia.	3.55	1.08	.054
	The government should be held responsible for the overdevelopment of high-rise apartment buildings in Australia.	3.59	1.102	.055
	The government should be blamed for the overdevelopment of high-rise apartment buildings in Australia.	3.46	1.158	.058
	Problems within the government caused the overdevelopment of high-rise apartment buildings in Australia.	3.35	1.1	.055
Diverse listening α = .961 M = 3.10 SD = 1.07 SE = .054	The government recognizes its diverse citizens as having legitimate rights to speak about its policies.	3.25	1.177	.059
	The government treats the voices of its diverse citizens with respect.	3.15	1.195	.06
	The government acknowledges and listens to what its diverse citizens say.	3.12	1.207	.06
	The government pays attention to the voices of its diverse citizens.	3.03	1.19	.059
	The government interprets what its diverse citizens say fairly and receptively.	3.08	1.186	.059
	The government considers suggestions from its diverse citizens.	3.12	1.171	.059
	The government responds to suggestions from its diverse citizens promptly and properly.	2.93	1.193	.06
Selective listening α = .963 M = 3.52 SD = 1.05 SE = .052	The government recognizes only some of its citizens as having legitimate rights to speak about its policies but ignores others.	3.41	1.162	.058
	The government treats the voices of only some citizens with respect but ignores others.	3.53	1.159	.058
	The government acknowledges and listens to only some of its citizens but ignores others.	3.53	1.176	.059
	The government pays attention to the voices of only some citizens but ignores others.	3.51	1.144	.057
	The government interprets the voices of only some citizens fairly and receptively and ignores others.	3.5	1.144	.057
	The government considers suggestions from only some citizens but ignores others.	3.59	1.134	.057
	The government responds to suggestions from only some citizens promptly and properly but ignores others.	3.53	1.126	.056

Figure 7.1 Hypothesized model to be tested

A conceptualization of the hypothesized model to be tested is sure in Figure 7.1. Weighted composites were created on SPSS version 28 for the data analysis. The relationships among the variables were tested using Structural Equation Modeling (SEM) on AMOS version 28.

Interviews

To test the factors that affected how public relations practitioners develop and implement organizational listening activities, 28 Australian public relations practitioners were recruited through snowball sampling and were interviewed on the phone in November 2020–February 2021. They were compensated with a gift card for their time. Of the 28 practitioners, 11 were male and 17 were female. Fourteen of them self-identified as engagement specialists. They had an average of 13.5 years of experience in the industry.

The interview guide included questions related to their views of organizations' motivations to invest in listening and their views of their roles in organizational listening (including how they ensure diverse voices are heard). Upon completion of the data collection, they were transcribed manually and analyzed using thematic analysis (Braun & Clarke, 2006).

Findings

Survey

The result from the testing of the hypothesized model is shown in Figure 7.2. As hypothesized, there is a positive relationship between problem recognition about the issue of high-rise over-development and attribution of responsibility to the Australian government for causing the issue ($\beta = .712^{***}$). A negative association between trust and attribution of responsibility was also found ($\beta = -.132^{***}$). Also, as hypothesized, a positive relationship between attribution of responsibility and selective listening was identified ($\beta = .393^{***}$). However, there was no association between attribution of responsibility and diverse listening. In addition to the paths in the hypothesized model, a positive relationship was also

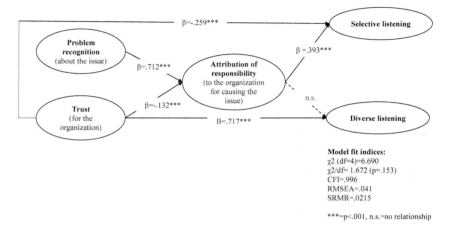

Figure 7.2 Results from the hypothesized model tested

found between trust and diverse listening (β = .717***). A negative relationship was found between trust and selective listening (β = −.259***). The model achieved satisfactory model fit indices (χ^2/df = 1.672, CFI = .996, RMSEA = .041, SRMR = .0215) based on Hu and Bentler's (1999) cutoff criteria (χ^2/df < 3, CFI > .95, RMSEA < .06, SRMR < .08).

The findings from the survey show that individuals' evaluations of an organization's listening efforts could be affected by their trust for an organization. Individuals' problem recognition of an issue and their attribution of responsibility to an organization for causing the issue also affected their evaluations of whether the organization listens selectively.

Interviews

To understand factors that influence how practitioners develop and implement an organization's listening efforts, the following findings highlighted the specific results that could influence how the listening efforts are evaluated.

Identifying Organizations' Goals and Motivations for Organizational Listening

Organizational listening in some organizations emphasize stakeholder-centric goals and organization-centric goals. Table 7.3 shows the organization- and stakeholder-centric goals identified from the interviews.

Specifically, Participant #9 noted that organizations invest resources in organizational listening either because of statutory requirements or because they see the genuine value in doing it. For those who do it for

Table 7.3 Stakeholder- and organization-centric goals identified from the interviews

Stakeholder-centric goals	Organization-centric goals
• To gather stakeholders' needs and expectations • To gain an understanding of the issues experienced by publics • To adjust organizational actions • To generate shared understanding to deliver outcomes desirable for both organizations and publics	• To inform communication strategy including the choice of messaging and channels • To obtain social license to operate • To ensure ongoing business through improvements • To reduce complaints and staff turnover

statutory requirements, such as in the government context, they may have a 20-day period for consultation. For those who see genuine value in practice, they think about the needs of the community and are dedicated to work collaboratively with a wide range of different stakeholders to achieve better outcomes for both the organization and its stakeholders. The latter does so to "build up the trust bank, which is critical to a social license to operate" (Participant #9). It is especially prevalent today because the advent of social media means that "stakeholders themselves have the power to influence and direct the content and the storyline of an organization" (Participant #13). Despite this, there are also some organizations that listen primarily to influence. Participant #15 notes from her experiences that listening is conducted "to ensure that communication strategies and the way that they are speaking to their stakeholders is effective."

Stakeholder Mapping and Choice of Channels

The practice of stakeholder mapping and prioritization of publics may cause organizational listening to be criticized. In the stakeholder mapping stage, practitioners identify stakeholders who are influenced or have a stake to influence a project or an issue. Participant #19 notes that stakeholder mapping would identify stakeholders including other organizations, shareholding ministers, government departments, regional organizations, community groups, and customers who are connected to the organization in some way and/or are impacted by it. But when it comes to the analysis process, she would prioritize based on (a) their influence on the project/issue, (b) their needs, (c) their motivations for engaging in the listening process, and (d) their mutual trust with the organization. She notes:

> Some people have a louder voice than others, and it doesn't mean that they should be spoken to first. You really have to work out if there are

groups or individuals that are less well represented and make a concerted effort to include them. So, yeah, mapping everybody that you could think of or every organization that that has some sort of touch point that you need to consider. And then that's the reason why you need to talk to them or listen to them and what it's about.

Participant #26 further notes that the choice of channels for listening is dependent upon the target stakeholder groups and the general sentiments within each group. Ultimately, the choice of channels will determine the stakeholders represented (and, thus, the voices heard). Participant #17 highlights that the role of the communicator is:

> to synthesize those different point of views and then present it to management. And particularly that process of synthesis to me is really bringing about meaning and understanding of what the various pieces of Insight's and data that are coming back from those tools mean to the executive to stick to the decision makers who they are presenting to, you know, a tweet which is posted by a person who could start a consumer backlash to the brand is very different to a tweet posted by someone with five followers who's never going to see the light of day.

Co-orientating with Stakeholders

While different stakeholder groups have different expectations, it was noted that listening needs to serve a purpose and that information should be provided to stakeholders before channels are set up to collect their feedback. Participant #6 pointed out the importance of providing information to stakeholders and thinking about what questions should be anticipated beforehand:

> When you're seeking people's feedback, it has to have a purpose because if you don't give them parameters, then you're going to have every man and their dog giving their opinion and then it might not be relevant. And you're wasting your time. You know, I've had experience on projects where things get blown out of proportion and the wrong information gets put out there, if you can control that in a way where your message is the one that's the source of truth and you're very clear about how to address people's concerns.

Likewise, Participant #9 notes that stakeholders may mistakenly believe that through participating in listening activities, they can change organizational decisions in the direction they desire. Considering that two-way communication is practiced during organizational listening, organizations also need to provide information and explanations. He notes that it is important to explain why certain feedback is not taken into consideration:

> If I say I want black, but the organization wants to deliver Y. It doesn't mean that they need to change from black to Y. That's not what. But they do need to know is that I've said that I want black and the reasons why I want black and is there are things that we can do to meet my needs as well as their needs.

Participant #23 highlights the differences between listening and hearing. During the listening process, organizations might reiterate their positions so that stakeholders would understand their positions and would provide feedback with consideration to those positions.

> Stakeholders might not like hearing the organization's position, but that is our position versus what they keep saying. Why don't you change a particular position on it? So I am listening, but I'm reiterating organization's position. If the stakeholder doesn't like what they're listening, that doesn't mean that I didn't listen. It is important to distinguish between listening and decision making. What I'm saying and communicating after I listen to stakeholder needs and what the positions organizations are. If they don't match, often the comment received is that organization didn't listen. They actually just didn't like it. They didn't like what they're hearing back from the organization.

Implications

The purpose of this study is to highlight enabling and disabling factors that lead to criticisms of the organizational listening process. The results from the survey indicated that individuals' preexisting perceptions about an issue and the organization involved affect whether they consider the organization to be responsible for causing the issue and whether the organization is listening selectively. This reflects that rather than *listen more, listen better*, there is a need to acknowledge individuals' motivations for engaging in the listening process. Extant research on cognitive dissonance has identified that individuals are more willing to accept information that is consistent with their preexisting beliefs and are more prone to reject information that is inconsistent with their preexisting beliefs (Tsang, 2019). This also dictates their choice of information and their communicative behaviors as they seek to reinforce their preexisting beliefs over time (Kim & Grunig, 2021). The findings from our study confirm the proposition that if an individual disagrees with an issue and associates an organization for causing the issue, it is likely that he/she will evaluate the organization as not listening or listening selectively.

Moreover, if he/she does not trust the organization to begin with, he/she will also evaluate the organization as not listening or listening selectively. These findings point to the need of identifying organizational listening practices to effectively "bridge" with stakeholders who do not trust an organization and/or have high problem recognition about an issue such as following the mutual gains approach to dealing with angry publics (Susskind & Field, 1996).

The results from the interviews showed that there are practices inherent in the process, which could cause an organization to be criticized for not listening or listening selectively. For example, organizations also have their motivations for investing in organizational listening. According to Macnamara (2016) and Meesters et al. (2021), these motivations are often organization-centric such as selling more products and services (Macnamara, 2016) and managing stakeholder expectations (Meesters et al., 2021). There could also be a tendency to favor agreements over disagreements (Ciszek, 2016). These organization-centric motivations could lead to tokenistic listening practices which do not translate into changes in decisions or behaviors (Tam et al., 2021). However, considering the different (and possibly conflicting) stakeholders' interests, it is also important to ensure that (a) organizations also convey their positions in the listening process and that (b) stakeholders are given some information about the issue or the project so that they are on the same page. After all, it is essential to generate inputs which are feasible and actionable. And lastly, the practice of stakeholder mapping and/or public segmentation has been a long-standing practice within public relations. Organizations have been criticized for prioritizing local, organized groups over non-local marginalized groups (Meesters et al., 2021). If practitioners only focus on one criterion such as influence, they will have a tendency of only listening to "the loud minority" and neglecting "the silent majority." Because this segmentation also affects the choice of channels used for listening, when reporting the feedback received during the listening process, practitioners should also report the limitations. This can include reporting the demographic data of the stakeholders who have been listened to and the channels used to collect their feedback. They should also consider reporting why some concerns have been incorporated into decision-making, and some have not.

Theoretical Implications

The findings from this study highlight a major problem: organizational listening seeks to serve the purpose of co-adaption to ensure shared decision-making and mutual benefits (Brunner, 2008), but it can result in perceptions of inauthentic listening (Sahay, 2021). These perceptions could be caused by factors beyond the control of organizations, such as individuals' preexisting problem perceptions and preferred outcomes about an issue and the discrepancies between individuals' and organizations' expectations of the process. From the perspectives of organizations, the listening process is not just about gathering feedback but also articulating their positions. From the perspectives of stakeholders, when they are invited to give feedback, they expect their concerns to be addressed and incorporated into organizations' decisions.

Organizational listening is aligned with the behavioral, strategic paradigm of public relations (Grunig, 2009a; Kim & Krishna, 2018) such that its purpose is to understand stakeholders' and publics' concerns properly and to reflect them in organizational decision-making. To bridge the gap between an organization and its stakeholders, adaptation is needed, which refers to "the willingness and ability of the organization to make changes necessary to create harmony between itself and its key publics" (Smith, 2013, p. 114). By employing principles of symmetrical communication and adapting themselves to the changes and concerns of stakeholders, organizations ensure their actions to be responsive to the stakeholders as well as responsible and ethical in their relationships with stakeholders (Kim & Krishna, 2018).

However, even though current research on public relations has consistently found positive outcomes of symmetrical communication in various contexts such as employee communication (e.g., Men & Sung, 2022) and crisis communication (e.g., Chon et al., 2022), its operations (in the form of organizational listening) may not be perceived positively. Ideally, symmetrical communication contributes to mutual understanding and mutually beneficial relationships (Grunig et al., 2002). But when both parties' expectations and experiences of organizational listening differ, the listening activities could be evaluated as inauthentic. Organizations' practice of symmetrical communication is only perceived as "symmetrical" if there are positive outcomes for stakeholders (e.g., organizations' addressing and incorporating their concerns into decisions). But when stakeholders have diverse views, some of which can be conflicting, the listening activities will not result in positive outcomes for *all* stakeholders.

While current research on symmetrical communication has operationalized the variable with measurement items testing perceptions of two-way communication in surveys (e.g., Chon et al., 2022; Men & Sung, 2022), future research should consider breaking down the construct into subdimensions such as the pursuit of mutual expectations, mutual understanding, and mutual benefits and should test the construct in relation to issues with which they may agree or disagree with an organization's positions. Furthermore, stakeholders' perceptions of organizations' efforts to pursue symmetrical communication with stakeholders who may agree or disagree with their positions on issues could also be tested using experiments in future research. On the one hand, organizations should pursue dissensus (rather than consensus) (Ciszek, 2016). On the other hand, if organizational listening results in the revelation of differences and disagreements that organizations cannot possibly address in the decisions they make, then it can be perceived as "inauthentic" (Sahay, 2021, p. 13) or "a manifestation of hypocrisy" (Andersen & Høvring, 2020, p. 421). Future research could examine the aims, processes, and outcomes of organizational listening separately and assess how alignment and misalignment could affect stakeholders' perceptions.

Recommendations for Practice

Like all organizational practices, organizational listening is subject to scrutiny and, thus, compliments and criticisms. Based on the findings of this study, the following recommendations are made for practice:

1 Prior to starting the process of organizational listening, practitioners should understand the organization's positions on the issue and their motivations for investing in organizational listening.
2 Rather than designing a listening process during which stakeholders can leave any feedback, practitioners should be cognizant of what the organization can and cannot do and ensure that the listening process does not give stakeholders the false expectations that all their feedback can be actioned.
3 Practitioners should provide stakeholders with some information about the issue before seeking feedback from them in order to ensure that the feedback collected has valuable information that can be incorporated into decision-making.
4 When doing stakeholder mapping, practitioners should clearly identify and justify their criteria for prioritizing some groups over others and their choice of channels for these groups.
5 Practitioners should seek to understand the stakeholders' motivations for engaging and *not* engaging in the listening process including their issue motivation, their trust for the organization, and their attribution of responsibility to the organization for causing the issue.
6 When synthesizing the listening report to management, practitioners should also report the limitations including the demographic data of the stakeholders who have been listened to and the groups that they might not have been able to reach.
7 At the conclusion of the listening process and/or decision-making process, practitioners should consider publishing a report that reports and explains the feedback that has been received and taken into consideration and the feedback that has been received but not taken into consideration.

References

Andersen, S. E., & Høvring, C. M. (2020). CSR stakeholder dialogue in disguise: Hypocrisy in story performances. *Journal of Business Research, 114*(August), 421–435. https://doi.org/10.1016/j.jbusres.2019.08.030

Bowen, S. A. (2008). A state of neglect: Public relations as "Corporate conscience" or ethics counsel. *Journal of Public Relations Research, 20*(3), 271–296. https://doi.org/10.1080/10627260801962749

Brandt, D. R. (2020). The current state of corporate voice of the consumer programs: A study of organizational listening practices and effectiveness. *International Journal of Listening, 34*(3), 156–177. https://doi.org/10.1080/10904018.2018.1482747

Brandt, D. R. (2021). Hierarchical and role-based differences in the perception of organizational listening effectiveness. *International Journal of Business Communication*. https://doi.org/10.1177/23294884211055839

Brandt, D. R., & Donohue, W. A. (2022). Perceived organizational listening effectiveness: A comparison of consumer intelligence provider and consumer intelligence user assessments. *International Journal of Business Communication*, 1–26. https://doi.org/10.1177/23294884221119168

Braun, V., & Clarke, V. (2006). Using thematic analysis in psychology. *Qualitative Research in Psychology, 3*(2), 77–101. https://doi.org/10.1191/1478088706qp063oa

Brown, K. A., & Ki, E. J. (2013). Developing a valid and reliable measure of organizational crisis responsibility. *Journalism and Mass Communication Quarterly, 90*(2), 363–384. https://doi.org/10.1177/1077699013482911

Brunner, B. R. (2008). Listening, communication & trust: Practitioners' perspectives of business/organizational relationships. *International Journal of Listening, 22*(1), 73–82. https://doi.org/10.1080/10904010701808482

Chon, M.-G., Kim, J.-N., & Tam, L. (2022). From messaging to behavioral strategy : Constructing a model of relationship- and action-focused crisis communication principles. *International Journal of Communication, 16*, 2103–2125. https://ijoc.org/index.php/ijoc/article/view/18185

Ciszek, E. L. (2016). Digital activism: How social media and dissensus inform theory and practice. *Public Relations Review, 42*(2), 314–321. https://doi.org/10.1016/j.pubrev.2016.02.002

Conrad, E., Cassar, L. F., Christie, M., & Fazey, I. (2011). Hearing but not listening? A participatory assessment of public participation in planning. *Environment and Planning C: Government and Policy, 29*(5), 761–782. https://doi.org/10.1068/c10137

Dyer, S. C. (1996). Descriptive modeling for public relations environmental scanning: A practitioner's perspective. *Journal of Public Relations Research, 8*(3), 137–150. https://doi.org/10.1207/s1532754xjprr0803_01

Fieseler, C., Lutz, C., & Meckel, M. (2015). An inquiry into the transformation of the PR roles' concept. *Corporate Communications: An International Journal, 20*(1), 76–89. https://doi.org/10.1108/CCIJ-02-2014-0013

Fitzpatrick, K. (2006). Baselines for ethical advocacy in the "marketplace of ideas." In K. Fitzpatrick & C. Bronstein (Eds.), *Ethics in public relations: Responsible advocacy* (pp. 1–18). SAGE Publications, Inc. https://doi.org/10.4135/9781452204208.n1

Grunig, J. E. (2006). Furnishing the edifice: Ongoing research on public relations as a strategic management function. *Journal of Public Relations Research, 18*(2), 151–176. https://doi.org/10.1207/s1532754xjprr1802

Grunig, J. E. (2009a). A general theory of excellent public relations. In J. E. Grunig, M. A. Ferrari, & F. França (Eds.), *Relações públicas: Teoria, contexto e relacionamentos (Public relations: Theory, context, and relationships)* (pp. 1–3 Chapter 2). Difusao Editora.

Grunig, J. E. (2009b). Paradigms of global public relations in an age of digitalisation. *PRism, 6*(2), 1–19. http://praxis.massey.ac.nz/prism_on-line_journ.html

Grunig, J. E. (2018). Strategic behavioral paradigm. In R. L. Heath, & W. Johansen (Eds.), *The international encyclopedia of strategic communication* (pp. 1–6). Wiley.

Grunig, L. A., Grunig, J. E., & Dozier, D. M. (2002). *Excellent public relations and effective organizations: A study of communication management in three countries*. Lawrence Erlbaum Associates.

Grunig, J. E., & Repper, F. C. (1992). Strategic management, publics, and issues. In J. E. Grunig (Ed.), *Excellence in public relations and communication management* (pp. 117–158). Lawrence Erlbaum Associates.

Hu, L. T., & Bentler, P. M. (1999). Cutoff criteria for fit indexes in covariance structure analysis: Conventional criteria versus new alternatives. *Structural Equation Modeling: A Multidisciplinary Journal, 6*(1), 1–55. https://doi.org/10.1080/10705519909540118

Jacobs, C., & Coghlan, D. (2005). Sound from silence: On listening in organizational learning. *Human Relations, 58*(1), 115–138. https://doi.org/10.1177/0018726705050938

Kim, J.-N. (2012). From relational quality to communicative actions of publics and stakeholders: Understanding causality loops between behaviors of organizations and behaviors of publics in strategic communication. *International Journal of Strategic Communication, 6*(1), 1–6. https://doi.org/10.1080/1553118X.2012.652010

Kim, J.-N., & Grunig, J. E. (2011). Problem solving and communicative action: A situational theory of problem solving. *Journal of Communication, 61*(1), 120–149. https://doi.org/10.1111/j.1460-2466.2010.01529.x

Kim, J.-N., & Grunig, J. E. (2021). Lost in informational paradise: Cognitive arrest to epistemic inertia in problem solving. *American Behavioral Scientist, 65*(2), 213–242. https://doi.org/10.1177/0002764219878237

Kim, S., & Kim, J.-N. (2016). Bridge or buffer: Two ideas of effective corporate governance and public engagement. *Journal of Public Affairs, 16*(2), 118–127. https://doi.org/10.1002/pa.1555

Kim, S., & Krishna, A. (2018). Unpacking public sentiment toward the government: How citizens' perceptions of government communication strategies impact public engagement, cynicism, and communication behaviors in South Korea. *International Journal of Strategic Communication, 00*(00), 1–22. https://doi.org/10.1080/1553118X.2018.1448400

Kim, J.-N., & Ni, L. (2010). Seeing the forest through the trees: The behavioral, strategic management paradigm of public relations and its future. In Robert L. Heath (Ed.), *The Sage handbook of public relations* (2nd ed., pp. 35–57). Sage.

Kim, J.-N., Ni, L., & Sha, B.-L. (2008). Breaking down the stakeholder environment: Explicating approaches to the segmentation of publics for public relations research. *Journalism & Mass Communication Quarterly, 85*(4), 751–768. https://doi.org/10.1177/107769900808500403

Larsen, P. V. (2005). Environmental scanning. In Robert L. Heath (Ed.), *Encyclopedia of public relations* (pp. 341–344). Sage. https://doi.org/10.4135/9781412952545.n142

Macnamara, J. (2015). *Organizational listening: The missing essential in public communication*. Peter Lang Publishing Inc.

Macnamara, J. (2016). Organizational listening: Addressing a major gap in public relations theory and practice. *Journal of Public Relations Research*, *28*(3–4), 146–169. https://doi.org/10.1080/1062726X.2016.1228064

Macnamara, J. (2018). Toward a theory and practice of organizational listening. *International Journal of Listening*, *32*(1), 1–23. https://doi.org/10.1080/10904018.2017.1375076

Macnamara, J. (2019). Explicating listening in organization–public communication: Theory, practices, technologies. *International Journal of Communication*, *19*, 5183–5204.

Meesters, M., Wostyn, P., van Leeuwen, J., Behagel, J. H., & Turnhout, E. (2021). The social licence to operate and the legitimacy of resource extraction. *Current Opinion in Environmental Sustainability*, *49*, 7–11. https://doi.org/10.1016/j.cosust.2020.11.002

Men, L. R., & Sung, Y. (2022). Shaping corporate character through symmetrical communication: The effects on employee-organization relationships. *International Journal of Business Communication*, *59*(3), 427–449. https://doi.org/10.1177/2329488418824989

Moon, B. B., & Yang, S.-U. (2015). Why publics terminate their relationship with organizations: Exploring antecedents of relationship dissolution in South Korea. *Asian Journal of Communication*, *25*(3), 288–306. https://doi.org/10.1080/01292986.2014.960876

Place, K. R. (2022). Toward a framework for listening with consideration for intersectionality: Insights from public relations professionals in borderland spaces. *Journal of Public Relations Research*, *34*(1–2), 4–19. https://doi.org/10.1080/1062726X.2022.2057502

Saffer, A. J., Yang, A., & Taylor, M. (2018). Reconsidering power in multistakeholder relationship management. *Management Communication Quarterly*, *32*(1), 121–139. https://doi.org/10.1177/0893318917700510

Sahay, S. (2021). Organizational listening during organizational change: Perspectives of employees and executives. *International Journal of Listening*, 1–14. https://doi.org/10.1080/10904018.2021.1941029

Smith, R. D. (2013). *Strategic planning for public relations*. Taylor and Francis.

Susskind, L., & Field, P. (1996). *Dealing with an angry public: The mutual gains approach to resolving disputes*. The Free Press.

Tam, L., Burns, K., & Barnes, K. (2021). Responsibilities and capabilities of health engagement professionals (HEPs): Perspectives from HEPs and health consumers in Australia. *Health Expectations*, *24*, 111–120. https://doi.org/10.1111/hex.13155

Tam, L., Kim, J.-N., Grunig, J. E., Hall, J. A., & Swerling, J. (2022). In search of communication excellence: Public relations' value, empowerment, and structure in strategic management. *Journal of Marketing Communications*, *28*(2), 183–206. https://doi.org/10.1080/13527266.2020.1851286

Taylor, M., & Kent, M. L. (2014). Dialogic engagement: Clarifying foundational concepts. *Journal of Public Relations Research*, *26*(5), 384–398. https://doi.org/10.1080/1062726X.2014.956106

Tsang, S. J. (2019). Cognitive discrepancy, dissonance, and selective exposure. *Media Psychology*, *22*(3), 394–417. https://doi.org/10.1080/15213269.2017.1282873

Zhao, X., Tsang, S. J., & Xu, S. (2022). Motivated responsibility attribution in a pandemic: Roles of political orientation, perceived severity, and construal level. *International Journal of Communication*, *16*, 2260–2282.

8 Improving Organizational Listening to Build Trust with Black Residents and Disrupt Racism in Local Government

Ashley E. English, Julie O'Neil, and Jacqueline Lambiase

Introduction

In the early morning hours of October 12, 2019, tragedy struck a family and a Fort Worth neighborhood. A long-time Fort Worth resident, James Smith, called a non-emergency police telephone number for a welfare check at his neighbor's home. While he waited on his front porch to talk with the police when they arrived, he missed connecting with them (Lopez, 2019). Police arrived, entering the neighboring home's yard quickly. One officer stood outside a window of the home, not identifying himself as a police officer but yelling for someone to "put your hands up." Almost instantaneous with the order, the officer shot into the window, killing 28-year-old Atatiana Jefferson. "I made the call, because I thought they would do what I called them to do," which was to check on his neighbor, said Smith a few days later (Lopez, 2019). Her killing sparked outrage in Fort Worth and across the nation as conversations about police brutality and excessive use of force continued to gain momentum after years of activism by Black Lives Matter and similar organizations.

Less than a year after Jefferson's killing, this activism gained more momentum after the murder of George Floyd by a Minneapolis police officer in May 2020, compelling government leaders in the United States to confront the reality of racism. An unprecedented wave of corporate activism and public policy discussions challenged local, state, and federal governments to address discrimination against Black people in policing, health care, education, economics, and more. Embedded in these cries for social justice were calls to listen, especially for government leaders.

While influencing the federal government may seem beyond the capability of most citizens due to their lack of trust in government, changes in local government may be seen as far more attainable and accessible, too (Rainie & Perrin, 2019; Trust in Government, 2020). Thus, local government could serve as an ideal place to foster listening and dialogue as ways to build a more just society. Doing so, however, necessitates that municipalities acknowledge that listening, and not just speaking, is a formal

DOI: 10.4324/9781003273851-11

duty, with accountability for the employees and elected officials officially designated as listeners.

Yet this shift from communicating well to listening well requires professional discipline and change-management strategies for cities. Public relations scholarship rarely examines listening (e.g., Macnamara, 2016, 2019; Place, 2019) and devotes even less academic attention to listening to minoritized publics such as Black residents. This chapter's case study and feedback from community members contribute to needed scholarship by examining the perceptions of Black residents and activists, their ideas about listening, and one large city's organizational listening practices.

The purpose of this chapter is three-fold. First, this chapter explores the current context of American racial and social justice efforts and scholarship on listening and trust. The second part of this chapter contains two types of research: a case study about the city's listening and actions before, during, and after the killing of Atatiana Jefferson, plus an analysis of interviews with 25 stakeholders, most of them Black, about the city's efforts at listening. Thirdly, this chapter concludes with recommendations to enhance a city's listening capacities, with special attention to the changes needed to demonstrate good faith and the possibility of building trust with minoritized communities.

Structural Racism, Trust, and Listening

While cries for social justice in the 21st century have intensified, discussions about racism in the American context are long-standing. Through government-sanctioned policies that impacted the ability of Black people to obtain housing, voting access, quality education, ethical medical care, equal employment opportunities, and economic security, the reality of structural racism is evident. This concept is defined by Lawrence and Keleher (2004):

> Structural racism in the United States is the normalization and legitimization of an array of dynamics – historical, cultural, institutional and interpersonal – that routinely advantage Whites while producing cumulative and chronic adverse outcomes for people of color. It is a system of hierarchy and inequity, primarily characterized by White supremacy – the preferential treatment, privilege and power for White people at the expense of Black, Latino, Asian, Pacific Islander, Native American, Arab and other racially oppressed people.
> (Lawrence & Keleher, 2004, p. 1).

Law enforcement is one institution in the United States at the forefront of discussions about the preferential treatment of Whites at the expense of Black people. Origins of policing in America included informal watch groups of White men who voluntarily protected property and controlled public safety, often in ways supporting economic interests rather than being rooted in the law or concerned with protecting individual rights (Brucato, 2020). In the American South, policing is traced by historians to "slave patrols," whose goal was to continue the oppression of White enslavers over enslaved Black people, which continued even after the abolition of slavery through Jim Crow and other racist laws (Platt, 1982).

The use of police to enforce oppressive, and often violent, policies aimed at patrolling and monitoring the movement of Black people is evident in modern times. In a 2020 Pew Research Center poll of 4,700 adults, 90% of Black respondents and 57% of White respondents indicated that police do a poor or fair job of treating racial and ethnic groups equally (Pew Research Center, 2020). In the same study, only 28% of Black people felt that the police do a good or excellent job protecting people from crime, compared with 67% of Whites. These different experiences among Black and White respondents could be attributed to structural racism. This feeling of normalized oppression of Black people has created a chasm of trust between local governments and Black people.

Trust, especially in government public relations, is an essential dimension of building positive relationships between government organizations and their relevant publics. Trust in the organization-public relationship (OPR) literature is defined as "one party's level of confidence in and willingness to open oneself to the other party" (Hon & Grunig, 1999, p. 3). There are three dimensions of trust that include: (1) integrity, or belief that the other party is fair and just; (2) dependability, or consistency, between an organization's words and actions; and (3) competence, or the degree to which each party believes that the other can do what it says it will do (Hon & Grunig, 1999). A fundamental contribution of OPR scholarship is that building trust leads to positive relationships with various publics, which is one of the primary purposes for public relations as a field and discipline. Bowen et al. (2016) argue that trust is an antecedent of OPRs, and the absence of ethics, consistency, and trust precludes organizations from developing positive, long-lasting relationships.

For many Black people, trust in the government is lacking. Waymer (2013) argues that Black people may indeed not want a relationship with the government due to the structural racism embedded in the history of government organizations and its perpetuation of oppression, violence, and harm. Modern government organizations, especially local entities, must prioritize building trust with Black people, especially since these entities still contain elements of structural racism. Thus, building trust with Black residents should be a priority for city governments, which manage law enforcement.

One means of improving trust and relational outcomes between municipalities and Black residents is to increase organizational listening efforts. According to Macnamara (2016), "organizational listening is comprised of the culture, policies, structure, processes, resources, skills, technologies, and practices applied by an organization to give recognition, acknowledgment, attention, interpretation, understanding, consideration, and response to its stakeholders and publics" (p. 52). Within the definition of organizational listening are elements that may be important to disrupting racist practices, including new policies and structures for listening, as well as appropriate responses after listening. The culture of organizations specifically focuses on the attitudes and actions of leadership during the processes of listening. In the case of government, this means emphasizing the important role of leaders in crafting a culture that gives consideration to others and establishes respect for listening. Unless leaders set the expectation for listening, the ability to hear the concerns of minoritized stakeholders is limited.

Additionally, the best organizational listening intentionally dismantles the usual politics of listening, with its connections to power. Within this better organizational framework, organizations pay close attention to who is listened to and who is not. The goal is to ensure organization leadership hears the broadest array of voices with a special effort to avoid pseudo-listening (Adler & Rodman, 2011, p. 136) or pretend listening (Bussie, 2011, p. 31), which is performative. At their best, organizations intentionally incorporate dissenting voices or minoritized voices as necessary sources for feedback and insight. It is through the disruption of politics that organizations may then establish policies for listening that "specify and require listening in an organization" (Macnamara, 2019, p. 5192). For example, this might mean requiring local governments to hear from residents from predetermined zip codes before making decisions or strategically targeting underrepresented communities as targets for listening to aid decision-making for city management, economic development professionals, or city council members. These policies mandate listening rather than giving a simple nod to listening.

After listening occurs, a fundamental step to close the loop on listening is offering an appropriate response, which means organizations should "have channels for the articulation of what was said to an organization to policy and decision making" (Macnamara, 2019, p. 5193). This step authenticates the listening process. Failure to make changes to an organization's policy-making or decision-making processes based on what an organization heard from stakeholders conveys that "voice has no value" (Ibid). Next, this study will use the framework of organizational listening to offer recommendations, after a two-pronged approach that uses a case study and an analysis of participant interviews.

Case Study: Fort Worth's Policing Issues in the Black Community from 2016 to 2020

Through the case-study method, we examine two critical incidents in 2016 and 2019 in the City of Fort Worth's policing activities. While researchers identified the 2019 killing of Atatiana Jefferson and the city's response as the key focus of the case study, participants during the interview process pointed to an earlier incident from 2016. Therefore, researchers built a case study using two critical incidents, instead of one, and included the City of Fort Worth's responses to both incidents. Between these incidents, the city established a city-appointed task force in 2017, and this case study also analyzes recommendations by and perceptions of that task force, and connections to listening and racial tension in the Black community. Using Lexis-Nexis searches of local media accounts, as well as creating an ethnographic account of actions by the community, activists, and the city itself, the research team created a narrative of events from 2016 through 2020, with updates through spring 2022 of further developments. However, the central focus of this case study remains the 2019 killing of Atatiana Jefferson, an innocent Black woman, at the hands of a White Fort Worth police officer.

Background

The city of Fort Worth, Texas, is among the largest cities in the United States with a 2019 population of 914,000 (DataUSA, 2022). It is considered a majority-minority city: 35% of residents are Hispanic, 20% Black, and 40% non-Hispanic White (Law, 2019). Even though Black and Hispanic residents constitute a majority of citizens, 65% of the police force is White as are the mayor, city manager, majority of the city council, and the police chief (Connelly, 2019). A 2016 racial profiling report revealed that although Blacks were 18.9% of residents, they comprised 26.3% of traffic stops by police (Fritsch & Trulson, 2016). Furthermore, in 2017, Black residents made up 41% of the arrests (Fernandez et al., 2019). The police department in Fort Worth has a history of involvement with high-profile incidents that relate to police violence, mistreatment, and excessive use of force, especially toward Black people (Lockhart, 2019). Compared to 11 U.S. cities of a similar size, "Fort Worth had the second-highest fatal police shooting rate per 100,000 people in 2019, and the third-highest such rate in 2018," while having the third-lowest violent crime rate of the comparison cities (Johnson, 2019).

Jacqueline Craig's Arrest and the Activist Community's Response

In December 2016, Fort Worth received national attention after resident Jacqueline Craig called the police to report her White neighbor for choking her son. Instead of being responsive to her complaint, the White responding officer pushed Craig to the ground and arrested her while her two daughters were detained; much of these actions against three Black women were caught on video (Lockhart, 2019; Mitchell et al., 2016). Shortly after Craig was arrested, the executive director of Texas'

ACLU said the city's police officer "ignored basic community policing standards and his own responsibility to de-escalate the confrontation" (Mitchell et al., 2016). The city's Black police chief at the time, Joel Fitzgerald, agreed that excessive force had been used and policing standards ignored, ordering the White officer to be suspended without pay for ten days (Osborne, 2017). Craig and her family also experienced harassment after the incident, including when three White protesters who came to her house with AK-47s (McFarland, 2017).

The arrest sparked criticism of the police chief and prompted several local and federal lawsuits by the Craig family and the police officer (The Editorial Board, 2017). The White neighbor was eventually found guilty of assaulting Craig's son (Fox 4 News, 2018). After Craig's arrest, city leaders learned that residents believed "law enforcement unfairly targets African-Americans" and that officers were not held responsible for misconduct and harassment (Lockhart, 2019). Deborah Peoples, a community activist and head of Tarrant County's Democratic Party, said in 2019 that "I have to believe that many of these folks want to do the right thing, but they come with preconceived notions about what happens in communities of color" (Johnson, 2019).

Fort Worth's Race and Culture Task Force

In response to activism and discussion surrounding Craig's arrest, the Fort Worth City Council invited members of the community to serve on a Task Force on Race and Culture during summer 2017, with these six focus areas: criminal justice, economic development, education, health, housing, and transportation (Baker, 2017; Simon, 2019; Tameez, 2018). One primary function of the task force was listening to the community for suggestions about the city's performance in these six focus areas. Council members specifically wanted this citizen review board to address "systemic, structural, and institutional racism" within these areas (Giving Citizens a Voice, 2021). After meetings with the community over more than a year, the task force presented more than 20 recommendations, with several that focused on civilian oversight of the city's police force and on hiring initiatives to bring more diversity to the police force. Yet most of these recommendations were not enacted until after the killing of Atatiana Jefferson (Lockhart, 2019).

The Killing of Atatiana Jefferson and the City of Fort Worth's Communication Efforts

On October 12, 2019, Atatiana Jefferson was playing video games with her 8-year-old nephew, Zion, when her neighbor called 311 around 2:30 a.m. to request a wellness check at her home because the front doors were open and the lights were on. Two minutes later, two officers from the Fort Worth Police Department arrived at Jefferson's home without announcing themselves. According to Zion, when the two heard noises outside, Jefferson grabbed her legally owned handgun from her purse and peered out the bedroom window to see what was happening outside (Branham & Emily, 2019). Within moments, after police officer Aaron Dean saw Atatiana Jefferson through the window, he shot her after shouting to "put your hands up, show me your hands" (Law, 2019). Minutes later, Jefferson, only 28 years old, was pronounced dead (Howland & Clarridge, 2019). Soon after the tragedy, Dean was fired from FWPD, arrested, and charged with murder. Dean's trial was scheduled to commence in August of 2021 after being delayed by the COVID-19 pandemic (Clarridge, 2020); it has since been delayed again and is scheduled to take place in December of 2022.

On the day of Atatiana Jefferson's death and for several days afterward, the city's communication was disconnected, with the mayor's office, police, and city communicators releasing information and apologies without coordination or strategy. Atatiana's first name was mispronounced in three or four different ways during spoken statements at press conferences and public gatherings. Following is a communication timeline:

- October 12, 2019
  - Atatiana Jefferson is killed in her home by Officer Dean at 2:36 a.m.
  - Later in the day, the police department releases a photo of Jefferson's gun and other evidence via social media.
  - The city issues a written statement about Jefferson's death at 12:20 p.m.
- October 14, 2019 – Mayor Betsy Price issues an open letter to the City of Fort Worth via social media apologizing to Jefferson's family and highlighting the need to rebuild trust with residents (Price, 2019).
- October 15, 2019 – Fort Worth Council Meeting proceeds with a business-as-usual agenda, with no discussion about Jefferson's death until the last 30 minutes.

Leadership in the City of Fort Worth struggled to communicate quickly and cohesively, waiting nearly 10 hours to make a statement after Jefferson was killed. On October 12, the police department released a photo of Jefferson's gun along with other evidence from the scene via social media, which social justice advocates and local residents criticized as an attempt to blame the victim and justify Dean's action. Fort Worth Mayor Betsy Price later lamented the release of the photos, and Police Chief Ed Kraus said the department's decision to release them was ill-advised (Saavedra, 2019).

Mayor Price released an open letter to the Fort Worth community via social media on October 14 and also delivered the contents of the letter at a press conference, apologizing to Jefferson's family (Price, 2019). She stated, "There is nothing to justify or explain what happened on Saturday morning. Nothing." She acknowledged the need to rebuild a sense of trust between Fort Worth residents, the city, and the police department, "action by action."

On October 15, hundreds of residents and protestors attended the first City Council meeting after Jefferson's death to discuss the safety of the Black community in Fort Worth, police accountability, and other issues affecting Jefferson's death (Fernandez et al., 2019). Despite national and local attention to Jefferson's killing, the city council meeting proceeded as usual and discussions about the incident were only permitted during the last 30 minutes of the meeting. This lack of commitment to listening to residents or hearing concerns enraged community members and leaders.

Residents specifically called for better training and policy changes for the Fort Worth Police Department along with a fully independent, community-driven police oversight board. The city would eventually hire Kim Neal as the police monitor and Christina Brooks as the diversity and inclusion director, both Black women with significant experience in previous roles (Connelly, 2020). The city also created a City Manager Mutual Accountability Group composed of "diverse community and police representatives," which began meeting in December 2020 to create a proposed community accountability model (Roberts, 2021).

Interviews: Perceptions among Black Residents

Between March and August of 2020, 25 stakeholders and activists (19 of them Black), who were sensitive to the needs of the Black community in Fort Worth, participated in virtual interviews to share their perspectives on the listening efforts of municipal leadership in the wake of Jefferson's death. Researchers used purposive and snowball selection to identify Fort Worth residents who had knowledge of either the city's efforts related to Atatiana Jefferson's shooting or other issues important to the Black community. These recorded interviews, handled via Zoom using institutional research protocols, lasted between 20 minutes and more than an hour and included people from many different professions and from many age groups.

Researchers analyzed the interviews using data reduction, data display, and conclusion drawing and verification (Miles & Huberman, 1994), as part of this project and a larger study. Researchers analyzed transcripts line-by-line to generate categories based upon the research questions and relationships to the case study for this project. Working together, researchers identified the major patterns and themes suggested by the coding categories, as well as suggested by events identified in the case study. Next researchers reread transcripts to code the material according to the identified categories and to capture representative stories and quotes.

During those interviews, participants shared insights about the city's efforts to rebuild trust with Black residents since Jefferson's killing, what city leadership could do to improve its relationship with Black residents, and how cities can better listen to Black residents. Concerning efforts from the city leadership to build trust, many participants failed to observe meaningful action. One theme was that change fosters trust, which necessitates creating new policies, or enacting policy changes, to authenticate the listening process and build trust. One participant and local pastor stated, "I'm waiting to see what they will do with police reform. I've heard them talk, but I want to know what actions will be taken. You've heard the people, now what are you going to do ... I measure listening by new actions." Without changes such as creating an independent, citizen review board, participants were not sure that trust could be rebuilt. Additionally, participants noted the city seemed to want to build trust without two-way communication, where the emphasis is on sharing information rather than building trust. A few participants did highlight the hiring of a diversity manager and police monitor and taking action on some of the Race and Culture Task Force recommendations as possible actions to build trust. However, not creating an independent civilian review board nor using an internal police monitor employed by the city was seen as silencing the community's voice, since these had been recommended by the Race and Culture Task Force.

When participants were asked how municipal leadership could build trust with Black residents, three themes emerged: (1) learning from past mistakes; (2) strategically improving representation; and (3) emphasizing listening and communicating with more authenticity and empathy.

Learning from past mistakes included acknowledging racist policies and implementing recommendations from previous engagement efforts; according to participants, these suggestions had been ignored. Participants wanted leadership to own and acknowledge the disparate impacts of government policies on communities of color, especially the Black community in Fort Worth. One participant noted, "At some point, they have to step forward and take action on the long history of racial profiling and use of force and mistreatment of people of color in Fort Worth. There's gonna have to be some recognition and atonement."

Participants in this study who were also involved with the Race and Culture Task Force highlighted the importance of city leaders acting on those recommendations and reporting back to the community what changed from that two-year project. One participant specifically emphasized the importance of continued and engaged communication, not simply adding information to a webpage that is hard to find on the city's website. "People who are most affected might not have access to a website. Bring the information to where the people are," the participant said. "Give us updates." Showing accountability, giving regular updates, and taking action on well-vetted ideas could help build trust, based on participant responses.

Another way to improve trust, according to participants, is to work on building relationships with the part of the community most impacted by the problem. A participant well-versed in city data indicated the importance of making data-driving decisions. By focusing on communities with high rates of arrests or signs of over-policing, city leadership can learn more about the experiences of those community members and how to repair relationships. Additionally, participants want different people on boards and commissions who might be more likely to express dissenting perspectives. One said that "there's an attitude that if you disagree with the city you're 'scum.' The city doesn't need to have resentment toward those who disagree with them, but bring them to the table for a broader range of ideas."

Participants frequently noted the tendency of Fort Worth leaders to contact and use Black churches when issues of policing or racial discrimination were focal topics. While churches have historically provided influence and leadership on issues impacting the Black community, some participants did not always trust clerical voices to present a full range of perspectives. "And in communicating with the various pastors they'll find, in my opinion, the avenue of least resistance. You know, where they think they can make the greatest inroads. So, and this is nothing against the, the pastors ... but they'll talk to the pastors because a lot of the pastors typically aren't necessarily going to be fiery outside of the pulpit." Building trust with younger residents in their teens and 20s and engaging more with those who disagree with city leadership are possible avenues for building trust.

Communicating with greater levels of empathy and transparency would build trust. Many participants felt the city did not fully acknowledge the humanity of Black people nor address the fears of being a victim of excessive use of force at the hands of police officers. Many wanted leaders to acknowledge the pain of losing a young life in this manner. One participant stated, "Why can't you cry with me? Why can't we hug each other and say, 'I can't believe this happened. I can't believe it. We're going to make it better for your kids and mine. We're going to work together, and we're going to make it better.' Instead of being so defensive, saying it's isolated, Back the Blue." Part of transparency includes a willingness to admit when mistakes happen. One participant noted, "It's okay to say, 'we're doing this wrong.... Let's talk about how to do it better. Let's take your opinions and try it. If it doesn't work, we'll try something else.' To be flippant about it and almost act like you're sick of hearing about it ... we're sick of living it." Admitting mistakes and reporting on actionable change are trust-building solutions when issues of policing, reform, and accountability. In another study based on different aspects of these interviews, participants said that public input at city council meetings had become an empty ritual, that privileged speakers had more power and were more likely to be given attention, and that many of the city's efforts at listening were simply publicity rather than meaningful dialogue (O'Neil et al., 2022).

Updates from the Case Study

Since the death of Atatiana Jefferson, many things have changed in the City of Fort Worth, including new leadership, renewed calls for justice, and actionable changes to policies. Two of these new leaders are White: Neil Noakes and Mattie Parker. In February of 2021, Noakes became the 27th police chief for the Fort Worth Police Department. He served for 20 years in the force before his appointment, and immediately acknowledged the necessity of police reform and building trust with the community as he took on his new role. In May of 2021, Fort Worth residents elected Mattie Parker to serve as mayor, making her the youngest mayor in Fort Worth history (Woodard, 2021). She had served as chief of staff to Betsy Price, the longest-serving mayor in Fort Worth, who served for ten years in that role. During Parker's June swearing-in, activists chanted Atatiana Jefferson's name and continued calls for justice. Parker thanked the activists for being there and acknowledged the need for unity, but stopped short of specifically referencing Black residents in the community (Woodard, 2021).

The death of George Floyd renewed calls for justice in Atatiana Jefferson's case. Local pastors, community activists, and Jefferson's family called for action to be taken to start the murder trial for former officer, Aaron Dean, whose court date was delayed due to the COVID-19 pandemic. Jefferson's sister, Ashley Carr, filed a wrongful death lawsuit against the City of Fort Worth in May of 2021 that alleged the city "failed to properly train, supervise, screen, discipline, transfer, counsel or otherwise properly equip and control officers including those who are known, or who should have been known, to engage in the use of excessive force and/or deadly force" (Hassan, 2021). Meanwhile, Dean has been out on bond since October 2019, and his trial has been delayed until summer 2022.

While Dean's murder trial stalls, the City of Fort Worth did make changes to hire more diverse officers and develop mechanisms for police oversight. The new Diversity and Inclusion Department, under the leadership of Chief Equity Officer and Director Christina Brooks, is actively working to close racial and gender gaps in contracting and procurement processes and presenting diversity-related learning opportunities for city employees and the community. In March 2020, the city also created the Office of the Police Oversight Monitor, under the leadership of Kim Neal.

The purpose of the office is to be a "proactive leader in law enforcement accountability to the Fort Worth Police Department and the population it serves" to ensure greater accountability and build public trust (Office of the Police Oversight Monitor, 2022). The department conducted perception surveys with both the community and active police officers to understand how each group perceives accountability and the state of the relationship between the community and FWPD.

Discussion and Recommendations for Practice

In examining the communication efforts of the City of Fort Worth after the death of Atatiana Jefferson at the hands of an FWPD officer, there are several implications for listening and trust-building efforts. In this section, we examine (1) missed opportunities for trust-building from the case study; (2) organizational listening efforts to mitigate negative outcomes connected to a racist past; and (3) specific opportunities to bolster OPRs between local government and Black residents.

Analysis of the city's communication efforts reveal missed opportunities from a process and policy standpoint to learn from the Race and Culture Task Force's deliberations and recommendations, after the group was commissioned by the Fort Worth City Council. Procedurally, some participants noted the facilitation of community conversations as being restrictive for participants of color. Community members were encouraged to "calm down" or lower their voices when engaging in listening sessions. These sentiments foreshadowed a visceral reaction during council meetings after Jefferson's killing, when protesters were arrested or escorted out of council chambers because of perceptions of aggression. Assuming a more aggressive nature among Black people is a known cultural stereotype that the city could mitigate by thoughtfully discussing the processes and policies for listening during community engagement discussions. Penalizing different forms of communication can breed distrust in Black residents because that practice is aligned with structural racism. Favoring standards of professionalism that favor Whites is indicative of "preferential treatment, privilege and power for White people at the expense of Black, Latino, Asian, Pacific Islander, Native American, Arab and other racially oppressed people" (Lawrence & Keleher, 2004). Additionally, the city council could have decided to suspend the intended agenda to allow time for residents to voice their concerns after Jefferson's killing. Or, council leaders could have set a time for community listening at the beginning of the council meeting to acknowledge the right of Fort Worth residents to speak after such a tragic event. Proceeding with the agenda as scheduled without modifications dehumanized the voices of the community. Other strategies for building capacity for better quality listening and more community input instead of formal council meetings or town halls are contained in Table 8.1.

Table 8.1 Six ideas for better listening by cities and for more quality input from residents

Curtail dependence on these activities	Add more of these listening activities
1 Traditional town-hall meetings	Trained listeners in breakout rooms
2 Heeding the voices of the loudest or most powerful residents and businesses	Scientific surveying of residents for representative input
3 Celebrations and state-of-the-city events for elites	Meetings with residents at their own special neighborhood events
4 One-way digital messaging in sometimes toxic spaces online	Face-to-face discussions and boots on the ground in underrepresented neighborhoods
5 Communicators pushing out content	Communicators as listeners-in-chief
6 One three-minute comment at a council meeting	Shorter but multiple structured inputs in special listening sessions with leaders

Source: Lambiase et al. (2021).

Organizational listening – which focuses on developing a culture of listening, attempts to hear from a broader cross-section of stakeholders, creates policies and structures for listening, and articulates listening efforts back to policy and decision-makers – can mitigate negative outcomes of a racist past. By engaging in organizational listening, municipal leadership can shift power back from the organization to minoritized publics. In this case, if the city council had chosen to add time to or to establish a separate listening meeting, rather than proceeding with the usual council meeting protocols, leadership would have better engaged those in attendance. By having a trained facilitator to lead listening efforts, designating a scribe to document the concerns of speakers, and predetermining a time to close the listening loop by reporting what people communicated back to policy and decision-makers (e.g., city council, mayor, city manager, chief of police), the voices of residents could become the powerful voices.

The City of Fort Worth could disrupt the politics of listening by giving close attention to who is speaking and creating avenues for participants to engage in a variety of formats (e.g., in-person, virtually, comment forms, video notes, etc.), thereby increasing the representation of diverse voices and perspectives. It would have been helpful to create listening events in partnership with Black organizations, businesses, or churches, to hear from the Black community in spaces that engender trust. Hearing specifically from Black stakeholders in spaces they are comfortable communicating would intentionally disrupt power imbalances that favor White stakeholders. Because structural racism routinely advantages Whites to the detriment of racially oppressed people, organizational listening becomes a tool to mitigate that advantage to welcome other voices.

Organizational listening is one method of increasing trust between Black stakeholders and municipal governments. Rather than highlight all of the possibilities when organizational listening happens, the city of Fort Worth case study provides instructive insight as to what happens when there is a failure to listen before, during, and after a crisis happens. Acknowledging the racist past of local governments and acting on known issues might have prevented the killing of Atatiana Jefferson by a police officer. To increase trust with minoritized communities, city leadership must shift the balance of power and disrupt processes to gain insight into innovation and change. They must add more and different opportunities for community input, some led or hosted by underrepresented and minoritized communities that have had the least power in the past. Finally, one of the best ways to build trust is to close the listening loop and articulate what organizations have heard and what will change because of the voice of the speaker.

References

Adler, R., & Rodman, G. (2011). *Understanding communication* (11th ed.). Oxford University.

Baker, S. (2017, July 25). Group chosen to fix "cruel reality" of race. *Fort Worth Star-Telegram*. https://www.star-telegram.com/news/local/fort-worth/article163638003.html

Bowen, S. A., Hung-Baesecke, C. F., & Chen, Y. R. (2016). Ethics as a precursor to organization–public relationships: Building trust before and during the OPR model. *Cogent Social Sciences, 2*(1), 1–19. https://doi.org/10.1080/23311886.2016.1141467

Branham, D., & Emily, J. (2019, October 15). Atatiana Jefferson pointed gun at window before Fort Worth officer killed her, nephew told authorities. Dallas Morning News. https://www.dallasnews.com/news/crime/2019/10/15/atatiana-jefferson-pointed-gun-out-windowbefore-fort-worth-officer-killed-her-nephew-told-authorities/?icid=ref_fark/

Brucato, B. (2020). Policing race and racing police: The origin of U.S. police in slave patrols. *Social Justice, 47*(3/4), 115–136.

Bussie, J. (2011). Reconciled diversity: Reflections on our calling to embrace our religious neighbors. *Intersections, 33*, 30–35.

Connelly, C. (2019, December 11). Why Fort Worth and other big cities struggle with police diversity. *KERA News*. https://www.keranews.org/texas-news/2019-12-11/why-fort-worth-and-other-big-cities-struggle-with-police-diversity

Connelly, C. (2020, Jan. 10). Fort Worth Names First Policy Monitor. https://www.keranews.org/news/2020-01-10/fort-worth-names-first-police-monitor

Clarridge, E. (2020, Oct. 12). Atatiana Jefferson's family waits for justice 1 year after Fort Worth police shooting. https://account.star-telegram.com/paywall/subscriber-only?resume=246294130&intcid=ab_archive

DataUSA. (2022). Fort Worth, Texas. *DataUSA*. https://datausa.io/profile/geo/fort-worth-tx/

Fernandez, M., Mervosh, S., & Bogel-Burroughs, N. (2019, October 20). Fort Worth police have more violence to answer for, residents say. *The New York*

Times. https://www.nytimes.com/2019/10/20/us/fort-worth-shooting-jefferson-dean.html

Fox 4 News. (2018, January 31). Neighbor who assaulted Jacqueline Craig's son found guilty. *Fox 4 News KDFW.* https://www.fox4news.com/news/neighbor-who-assaulted-jacqueline-craigs-son-found-guilty

Fritsch, E. J., & Trulson, C. R. (2016). Fort Worth Police Department 2016 racial profiling analysis. *Professional Development Institute: University of North Texas.* https://police.fortworthtexas.gov/UI/Repository/Documents/2018/92658542/Full%20Final%20Racial%20Profiling%20Report%20Fort%20Worth%20PD%202016.pdf

Giving Citizens a Voice. (2021, May 24). Giving Citizens a Voice, *Fort Worth Weekly.* https://www.fwweekly.com/2021/03/24/giving-citizens-a-voice/

Hassan, C. (2021, May 22). The sister of a woman killed by a police officer who fired into her Texas home files a wrongful death lawsuit. *CNN.* https://www.cnn.com/2021/05/22/us/atatiana-jefferson-wrongful-death-lawsuit/index.html

Hon, L., & Grunig, J. (1999). Guidelines for measuring relationships in public relations. Institute for Public Relations. https://www.instituteforpr.org/wp-content/uploads/Guidelines_Measuring_Relationships.pdf

Howland, J., & Clarridge, E. (2019). October 12). Woman killed in own home when Fort Worth officer shoots her, police and witness say. Fort Worth Star-Telegram. https://www.startelegram.com/news/local/fort-worth/article236067328.html

Johnson, K. (2019, November 14). Do Fort Worth police shoot, kill at a disproportionate rate? Here's what the data says. *Fort Worth Star-Telegram.* https://www.star-telegram.com/news/local/crime/article236822538.html

Lambiase, J., Lyons, K., & English, A. E. (2021, March 1–5). Community input [Conference presentation]. Govapalooza annual conference. (Virtual). https://www.baldrigeinstitute.org/events/event-description?CalendarEventKey=67c5c275-9313-402f-b94e-046b308c3f7d&Home=%2Fevents%2Fcalendar

Law, T. (2019, October 15). Fort Worth officer who killed Atatiana Jefferson charged with murder: Here's what to know about the police shooting. *Time Magazine.* https://time.com/5699843/fort-worth-shooting-atatiana-jefferson/

Lawrence, K., & Keleher, T. (2004). *Structural racism – Chronic Disparity: Strong and pervasive evidence of racial inequalities poverty outcomes* [Conference presentation]. Race and Public Policy Conference. https://www.intergroupresources.com/rc/Definitions%20of%20Racism.pdf

Lockhart, P. R. (2019, October 16). Fort Worth police had problems way before the Atatiana Jefferson shooting. *Vox.* https://www.vox.com/identities/2019/10/16/20916101/fort-worth-police-department-atatiana-jefferson-shooting-history

Lopez, R. (Reporter). (2019, October 15). "I'm devastated," says neighbor who called police before Atatiana Jefferson was shot, killed [Video file]. *WFAA-Channel 8.* Retrieved from https://www.youtube.com/watch?v=1FqVYOAOIgE

Macnamara, J. (2016). *Organizational listening: The missing essential in public communication.* Peter Lang.

Macnamara, J. (2019). Explicating listening in organization-public communication: Theories, practices, and technologies. *International Journal of Communication, 13,* 5183–5204.

McFarland, S. (2017, January 22). Fort Worth police detain armed men outside home of Jacqueline Craig. *Fort Worth Star-Telegram (TX)*. NewsBank: Access World News – Historical and Current: https://infoweb.newsbank.com/apps/news/document-view?p=WORLDNEWS&docref=news/16214C926BCF06E0

Miles, M. B., & Huberman, A. M. (1994). *Qualitative data analysis: An expanded sourcebook* (2nd ed.). Sage.

Mitchell, M., Branson, A., Boyd, D., & Osborne, R. (2016, December 22). In Fort Worth police incident that went viral, "racism is still all over it." *Fort Worth Star-Telegram*. NewsBank: Access World News – Historical and Current: https://infoweb.newsbank.com/apps/news/document-view?p=WORLDNEWS&docref=news/1617242FE61E2DC0

O'Neil, J., English, A. E., & Lambiase, J. (2022). After the killing of Atatiana Jefferson: Black stakeholder experiences within a municipal listening structure. *Journalism and Mass Communication Quarterly*, *99*(3) 802–825.

Office of the Police Oversight Monitor. (2022). City of Fort Worth. Retrieved from https://www.fortworthtexas.gov/departments/opom#:~:text=Kim%20Neal%2C%20was%20appointed%20as,and%20the%20population%20it%20serves

Osborne, R. (2017, January 9). Officer in viral video suspended 10 days for "multiple errors of judgment." *Fort Worth Star-Telegram*. NewsBank: Access World News – Historical and Current: https://infoweb.newsbank.com/apps/news/document-view?p=WORLDNEWS&docref=news/161CF7440E0854B8

Pew Research Center. (2020). Majority of public favors giving civilians the power to sue police officers for misconduct. https://www.pewresearch.org/politics/2020/07/09/majority-of-public-favors-giving-civilians-the-power-to-sue-police-officers-for-misconduct/

Place, K. R. (2019). Listening as the driver of public relations practice and communications strategy within a global public relations agency. *Public Relations Journal*, *12*(3), 1–18.

Platt, T. (1982). Crime and punishment in the United States: Immediate and long-term reforms from a Marxist perspective. *Crime and Social Justice*, 18, 38–45. http://www.jstor.org/stable/29766165

Price, B. [@betsypriceftw]. (2019, October 14). *My open letter to the community. -Mayor Betsy* [Tweet]. Twitter. https://mobile.twitter.com/BetsyPriceftw/status/1183811468409671682?lang=fr

Rainie, L., & Perrin, A. (2019, July 22). Key findings about Americans' declining trust in government and each other. *Pew Research Center*. https://www.pewresearch.org/fact-tank/2019/07/22/key-findings-about-americans-declining-trust-in-government-and-each-other/

Roberts, K. (2021, May 17). Fort Worth Police Oversight Monitor Focuses on Community Outreach During First Year. https://thetexan.news/fort-worth-police-oversight-monitor-focuses-on-community-outreach-during-first-year/

Saavedra, M. (2019, October 13). Fort Worth Police Officers Association responds to fatal shooting of Atatiana Jefferson. WFAA News. https://www.wfaa.com/article/news/local/fort-worth-police-officers-association-responds-to-fatal-shooting-of-atatianajefferson/287-5043b50f-8b6a-4000-9637-fff6e3690f5d

Simon, D. (2019, October 15). Before a Fort Worth police officer shot Atatiana Jefferson in her home, relations with the community were already tense. *CNN News*. https://www.cnn.com/2019/10/15/us/fort-worth-police-department/index.html

Tameez, H. (2018, August 20). Race, culture task force has exposed racial inequities. Here's how they plan to fix them. *Fort Worth Star-Telegram* (TX). NewsBank: Access World News – Historical and Current: https://infoweb.newsbank.com/apps/news/document-view?p=WORLDNEWS&docref=news/16DF06C16C08D3C0

The Editorial Board. (2017, January 17). Officer's choice: Lighter discipline, even promotion. *Fort Worth Star-Telegram (TX)*. NewsBank: Access World News – Historical and Current: https://infoweb.newsbank.com/apps/news/document-view?p=WORLDNEWS&docref=news/161FAF3EC2EA6A08

Trust in Government. (2020). Gallup Poll. https://news.gallup.com/poll/5392/trust-government.aspx

Waymer, D. (2013). Democracy and government public relations: Expanding the scope of "Relationship" in public relations research. *Public Relations Review*, *39*(4), 320–331. https://doi.org/10.1016/j.pubrev.2013.07.015

Woodard, T. (2021, June 15). "It's go-time in Fort Worth": Mattie Parker sworn in as youngest mayor of any major US city. WFAA. https://www.wfaa.com/article/news/local/fort-worth-mattie-parker-sworn-in-as-youngest-mayor-of-any-major-us-city/287-695309fe-de85-4077-97bf-974fbaf3bdb5

9 Organizational Social Listening and Corporate Climate Advocacy
Amazon and Amazon Employees for Climate Justice

Ioana A. Coman and Rosalynn Vasquez

Introduction

In today's highly political and polarized society, more and more companies are taking a stand on controversial issues ranging from gun control to same-sex marriage to immigration, and oftentimes doing so whether the social issue aligns with their corporate mission or not. For Amazon, one of the largest global tech companies and leading online retailers, taking a stand on climate change is an unprecedented step for a company with a historically large carbon footprint. However, in recent years corporations have become primary targets for bold climate change leadership, especially due to their enormous carbon footprints and access to resources and capital. As the climate crisis continues to weigh heavily on the minds of civilians and nation leaders, companies are also taking notice and becoming agents of change. This study contributes to the growing phenomenon known as corporate climate change communication (Vasquez, 2022) by examining how a global corporation, such as Amazon, communicates about climate change and engages with one of its primary stakeholders—its employees. In this chapter, we explore what happens when a company's stakeholders (e.g., employees) are calling for authentic climate change leadership and yet the company does not seem to listen, and what are the ramifications for lack of social listening and authentic engagement in times of abounding social change.

Corporate Social Advocacy, Climate Change, and Corporate Climate Advocacy

Many companies adopt corporate social responsibility (CSR) issues in an effort to be more socially responsible (Coombs & Holladay, 2012). This includes supporting causes in the realms of accessibility, protection of human and civil rights, and particularly, protection and maintenance of the environment. CSR is not a new phenomenon, as it has long been regarded as a key public relations tool for creating mutually beneficial relationships with various stakeholders (Grunig 1994). In fact, CSR has been viewed as a company's voluntary actions to pursue its mission and fulfill its societal obligations to various stakeholders (Coombs & Holladay, 2012). However, in light of social changes over time, the CSR actions started to seem insufficient, and corporate social advocacy or even activism emerged. As previous studies have shown, corporate social advocacy occurs when a company takes a public stance on a polarized, political, or controversial issue, whether the issue aligns with the brand or not (Dodd & Supa, 2014). Recent studies have shown that as audiences expectations are changing, companies are expected to take a stance on often controversial issues perceived as major social issues (Coman et al., 2022; Maicon, 2020).

Since climate change is heavily perceived as a politically polarizing issue in the US (Dunlap & McCright, 2008) it provides a new and relevant context for this study to examine corporate climate advocacy. Human-caused climate change is one of the most pressing concerns in our society (Allen & Craig, 2016), and has increasingly become a politically polarized issue in the public sphere (Pew Research Center, 2020). However, as the climate crisis continues to disrupt the public's overall livelihoods concerning business, health, economy, and security, there is a growing urgency to communicate the scientific information accurately and seek solutions. Over the last several years, the climate crisis has gained momentum with several influential global efforts (e.g., Pope Francis' Encyclical in 2015, the People's Climate March in 2017, the Paris Climate Agreement in 2017, Greta Thunberg's Fridays for Future youth climate strikes in 2018) and gained increased significance in 2020 with the COVID-19 outbreak and ongoing effects (Vasquez, 2022). As societal issues evolve, people are increasingly turning to corporations, expecting them to step up and take a stand on major social issues (Barometer, 2022; Gaither et al., 2018). With its increasing importance around the globe and heightened scrutiny from internal and external stakeholders, the climate crisis presents both a timely and relevant context through which to examine a company's climate advocacy efforts.

Organizational Listening, Dialogical Communication, and Social Media

Social media is increasingly seen as a credible source of information that is more trustworthy than traditional forms of communication (Foux, 2006). The changing digital landscape enables social media as a unique tool for engaging audiences in relationship-building, including the capability to respond directly to and interact with the public (Saffer et al., 2013). On social media platforms, the public can express support for or disapproval of messages, and these expressions become visible through information cues (e.g., number of likes, shares, or comments). As a powerful and evolving online platform for companies, social media presents an invaluable opportunity for companies to practice listening, an important but underutilized practice (Place, 2019; 2022), and to further engage stakeholders (both internal and external) with messages concerning an important social issue. In fact, with the continued evolution and influence of social media, the public is becoming more aware and concerned about social issues, and how companies are behaving and engaging in a real-time and authentic dialogue with brands.

Among the multiple theoretical models in public relations, excellence theory (Grunig & Hunt, 1984), with its subsequent developments until the final synthesis (Grunig et al., 2006) proved to be one of the most enduring and often used in research and reflection in this domain. The two-way symmetric communication model is viewed as the most ethical method for practicing PR and balancing the needs of an organization and its stakeholders (Macnamara, 2016a). Additionally, this model emphasizes the fact that communication takes place in two directions (public–organization; organization–public), with a special emphasis on public reactions—not to identify how these reactions can be changed, but to change the behavior of the organization. This model is based on mutual understanding and leads to the resolution of possible conflicts through communication. Obviously, this involves listening to the various voices from the various publics of an organization, as an essential element of creating and maintaining reputation. On the other hand, by emphasizing the role of feedback from the public, this model empowers internal and external stakeholders to become an essential factor in the decision-making process.

International Listening Association (ILA) proposed a definition of organizational listening as "the process of receiving, constructing meaning from, and responding to spoken and/or nonverbal messages" (ILA, 1995, in Macnamara, 2016b, p. 151). Further, organizational listening is characterized by four distinct notes: (a) it is delegated to some organizational functions (from customer relations to social media monitoring); (b) it is mediated, the weight of interpersonal relationships being insignificant compared to the messages received through the mass media and/or social media; (c) it is asynchronous: it rarely happens in real time and dynamically, most often the messages are analyzed after their reception; (d) it involves a problem of scale, because some organizations have to listen to less numerous audiences, while corporations and governments have to listen to hundreds of thousands, even millions of peoples (Macnamara, 2018, p. 3). Organizational listening can also be oriented toward external or internal audiences (employees)—in this situation, one can distinguish between organization-wide listening, usually initiated by communication department and supervisory listening, initiated by leaders placed at different levels (Qin & Men, 2021, p. 366). Adapting the definitions and models from the field to the topic of corporate communication, Borner and Zerfass (2018, p. 13) consider that corporate listening "is a strategic mode that represents the inbound dimension of corporate communications" in which "articulated impulses from stakeholders as well as relevant context variables are intentionally and selectively perceived, interpreted and evaluated in order to support corporate decision-making." From this point of view, it would be expected that, after the launch of the AECJ's actions online and offline, Amazon would follow "articulated impulses" from one of its most important stakeholders—the employees.

Dialogue is heavily valued in public relations theories, because it is considered one of the most ethical forms of communication (Taylor & Kent, 2014), because it involves participants exchanging ideas and decision-making. The idea of dialogue is involved in the public relations definitions that speak either of relationships, symmetrical communication, mutual understanding, or of negotiation and compromise (Pieczka, 2011). Dialogue refers to "any negotiated exchange of ideas and opinions" (Kent & Taylor, 2002) and represents efforts by parties in a relationship to engage in an honest, open, and ethically based give and take (Bortree & Seltzer, 2009; Broom, 2009). Starting from here, a dialogic organization communication strategy can be built, which includes a number of measures to create a communicative environment based on respect and responsibility. In other words, simply responding to some questions or critical remarks of stakeholders is not evidence of a culture of dialogue, nor of a dialogical public relations strategy (Johnston, 2014; Taylor & Kent, 2014).

Social media has a special place when it comes to organizational communication and listening due to its "potential to facilitate two-way communication and dialogue" (Macnamara, 2016a, p. 161). Traditionally, the ability of social media to facilitate two-way communication is continuously underutilized by organizations (Hallahan, 2000; Taylor & Kent, 2014). As the public's interest and investment in organizations are increasing, so are the expectations for transparent communications becoming more important and necessary to build trust and long-term viability. Many organizations have adopted efforts to be more socially responsible. In fact, in recent years, there has been an increase in environmental awareness and activism that focus on the maintenance and protection of the environment. With the public's environmental consciousness growing, more people and organizations are stepping forward and using various communication strategies, such as social media, to expand their reach.

Indeed, the increase of social and political activism has been further amplified on social media, giving voice to a variety of stakeholders who expect organizations to uphold their values and take a stand on social issues (Wilcox, 2019). Thus, socially responsible companies are increasingly expected to communicate well with their stakeholders and create opportunities for deliberation and change, a responsibility that rests with public relations professionals (Wilcox, 2019). This is in line with dialogic communication principles that espouse the importance of dialogic communication between the company and its stakeholders. However, in Amazon's case, there appeared to be a disconnect with the employee activist group, which goes against dialogic communication and does not support the goal behind organizational listening. "Just saying we're listening is not enough. Listening requires a range of actions and interactions" (Macnamara, 2016a, p. 48).

The Context: Amazon and Amazon Employees for Climate Justice

The Amazon Employees for Climate Justice (AECJ) employee activist group was formed in 2019 by two former Amazon employees, Maren Costa and Emily Cunningham (Savransky, 2020). Both had worked at Amazon for a number of years as user experience designers and began to get involved in the climate crisis debate upon seeing no action or leadership from Amazon. For Costa, the issue was too important and worth the risk. As a mother of two, she had worked at Amazon for 15 years and wanted to "help the company become a leader on the issue" (Savransky, 2020). Members of the AECJ group developed a climate change proposal to share with the Amazon leadership team, but the company asked them to withdraw it. Refusing to be silenced, Costa spoke to the media about the climate change proposal and was threatened with termination for violating Amazon's external communication policies (Savransky, 2020).

On September 19, 2019, CEO Jeff Bezos announced Amazon's first official pledge to fight climate change and become carbon neutral by 2040 (Thorbecke, 2019). While this was certainly a win for employees representing the AECJ, the timing of this corporate announcement was conspicuously perceived to be more reactive than proactive and lacking authentic climate leadership. The next day (as previously planned), 3,000 Amazon employees walked out of company headquarters in support of the Global Climate Strike, as a sign of protest for the company's lack of real climate change leadership (Garcia, 2019). This organized protest was a planned, bottom-up, grassroots effort that began inside the company to demand companywide policy changes (e.g., reduce carbon footprint, cancel fossil fuel company contracts, end lobbying for climate change deniers) (Ghaffary, 2019) and placed Amazon in the accountability spotlight. This was not the first time that company employees took a stand on climate change and received inadequate responses. During the company's annual shareholder's meeting in May 2019, employees vocalized their concerns for the company's lack of climate action and metrics (Garcia, 2019). And in January 2020, several Amazon employees revealed that their jobs had been threatened because of their climate change activism efforts (Thorbecke, 2019), creating more friction (than fusion) between the company and its number one brand ambassadors. Despite these organized protests aimed to contradict Amazon's desire to be perceived as a climate change leader and question the company's organizational listening, Amazon launched The Climate Pledge. As Jeff Bezos stated in the corporate press release (appearing in the company's press center) on Sept. 19, 2019, The Climate

Pledge was the company's first highly visible commitment to become a climate leader by calling on signatories to be net zero by 2040.

> "We're done being in the middle of the herd on this issue—we've decided to use our size and scale to make a difference. If a company with as much physical infrastructure as Amazon—which delivers more than 10 billion items a year—can meet the Paris Agreement 10 years early, then any company can. I've been talking with other CEOs of global companies, and I'm finding a lot of interest in joining the pledge. Large companies signing The Climate Pledge will send an important signal to the market that it's time to invest in the products and services the signatories will need to meet their commitments."
>
> (Amazon, 2019)

As part of its communication efforts, Amazon launched its sustainability website to report progress, metrics, and ongoing performance of the company's Climate Pledge. Meanwhile, AECJ took to social media to create its communication platforms to not only openly criticize Amazon's lack of climate change action and leadership but also to galvanize others into collective action. The employees who had organized the company walkout on Sept. 20, 2019 had circulated an internal email weeks in advance to invite and encourage more employees to join the climate change fight. The employees stated: "We need bold, immediate climate action. As a large, global company, we must demonstrate real climate leadership" (Ghaffary, 2019).

Consequently, this chapter examines both organizations' climate change communication and engagement with their respective commenters.

Approach

This chapter focused on Amazon and AECJ and their respective climate change communication efforts as visible on their Facebook communications. Using a qualitative content analysis approach (Creswell & Poth, 2018), this study examined both Amazon's and AECJ's Facebook posts and related forms of engagement, including reactions, comments, and replies, from September 2019 to September 2020. This timeframe allowed for a longer examination into the way Amazon and AECJ have been using Facebook to engage in climate change advocacy and engage with the public. Facebook was chosen as the primary social media platform because both organizations used it for their communication, and it allows for longer and richer engagement. A total of 10 posts and 11.509 comments for Amazon, and 4 posts and 208 comments for AECJ were collected. We then analyzed the engagement variables by aggregating the Facebook "reactions" (i.e., likes, love, anger), reposts, and number of comments for each post by each organization (see Tables 9.1 and 9.2). Additionally, topic and engagement were broken down (Figures 9.1 and 9.2). Further,

Table 9.1 Amazon's climate-related posts, included hashtags, links, replies, shares, reactions, and reactions breakdown

Date	Topic of post	Hashtag in post frequency	Link frequency	Reply (comments) frequency	Shares frequency	Reaction frequency	Likes frequency	Loveheart frequency	Sad frequency	Anger frequency	Laugh frequency	Care frequency	Wow frequency
September 19, 2019	Announce commitment Climate Pledge	1	1	1600	333	2400	1600	263	6	44	473	0	23
January 22, 2020	Fully electric delivery vehicles Jeff driver joke	1	0	1100	332	2200	1700	149	0	13	204	0	72
April 22, 2020	Protecting people and planet—Climate Pledge plans and actions	2	1	916	47	949	828	65	1	20	28	3	4
May 21, 2020	Actions/changes—wind projects in Texas to solar projects in Shandong	0	1	952	78	781	684	55	1	17	18	4	2
June 26, 2020	Climate Pledge commitment carbon blog promotion	1	1	1700	283	2000	1500	188	4	44	194	22	14
June 26, 2020	Feel good story climate pledge arena	1	1	1900	519	4100	3000	414	10	19	504	29	122
August 24, 2020	Feel good story highlighting employee	0	1	1100	188	1300	1200	140	1	12	11	20	10
August 31, 2020	Feel good story highlighting employee	0	1	560	88	662	553	49	1	7	33	13	6
September 24, 2020	Climate Pledge friendly new program for customers	0	1	982	129	1000	915	73	1	17	4	6	8
October 8, 2020	First custom electric delivery vehicle	1	1	659	178	946	800	101	1	7	10	8	19

Table 9.2 AECJ's posts, included hashtags, links, replies, shares, reactions, and reactions breakdown

Date	Topic of post	Reply (comments) frequency	Shares frequency	Reaction frequency	Likes frequency	Love/Heart frequency	Sad frequency	Anger frequency	Laugh frequency	Care frequency	Wow frequency
April 23, 2020	Criticizing Amazon for firing employees and trying to stop AECJ to protest/host panels	1	8	9	7	1	0	0	1	0	0
April 24, 2020	Live panel with fired employees and about walkout	70	60	62	38	23	0	1	0	0	0
April 24, 2020	Part II of the live	124	48	55	36	18	0	0	1	0	0
May 26, 2020	Criticizing Amazon for environmental racism and climate issues	13	15	12	9	0	0	1	2	0	0

Organizational Social Listening and Corporate Climate Advocacy 165

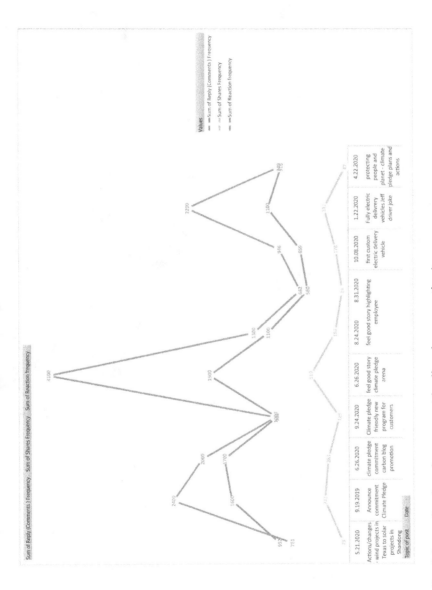

Figure 9.1 Breakdown of topic and engagement (replies, shares, reactions)

166 *Ioana A. Coman and Rosalynn Vasquez*

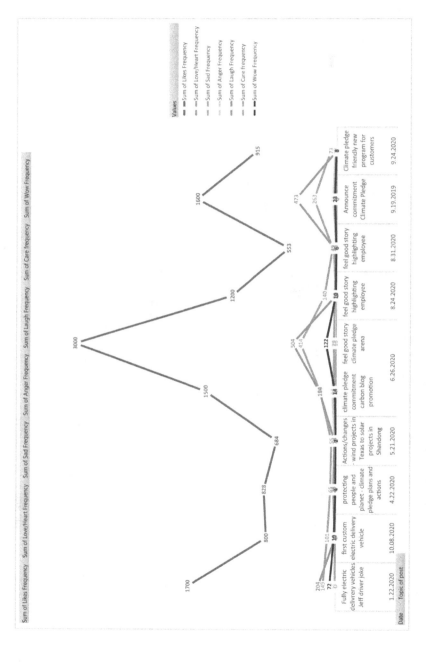

Figure 9.2 Breakdown of topic and different reactions

we analyzed through an inductive and iterative process, following a qualitative data analysis methodology (Creswell & Poth, 2018). The listening, dialogical, and CSA literature served as theoretical lenses, but no a priori coding sheets were used, to allow for the emergence of findings from the data. Data were read and re-read multiple times, each time pinpointing and refining codes, comparing and contrasting, and eventually leading to themes. This process was followed until redundancy and clarity were reached. Quotes that best exemplified these themes were chosen and everything was further classified, making sure that rigor and credibility of the data were indeed achieved.

Key Findings

Our main goal for this chapter was to examine how Amazon and AECJ's communicated with their publics on Facebook about climate change advocacy, and if/how Amazon responded to AECJ's calls for climate change advocacy. We explored both organizations' social media posts and comments on Facebook. Our analysis revealed five main themes across both companies' posts and publics' comments: Amazon positioning itself as a hero/leader; climate change takes back seat to customer service and other issues among Amazon's posts commenters; AECJ paints Amazon as villain; supporting climate justice among AECJ's posts commenters; Amazon-AECJ lack of engagement. In the following sections, we present all these key findings, we discuss them in the context of our theoretical lenses, and we conclude with recommendations for the public relations practice.

Positioning Amazon as a Hero/Leader

Over the analyzed year, Amazon kept its communication about climate change to the minimum (ten posts total within our timeline). However, the company did increase volume compared to the previous year (see Table 9.1).

Certain topics attracted more engagement and different types of reactions, such as liking, or loving a post (see Figures 9.1 and 9.2). For example, feel-good type stories about Amazon's climate pledge-specific outcomes (such as a climate-friendly arena) garnered more replies, shares, and positive reactions (see Figures 9.1 and 9.2).

Amazon's original posts mainly focused on the positive changes the company has made (or is making) to combat climate change, especially in light of announcing its first Climate Pledge. For example, the first post from September 19, 2019 simply stated: *Today we announced our commitment to meet the Paris Agreement 10 years early. Find out what that means: sustainability.aboutamazon.com#ClimatePledge* (Amazon post, September 19, 2019). Most of the company's posts were brief, generally included a link to view more information, and emphasized the company's current or future actions or plans. The following two examples illustrate: (a) *From wind projects in Texas to solar projects in Shandong, we're making big changes to reduce carbon emissions. See our latest projects: https://amzn.to/2ZnJpwi* (Amazon post, May 21, 2020); and (b) *Amazon today announced Climate Pledge Friendly, a new program to help make it easy for customers to discover and shop for more sustainable products. http://amazon.com/climatepledgefriendly?utm_source=social...* (Amazon post, September 24, 2020).

Some of the posts were more personal and story focused. They emphasized how Amazon is committed and caring. They self-portrayed the company as a hero and a leader, through personal stories about existing (and future) efforts and policies. For example, one post paints Amazon as a protected and innovator: *Protecting our people. Protecting our planet. We're committed to both. From renewable energy to reinventing packaging, we're pushing forward on the goals of The Climate Pledge. See how we'll get to carbon neutral by 2040: sustainability.aboutamazon.com #climatepledge #EarthDay50* (Amazon post, April 22, 2020). Another post's narrative focuses on a specific outcome: *Imagine a sports arena where hockey players skate on ice from reclaimed rainwater. Where solar panels generate power. Where most of the food is sourced locally. It's becoming a reality. Here's a first look at the Climate Pledge Arena, a green sports and events venue from Amazon, Oak View Group, & NHL Seattle that will be home to Seattle's new NHL franchise – setting a new sustainability bar for sports and events. #ClimatePledge https://amzn.to/37YbUmK* (Amazon post, June 26, 2020).

Along the same lines, a few stories also focused on showcasing employees involved in the Amazon climate efforts in various capacities, and their personal stories or purpose. Most highlighted the legacy Amazon will have for the employees' children and future generations. For example, on post states: *Hector doesn't just like to run outside, he lives for it. He wants his daughters to grow up seeing the same beauty in nature, so he's helping Amazon roll out a new electric fleet as a Delivery Operations Manager. See Hector's story: https://amzn.to/3hizSg9* (Amazon post, August 24, 2020). And another post emphasizes yet another employee's efforts: *A love of both nature and complex problems led Joe to a career in sustainability. He wants to leave a lasting impact for his son, which is why he's helping Amazon reduce its carbon footprint as a Sustainability Science Researcher. See Joe's story: https://amzn.to/2EwLzlm* (Amazon post, August 31, 2020).

Climate Change Takes Back Seat to Customer Service and Other Issues

Amazon's posts included high public interaction in the form of comments. However, the nature of the comments was focused primarily on specific customer service issues rather than about the posts' content or in response to its climate change efforts. Comments directly related to Amazon (or its efforts) were both positive and negative. For example, some commenters applaud Amazon's efforts while acknowledging no company can be fully climate neutral:

> Amazon hasn't been the cheapest option for almost a decade now. Now that pretty much every single organization out there has figured out how Amazon has done it, they are now copying that method. Take Chewy for example. Doing pretty much what Amazon is doing but for Pet food. Yet you can get the same stuff on Amazon as Chewy, but I find that the prices to be about the same. Amazon isn't some miracle machine churning out the products, they still get them from the same places everyone else does. The only difference is that they are at least attempting to reduce their impact on the planet, which is exactly what needs to happen. Instead of Nations flying their nations so called climate specialists on expensive private jets that pour a ton of CO_2 into the air, corporations should be leading the way. At least on paper, Amazon seems to grasp that.

Those who criticize Amazon, do so on climate and business choices: *"So China is the BIGGEST World contribute to Global Climate Damage, and it is the 95% supplier to Amazon sold products!"* Some go beyond climate, into other employee issues:

> Which seems to include starvation wages for your employees, ensuring that they cannot afford to be a part of the climate solution easily, and getting rid of health care for part-time Whole Foods employees so they can't afford to get the medical help they need until things get bad (also bad for climate issues). Great job there Bezos. No one would suspect the world's richest person of being a miserly narcissist. You should change your name to Ebinezar.

Unsurprisingly, many of the commenters engaged in debating social issues beyond Amazon and speaking on the wider issue of climate change with both skeptics/deniers and supporters. For the most part, Amazon was responsive throughout these comments regardless of the topic, which indicates the company was listening and engaging in dialogue or problem-solving:

> **Commenter:** *The mentioning of the new electric vehicles is great but I wish they would have talked about packaging and putting pressure on the manufacturers to become carbon free.*
> **Amazon response:** *Hey there, Raven! Thanks for the feedback. We've forwarded this to our packaging team for review. We're always looking for ways to improve and your feedback is always appreciated.— [Name of responder].*

Amazon as Villain

AECJ's posts on Facebook were minimal (a total of four posts). These included going live posts (see Table 9.2).

Certain topics and the live posts attracted more engagement and different reactions, especially their live post (see Figures 9.3 and 9.4).

When the group did communicate on Facebook, the posts were often very critical of Amazon. Employees focused mainly on the idea that Amazon is hurting the environment, its employees, and the communities, especially people from marginalized communities. The following example illustrates this sentiment: *Amazon's operations are complicit in environmental racism. Amazon's logistics network of trucks spew climate-change-causing greenhouse gases and toxic particles as they drive to and from warehouses that are concentrated near Black, Latinx, and Indigenous communities* (AECJ post, May 26, 2020). Moreover, once the two founders of the group were fired, the post focused on Amazon's trying to shut them down: *Amazon fired Emily Cunningham and Maren Costa to try to scare us and stop us from hosting the panel with Naomi Klein and our warehouse coworkers last week. Join us tomorrow (Friday) to tell Amazon: Stop firing workers for speaking up! Details here: https://medium.com/@amazonempl.../amazon-sick-out-3d61b5a7ebfa* (AECJ post, April 23, 2020).

However, these posts garnered minimal engagement and comments. Of the few comments gathered, most of them were positive toward AECJ's efforts: (a) *Check out the Tax Amazon movement in Seattle! #TechSolidarity ● www.taxamazon.net.sign*; (b) *Climate justice = worker justice, racial justice, economic justice, and social justice;* (c) *(...) Will do absolutely whatever we can to support you in your hugely important fight.*

AECJ was responsive with the comments, often using these as an opportunity to engage in further listening, add news or information, or organize collective support. The following examples illustrate this approach: (a) *Amazonians are powerful together. Respond to this survey to show support for fired workers and warehouse workers (you can keep your identity hidden). We want to know you're listening in the livestream! https://bit.ly/Amazon-Listen*; (b) *Here's a link to a Seattle Times article that talks about environmental racism: https://www.seattletimes.com/.../coronavirus-risk-and.../;* (c) *Microsoft Workers four Good has done excellent work on worker issues, and many of them joined the Climate Strike last September. https://twitter.com/msworkers4?lang=en.*

Sweeping Aside Criticism and AECJ

While AECJ's sole social media focus was criticizing Amazon and organizing protests and petitions on- and offline, Amazon's posts never contained responses to (or mentions) of AECJ protests or anything

Organizational Social Listening and Corporate Climate Advocacy 171

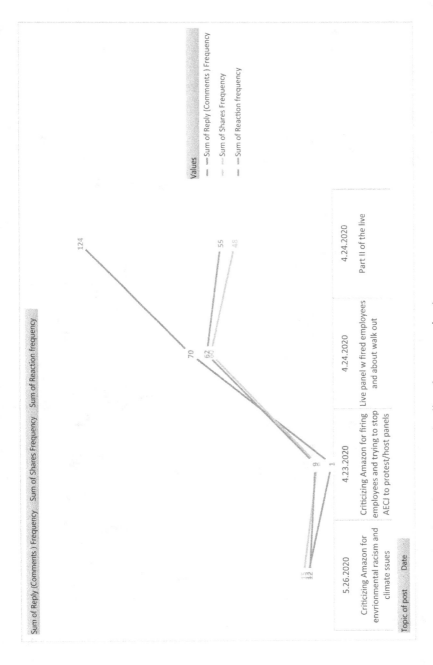

Figure 9.3 Breakdown of topic and engagement (replies, shares, reactions)

172　*Ioana A. Coman and Rosalynn Vasquez*

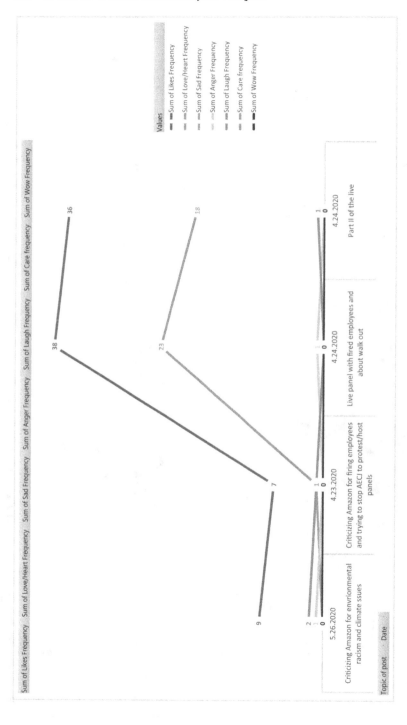

Figure 9.4 Breakdown of topic and different reactions

else associated with the organization and its efforts. These posts never alluded to any controversial issues, countered AECJ claims or accusations, or addressed anything else other than Amazon's corporate climate change efforts and positive changes underway. Additionally, there did not appear to be any direct interaction between Amazon and AECJ on social media. In fact, AECJ did not post comments in response to Amazon's original posts. Both organizations maintained their unique communication channels, images, and agendas. Amazon continued to highlight its inaugural Climate Pledge and plans, while AECJ continued to criticize and scrutinize the initiative that was perceived to be a scam and called for real climate leadership.

Discussion and Conclusion

This analysis contributes to the understanding of organizational social listening and dialogic communication, by examining Amazon's response (or lack of) to the employee advocacy group known as the AECJ in the context of climate change activism.

Using the typology proposed by Borner and Zerfass (2018), we can say that Amazon behaved as "insensitive organizations" that "restrict themselves to absorb obvious impulses which cannot be ignored (e.g., in crisis situations) and thus act mostly reactively" (p. 10) Amazon's reactions do not seem to indicate or show the existence of a corporate strategy oriented toward organizational listening: the answers are formal, valid for any kind of controversial situations, focused on reaffirming corporate values and not on anticipating stakeholder aspirations and confirming them by announcing appropriate actions.

Furthermore, Amazon's reactions to the comments also seem to indicate the lack of an affective commitment in the dialogue with the internal audience, which cannot lead to the point of maximum fulfillment of organizational listening: the empowerment of employees as, on the one hand, dialogue partners and, on the other hand, participants in the climate change actions designed and implemented by the corporation. These things are all the more important as studies have shown that "organizational listening is more effective in identifying and addressing the trend or common themes of employee voices regarding organization-related issues, long-term planning, and broader goals" (Qin & Men, 2021, p. 380). Overall, this analysis reveals the absence of a true "architecture of listening." As Macnamara (2016b) points out, corporations have implemented strong "architectures of speaking" that involve "structures, systems, resources, tools, and technologies such as websites, databases, mailing lists, events, presentations, videos, media campaigns, speeches, reports, newsletters, brochures, and so on" (p. 161). The scarcity of Amazon reactions, the lack of dialogue (and of a dialogic "philosophy") are proof that there were no "policies, systems, structures, resources, and a range of processes, technologies, and specialist skills to enable and facilitate delegated, mediated, large-scale listening" (Macnamara, 2018, p. 3).

This chapter provides new insight and direction to future PR researchers and practitioners to explain how to better understand the importance of listening to both external and internal stakeholders, and creating authentic and consistent communication initiatives on social issues. As one of the largest companies in the world, Amazon is still in the early stages of building its sustainability presence and legacy, which makes it an ideal case to explore as it communicates and engages with its stakeholders to address and combat the climate crisis.

Overall, this study provides insights into this growing phenomenon of corporate climate change communication and advocacy, especially in the digital environment. Social media continues to amplify global societal issues and problems and companies are no longer staying silent. Companies are appearing at the forefront of global climate change and working together to generate awareness and change (Allen & Craig, 2016). With the increased need for transparency and accountability for companies, we hope to see corporate leaders move beyond the minimum standards of compliance and communication and demonstrate higher levels of commitment as visible advocates and bold leaders for climate change (Vasquez, 2022).

Recommendations for Public Relations Practice

- A commitment to organizational social listening and dialogic communication are essential for companies to build and maintain mutually beneficial relationships with stakeholders.
- Internal stakeholders are just as important as external stakeholders and should not be overlooked or ignored. Create open forums and opportunities to hear their voices and concerns, and create feedback mechanisms to close the listening loop.
- Companies should continue to monitor socio-political issues and create authentic, consistent, and transparent communications in their positioning.
- Public relations practitioners and company leaders should be aware of the rise of employee activist groups who advocate for social issues, and create an organizational culture for open communication and listening.

References

Allen, M. W., & Craig, C. A. (2016). Rethinking corporate social responsibility in the age of climate change: A communication perspective. *International Journal of Corporate Social Responsibility*, *1*(1), 1. https://doi.org/10.1186/s40991-016-0002-8

Amazon (2019). *Amazon co-founds the climate pledge, setting goal to meet the Paris Agreement 10 years early. Amazon.com.* https://www.businesswire.com/news/home/20190919005609/en/Amazon-Co-founds-The-Climate-Pledge-Setting-Goal-to-Meet-the-Paris-Agreement-10-Years-Early

Barometer, E. T. (2022). Societal leadership is now a core function of business/Edelman: https://www.edelman.com/trust/2022-trust-barometer

Borner, M., & Zerfass, A. (2018). The power of listening in corporate communications: Theoretical foundations of corporate listening as a strategic mode of communication. In S. Bowman, A. Crookes, Ø. Ihlen & S. Romenti (Eds), *Public relations and the power of creativity: Strategic opportunities, innovation and critical challenges.* Emerald Group Publishing.

Bortree, D. S., & Seltzer, T. (2009). Dialogic strategies and outcomes: An analysis of environmental advocacy groups' Facebook profiles. *Public Relations Review, 35*(3), 317–319. https://doi.org/10.1016/j.pubrev.2009.05.002

Broom, B. J. (2009). Dialog theories. In S. W. Littlejohn & K. A. Foss (Eds), *Encyclopedia of communication theory.* Sage.

Coman, I. A., Yuan, S., & Tsai, J.-Y. (2022). Toward an audience-centric framework of corporate social advocacy strategy: An exploratory study of young consumers from generation Z. *Sustainability, 14*(7), 4099. https://doi.org/10.3390/su14074099

Coombs, W. T., & Holladay, S. J. (2012). Fringe public relations: How activism moves critical PR toward the mainstream. *Public Relations Review, 38*(5), 880–887.

Creswell, J. W., & Poth, C. N. (2018). *Qualitative inquiry and research design: Choosing among five approaches.* Sage.

Dodd, M. D., & Supa, D. W. (2014). Conceptualizing and measuring "corporate social advocacy" communication: Examining the impact on corporate financial performance. *Public Relations Journal, 8*(3), 2–23.

Dunlap, R. E., & McCright, A. M. (2008). A widening gap: Republican and Democratic views on climate change. *Environment: Science and Policy for Sustainable Development, 50*(5), 26–35. https://doi.org/10.3200/ENVT.50.5.26-35

Foux, G. (2006). Consumer-generated media: Get your customers involved. *Brand Strategy, 8*(202), 38–39.

Gaither, B. M., Austin, L., & Collins, M. (2018). Examining the case of DICK's sporting goods: Realignment of stakeholders through corporate social advocacy. *The Journal of Public Interest Communications, 2*(2), 176.

Garcia, A. (2019). *Amazon workers walk out to protest climate change inaction. CNN Business.* Retrieved from https://www.cnn.com/2019/09/20/tech/amazon-climate-strike-global-tech/index.html

Ghaffary, S. (2019). *Hundreds of Amazon employees plan to walk out of work in protest of Amazon's environmental policies. Vox.* Retrieved from: https://www.vox.com/recode/2019/9/9/20857030/amazon-employees-walkout-environmental-policies

Grunig, J. E. (1994). World view, ethics, and the two-way symmetrical model of public relations. *Normative Aspekte der Public Relations: Grundlegende Fragen und Perspektiven. Eine Einführung,* 69–89.

Grunig, J. E., & Hunt, T. (1984). *Managing public relations.* Holt, Rinehart & Winston.

Grunig, J. E., Grunig, L. A., & Dozier, D. M. (2006). The excellence theory. In C. H. Botan & V. Hazelton (Eds.), *Public relations theory II* (pp. 21–30). Routledge.

Hallahan, K. (2000). Enhancing motivation, ability, and opportunity to process public relations messages. *Public Relations Review*, *28*(4), 463–480. https://doi.org/10.1016/S0363-8111(00)00059-X

Johnston, K. A. (2014). Public relations and engagement: Theoretical imperatives of a multidimensional concept. *Journal of Public Relations Research*, *26*(5), 381–383. https://doi.org/10.1080/1062726X.2014.959863

Kent, M. L., & Taylor, M. (2002). Toward a dialogic theory of public relations. *Public Relations Review*, *28*(1), 21–37. https://doi.org/10.1016/S0363-8111(02)00108-X

Macnamara, J. (2016a). *Organizational listening. The missing essential in public communication*. Peter Lang Verlag.

Macnamara, J. (2016b). Organizational listening: Addressing a major gap in public relations theory and practice. *Journal of Public Relations Research*, *28*(3–4), 146–169. https://doi.org/10.1080/1062726X.2016.1228064

Macnamara, J. (2018). Toward a theory and practice of organizational listening. *International Journal of Listening*, *32*(1), 1–23. https://doi.org/10.1080/10904018.2017.1375076

Maicon, L. (2020). *Purpose is not enough: brand action through advocacy*. Edelman. Available online: https://www.edelman.com/research/purpose-not-enough

Pew Research Center (2020). *As economic concerns recede, environmental protection rises on the public's policy agenda*. Retrieved from: https://www.people-press.org/2020/02/13/as-economic-concerns-recede-environmental-protection-rises-on-the-publics-policy-agenda/

Pieczka, M. (2011). Public relations as dialogic expertise? *Journal of Communication Management*, *15*(2), 108–123.

Place, K. R. (2019). Listening as the driver of public relations practice and communications strategy within a global public relations agency. *Public Relations Journal*, *12*(3), 1–18.

Place, K. R. (2022). Toward a framework for listening with consideration for intersectionality: Insights from public relations professionals in borderland spaces. *Journal of Public Relations Research*, 1–16. https://doi.org/10.1080/1062726X.2022.2057502

Qin, Y. S., & Men, L. R. (2021). Why does listening matter inside the organization? The impact of internal listening on employee-organization relationships. *Journal of Public Relations Research*, *33*(5), 365–386. https://doi.org/10.1080/1062726X.2022.2034631

Saffer, A. J., Sommerfeldt, E. J., & Taylor, M. (2013). The effects of organizational Twitter interactivity on organization–public relationships. *Public Relations Review*, *39*(3), 213–215. https://doi.org/10.1016/j.pubrev.2013.02.005

Savransky, B. (2020). *A Seattle-based Amazon employee spoke up for workers' rights. Then, she was fired*. Seattle PI. Retrieved from https://www.seattlepi.com/coronavirus/article/amazon-employee-maren-costa-fired-workers-rights-15254473.php

Taylor, M., & Kent, M. L. (2014). Dialogic engagement: Clarifying foundational concepts. *Journal of Public Relations Research*, *26*(5), 384–398. https://doi.org/10.1080/1062726X.2014.956106

Thorbecke, C. (2019). *Amazon workers claim their jobs were threatened for speaking out about climate change*. Retrieved from https://abcnews.go.com/Business/amazon-workers-claim-jobs-threatened-speaking-climate-change/story?id=68049064

Vasquez, R. (2022). CSR, CSA, or CPA? Examining corporate climate change communication strategies, motives, and effects on consumer outcomes. *Sustainability, 14*(6), 3604.

Wilcox, D. L. (2019). Dialogic communication theory in the age of corporate activism: A postmodern perspective. *Communication and Media in Asia Pacific (CMAP), 2*(1), 1–10.

Unit 3
Organizational Listening for Diversity, Equity, and Inclusion

10 Organizational Listening for Diversity, Equity, and Inclusion

Katie R. Place

Introduction

A 2021 "Language of Diversity" report co-authored by The Wakeman Agency and Institute for Public Relations described diversity, equity, and inclusion (DE&I) in public relations as the acknowledgment of the presence, fluidity, and intersections of different needs and identities, the promotion of justice and fairness with respect to different needs and identities, and the development of an environment where different needs and identities are respected, welcomed, valued, and *heard* (The Language of Diversity, 2021, p. 5). Interestingly, only 46% of the report's survey respondents said their organization's communications functions worked very closely with the functions responsible for DE&I, indicating a potential area of improvement.

Listening is a practice involving the receiving, constructing of meaning from, and responding to spoken or nonverbal messages (Bentley, 1996). In an organization, listening embodies the culture, structure, skills, policies, and personnel for being responsive to the needs of organizational publics, particularly via two-way flows of communication (Macnamara, 2016a, 2016b; Worthington & Fitch-Hauser, 2018). Listening in organizations may promote respect for all partners engaged in dialogue, commitment to understanding shared messages, hearing of diverse voices across contexts, and openness to multiple narratives (Parks, 2019), thus bridging strategic communication and DE&I efforts.

The purpose of this chapter is to explore organizational listening for DE&I in public relations and strategic communication contexts. First, the chapter reviews literature pertaining to organizational listening and DE&I. Next, the chapter reviews the qualitative method utilized to explore the concepts of organizational listening and DE&I and a discussion of the key findings of the study. Lastly, the chapter concludes with implications for strategic communications and public relations practice and directions for future research.

DOI: 10.4324/9781003273851-14

Literature

Organizational Listening

Listening can be described as a complex human communication phenomenon involving affective processes, behavioral processes, and cognitive processes for the purpose of relating to, contributing to, and understanding each other (Bodie, 2016; Claro, 2022). In organizational contexts, listening may occur in evolving, demanding, and competitive environments in which stakeholders have a vested interest (Claro, 2022). Organizational listening includes a variety of cultural, structural, procedural, technological, and skills- or resource-based practices to understand, acknowledge, and respond to organizational publics (Macnamara, 2016a). It can be defined as a management function that develops and applies listening policies and research methodologies to gather, understand, interpret, and evaluate input from stakeholder publics to fulfill tactical or strategic objectives (Falconi, 2016, p. 2). Particularly important to organizational listening are the processes of identifying and activating listening channels, acknowledging stakeholders' expectations and considering them in organizational strategy before taking action, and genuinely listening as actions are taken in pursuit of strategies (Global Alliance, 2012, pp. 3–4).

Organizational listening is most often implemented via supportive cultures, face-to-face interactions applying dialogic skill sets, formative and summative research, informal public consultations, and formal public consultations such as meetings, forums, suggestion boxes, online inquiries, or telephone calls (Macnamara, 2016a, p. 135). However, organizational listening must be facilitated by a supportive, empathetic, and ethical culture (Claro, 2022; Macnamara, 2016a; Neill & Bowen, 2021a, 2021b; Sahay, 2021; Worthington & Bodie, 2018). Macnamara (2016a) and Worthington and Bodie (2018), for example, suggest that organizational culture—championed by leaders who champion listening-based values, support two-way communication, and value collaborative inquiry—is integral to effective organizational listening. Knowledgeable, ethical, and research-oriented communication professionals who advocate for listening in such organizational cultures are also key (Macnamara, 2016a, p. 238). Claro (2022) and Sahay (2021) both suggest that empathetic listening skills are critical for organizational listening, as such skills embody sincere and inclusive dialogic engagement, expression of understanding and acknowledgment, and acceptance and investment of time listening, interpreting, and responding to others. Amid a global pandemic, organizational listening may particularly need to rely on frequent pulse surveys, video conferencing technologies, or mobile applications to instill a culture of trust and connection among organizations and publics, particularly employees (Neill & Bowen, 2021b).

Architecture of Listening

To best support a culture of listening and counteract a predominance of speaking, organizations can implement an architecture of listening that proactively champions listening, addresses the politics of listening, develops policies and procedures for listening, builds systems that are open, interactive, and conducive to listening, uses technologies to facilitate listening, utilizes resources and staff and systems for listening, and articulates the voices of stakeholders and publics to decision makers (Macnamara, 2018; Sahay, 2021). An architecture framework provides structure for organizational listening, leaves room for creativity and diversity of listening styles, and ensures that various organizational constituents have a right to consideration (Macnamara, 2016a). Specific resources, structures, and processes for listening include a clear timeline, budget, and designation of to whom responsibilities of listening are delegated (Claro, 2022; Macnamara, 2015). Such responsibilities may be assigned to an organization's human resources, marketing, communications, or digital communication teams (Macnamara, 2015). An architecture of listening approach also calls for a variety of skills and training for listening, such as knowledge of feedback mechanisms, expertise in quantitative and qualitative research methods, understanding of consulting techniques, and facility with psychological, sociological, and anthropological techniques (Macnamara, 2015, 2016a). Listening policies should address who is being listened to and how, both externally and internally (Claro, 2022; Macnamara, 2015). Even with policies, structures, and resources present, Macnamara (2013) cautions that the work to carry out an effective and appropriate architecture of listening is challenging, time-consuming, complex.

Recent research has expanded our understanding of an architecture of listening in strategic communication contexts. Place (2019), for example, explored how an international public relations agency fostered an architecture of listening via structural accommodations to encourage listening, programs and policies to facilitate listening and dialogue, and technology and tools to support listening. A culture of listening was also championed across organizational literature with keywords "conversation, collaboration, voice, respect, engagement, truth, trust, and inclusion." Neill and Bowen's (2021b) study of ethical listening similarly found that organizations employed varied systems, technologies, and resources for listening including group and face-to-face meetings, electronic surveys, and videoconferencing tools.

Diversity, Equity, and Inclusion

DE&I acknowledges the presence, fluidity, and intersections of different needs and identities, promotes justice and fairness with respect to different needs and identities, and fosters an environment where different needs and identities are respected, welcomed, valued, and heard (The Language of Diversity, 2021). Specifically, diversity can be defined as the presence and intersection of differences in demographics, such as gender, ethnicity, nationality, age, language, education, socioeconomic status, religion, or political affiliation and psychographics, such as cognitions, values, attitudes, experiences, and personal background (The Language of Diversity, 2021, p. 6). It is a social construction that reflects individual and group characteristics and power differences, as well as negotiations of identities, cultural memberships, attitudes, and past experiences (Grunig, 2006; Place & Vanc, 2016; Tsetsura, 2011). Specifically, equity involves the promotion of fairness, justice, and equality by recognizing and correcting imbalances of power and ensuring fair distribution of resources (The Language of Diversity, 2021, p. 6). Inclusion is defined as an outcome where individuals feel welcomed, heard, accepted, empowered, and respected in an environment (The Language of Diversity, 2021, p. 6). Inconsistencies remain regarding how public relations and strategic communication professionals define DE&I in professional settings (The Language of Diversity, 2021). Additionally, the range of studies regarding DE&I has been historically limited to topics of gender, ethnicity, and race (Ertem-Eray & Ki, p. 4).

Recent scholarship has analyzed DE&I from a variety of practical and theoretical approaches. Vardeman-Winter and Place (2017), assessing extant literature on diversity in public relations, found that various facets of identity and lived experience are often left out of research on the field, such as ability. The authors called for additional intersectional research incorporating a variety of research methods to achieve a more accurate picture of diversity in public relations. More recently, Bardhan and Engstrom (2021) conducted a rhetorical analysis of "Diverse Voices: Profiles in Leadership" and found that minority public relations professionals often had to do extra work to fight for systemic change and often had to take on DE&I work as an individual quest rather than as part of an organization-wide or industry-wide effort. Bardhan and Engstrom (2021) urged for DE&I research to extend beyond the descriptive level to suggestions for actionable change and intervention for complex diversity-related issues. Lee et al. (2021) explored how diversity-oriented leadership and internal communication achieve organizational DE&I goals. The authors found that diversity-oriented leadership that values inclusiveness and recognizes employees' diverse backgrounds in decision-making may enhance racial minorities' perceptions of justice in the workplace. Building theory to address DE&I, Logan (2021) asserted that corporations have a responsibility to address racial injustice and work to improve race relations, because they have historically capitalized upon or perpetuated racial oppression (p. 13). Organizations employing a corporate responsibility to race (CRR) approach should consider authentic CRR, promote racial equity, allyship, and accountability, and consider needs of society over the economic needs of the corporation (Logan, 2021, pp. 13–15).

Organizational Listening for DE&I

Organizational listening in support of DE&I remains an understudied concept in strategic communication and public relations. Macnamara (2016a) suggested that organizational listening must better focus on marginalized voices and listen across differences of culture, language, ability, faith, and identity to promote social equity, fair representation, and justice. To effectively do so, Place (2022) argued for the application of intersectional listening strategies in strategic communication and public relations contexts. Her study participants suggested that practitioners listen in support of intersectionality by being reflexive of their own intersecting identities and lived experiences, being sensitive to differing levels of experience, power, and positionality, being knowledgeable of organizational methods to listen to diverse intersecting identities, and listening "coalitionally" for disempowerment and oppression across communities.

Organizational listening in support of DE&I must center around social equity and ethics by addressing which groups are denied a voice, disadvantaged, underrepresented, or ignored (Macnamara, 2015). Parks (2019) suggests that listening must acknowledge contextual and social situations, as dialogue is performed amid "dynamic stories and identities which impact the discursive construction of meaning and value" (p. 15). Communications professionals must listen out for how privileges may be withheld or given based on the way meanings are assigned—by individuals who reinforce or perpetuate socially constructed categories of difference (p. 16). The restoration of marginalized voices and creation of spaces where individuals can be heard may be especially facilitated by authentic and attentive listening that supports meaning-making and understanding (Tyler, 2011). Authentic listening applies empathy and avoidance of judgment to achieve engagement rather than functionalist or hegemonic outcomes.

Drawing from literature regarding organizational listening and DE&I, the research question guiding this research was: How does organizational listening support DE&I in public relations and strategic communication?

Method

A qualitative method was used for this study of organizational listening and DE&I, particularly as it enables rich description of phenomena and acknowledges research as an interactive and socially constructed activity shaped by history, gender, race, and class (Denzin & Lincoln, 2003). This chapter represents a segment of findings from a larger study regarding organizational listening in strategic communication and public relations.

Sampling and Recruitment

Professionals responsible for an organization's strategic communication and public relations efforts were recruited using both purposive and snowball sampling methods. First, a purposive sampling method was used to enlist participants across the United States. Practitioners received an email recruitment letter inviting them to participate in the study. Later, other interviewees were recruited using a snowball sampling method, as earlier participants recommended individuals to participate in the study.

The sample of participants included 54 strategic communication and public relations professionals and executives representing nonprofit (32), agency (11), corporate (5), education (3), and governmental (3) organization types from the East Coast, Mid Atlantic, Southern and Midwestern, and West Coast regions of the United States. Regarding gender identity, 34 participants identified as women, 18 participants identified as men, 1 participant identified as nonbinary, and 1 participant identified as transgender. Regarding race and ethnicity, 10 participants identified as Black, 4 participants identified as Latinx, 1 participant identified as Asian, 1 participant identified as Arab American, and 38 of the participants identified as White. Most participants (30) represented senior- or executive-level positions responsible for strategic communication or public relations within their organizations. The remainder (8) represented mid-level communications professionals who oversaw the public relations or communications functions. Some participants representing an Executive Director level of leadership were also included in the sample because they also managed communication efforts for their respective organizations.

Procedure

Interviews were conducted between February and May 2021 and guided by a 16-question interview protocol featuring a variety of rapport-building or open-ended questions in a pre-determined order (Rubin & Rubin, 2005). Additionally, probes and follow-up questions, such as "Why?" "How?" or "Could you elaborate on..." were used to encourage participants to elaborate upon their responses and offer examples. All interviews were audiotaped, conducted via Zoom due to the COVID pandemic, and ranged from approximately 40 minutes to 90 minutes in length.

Analysis

After interviews were transcribed professionally, they were analyzed and coded word-for-word. Using a thematic analysis approach (Boyatzis, 1998), the transcripts were read and re-read multiple times for themes related to listening and trauma. Annotations and memos were also written in comment boxes among the transcripts to identify connecting themes or to highlight features of the themes (Corbin & Strauss, 2008; Miles & Huberman, 1994). Lastly, member checks (e.g., Lincoln & Guba, 1985) were used to confirm or check the meanings of particular responses. Some quotations were edited to remove verbal placeholders, but original meanings of passages remain.

Findings

Analysis revealed five key themes regarding organizational listening to support DE&I in strategic communication and public relations. Participants described the importance of (a) formal surveys and meetings, (b) employee resource groups (ERGs), (c) designated organizational listeners, and (d) invoking a grassroots approach. Additionally, participants described a sense of futility regarding listening for DE&I. Each theme is explored in-depth below:

Formal Surveys and Meetings

Participants indicated that formal surveys and meetings (such as departmental meetings and focus groups) were often the first means that organizations utilized to listen in support of DE&I. Surveys or meetings were implemented both annually or periodically to listen to internal and external publics' feedback, concerns, and needs. Surveys used to elicit DE&I feedback were distributed to broad publics, such as all organizational employees, or sometimes only to segmented publics by identity or lived experience. A corporate senior vice president of digital communications, for example, described the annual and periodic surveys that they implemented to convey empathy and develop a more trusting relationship between the organization and its diverse employees. She stated that surveys, "foster the sense of listening, you know, 'what are your needs in the organization and then how can the organization respond to those needs? What can we do better?' It makes it intentional like that. That listening is not done just so they can you know, people can like bellyache, but the organization really cares about what you think." The executive director of a nonprofit serving low-income and homeless publics also shared the importance of surveys for DE&I listening, emphasizing the importance of valuing, utilizing, and acting upon the feedback. She explained that her organization sends individuals receiving their services a survey asking how they were treated or could be better served. She elaborated, saying,

> We send a self-addressed stamped envelope for them to do a survey because we care about how they felt about the job we did and packing their suitcase when we never met them. Never ask a question to gain

information that you're not going to need. Don't even waste your time. Don't ask them this if you're not going to listen to the answer and do something about it.

Formal meetings and focus groups were described as equally effective for fostering an intentional and collaborative space for listening and dialogue in support of DE&I and empowering diverse organizational publics. Speaking to the importance of formal meetings to support DE&I efforts, the chief executive officer of a community-based services nonprofit shared,

> We're trying to be very intentional about providing spaces for our clients to provide us with feedback about what they're experiencing in our programs. In the residential programs, a lot of that has to do with having meetings where people can voice their concerns or their ideas for how to improve the programs. We serve young people that are in the foster care system and, you know, it's important for us to make sure that the youth voices are heard and that they can come to the table and feel that they have some say in what's happening with their treatment or what's happening with their experience with the program. That's of critical importance.

Likewise, the director for a regional food bank shared the importance of focus groups to ensure her organizational leaders avoid making assumptions about the needs of the diverse, often marginalized, publics they serve. Listening via focus groups embodied her organization's core value of "nothing about us without us." She explained,

> We all need to be reminded that all the time, as we will often have ideas of what people with people who are facing food insecurity need. And we find out that we are so wrong about it. And after the process of setting some program up or developing, something has begun. It's too late. It has to be right from ground, you know, ground zero... We set up focus groups and that's growing all over the region and just asking, you know, 'Are we doing OK? What do you need? How are our member agencies doing? How hard is it for you to get to a grocery store? How hard is it for you to get SNAP benefits or any of any of that?'

The executive director of a nonprofit serving low-income and homeless publics similarly touted the effectiveness of both focus groups and surveys for listening in support of DE&I efforts for their diverse constituents. After the organization's first focus group with members of the homeless community, the director recounted the sense that it had offered their publics a space to be heard and feel like, "I have something valuable to give because I'm helping this organization serve people in my situation better."

Employee Resource Groups

Though less commonly implemented than surveys or meetings, participants championed the effectiveness of ERGs or affinity groups for listening in support of DE&I. Such groups were touted as providing appropriate spaces for listening to or among diverse publics and addressing instances of (particularly racial) inequity or marginalization. A nonprofit communications manager, for example, championed employee affinity groups as being a potential space for inclusive engagement and listening to and among members of marginalized communities. They shared:

> I was the only visible out trans person on staff in my department at [organization]. And I had a few other people come to me and say, 'I'm trans and I like to be able to come out and be respected and my identity at work.' And I think allowing space for an affinity group to form, whether it's for LGBTQ employees or disabled employees, or whoever, and letting them have a seat at the table and make decisions... Saying, 'this is a decision that's going to harm our community by allowing employees to staff members to advocate for themselves.' I think this is the biggest thing that corporate America can do to really listen to marginalized communities.

Similarly, a corporate senior vice president of communications described the impact of a Black ERG and the importance of ensuring that organizations listen to and heed feedback from such groups. She explained, "After the George Floyd incident, there was an informal group that was set up by our Black employees to have them kind of listen and share information. And they've kept that going, which has been super cool ... it's designed to resolve issues or move things forward." Indeed, ERGs may best facilitate organizational listening in support of DE&I, particularly if other structures in an organization do not model respectful listening. A Black agency account executive shared his frustration when human resources asked him and his Black colleagues to take an enneagram survey in the wake of social unrest and Black Lives Matter events in the summer of 2020. He touted the firm's Black ERG as a safe space for having his frustrations heard:

> And it was just kind of like with everything that's gone on, 'You want us to take a 90-minute test and get more work? And it's just like that's the opposite of what I want to be doing right now!' But I can respect that they were trying. Like I get what they were trying to do, but maybe approach it like this. Maybe listen to this, get the employee

resource group. Our resource group functions in a way that will allow us to grow both mentally, emotionally, and professionally...

ERGs may also be especially important for personal reflection to address racial bias and hone listening skills for DE&I. A nonprofit communications director touted the ERG as a space for her listening and reflection work as a White person in power. She said,

> Employee resource groups. There's a group for people who identify as White and one for those who identify as multiracial to come together and do our own work separately so that we're not doing harm while we're doing our work. There are some processes in place that allow us to be better at [DE&I] ourselves, especially for me as a White person in a position of power at the organization. As a gatekeeper, I recognize that that's something I really need to work on and I'm not great at working on.

Designated Organizational Listeners

Participants also championed formal and informal designated listeners as a vital means of organizational listening for DE&I. Designated listeners served as the point-people for listening, connecting, interpreting, and relaying insights about DE&I or diverse publics to decision-makers in the organization. One corporate senior vice president of communications championed the effectiveness of formal review and advisory committees comprised of external community and industry leaders for listening and conveying DE&I insights to organizational executives. Of the formal committees, she shared, "so it's like they could foreshadow or foresee what issues that are going to be most critical, relay the actions we will need to take on, and talk about how things are going and what we're doing. So ways to listen to different perspectives and have weigh-in." Internal employees were also described as key to formal listening for DE&I. A communications director for a regional school system, for example, shared the importance of formal caseworkers for listening to diverse families in the school district who are experiencing food or housing insecurities, language barriers, or differences in citizenship status. She explained,

> Every family has its own case worker, and they do a couple of home visits at the very beginning of the year. Their goal is to sit with the family and ask them 'what are your needs?' So, it is a very individual process for the families and those social workers or family workers work with the family. Through the school year, they're not only checking on the kids, but also the parents and making sure that they're moving toward those goals...that's our job to communicate, to *listen*.

Organizational Listening for Diversity, Equity, and Inclusion 191

Participants underscored the importance of having internally designated listeners who possessed lived experiences or identity facets that overlapped with the diverse stakeholders to whom an organization wished to listen. Those critical listeners "bridge a gap" between an organization and its publics. A director of communications and community engagement at an immigration nonprofit shared, for example:

> I think one of the really great things is that we have immigrants and refugees on our staff that help with listening and connecting to clients. They can speak to the clients, maybe in their native language, and they'll just pick up on nuances that someone else will not pick up on. And then that way they can sort of let the broader staff know about what's going on.

Similarly, the director of communications for a US Senator described the importance of staff members who hold overlapping lived experiences or identity facets of diverse constituent groups. He shared that his office listens for DE&I by, "...having staff that is representing the local community, having staff that reflects the community and understands their language and understands their traditions and ways of ways of interacting ... So having them reach out and sort of bridging that gap and so forth. That's so good."

Informal designated listeners were also described as important for organizational listening for DE&I, such as partnering organizations, peer groups, or volunteers. The regional director of a social services nonprofit shared the importance of community peers for listening to marginalized communities during COVID to better understand barriers or misconceptions surrounding vaccines. She explained,

> We know that a lot of the African American communities right now are underserved and under vaccinated. And some of that is a lack of trust for government. Some of that is that they're afraid of the vaccine...We have peers in the community who hit the streets. Smaller groups who actually go knock on doors, asking, "Tell us, have you gotten the vaccine and if not, why? What are your fears? Can we put those to ease?" So really going right to the source, if you will, to collect the information. We think we know, but [our peers in the community] tell us for real, which makes it special.

Grassroots Organizing Lens

Complementing the designated listeners' theme, participants described the importance of a grassroots organizing approach for engaging in listening for DE&I grounded in authentic, organic connections to the community. The director of a nonprofit serving the LGBTQ+ community shared the importance of a community organizing lens for DE&I purposes. He noted how some large nonprofit organizations often embody a lack of listening and a disconnect from the communities they serve. He urged,

> ...if organizations big or small, for profit, non for profit, really listened and did their work - their communications work through a community organizing lens where they were actually participating in the community - they would just have this more meaningful relationships and thus be able to connect with people, particularly marginalized people, in a very different way than they do.

Similarly, the director of communications for a US Senator underscored the importance of listening for DE&I in concert with community members, leaders, and organizations. He shared his office's approach stating,

> We've tried to listen and speak with the minority community leaders to understand how they want information in their communities. It can't just be those of us in elected office or in the government bureaucracy making these decisions, so we really need to engage the boots on the ground, community leaders. And that's pastors of the local churches, that's local business leaders who live in these communities and work in these communities. They understand what their communities need more so than those of us who work in offices downtown.... And listening to them is highly important.

Ultimately, an educational nonprofit director explained that a grassroots approach to listening for DE&I centers on *how* you listen on a relational level. She explained,

> It's the way you listen... When working with certain communities, you do not come in and say, 'you know, I have a master's degree. I know what's right and I'm going to help!' It's 'I'm a parent too, so how can we talk?' It's always about building a relationship. And a strong relationship is worth more to me than any information that I would be able to solicit. I mean, having communities say you've listened to them and you heard their concerns...

Listening Futility

Unexpectedly, many participants described a sense of futility regarding listening to support DE&I efforts, using comments like "we can do better" "we are just not there yet" or "we have a long way to go." Many sentiments were espoused by organizational leaders or chief executives, who expressed difficulty harnessing adequate resources, time, tools, or "buy in" to listen appropriately. Organizational narratives and leadership teams lacking racial diversity were also described as barriers to listening in support of DE&I. When asked how their organization listens in support of DE&I, a regional communications manager for a nonprofit humanitarian organization confessed that his organization needed to listen better, hire individuals to do DE&I work, and to hire a more racially diverse workforce. He commented,

> I think between us, we could still do a better job with diversity and inclusion. I think that's still an area where they are heading in the right direction with that, but they still are not there. They need to make a concerted effort to get more professionals in more diversity and inclusion roles. I've had my colleagues who were Black that said, you know, 'I love working here, but I don't see anybody that looks like me that's in a VP or leadership role.'

Similarly, the executive director of a nonprofit tackling housing and food insecurity discussed the difficulty that some organizational leaders have with listening to critical feedback from publics regarding DE&I. She described their hesitancy to listen, acknowledging the lack of racial diversity among the organization's leadership team. She explained,

> I think you have to be ready to hear hard things. I'm sure you've noticed so far, we are White people running an organization that serves predominantly Black and Latino folks. And so, you know, it is very possible that one of the things we'll hear is, you know, 'that's kind of a Whitecap organization.' So it's easy for people to feel fragile about that. Well, that's the truth. And yet you dip your toes into wanting to listen more deeply and help and begin to raise questions and items and issues that are a little more. It's sensitive. It's hard to listen.

A Black agency senior communications strategist critiqued organizations for not having leadership, structures, and tools in place for listening in support of DE&I. She urged organizational leaders to step up and "do the work" of listening for DE&I, sharing:

> Sometimes we move so slow because we are constantly interrogating every action. There is an interrogation about what impact it's going to have on the people who are connected to it and who is not here. And it's because we're marginalized. We constantly think about it. It's at the forefront of our minds and it's a labor that we naturally engage in. But this is where our White allies and folks who want to do better need to work. This is the work. You know, connecting with people, doing the reading, not expecting Black people or for people

who are marginalized to do the thinking for you. So it definitely seems like there's got to be a structure in place, there's got to be a group of people at that executive level who's going to listen. There's got to be all sorts of tools and structures and people in place to help.

Discussion

This qualitative, exploratory study examined how 54 strategic communication and public relations professionals made sense of organizational listening in support of DE&I. Participants touted organizational listening features such as formal surveys and meetings, employee affinity or resource groups, designated listeners, and grassroots or community-driven orientations as particularly support of DE&I. Findings of this study build upon our understanding of which organizational listening and architecture of listening elements are currently implemented in strategic communication and public relations contexts to address DE&I. Formal tools and programming to support listening for DE&I, such as surveys and meetings, were most frequently utilized. Surveys provide excellent opportunities for routine and anonymous collection and analysis of publics' feedback. However, organizations must utilize surveys for intentional and authentic DE&I listening to act, when appropriate, on feedback or concerns. As one practitioner put it, "Don't ask if you're not going to listen to the answer and do something about it." Because surveys are mediated and anonymous, meetings offer alternative real-time, dialogic, and co-creational listening opportunities for DE&I in the spirit of "nothing about us without us." Organizations must ensure that meetings are led by facilitators who have undergone appropriate listening and DE&I training and adhere to policies and procedures guiding respectful, equitable dialogue. Tapping into the community organizing theme, organizations may wish to hold meetings that foster dialogue and listening to address racial equity, diversity, and inclusion among various external stakeholder groups such as partnering organizations, community groups, places of worship, governmental agencies, or policy leaders. Such a coalitional or community approach may particularly allow organizations to listen for intersecting forms of oppression, power imbalances, and inequities across the populations or regions they serve (Place, 2022). Whereas meetings and surveys are often fleeting or periodic, ERGs or affinity groups offer permanent and longstanding means for DE&I-centered listening, reflection, dialogue, and action built into an organization's structure. Ultimately, as one participant suggested, it's all about *how* you listen in support of DE&I—emphasizing the importance of ensuring that organizational listening practices are backed up with an authentic intent to hear and foster relationships.

This study exposed a sense of futility associated with organizational listening in support of DE&I, suggesting that development of DE&I

architecture of listening frameworks and support systems is needed. DE&I is not only the promotion of different and intersecting needs and identities, but also the intentional promotion of justice, fairness, respect, and valuing of those different and intersecting needs and identities. Therefore, organizations should listen in support of DE&I by implementing an architecture of listening that facilitates the promotion of difference, justice, fairness, and respect while attending to complex power, culture, or attitude differences (i.e., Grunig, 2006). Building out such a listening architecture for DE&I may contribute to more systematic, intentional, ethical, and authentic listening that builds trust and enchantment among diverse organizational stakeholders (i.e., Lee et al., 2021; Tyler, 2011).

Specifically, an architecture of listening for DE&I must include components that foster a supportive culture of listening and others' right to speak, policies that specify and support listening, open and interactive organizational communication systems, technologies and monitoring tools to aid listening, sufficient resources, staff, space, and skills to do the work of (Macnamara, 2016b, p. 163; Macnamara, 2018, pp. 11–12). Such an architecture must address both internal and external publics, and prioritize listening that holds space for multiple, diverse, and intersecting narratives (Parks, 2019; Place, 2022). An architecture guided by a corporate commitment to race (CRR) (Logan, 2021) may best drive intentional organizational listening to acknowledge and eliminate forms of oppression and racial injustice. An architecture of listening for DE&I, guided by a CRR approach, would employ structures, policies, resources, skills and knowledge bases, and cultural features that enable authentic dialogic exchanges promoting racial equity, accountability, allyship, and meeting of societal needs over economic ones (Logan, 2021, pp. 13–15).

In order to implement an architecture of listening for DE&I, supported by a CRR approach, listening to embody racial equity, allyship, and accountability should be championed across organizational structures, among leadership and personnel, throughout strategic or tactical communications, and during ongoing evaluation of practices and communications. Listening for DEI, supported by a CRR approach, needs to be embodied by the leadership of an organization to successfully model necessary behaviors and champion corporate values. Evidence from this study suggested that most of the designated listeners were staff members, case workers, and marginalized or racial minority individuals within the organization. Organizations must be cognizant not to put the work of listening for DE&I solely on marginalized employees or stakeholders and should never seek to instrumentalize or "use" employees or stakeholders to achieve organizational goals. This was particularly illustrated by the public relations agency practitioner's frustration that that his organization was putting more work on Black employees to take a survey to "listen." In alignment with current trends, organizations may wish to elect a "Chief Listening Officer" who ensures that listening is conducted in a consistent, appropriate, and respectful manner. Chief listening officer roles have been touted as the "must-have position for organizations" (DiRenzo, 2022), but are often associated with social media listening for tapping into trends and tones of conversations among external stakeholders. Findings from this study suggest that designated listeners, such as chief listening officers, must also listen with a DE&I lens to hear different perspectives, address intersecting forms of oppression or barriers, and bridge dialogic gaps between organizations and diverse publics.

In conclusion, this exploratory study analyzed interviews from 54 strategic communications and public relations professionals to understand how they made meaning of organizational listening in support of DE&I. As Bardhan and Engstrom (2021) suggest, DE&I should not be an individual quest, but a responsibility shared among all members of an organization or industry. Findings suggest that organizations can take responsibility for listening in support of DE&I via structural enhancements, programming, personnel, and a community organizing lens. Because this study also noted a sense of futility or hesitancy expressed by some participants, future research must be carried out to better identify organizational leaders' meaning making of listening in support of DE&I and to better understand organizational barriers to developing protocols or architectures to listen in support of DE&I. Organizational listening architectures in support of DE&I, in alignment with intersectional and CRR approaches, may provide particularly effective paths forward for developing authentic, equitable, and social-justice oriented listening practices in strategic communications and public relations contexts.

References

Bardhan, N. R., & Engstrom, C. L. (2021). Diversity, inclusion, and leadership communication in public relations: A rhetorical analysis of diverse voices. *Public Relations Journal, 12*(4), 1–27.
Bentley, S. (1996). The all new, state-of-the-art ILA definition of listening: NoW that we have it, what do we do with it? https://www.listen.org/resources/Documents/56_Apr_96Spring.pdf
Bodie, G. (2016). Listening. Oxford Research Encyclopedia entry. Accessed January 12, 2018 at http://communication.oxfordre.com/view/10.1093/acrefore/9780190228613.001.0001/acr
Boyatzis, R. E. (1998). *Transforming qualitative information: Thematic analysis and code development*. Sage.
Claro M. C. (2022). Organizational listening and its implementation in the Chilean multi-store sector. *Public Relations Inquiry, 11*(2), 221–239. https://doi.org/10.1177/2046147X221081173
Corbin, J., & Strauss, A. (2008). *Basics of qualitative research* (3rd ed.). Sage.
Denzin, N. K., & Lincoln, Y. S. (2003). *The landscape of qualitative research theories and issues*. Sage.

DiRenzo, Z. (2022, Feb. 18). Chief listening officer: The must-have position for every organization in 2022. https://www.cnbc.com/2022/02/18/chief-listening-officer-the-must-have-position-for-every-organization.html

Ertem-Eray, T., & Ki, E. J. (2021). The status of diversity research in public relations: An analysis of published articles. *PRism, 17*(1), 1–21.

Falconi, T. (2016). Organizational listening. In C.E. Carroll (Ed.), *The SAGE encyclopedia of corporate reputation* (pp. 543–546). Sage.

Global Alliance. (2012). *The Melbourne Mandate.* https://www.globalalliancepr.org/melbourne-mandate

Grunig, L. A. (2006). Feminist phase analysis in public relations: Where have we been? Where do we need to go? *Journal of Public Relations Research, 18,* 115–140. https://doi.org/10.1207/s1532754xjprr1802_3

Lee, Y., Li, J. Y., & Sunny Tsai, W. H. (2021). Diversity-oriented leadership, internal communication, and employee outcomes: A perspective of racial minority employees. *Journal of Public Relations Research, 33*(5), 314–334. https://doi.org/10.1080/1062726X.2021.2007388

Lincoln, Y. S., & Guba, E. G. (1985). *Naturalistic inquiry.* Sage.

Logan, N. (2021). A theory of corporate responsibility to race (CRR): Communication and racial justice in public relations. *Journal of Public Relations Research, 33*(1), 6–22. https://doi.org/10.1080/1062726X.2021.1881898

Macnamara, J. (2013). Beyond voice: Audience-making and the work and architecture of listening as new media literacies. *Continuum, 27*(1), 160–175. https://doi.org/10.1080/10304312.2013.736950

Macnamara, J. (2015). *Creating an architecture of listening in organizations.* University of Technology, Sydney. 1–76. https://www.uts.edu.au/sites/default/files/fass-organizational-listening-report.pdf

Macnamara, J. (2016a). *Organizational listening: The missing essential in public communication.* Peter Lang.

Macnamara, J. (2016b). Organizational listening: Addressing a major gap in public relations theory and practice. *Journal of Public Relations Research, 28*(3–4), 146–169. https://doi.org/10.1080/1062726X.2016.1228064

Macnamara, J. (2018). Toward a theory and practice of organizational listening. *International Journal of Listening, 32*(1), 1–23. https://doi.org/10.1080/10904018.2017.1375076

Miles, M. B., & Huberman, A. M. (1994). *Qualitative data analysis: An expanded sourcebook.* Sage.

Neill, M. S., & Bowen, S. A. (2021a). Employee perceptions of ethical listening in US organizations. *Public Relations Review, 47*(5), 102123. https://doi.org/10.1016/j.pubrev.2021.102123

Neill, M. S., & Bowen, S. A. (2021b). Ethical listening to employees during a pandemic: New approaches, barriers and lessons. *Journal of Communication Management, 25*(3), 276–297. https://doi.org/10.1108/JCOM-09-2020-0103

Parks, E. S. (2019). *The ethics of listening: Creating space for sustainable dialogue.* Lexington Books.

Place, K. R. (2019). Listening as the driver of public relations practice and communications strategy within a global public relations agency. *Public Relations Journal, 12*(3), 1–18.

Place, K. R. (2022). Toward a framework for listening with consideration for intersectionality: Insights from public relations professionals in borderland

spaces. *Journal of Public Relations Research*, 1–16. https://doi.org/10.1080/1062726X.2022.2057502
Place, K., & Vanc, A. M. (2016). Exploring diversity and client work in public relations education. *Journal of Public Relations Education*, 2(2), 83–100.
Rubin, H. J. & Rubin, I. S. (2005). *Qualitative interviewing: The art of hearing data*. Sage.
Sahay, S. (2021). Organizational listening during organizational change: Perspectives of employees and executives. *International Journal of Listening*, 1–14. https://doi.org/10.1080/10904018.2021.1941029
The Language of Diversity. (2021). https://instituteforpr.org/defining-diversity-equity-inclusion-report/
Tsetsura, K. (2011). How understanding multidimensional diversity can benefit global public relations education. *Public Relations Review*, 37(5), 530–535. https://doi.org/10.1016/j.pubrev.2011.09.020
Tyler, J. A. (2011). Reclaiming rare listening as a means of organizational re-enchantment. *Journal of Organizational Change Management*, 24(1), 143–157. https://doi.org/10.1108/09534811111102328
Vardeman-Winter, J., & Place, K. R. (2017). Still a lily-white field of women: The state of workforce diversity in public relations practice and research. *Public Relations Review*, 43(2), 326–336. https://doi.org/10.1016/j.pubrev.2017.01.004
Worthington, D. L., & Fitch-Hauser, M. E. (2018). *Listening: Processes, functions, and competency*. Routledge.

11 Listening in Polarized Times

Centering Presence in Arendt's Actualized Plurality for Organizational Listening

Luke Capizzo

Introduction

Organizational listening theory promotes practices, skills, resources, and cultures that facilitate openness within organizations (e.g., Macnamara, 2016b; Place, 2019b). It emphasizes the central role of public relations in helping gather, analyze, and share the insights gleaned in the processes of listening. Many of today's public and strategic communication practitioners work in democratic societies facing high polarization and politicization (Hill, 2020) as well as a multitude of risks and challenges to free speech, free press, and basic voting rights. In this context, organizational listening has the potential to fulfill a larger purpose. Listening can act as a lens through which organizations view the issues and risks prioritized by stakeholders and communities—not simply the needs of the organization itself. Listening has the potential to open doors to stakeholders and publics whose voices have not been heard by organizations in the past (e.g., Ciszek & Rodriguez, 2020; Logan, 2021; Place, 2022; Place & Ciszek, 2021). It can be a vehicle for organizations to fulfill, through public relations, their civic responsibilities in the contexts of civil society (e.g., Saffer, 2019; Sommerfeldt, 2013; Taylor, 2011, 2018) and democratic discourse (Edwards, 2016; Macnamara, 2020; Motion & Leitch, 2009; Palazzo & Scherer, 2006) and to be better aware of (and address) the power inequities among organizations and subaltern publics (e.g., Munshi et al., 2017; Place, 2019a, 2022; Place & Ciszek, 2021).

This chapter takes up Hannah Arendt's concept of *plurality* and its impact on the framework of organizational listening. A core topic in Arendt's philosophy, her definition of plurality puts it at the center of her understanding of politics and political life—beyond *pluralism* or a valuing of the multiplicity of opinions and perspectives (Loidolt, 2018), plurality is "a sense of We" (Arnett, 2013, p. 239) or being, thinking, and acting among others who are inherently different from ourselves. Plurality is ever-present but must be cultivated through conscious tending and maintenance of "interspaces" between public and private life (Arendt, 2005). As Arnett (2013) explains, "for Arendt, the realm of politics is the space

DOI: 10.4324/9781003273851-15

between persons in the public domain that actually creates a common world" (p. 192). This commonality of understanding is clearly sought as a goal of organizational listening. Examining Arendt's plurality provides a bridge to a more discursive and deliberative democratic enactment of organizational listening theory, building on recent scholarship (e.g., Macnamara, 2020; Place, 2019b, 2022).

Yet, Arendt (1951) clearly defines plurality's limits, ensuring a clear line between potentially useful disagreement among perspectives and destructive displacement of others. A better knowledge of who we are—as individuals and organizations—is only possible through a deeper understanding of those around us, which must reflect a genuineness and openness toward their existence—not a strategic mindset. While mentioned as a possibility by Macnamara (2016b, 2020), the scope of this democratic, discursive, and deliberative purpose for organizational listening has yet to be fully explored. Timely enactment of plurality provides a crucial augmentation for organizational listening to achieve its community-centered potential. The next section provides an overview of relevant public relations theory, within and adjacent to organizational listening and listening scholarship, before turning to Arendt's concept of *actualized plurality*. Arendt gives us a perspective on the purpose and value of listening for organizations as part of a full understanding of societal responsibility and social contributions.

Literature

Organizational Listening in Public Relations

Organizational listening theory and the Organizational Listening Project remind practitioners and scholars of public relations of the importance of listening—and not just speaking—in our work to understand and improve the ways in which organizations communicate and act in their communities (e.g., Macnamara, 2016a, 2016b; Place, 2019b). A more civic-minded approach to organizational listening that centers pluralism as a core value has the potential to contribute to organizational citizenship and social responsibility in both communication and action.

Architecture of Listening

In his landmark book, *Organizational Listening: The Missing Essential in Public Communication*, Macnamara (2016b) outlines the rationale for listening as a central value and action of the public relations function. To counteract the loosely defined and often disingenuously applied practices of listening described in the project, Macnamara developed the "architecture of listening" as a practical roadmap enabling professional communicators to apply the values and tasks of listening to their work. The seven facets of the architectures are (1) culture, (2) politics/policies, (3) open systems, (4) technologies, (5) resources, (6) skills, and (7) articulation of insights to organizational decision-making (e.g., Macnamara, 2016a, 2016b). In this normative framework, organizations should (1) demonstrate a cultural openness and responsiveness to listening and new ideas (Gregory, 2015; Husband, 2009). Organizations should (2) adopt policies that require listening processes and empower listening-based knowledge (Dreher, 2009). Organizations should (3) maintain open systems for adaptation and implementation of feedback (Macnamara, 2016a; Place, 2019b). Organizations should provide team members with (4) the tools and (5) resources to gather listening-based data (Gregory & Halff, 2020; Macnamara, 2018) as well as with (6) the individual skills to listen effectively (Wolvin, 2010; Wolvin & Coakley, 1991). Finally, organizations should develop the structures, processes, and expertise to (7) analyze and share data from organizational listening efforts across the organization (Gregory & Macnamara, 2019; Macnamara & Gregory, 2018; Volk, 2016).

Properly understood and implemented, an architecture of listening can emphasize inclusiveness rather than strategic or organization-centric ends: As Macnamara (2019) points out, "an organization should listen to all who wish to communicate with it" (p. 5192), rather than prioritizing the stakeholders' organizational leaders deem to be important. Yet, as organizational listening scholars have emphasized, organizations often don't live up to the stated values and processes articulated in the architectures (e.g., Claro, 2022; Macnamara, 2016b; Place, 2019b). A complete understanding and enactment of listening must include "recognition, openness, acknowledgement, attention, understanding, consideration, and response" (Macnamara, 2020, p. 393). While the Organizational Listening Project and subsequent research (Macnamara, 2020; Place, 2019b, 2022) have moved the theory toward its societally centered potential, the full impact of organizational listening as a conduit for civic good through organizational engagement has yet to be realized.

Organizational Listening and Deliberative Society

Building on the initial studies, Macnamara (2020) established a clearer connection between organizational listening and the discursive and deliberative responsibilities of all types of organizations. Deliberative societies require the spaces and systems needed for productive discourse, and public relations can be a contributor to increasing the overall deliberative capacity of democratic systems (Edwards, 2016; Heath et al., 2013). Again, public relations efforts have failed to live up to these optimistic or normative conceptions of useful deliberative democratic contributions (e.g., Aronczyk & Espinoza, 2021; Habermas, 1991; Leitch & Motion, 2010). Lack of fully realized organizational listening values, systems, and resources are significant contributors, but this gap also reflects the degree to which organizations and organizational leaders may not have any desire to listen with genuineness and presence to perspectives that might contradict their own. As in dialogue, individuals and organizations take on risk by allowing themselves to fully listen to publics and stakeholders (Kent & Taylor, 2002; Theunissen & Wan Noordin, 2012).

Pluralism in Public Relations

While this chapter addresses Arendt's concept of plurality, the closest fully articulated concept within public relations scholarship is *pluralism*. While not often a central topic in public relations theory, pluralism has made its way into public relations research including in contexts of agonism (Davidson, 2016, 2018; Davidson & Motion, 2018), participative public relations (Motion, 2005), culture/intercultural public relations (Dutta & Elers, 2020; Gregory & Halff, 2013), lobbying (Davidson, 2015), and deliberative democracy (Aronczyk et al., 2017; Edwards, 2016; Ramsey, 2015).

In an agonistic context, pluralism is constitutive of democratic or deliberative processes and discourses (Davidson, 2016). In particular, what Davidson (2016) terms "contemporary agonism" centers radical pluralism and contention as the natural democratic state—understanding consensus and agreement as extremely contingent and temporary. This empowers the public relations function to act in a more fully postmodern model—embracing dissensus over having consensus as a primary objective (Ciszek, 2016; Holtzhausen, 2000; Holtzhausen & Voto, 2002). In addition to the mindset shift of favoring agonistic and dissensus-oriented strategies and tactics in working toward social justice causes on behalf of the organization (e.g., Ciszek & Logan, 2018), a postmodern model can reflect the individual acts of resistance practitioners can take, such Pompper's (2015) insider-activist role. This mindset positions social, environmental, and community-oriented goals and perspectives as a central part of what the public relations function can advocate for and bring to organizations. Thus, a pluralistic approach to public relations seeks to solve the existing shortcomings of an issues management mindset—such as an over-reliance on rational argument and a devaluing of emotion, gender, and individual experience (Madden, 2019)—through acknowledgment and engagement of dissenting opinions and perspectives.

The economic and power contexts of these discourses and voices matter as well. One useful thread is the distinction, raised by Davidson (2015) in a lobbying context, of pure pluralism and the more power-aware *neopluralism*. In short, ideas are not the only discursive currency—power and resources matter and often, but not always, influence discourse in a public affairs context (Baumgartner et al., 2009; Godwin et al., 2012; Ihlen, 2002). A power-aware pluralism appreciates the context and circumstances of publics and stakeholders—not just the logical value of their arguments. Public relations is never a power-neutral enterprise, particularly in its implications for deliberative and democratic discourse (Berger, 2005; Edwards, 2006). Bringing power imbalances and discursive inequities inherent in most deliberative discourse to light (e.g., Weder, 2021) makes the case for a representation-minded pluralism in public relations theory and moves an important step closer to a more ecological understanding, approaching Arendt's *plurality*.

Propinquity and Presence in Public Relations

The last part of this literature review turns to a final central component to connect organizational listening to *plurality*: Presence. The value of *propinquity* represents the centrality of presence, timeliness, and engagement for public relations practitioners, generally construed as part of dialogue (Kent & Taylor, 2002; Theunissen & Wan Noordin, 2012) and engagement (Dhanesh, 2017; Taylor & Kent, 2014). Dhanesh (2017) defines the concept as "an organization's openness to interacting with publics and to the idea that publics ought to be consulted in a timely and relevant manner" (p. 926), reflecting both the act of engagement as well as the recognition and prioritization of the information received. As Lane and Bartlett (2016) explain, "the presumption behind the principle of propinquity must be that decision makers (arguably the organization in most public relations instances) are prepared to rescind—or at least devolve—their power in this regard to others" (p. 477). Kent and Taylor (2002) understand propinquity as composed of three facets: "immediacy of presence, temporal flow, and engagement" (p. 26). Thus, organizations should actively seek and consciously value the perspectives of stakeholders and publics—not only when it is convenient but also when it matters most to those stakeholders and publics.

Asked directly about propinquity, Australian practitioners noted the importance of timeliness in seeking public input on certain issues, but questioned their ability to be genuinely present and responsive in conversations with stakeholders given their organizational mandates and objectives (Russmann & Lane, 2020). In addition to this interpersonal sense of propinquity, public expressions of plurality—as outlined by Arendt (2018)—reflect an inherent publicness that mirrors understandings of open dialogue in public relations as a potentially transformative and cumulative shared force (Capizzo, 2018; Madden & Alt, 2021). To effect change, activist use of open dialogue is concurrent and reinforcing (Madden & Alt, 2021).

Presence in Listening

Outside of public relations research, scholarship on listening has supported an emphasis on the value of presence (e.g., Bodie, 2012; Tompkins,

2009). Husband (2009) understands listening as "an act of attention, a willingness to focus on the other, to heed both their presence and their communication" (p. 441). In Parks' (2018) book *The Ethics of Listening: Creating Space for Sustainable Dialogue*, she emphasizes that "ethical listening engagement demands presence" (p. 130). At different points in the text, she refers to "active presence" (p. 4), "intentional presence" (pp. 171–172), and "narrative presence" (p. 150) to emphasize the nuances of giving attentiveness and engagement. The most central of these for Parks, *intentional presence*, provides reasonable guidance for listeners including (1) prioritizing the speaker's priorities, (2) efficiency of conversation, (3) information retention, and (4) appropriate reactions and responses (see p. 114). While much more concrete and attainable than propinquity in public relations conceptualizations of dialogue (e.g., Kent & Taylor, 2002; Lane, 2020), this line of inquiry mirrors the valuing and centrality of both attendance and attentiveness in listening practice. To augment existing conceptions of genuine and representative organizational listening, the paper now turns to the concept of plurality and the work of Hannah Arendt as a resource and guide.

Hannah Arendt

The following section examines the political theory of Hannah Arendt, in particular her concept of *actualized plurality*, in order to inform public relations theory around organizational listening. Arendt's work is analyzed with the help of several secondary sources, primarily scholars from outside of the public relations discipline, to provide additional context, insight, and grounding for the interpretation. Two significant guides for this analysis are Arnett's (2013) book *Communication Ethics in Dark Times: Hannah Arendt's Rhetoric of Warning and Hope*, which interprets Arendt in the context of communication scholarship, and Loidolt's (2018) book *Phenomenology of Plurality: Hannah Arendt on Political Intersubjectivity*, which focuses on the role of plurality in her thought and writing. Both books attempt to view Arendt's thought holistically across her decades of work. This section introduces Arendt's definition of plurality, before turning to *actualized plurality* and differentiating between *plurality* and *pluralism*, and, finally, seeking her understanding of plurality's limits.

Hannah Arendt and Plurality

Hannah Arendt was an outsider: a Jewish woman in Weimar, Germany; an immigrant in the United States; an itinerant academic with a broad public audience; and a leading political theorist of her generation. Her work addresses these topics explicitly in her writings on the *parvenu* or societal pariah (Arnett, 2013) and undergirds her recurring focus on being and belonging to the world (Loidolt, 2018). She fled to the United States, her home from 1941 until the end of her life, and wrote, lectured, and witnessed the middle of the 20th century as a university faculty member based primarily in New York City. She first came to public prominence in 1958 for her acclaimed book *The Human Condition* and continued to publish and provoke with work centered on the darkness and light of existence, the outsider—a refugee herself until she gained US citizenship in 1950—and the challenges of modernity for human and political life (Arnett, 2013; Young-Bruehl, 2004).

In introducing the concept of *plurality*, Arendt forced a paradigm shift within the field of political theory, breaking with a more philosophically oriented tradition in political thought that sought individualized answers for questions concerning the shared spaces and places of human existence (Loidolt, 2018). Most directly addressed as part of *The Human Condition* (2018) and *The Life of the Mind* (1978), plurality faces the tension between individuality and similarity: "Plurality is the condition of human action because we are all the same, that is, human, in such a way that nobody is ever the same as anyone else who has ever lived, lives, or will live" (Arendt, 2018, p. 8). In this way, Arendt's plurality "is not something that simply is, but essentially something we have to take up and do" (Loidolt, 2018, p. 15). Plurality is "the condition—not only the *conditio sine qua non*, but the *conditio per quam*—of all political life" (p. 7), both the indispensable condition of and the cause or genesis for our common or social existence.

Plurality is intrinsic and exists within individuals and organizations as well as among them: "In our terms, wherever there is a plurality—of living beings, of things, of ideas—there is difference, and this difference does not arise from the outside but is inherent in every entity in the form of duality, from which comes unity as unification" (Arendt, 1978, p. 184). In Arendt's posthumously edited collection, *The Promise of Politics* (2005), she explained that "the faculty of speech and the fact of human plurality correspond to each other, not only in the sense that I used words for communication with those with whom I am together in the world, but in the even more relevant sense that speaking with myself I live together with myself" (p. 20). Plurality therefore exists inside individuals and as part of the fabric of organizations in addition to the differences between and among distinct individuals and entities. As Macnamara (2016b, 2020) posits in the context of organizational listening, an understanding of others (a prerequisite to acting in ways that reflect common goals and interests) is both intrinsic to organizational life and potentially lacking in its connectivity and understanding of diverse stakeholders. While *pluralism* speaks to a tolerance for a diversity of perspectives and options, *plurality*—particularly Arendt's actualized plurality—emphasizes the action, engagement, and presence needed to fully (1) understand the viewpoints of others (and those within ourselves) and (2) act with regard for others as a community and societal citizen.

Actualized Plurality

The experience of actualized plurality, for Arendt, rests on the interrelated concepts of *intentionality* and *subjectivity* (Loidolt, 2015, 2018). Plurality cannot be actualized if it is implicit (as opposed to specifically and deliberately part of consideration and action and must also be informed through the insights and perspectives of others. Therefore, to be actualized, plurality must be enacted (1) consciously, (2) among others, and (3) through a decentering of the self and a distancing (or, at least, contextualization) of self-interest. As Loidolt (2018) argues, "intentional presence is the basic event, a state of actuality, from which subjectivity, world, and intersubjectivity emerge as interrelated elements" (p. 77). In the context of organizational life, this references the importance of showing up—of being present for important discussions as an organization—as well as being wholly cognizant of other individuals and organizations that have done the same. It represents an awareness of our being among others, an action of engagement with the broader world. It is only actualized as a public or external action: "Plurality is not something that simply is, but essentially something we have to take up and do. Therefore, it manifests itself only as an actualization of plurality in a space of appearances" (Loidolt, 2018, p. 2). In all of these ways, plurality is about publicness—being and acting with or among others in communities. In the context of organizational listening and public relations, this means that it is not enough to listen, but organizations must listen visibly and transparently—disclosing their architectures.

Actualized plurality is an ongoing process that occurs through action, rather than a passive stance or perspective. As Loidolt (2018) explains, "it is important to note that it does not primarily describe a concept (as if Arendt had 'discovered' the 'concept of plurality'), but something that happens in a verbal sense like an activity, e.g. the activity of dancing or conducting a conversation" (p. 51). Action happens (and has consequences) among members of a community "in which a We is always engaged in changing our common world, stands in the sharpest possible opposition to the solitary business of thought, which operates in a dialogue between me and myself" (Arendt, 1978, p. 200). In this way, the inclusion of both internal dialogue and discourse among individuals and groups serves as a prerequisite for plurality through action.

Finally, presence and appearance are central concepts to achieve actualized plurality. Our understanding of reality exists due to the public presence of others: "For without a space of appearance and without trusting in action and speech as a mode of being together, neither the reality of one's self, of one's own identity, nor the reality of the surrounding world can be established beyond doubt" (Arendt, 2018, p. 208). Thus, plurality is linked to presence in public life and discourse. According to Loidolt (2018), relative to prior understandings of *appearance* in political thought, "Arendt transforms them from an appearance for someone (in the intentional relation) to worldly appearance for many. This entails an investigation of three of Arendt's central theses: To be real means to appear; to be a self means to appear; to 'be of-the-world' means to fundamentally belong to the realm of appearance" (p. 53). This emphasizes the fundamental publicness necessary for political life—for being together and acting together.

Plurality and Pluralism

Arendt's concept of *plurality* goes beyond the common political or democratic understanding of pluralism as an acceptance of difference. Plurality is grounded in the truth that we live in the world together, not as wholly separate individuals. Our actions and communication have consequences for others, and we depend on others for our own survival. For Arendt, an individual's perspectives matter, but their full humanity and being are only fully realized as part of a community, with the interdependence, compromise, and discourse that such membership (or citizenship) entails. Beyond pluralism, plurality reflects a "two-fold character of equality and distinction" (Arendt, 2018, p. 175): (1) A presumption of equality is necessary for understanding and discourse, and (2) if we weren't different, we wouldn't need to communicate. Thus, "the actualization of the human condition of plurality, that is, of living as a distinct and unique being among equals" (p. 178). Her understanding of political community grows from the need to accept the essential humanness of others in order to build shared spaces and societies. If *pluralism* is an acceptance of others and their distinct or disparate beliefs and perspectives, *plurality* is an embrace of their equal standing and value in a community.

Ethics and Limits of Plurality

The concept of an actualized plurality holds the potential for significant ethically positive contributions in deliberative and political contexts (Loidolt, 2018). While plurality itself is inescapable, an actualized plurality requires consistent engagement and nurturing. Its limits or inherent fragility are, in essence, at the heart of its ethical contribution. Arendt's plurality necessitates (1) self-limitation, (2) protection of interspaces, and (3) "inherent conditions for success that are of an ethical nature" (p. 235). It is a perspective that prioritizes "visibility and interruption" (p. 237). Thus, plurality requires multiple qualities (referred to by Loidolt and "attitudes" and "virtues") that undergird its ethical nature. These include courage (or risk taking), truth (in the sense or a shared understanding of reality), and trust (or belief in promises and follow-through of others). In these ways, plurality is a contextualizing force—a way for individuals and organizations to more fully grasp the needs of the communities and societies they inhabit. Arendt places this embeddedness in stark contrast to the ideas of alienation and "worldlessness" that flow through much of her work (e.g., Arendt, 1951, 1997; Arnett, 2013). Existing ethically in political communities requires active engagement toward such an understanding. By contrast, the conformity of mass society as well as the "conditions of radical isolation" can undermine plurality (Arendt, 2018, p. 58).

Loidolt (2018) posits that, in contrast to explicitly agonistic theorists such as Chantal Mouffe and Ernesto Laclau, Arendt does not see discussion or policy implementation of ethics as harming or limiting the nature of plurality, except for those—on one hand—who would attempt to remove or minimize conflict in public spaces, prioritizing "excessively harmonizing" (p. 233) or on the other, those who consciously spread known falsehoods (Arendt, 1983). Loidolt (2018) summarizes Arendt's approach by explaining that "we need the experiences of speaking, acting, and judging in public, in order to develop and keep up a sense of individual relevance against a logic of dealing with the masses that has the ethically erroneous but unerring tendency to become monstrous" (p. 244).

It is in this context that Arendt's pluralism speaks most directly to the 21st century concerns of increasing political polarization (e.g., Barberá, 2020; Sunstein, 2018; Zhou, 2019) and dis- and mis-information (e.g., Boman, 2021; Boman & Schneider, 2021; Ihlen et al., 2019; Pamment et al., 2018). Public relations practitioners may find themselves in the middle or on multiple sides of a variety of highly polarized issues and contexts, from the Women's March (Vardeman & Sebesta, 2020) to Black Lives Matter and racial justice (Ciszek & Logan, 2018; Edrington, 2022; Edrington & Lee, 2018; Logan, 2021), to LGBTQ rights (Capizzo, 2020; Ciszek, 2017, 2020; Place et al., 2021; Zhou, 2021). While organizations and practitioners may not (and should not) embrace all perspectives or the views of all stakeholders, these polarized issues force many organizations to see the spectrum of pluralistic viewpoints that they may have skirted in the past. Arendt emphasizes plurality as a way of being in the world that directly opposes the horrors she lived through: The displacement and mass migration of world wars, the antisemitism of Weimar Germany, and the dehumanization and mass murder of the holocaust (Arnett, 2013; Young-Bruehl, 2004).

In contrast, Arendt's ideal politics emphasizes "spontaneity, imagination, participation, and empowerment" (Benhabib, 1992, p. 81). Loidolt (2018) compares the rules of implementing an actualized plurality to playing and improvising in jazz ensembles—structures, norms, and standards exist and are known to the participants but can be revised or broken in certain contexts. The goal is not victory or defeat, but a communal understanding of success or "a willingness to maintain a common world together" (p. 236). Success relies on the skill and training of the participants, the adjustment to each other's actions, and a degree of respect for the autonomy of others. This does not make the space of public contention any less "turbulent and fragile" (p. 236), but it does contribute to an inherently more communally ethical discourse, more open to an understanding and valuing of others. Again, there is room for perspective, but such standpoints have their limits: "Facts inform opinions and opinions, inspired by different interests and passions, can differ widely and still be legitimate as long as they respect factual truth" (Arendt, 1983, p. 238). The further removed such discourse becomes from a space of commonality, the more plurality is destabilized (Loidolt, 2018). Awareness of this fragility or vulnerability contributes to an understanding of ethical communication, action, and engagement in shared spaces. This speaks to the individual or organizational potential for "reflective judgment" or stance-taking that embraces the complexity of ecologically interconnected communities (p. 251). Organizations participating in society have an obligation and responsibility to seek the perspectives of others. Arendt's actualized plurality examines this mandate in all of its precarity but also uncovers its potential to seed more holistic and ethical engagement with the world.

Discussion: Arendt's Plurality in Public Relations and Organizational Listening

Organizational listening is a framework for guiding organizations to be more complete citizens within their communities and societies (Macnamara, 2016b, 2020). It speaks to the specific shortcomings of public relations as a discipline—one historically and primarily focused on organizational speaking rather than full engagement (Macnamara, 2016a). It opens a door to the public relations function prioritizing a less organization-centric worldview, and one more aware of power and inequity (Place, 2022). The work of Hannah Arendt provides a lens that extends organizational listening toward a more complete awareness and embrace of organizational citizenship and organizational contributions to civil society. This final section addresses theoretical and practical implications of Arendt's actualized plurality for organizational listening in public relations.

Theoretical and Practical Implications

Public relations practitioners doing the ongoing work of organizational listening face significant challenges, particularly in a time of high political polarization and challenges to democratic norms and journalistic freedoms within many countries. The public relations function can act to support civil society and build social capital (e.g., Saffer, 2019; Sommerfeldt, 2013; Taylor, 2011, 2018) and make substantive, productive contributions to democratic discourse and civic debate (Davidson, 2016; Edwards, 2016; Ramsey, 2015), but it needs a holistic understanding of communities and societies in order to achieve these contributions. Organizational listening has the potential to aid the public relations function in this mandate (Macnamara, 2016b, 2020)—and *plurality* is a useful supplement and outcome. While public relations scholarship has addressed *pluralism* (e.g., Davidson, 2015; Davidson & Motion, 2018; Motion & Leitch, 2009), plurality goes beyond a passive acceptance of multiple viewpoints to embrace an active, ongoing process of understanding others as fundamental to community citizenship (Arendt, 2018). Arendt's actualized plurality (i.e., Loidolt, 2015, 2018) provides four central takeaways in the context of public relations—tenets of plurality for organizational listening: (1) the necessity to address information and perspectives gathered by listening architectures; (2) the value of actively listening for the outsider; (3) the organizational imperative to hear, listen, and act as part of an interconnected community ecology; and (4) the responsibility of intentional presence (and accompanying risks) in listening activities.

The listening imperative, as underscored by Macnamara (2016a, 2016b, 2018) and Place (2019b, 2022), requires that listening not just be a one-way accumulation of information but must be done with genuine interest, engagement, and willingness to be open to other perspectives—and utilize them in organizational decision making. First, this means an understanding of complexity of identities and resulting needs for listening that are "intimate, synchronous, or personalized" (Place, 2022, p. 15). Intersectional lenses for listening empower the public relations function to better see and address power differentials (Ciszek & Rodriguez, 2020; Place, 2022; Place & Ciszek, 2021). Rather than only large-scale, systematic data-gathering approaches, listening practices must range from intimate to mass and take into account the structural challenges faced at interpersonal, organization, and societal levels. From Arendt's perspective, this prioritizes a focus on listening as part of the maintenance of interspaces, the gaps between our private and public selves (and the spaces in which we enact these selves) that allow for the individual-level maintenance of differences and that allow citizens to be themselves (Arendt, 2018; Arnett, 2013) to understand what distinct individuals and groups need in order to fully contribute their perspectives to organizational discussions. In this way, the imperative can be framed as part of expanded understandings of an organization's societal responsibilities (e.g., Logan, 2021; Palazzo & Scherer, 2006).

Arendt's actualized plurality is reflective of her life as an outsider and refugee, and her extensive writing on the *parvenu* and the importance of understanding those excluded from certain circles or societies (Arendt, 1997; Arnett, 2013). This line of reasoning reminds practitioners of organizational listening of the significant potential barriers for inclusion in organizational discourse and decision-making. It emphasizes that listening for the "outsider" is an active, additional step in holistic understandings of communities and that actualized plurality requires the work of understanding, contextualizing, and applying perspectives beyond those embedded in the organization itself. Organizational listening provides tools for recognizing *appearance* of a wide variety of stakeholders (Arendt, 2018; Loidolt, 2018) and thus exposing the organization to a better understanding of its environment as well as a broader array of perspectives. This entails looking for opportunities beyond existing or accepted stakeholder relationships, in particular allow for the prioritization of subaltern groups, counterpublics, and others whose perspectives organizations may not have traditionally valued (Place, 2019a; Place & Ciszek, 2021). In this way, organizational listening provides space for public relations practitioners to embrace their own understanding of resistance and activism in their work (Ciszek & Rodriguez, 2020; Dutta & Elers, 2020; Holtzhausen & Voto, 2002; Pompper, 2015), pushing back against the organizational "banal" when such banality masks injustice (Arendt, 1964; Aronczyk & Espinoza, 2021). In this way, public relations can more fully embody its role as a "steward of democracy" by improving organizational understandings of community ecologies (Heath et al., 2013, p. 278).

A more fully holistic perspective of organizational listening, drawn from actualized plurality, leads to a clearer acceptance of dissensus and radical pluralism (e.g., Ciszek, 2016; Davidson & Motion, 2018). Organizations better understand their situated place within a community or society, including the resources they and others have or lack (Ihlen, 2002). It allows for a wider range of opinions, perspectives, and platforms to be included in organizational decision-making, as well as supporting a more open-ended understanding of measuring organizational success (e.g., Capizzo, 2022; Gregory & Macnamara, 2019; Macnamara & Gregory, 2018; Volk, 2016)—defining and measuring success with and among others. It connects with the practical questions and needs of organizations, rather than only interacting at a theoretical level (Claro, 2022; Place, 2019b). An overreliance on big data and quantitative approaches at the expense of qualitative and power-informed understandings creates (Gregory & Halff, 2020).

Finally, actualized plurality moves ethically informed organizational listening closer to genuine dialogue (e.g., Kent & Taylor, 2002; Lane, 2020; Taylor & Kent, 2014) in emphasizing presence of engagement (e.g., Bodie, 2012; Parks, 2018; Tompkins, 2009) and the potential associated risks of propinquity (Kent & Taylor, 2002). It also reflects the inherent publicness and shared spaces of open dialogue (Capizzo, 2018; Madden & Alt, 2021). For Arendt, embracing plurality requires the contextualization of action among everyone affected by its potential outcomes. Such knowledge comes from the mutual understanding created in moments of propinquity, reflecting those organizations stretching for genuine dialogue

(Lane, 2020). Augmenting organizational listening practice with these values provides additional support for hearing and understanding the perspectives of diverse internal and external stakeholders, and—most critically—acting on such knowledge with an awareness of power imbalances and intersectional identities (Place, 2022).

Conclusion

Building from community-oriented and stakeholder-centered conceptions of organizational management, a more radical, holistic implementation of organizational listening can harness the full potential of public relations to inform and lead more ethical, caring, and just organizations. Deeper understandings of a wider range of organizational publics and stakeholders help organizations act and communicate more ethically, particularly in a growing environment of mis- and dis-information (Boman, 2021; Boman & Schneider, 2021; Ihlen et al., 2019). Actualized plurality, based on Arendt's political theory, provides a clear rationale for empowered organizational listening as activist public relations (e.g., Coombs & Holladay, 2012; Holtzhausen, 2000). It opens the door for listening as a tool of resistance for practitioners (e.g., Ciszek & Rodriguez, 2020; Dutta & Elers, 2020; Holtzhausen & Voto, 2002; Munshi et al., 2017; Pompper, 2015). It prioritizes seeing publics and stakeholders as equals and helps practitioners understand them in light of how they see themselves. It reminds us that ethical and constructive organizational listening begins from intentional presence in conversations and communities—a step every organization and every public relations practitioner can take as they enter the larger world.

References

Arendt, H. (1951). *The origins of totalitarianism.* Harcourt.
Arendt, H. (1964). *Eichmann in Jerusalem: A report on the banality of evil.* Viking Press.
Arendt, H. (1978). *The life of the mind.* Harcourt.
Arendt, H. (1983). *Between past and future: Eight exercises in political thought.* Penguin.
Arendt, Hannah (1997) [1958]. *Rahel Varnhagen: The life of a Jewess.* Johns Hopkins University Press. *ISBN 978-0-8018-5587-0.*
Arendt, H. (2005). *The promise of politics.* Schocken Books.
Arendt, H. (2018). *The human condition.* University of Chicago Press. (Original work published 1958.)
Arnett, R. C. (2013). *Communication ethics in dark times: Hannah Arendt's rhetoric of warning and hope.* Southern Illinois University Press.
Aronczyk, M., Edwards, L., & Kantola, A. (2017). Apprehending public relations as a promotional industry. *Public Relations Inquiry, 6*(2), 139–155. https://doi.org/10.1177/2046147X17706411

Aronczyk, M., & Espinoza, M. I. (2021). *A strategic nature: Public relations and the politics of American environmentalism*. Oxford University Press.

Barberá, P. (2020). Social media, echo chambers, and political polarization. In N. Persily & J. A. Tucker (Eds.), *Social media and democracy: The state of the field, prospects for reform* (pp. 34–55). Cambridge University Press.

Baumgartner, F. R., Berry, M., Hojnacki, M., Leech, B., & Kimball, D. (2009). *Lobbying and policy change: Who wins, who loses, and why*. University of Chicago Press.

Benhabib, S. (1992). Models of public space: Hannah Arendt, the liberal tradition, and Jurgen Habermas. In C. Calhoun (Ed.), *Habermas and the public sphere* (pp. 73–98). MIT Press.

Berger, B. K. (2005). Power over, power with, and power to relations: Critical reflections on public relations, the dominant coalition, and activism. *Journal of Public Relations Research*, *17*(1), 5–28. https://doi.org/10.1207/s1532754xjprr1701_3

Bodie, G. D. (2012). Listening as positive communication. In T. Socha & M. J. Pitts (Eds.), *The positive side of interpersonal communication* (pp. 109–125). Peter Lang.

Boman, C. D. (2021). Examining characteristics of prebunking strategies to overcome PR disinformation attacks. *Public Relations Review*, *47*(5), 102105. https://doi.org/10.1016/j.pubrev.2021.102105

Boman, C. D., & Schneider, E. J. (2021). Finding an antidote: Testing the use of proactive crisis strategies to protect organizations from astroturf attacks. *Public Relations Review*, *47*(1), 102004. https://doi.org/10.1016/j.pubrev.2020.102004

Capizzo, L. (2018). Reimagining dialogue in public relations: Bakhtin and open dialogue in the public sphere. *Public Relations Review*, *44*(4), 523–532. https://doi.org/10.1016/j.pubrev.2018.07.007

Capizzo, L. (2020). The right side of history, inc.: Social issues management, social license to operate, and the Obergefell v. Hodges decision. *Public Relations Review*, *46*(5), 101957. https://doi.org/10.1016/j.pubrev.2020.101957

Capizzo, L. (2022). What counts amid contention? Measuring perceived intractable problems in public relations. *Public Relations Review*, *48*(2), 102179. https://doi.org/10.1016/j.pubrev.2022.102179

Ciszek, E. (2020). "We are people, not transactions": Trust as a precursor to dialogue with LGBTQ publics. *Public Relations Review*, *46*(1), 101759. https://doi.org/10.1016/j.pubrev.2019.02.003

Ciszek, E. L. (2016). Digital activism: How social media and dissensus inform theory and practice. *Public Relations Review*, *42*(2), 314–321. https://doi.org/10.1016/j.pubrev.2016.02.002

Ciszek, E. L. (2017). Activist strategic communication for social change: A transnational case study of lesbian, gay, bisexual, and transgender activism. *Journal of Communication*, *67*(5), 702–718. https://doi.org/10.1111/jcom.12319

Ciszek, E., & Logan, N. (2018). Challenging the dialogic promise: How Ben & Jerry's support for black lives matter fosters dissensus on social media. *Journal of Public Relations Research*, *30*(3), 115–127. https://doi.org/10.1080/1062726X.2018.1498342

Ciszek, E., & Rodriguez, N. S. (2020). Power, agency and resistance in public relations: A queer of color critique of the Houston equal rights ordinance. *Communication, Culture and Critique*, *13*(4), 536–555. https://doi.org/10.1093/ccc/tcaa024

Claro, M. C. (2022). Organizational listening and its implementation in the Chilean multi-store sector. *Public Relations Inquiry, 11*(2), 221–239. https://doi.org/10.1177/2046147X221081173

Coombs, W. T., & Holladay, S. J. (2012). Privileging an activist vs. a corporate view of public relations history in the US. *Public Relations Review, 38*(3), 347–353. https://doi.org/10.1016/j.pubrev.2011.11.010

Dhanesh, G. S. (2017). Putting engagement in its PRoper place: State of the field, definition and model of engagement in public relations. *Public Relations Review, 43*(5), 925–933. https://doi.org/10.1016/j.pubrev.2017.04.001

Davidson, S. (2015). Everywhere and nowhere: Theorising and researching public affairs and lobbying within public relations scholarship. *Public Relations Review, 41*(5), 615–627. https://doi.org/10.1016/j.pubrev.2014.02.023

Davidson, S. (2016). Public relations theory: An agonistic critique of the turns to dialogue and symmetry. *Public Relations Inquiry, 5*(2), 145–167. https://doi.org/10.1177/2046147X16649007

Davidson, S. (2018). Organizational rhetoric in deeply pluralistic societies. In Ø. Ihlen & R. L. Heath (Eds.), *The handbook of organizational rhetoric and communication* (pp. 301–313). Wiley. https://doi.org/10.1002/9781119265771.ch21

Davidson, S., & Motion, J. (2018). On Mouffe: Radical pluralism and public relations. In Ø. Ihlen & M. Fredriksson (Eds.), *Public relations and social theory* (pp. 394–413). Routledge.

Dreher, T. (2009). Listening across difference: Media and multiculturalism beyond the politics of voice. *Continuum: Journal of Media & Cultural Studies, 23*(4), 445–458. https://doi.org/10.1080/10304310903015712

Dutta, M. J., & Elers, S. (2020). Public relations, indigeneity and colonization: Indigenous resistance as dialogic anchor. *Public Relations Review, 46*(1), 101852. https://doi.org/10.1016/j.pubrev.2019.101852

Edrington, C. L. (2022). Social movements and identification: An examination of how black lives matter and March for our lives use identification strategies on Twitter to build relationships. *Journalism & Mass Communication Quarterly, 99*(3), 643–659. https://doi.org/10.1177/10776990221106994

Edrington, C. L., & Lee, N. (2018). Tweeting a social movement: Black lives matter and its use of Twitter to share information, build community, and promote action. *The Journal of Public Interest Communications, 2*(2), 289–289. https://doi.org/10.32473/jpic.v2.i2.p289

Edwards, L. (2006). Rethinking power in public relations. *Public Relations Review, 32*(3), 229–231. https://doi.org/10.1016/j.pubrev.2006.05.013

Edwards, L. (2016). The role of public relations in deliberative systems. *Journal of Communication, 66*(1), 60–81. https://doi.org/10.1111/jcom.12199

Godwin, R. K., Ainsworth, S., & Godwin, E. K. (2012). *Lobbying and policymaking*. CQ Press.

Gregory, A. (2015). Practitioner-leaders' representation of roles: The Melbourne mandate. *Public Relations Review, 41*(5), 598–606. https://doi.org/10.1016/j.pubrev.2014.02.030

Gregory, A., & Halff, G. (2013). Divided we stand: Defying hegemony in global public relations theory and practice? *Public Relations Review, 39*(5), 417–425. https://doi.org/10.1016/j.pubrev.2013.04.006

Gregory, A., & Halff, G. (2020). The damage done by big data-driven public relations. *Public Relations Review*, *46*(2), 101902. https://doi.org/10.1016/j.pubrev.2020.101902

Gregory, A., & Macnamara, J. (2019). An evaluation U-turn: From narrow organisational objectives to broad accountability. *Public Relations Review*, *45*(5), 101838. https://doi.org/10.1016/j.pubrev.2019.101838

Habermas, J. (1991). *The structural transformation of the public sphere: An inquiry into a category of Bourgeois society*. In T. Burger (Trans.). MIT Press. (Original work published 1962.)

Heath, R. L., Waymer, D., & Palenchar, M. J. (2013). Is the universe of democracy, rhetoric, and public relations whole cloth or three separate galaxies? *Public Relations Review*, *39*(4), 271–279. https://doi.org/10.1016/j.pubrev.2013.07.017

Hill, S. (2020). Politics and corporate content: Situating corporate strategic communication between marketing and activism. *International Journal of Strategic Communication*, *14*(5), 317–329. https://doi.org/10.1080/1553118X.2020.1817029

Holtzhausen, D. R. (2000). Postmodern values in public relations. *Journal of Public Relations Research*, *12*(1), 93–114. https://doi.org/10.1207/S1532754XJPRR1201_6

Holtzhausen, D. R., & Voto, R. (2002). Resistance from the margins: The postmodern public relations practitioner as organizational activist. *Journal of Public Relations Research*, *14*(1), 57–84. https://doi.org/10.1207/S1532754XJPRR1401_3

Husband, C. (2009). Commentary: Between listening and understanding. *Continuum: Journal of Media & Cultural Studies*, *23*(4), 441–443. https://doi.org/10.1080/10304310903026602

Ihlen, Ø. (2002). Rhetoric and resources: Notes for a new approach to public relations and issues management. *Journal of Public Affairs*, *2*(4), 259–269. https://doi.org/10.1002/pa.118

Ihlen, Ø., Gregory, A., Luoma-aho, V., & Buhmann, A. (2019). Post-truth and public relations: Special section introduction. *Public Relations Review*, *45*(4), 101844. https://doi.org/10.1016/j.pubrev.2019.101844

Kent, M. L., & Taylor, M. (2002). Toward a dialogic theory of public relations. *Public Relations Review*, *28*(1), 21–37. https://doi.org/10.1016/S0363-8111(02)00108-X

Lane, A. B. (2020). The dialogic ladder: Toward a framework of dialogue. *Public Relations Review*, *46*(1), 101870. https://doi.org/10.1016/j.pubrev.2019.101870

Lane, A., & Bartlett, J. (2016). Why dialogic principles don't make it in practice-and what we can do about it. *International Journal of Communication*, *10*, 4074–4094. https://ijoc.org/index.php/ijoc/issue/view/12

Leitch, S., & Motion, J. (2010). Publics and public relations: Effective change. In R. L. Heath (Ed.), *The SAGE handbook of public relations* (pp. 99–110). Sage Publications.

Logan, N. (2021). A theory of corporate responsibility to race (CRR): Communication and racial justice in public relations. *Journal of Public Relations Research*, *33*(1), 6–22. https://doi.org/10.1080/1062726X.2021.1881898

Loidolt, S. (2015). Hannah Arendt's conception of actualized plurality. In T. Szanto & D. Moran (Eds.), *Phenomenology of sociality* (pp. 42–55). Routledge.

Loidolt, S. (2018). *Phenomenology of plurality: Hannah Arendt on political intersubjectivity*. Routledge.

Macnamara, J. (2016a). Organizational listening: Addressing a major gap in public relations theory and practice. *Journal of Public Relations Research*, *28*(3–4), 146–169. https://doi.org/10.1080/1062726x.2016.1228064

Macnamara, J. (2016b). *Organizational listening: The missing essential in public communication*. Peter Lang.

Macnamara, J. (2018). Toward a theory and practice of organizational listening. *International Journal of Listening*, *32*(1), 1–23. https://doi.org/10.1080/10904018.2017.1375076

Macnamara, J. (2019). Explicating listening in organization-public communication: Theory, practices, technologies. *International Journal of Communication*, *13*, 5183–5204. https://ijoc.org/index.php/ijoc/article/view/11996

Macnamara, J. (2020). Listening for healthy democracy. In D. L. Worthington & G. D. Brodie (Eds.), *The handbook of listening* (pp. 385–395). Wiley. https://doi.org/10.1002/9781119554189.ch26

Macnamara, J., & Gregory, A. (2018). Expanding evaluation to progress strategic communication: Beyond message tracking to open listening. *International Journal of Strategic Communication*, *12*(4), 469–486. https://doi.org/10.1080/1553118X.2018.1450255

Madden, S. (2019). The issue with issues management: Considering the emotional and gendered core of issues. *Public Relations Inquiry*, *8*(3), 299–317. https://doi.org/10.1177/2046147X19872

Madden, S., & Alt, R. A. (2021). Know her name: Open dialogue on social media as a form of innovative justice. *Social Media + Society*, *7*(1). https://doi.org/10.1177/2056305120984447

Motion, J. (2005). Participative public relations: Power to the people or legitimacy for government discourse? *Public Relations Review*, *31*(4), 505–512. https://doi.org/10.1016/j.pubrev.2005.08.009

Motion, J., & Leitch, S. (2009). The transformational potential of public policy discourse. *Organization Studies*, *30*(10), 1045–1061. https://doi.org/10.1177/0170840609337940

Munshi, D., Kurian, P., & Xifra, J. (2017). An (other) "story" in history: Challenging colonialist public relations in novels of resistance. *Public Relations Review*, *43*(2), 366–374. https://doi.org/10.1016/j.pubrev.2017.02.016

Palazzo, G., & Scherer, A. G. (2006). Corporate legitimacy as deliberation: A communicative framework. *Journal of Business Ethics*, *66*(1), 71–88. https://doi.org/10.1007/s10551-006-9044-2

Pamment, J., Nothhaft, H., Agardh-Twetman, H., & Fjällhed, A. (2018). *Countering information influence activities: The state of the art*. Lund, Department of Strategic Communication. Available online: https://www.msb.se/RibData/Filer/pdf/28697.pdf

Parks, E. S. (2018). *The ethics of listening: Creating space for sustainable dialogue*. Lexington Books.

Place, K. R. (2019a). Exploring digital, social and mobile dialogic engagement with low-income publics. *Public Relations Journal*, *12*(4), 1–17. https://m.lunyim.com/prjournal/wp-content/uploads/Exploring-Digital-Updated-090519.pdf

Place, K. R. (2019b). Listening as the driver of public relations practice and communications strategy within a global public relations agency. *Public Relations Journal*, *12*(3), 1–18. https://prjournal.instituteforpr.org/wp-content/uploads/katieplace_listening.pdf

Place, K. R. (2022). Toward a framework for listening with consideration for intersectionality: Insights from public relations professionals in borderland spaces. *Journal of Public Relations Research*, 1–16. https://doi.org/10.1080/1062726X.2022.2057502

Place, K. R., & Ciszek, E. (2021). Troubling dialogue and digital media: A subaltern critique. *Social Media + Society*, 7(1), 1–11. https://doi.org/10.1177/2056305120984449

Place, K. R., Edwards, L., & Bowen, S. A. (2021). Dignity and respect or homocommodification? Applying moral philosophy to LGBTQ public relations. *Public Relations Review*, 47(4), 102085. https://doi.org/10.1016/j.pubrev.2021.102085

Pompper, D. (2015). *Corporate social responsibility, sustainability and public relations: Negotiating multiple complex challenges*. Routledge.

Ramsey, P. (2015). The public sphere and PR: Deliberative democracy and agonistic pluralism. In J. L'Etang, D. McKie, & N. Snow (Eds.), *The Routledge handbook of critical public relations* (pp. 65–75). Routledge.

Russmann, U., & Lane, A. B. (2020). Mandating dialogue? International perspectives on differences between theory and practice. *Public Relations Review*, 46(1), 101819. https://doi.org/10.1016/j.pubrev.2019.101819

Saffer, A. J. (2019). Fostering social capital in an international multi-stakeholder issue network. *Public Relations Review*, 45(2), 282–296. https://doi.org/10.1016/j.pubrev.2019.02.004

Sommerfeldt, E. J. (2013). The civility of social capital: Public relations in the public sphere, civil society, and democracy. *Public Relations Review*, 39(4), 280–289. https://doi.org/10.1016/j.pubrev.2012.12.004

Sunstein, C. (Ed.). (2018). *#Republic: Divided democracy in the age of social media*. Princeton University Press. https://doi.org/10.1515/9781400890521

Taylor, M. (2011). Building social capital through rhetoric and public relations. *Management Communication Quarterly*, 25(3), 436–454. https://doi.org/10.1177/0893318911410286

Taylor, M. (2018). Reconceptualizing public relations in an engaged society. In K. A. Johnston & M. Taylor (Eds.), *The handbook of communication engagement* (pp. 103–114). John Wiley & Sons, Inc.

Taylor, M., & Kent, M. L. (2014). Dialogic engagement: Clarifying foundational concepts. *Journal of Public Relations Research*, 26(5), 384–398. https://doi.org/10.1080/1062726X.2014.956106

Theunissen, P., & Noordin, W. N. W. (2012). Revisiting the concept "dialogue" in public relations. *Public Relations Review*, 38(1), 5–13. https://doi.org/10.1016/j.pubrev.2011.09.006

Tompkins, P. S. (2009). Rhetorical listening and moral sensitivity. *The International Journal of Listening*, 23(1), 60–79. https://doi.org/10.1080/10904010802591912

Vardeman, J., & Sebesta, A. (2020). The problem of intersectionality as an approach to digital activism: The Women's March on Washington's attempt to unite all women. *Journal of Public Relations Research*, 32(1–2), 7–29. https://doi.org/10.1080/1062726X.2020.1716769

Volk, S. C. (2016). A systematic review of 40 years of public relations evaluation and measurement research: Looking into the past, the present, and future. *Public Relations Review*, 42(5), 962–977. https://doi.org/10.1016/j.pubrev.2016.07.003

Weder, F. (2021). Strategic problematization of sustainability reframing dissent in strategic communication for transformation. *Public Relations Inquiry*, *11*(3), 337–360. https://doi.org/10.1177/2046147X21102685

Wolvin, A. (2010). Response: Toward a listening ethos. *The International Journal of Listening*, *24*(3), 179–180. https://doi.org/10.1080/10904018.2010.513657

Wolvin, A., & Coakley, C. G. (1991). A survey of the status of listening training in some fortune 500 corporations. *Communication Education*, *40*(2), 152–165. https://doi.org/10.1080/03634529109378836

Young-Bruehl, E. (2004). *Hannah Arendt: For love of the world*. Yale University Press.

Zhou, A. (2019). Bring publics back into networked public relations research: A dual-projection approach for network ecology. *Public Relations Review*, *45*(4), 101772. https://doi.org/10.1016/j.pubrev.2019.03.004

Zhou, A. (2021). Communicating corporate LGBTQ advocacy: A computational comparison of the global CSR discourse. *Public Relations Review*, *47*(4), 102061. https://doi.org/10.1016/j.pubrev.2021.102061

12 Listening to Historically Marginalized Publics

A Conceptualization of Perceived Organizational Listening in LGBTQ Advocacy

Hayoung Sally Lim, E. Ciszek, and Won-Ki Moon

Introduction

Over the past several years, organizations have made progress in LGBTQ communication, with growth in LGBTQ communication campaigns and improvements in organizational policies and practices. However, as recent Pride campaigns suggest, some organizations continue to fall short when it comes to corporate allyship. Rainbow campaigns in June remind us what began as an anti-capitalist, anti-carceral riot for queer liberation, has faded to a month of corporations "selling LGBTQ people their own identity" (Cheung, 2022, para. 1). Burger King's Austrian restaurants served two "top" and "bottom" buns as part of a public relations campaign that was a much-ridiculed and tone-deaf campaign announcing the "Pride Whopper." The campaign, which was launched on Burger King Austria's Instagram page included a burger with two bun tops and another with two bottoms, a misinformed signal to sex within the gay community. In a LinkedIn post, Jung von Matt Donau, the German agency responsible for the campaign, noted: "We've heard your voices and listened carefully." They acknowledged the campaign's missteps and took accountability for their actions: "Unfortunately, we still messed up and didn't check well enough with community members on different interpretations of the Pride Whopper. That's on us." As corporate pride campaigns are increasingly more mainstream, organizations are experiencing pressure for more tangible commitments to LGBTQ communities. Employees play a particularly prominent role in getting companies to speak out against anti-LGBTQ government policy proposals, pushing their employers to reexamine business practices.

At a March 2022 town hall for employees, after internal uproar over the company's response to a Florida bill barring schools from discussing sexual orientation, Walt Disney Co. Chief Executive Officer Bob Chapek announces a global listening tour with employees in an effort

DOI: 10.4324/9781003273851-16

to understand internal perspectives. Earlier in the month, Chapek said Disney wouldn't take a public stance on the Florida legislation, prompting protests from employees, a decision he later reversed. Disney's initial decision not to respond to the bill led some employees to stage a week of internal protests and a full-day walkout. Christopher Grimes of the Financial Times notes that Disney is facing "perhaps the worst public relations crisis in its 100-year history" (2022, para. 3) that has enraged individuals across the political spectrum. The company's botched response to Florida's proposed "Don't Say Gay" law, has angered employees despite the goodwill it created with LGBTQ employees. Failing to speak out against the discriminatory, Disney's silence resulted in employee walkouts and an outcry by activists. However, when the company publicly condemned the bill, Disney found itself in the crosshairs of a political and cultural war. Florida's governor Ron DeSantis and state Republican leaders – many of whom have received campaign contributions from Disney – turned on the company, while conservative journalists declared a "moral war against Disney" (by Halaschak, 2022, para. 8). Disney officials acknowledge this organizational crisis was the result of avoiding taking a public stand on a divisive issue and a failed attempt to pacify its employees.

In early March, Chapek met with a group of Disney LGBTQ leaders to discuss the bill, after issuing a memo to staff acknowledging employee disappointment that Disney had not condemned the bill. The bill passed the Florida legislature the day after the memo was released, and angry employees organized walkouts pressing Disney about campaign contributions to Republicans who voted for the bill. In an email to employees, Chapek wrote: "You needed me to be a stronger ally in the fight for equal rights and I let you down. I am sorry," announcing that the company would suspend political contributions in Florida and review its donation strategy in future. Reflecting on the crisis, in an interview with the Financial Times, a Florida Republican senator criticized the company: "Disney was listening to certain stakeholders and got the wrong comms advice. They should have stayed quiet" (Grimes, 2022). Chapek embarked on a global listening tour with employees of Pixar, ESPN, Disney World, and other divisions of the company and created an LGBTQ task force comprised of 30 executives to examine Disney's content and culture – and met with small groups of LGBTQ employees who shared stories about facing discrimination. In July 2022, "Don't Say Gay" – one of the most prominent pieces of anti-LGBTQ+ legislation – went into effect in Florida, threatening the well-being of LGBTQ+ communities.

Recent events at the Walt Disney Co. are part of a broader social climate in which LGBTQ stakeholders feel ignored, disregarded, and marginalized. As demonstrated by the case of Disney and "Don't Say Gay," when organizations' political contributions and values are out of alignment, employees demand a commitment to the protection of

LGBTQ+ communities. This chapter explores what extent PR research on LGBTQ publics tell us about organizational listening and the gaps that exist in research and practice. As Toledano (2018) reminds us that public relations professionals are obligated to ensure that publics, regardless of differences and disparities, have an equal opportunity to be heard, respected, and engaged. Organizational listening is a significant practice for organizations wanting to move away from performative support to organizational allyship. In the first part of this chapter, we consider organizational listening in LGBTQ communication and public relations. In the second section, we examined how LGBTQ and non-LGBTQ publics perceive organizational listening within the context of an LGBTQ campaign. We consider how sexual orientation, gender identity, race, and ethnicity affect perceptions of organizational listening. We conclude the chapter by considering implications for theory and practice, particularly as it relates to perceptions of organizational listening and LGBTQ publics.

LGBTQ Public Relations

LGBTQ Employees

Historically, corporations have failed to engage authentically with LGBTQ stakeholders (Ciszek, 2020; Ciszek & Pounders, 2020), with sexual and gender minorities experiencing harassment and discrimination (Tindall, 2013; Tindall & Waters, 2012; Waters, 2013) and exploitation (Ciszek & Pounders, 2020; Gudelunas, 2013; Sender, 2004) in the workplace, and being misrepresented and stereotyped in communication campaigns (Alwood, 2015; Chavez & Place, 2013; Ciszek, 2017; Comefero, 2013). Within communication and media spaces, LGBTQ professionals have experienced discrimination and harassment, as well as facing tokenization, bigotry, marginalization, and prevention of career advancement (Tindall, 2013; Tindall & Waters, 2012; Waters, 2013). In their study of LGBTQ public relations practitioners, Tindall and Waters (2012) found that participants faced micro and macro aggressions including threatening phone calls or notes, physical or sexual abuse, exclusion from workplace conversations or activities, and withholding of pay raises or promotions (see also Tindall, 2013; Waters, 2013). Scholars have pointed to an underlying culture and institutional climate of heteronormativity in public relations (Edwards & L'Etang, 2013), that reproduces dominant practices and reinforces the status quo.

LGBTQ Media and Representation

The historical misrepresentation of sexual and gender minorities by mainstream news outlets, resulted in damaging imagery and stereotypes that permeated popular culture (Alwood, 2015). In advertising, campaigns in the 1990s and early 2000s projected homophobic messaging, situating sexual and gender minorities as the butt of jokes (Comeforo, 2013). When brands did feature gay or lesbian imagery in campaigns, visibility often circulated monolithic imagery of gay culture that relied upon a trope of the affluent, White gay male as seen in Absolut's "No Label" campaign (Chavez & Place, 2013). Over the past two decades, rainbow imagery has been used by corporations to market to LGBTQ consumers, rather than investing in issues and needs of sexual and gender minorities (Ciszek & Pounders, 2020; Gudelunas, 2013). This rainbow-washing – the employment of LGBTQ imagery without contributing to efforts that support LGBTQ communities – is perceived by both LGBTQ and non-LGBTQ stakeholders as inauthentic and tone-deaf (Lim et al., 2022). Employing inauthentic representations of sexual and gender minorities results in distrust by LGBTQ publics (Ciszek, 2020 Kaur, 2016; Owusu & Mathenge, 2017).

LGBTQ public relations has become an important practice in which organizations can articulate a position on issues faced by sexual and/or gender minorities (e.g., marriage equality, employment nondiscrimination). However, while Pride Month is one time for organizations to convey their support of LGBTQ communities, consumers are skeptical of organizations that use social issues for self-promotion. Place et al. (2021) have critiqued this practice as unethical and a form of homocommodification. Relationships with LGBTQ publics must be grounded in an ethic of trust and that is underpinned by integrity, thoughtfulness, and purpose, with a commitment to inclusion and equity (Ciszek, 2020).

Organizational Listening

As we know, organizational listening is fundamental to public relations in issues management and ethics counsel. Within extant research, organizational listening has been conceptualized as comprising at least three dimensions: cognitive, behavioral, and affective (Lipetz et al., 2020). While the cognitive dimension refers to practices such as understanding, receiving, and interpreting a message, the behavioral dimension encompasses verbal and nonverbal responses such as asking questions to clarify information, and the affective dimension encapsulates emotions such as empathy and respect (Lipetz et al., 2020). Organizational communication scholar Laurie Lewis (2020) defines strategic organizational listening as "a set of methodologies and structures designed and utilized to ensure that an organization's attention is directed toward vital information and input to enable learning, questioning of key assumptions, interrogating decisions, and ensuring self-critical analysis" (p. xvi). This definition requires senior leadership to be sincere in their desire to learn and gain insights from listening. Lewis (2020) pointed out that this type of organizational listening can result in improvements in trust, commitment, and performance.

Our Research

The first question guiding our research examines the dimensions that comprise perceived organizational listening within the context of LGBTQ communication. In our second research question, we consider whether organizational listening plays a role in how sexual and gender minorities perceive organizations. Additionally, we attend specifically whether the level of perceived organizational listening varies by the social group based on sexual orientation, gender, and race, e.g., do historically marginalized groups (sexual/gender/racial minorities) perceive organizational listening differently than individuals from dominant social groups (heterosexual/cisgender/white). To do so, we draw on Macnamara's (2016) conceptions of organizational listening and extant LGBTQ communication literature. These questions explore the dimensionality of perceived organizational listening with a historically marginalized public to develop a robust measure of perceived organizational listening from the perspective of LGBTQ stakeholders that can be adopted and adapted to other social groups.

In an experimental study, we developed a stimulus featuring an LGBTQ Pride campaign launched by Skittles, an American brand of fruit-flavored candy produced by parent company Wrigley. Our sample of 339 participants, generated through an online panel service, were asked to read a news article about an LGBTQ campaign launched by Skittles during Pride month. According to the article, Skittles replaced their signature rainbow candy for a colorless variety, promoting "only #OneRainbow matters" on social media channels. For each pack purchased, parent company Wrigley donated $1 to GLAAD, a LGBTQ American NGO. The article highlighted the expected impact of the campaign on LGBTQ communities and incorporated corporate comments regarding Pride and the partnership with GLAAD. After reading the news article, participants assigned to the second condition group were also shown a short Instagram video produced by Skittles. In the video post, Todrick Hall, an American Black gay celebrity, talks about his year-long partnership with Skittles and Wrigley's donation of $100,000 to the National Black Trans Advocacy Coalition.

Notably, given the focus of our study, we oversampled in regard to sexual and gender minorities, with 48.7% of participants identifying as LGBTQ and 51.3% identifying as non-LGBTQ compared to a national average of 5.6% (Jones, 2021). A majority of LGBTQ participants identified as gay ($n = 78$, 46.7%), followed by bisexual ($n = 44$, 26.3%), lesbian ($n = 22$, 13.1%), agender ($n = 11$, 6.5%), queer ($n = 5$, 2.9%), and others including pansexual ($n = 5$, 2.9%), same-gender loving ($n = 2$, 1.19%), etc. ($n = 2$, 1.19%). Participants who identified as heterosexual ($n = 172$, 50.7%) or heteroflexible ($n = 2$, 0.6%) were included in the non-LGBTQ group. Age ranged from 18 to 83 ($M = 51.6$, $SD = 16.7$). The median education level was a 4-year college degree, including BA, BS, or BFA. Participants' reported ethnicities were 272 Caucasian (80.2%), 23 Asian (6.8%), 20 African American (5.9%), and 23 others (6.8%).

Results

Our scale development resulted in a 17-item perceived organizational listening scale measuring four dimensions (see Table 12.1). After developing the items, we tested the reliability and validity of the scale ($N = 339$ after data cleaning). As a result, the scale had acceptable estimates in terms of exploratory factor analysis (EFA), confirmatory factor analysis (CFA),

Table 12.1 Perceived organizational listening measurement items

Items	M	SD	α
Perceived organizational listening	4.60	1.44	.98
Listening orientation	4.79	1.63	.98
1 This organization seeks my insights and feedback.			
2 I feel my insights and feedback are valued by this organization.			
3 This organization listens to me and cares about what I have to say.			
4 This organization genuinely wants to hear my point of view.			
Understanding my (social groups') value	4.97	1.60	.97
5 This organization is interested in more than just selling me something to make a profit.			
6 I believe this organization thinks I am a consumer with whom they need to engage with.			
7 I feel like this organization respects my perspective.			
8 In general, this organization values me for who I am.			
Perceived efficacy in communication	3.86	1.77	.91
9 I can get the organization to do what I want.			
10 I think I have a great deal of power over the organization.			
11 I believe I have the ability to have meaningful input into decisions of the organization.			
Online listening efforts	4.46	1.42	.96
12 This organization listens to what I have to say on the review websites.			
13 This organization listens to what I have to say on social media posts.			
14 This organization listens to what I have to say in website comments.			
15 This organization listens to what I have to say in complaint departments.			

and discriminant validity test. Specifically, our EFA result shows that no dimensions include items having factor loadings as lower than .4 and over .4 from one more dimension. The Cronbach alphas of all dimensions were more than .900 (over .75 alpha indicates good reliability in general). We created a CFA model using these items to analyze subsequent structural testing. Model fit indices show that the model has a good fit: CFI = .983, SRMR = .031, RMSEA = .060 (criteria of fits: CFI > .95, SRMR < .05, RMSEA < .08). We also tested the discriminant validity of the scale with other relevant scales such as perceived organizational authenticity and attitudes toward organizations. The result suggested perceived organizational listening scale included no issues of discriminant validity and convergent validity.

To extend the concept of organizational listening in public relations and develop items that account for several dimensions of organizational listening, we also examined studies from diverse areas, such as organizational online listening efforts (Navarro et al., 2018), listening orientation (Aurier & de Lanauze, 2012), organizational respect (Place, 2019), and symmetrical communication (Roper, 2005). The perceived organizational listening scale can be used to measure the effectiveness of organizational listening as well as stakeholder perception of listening. This study provides not only empirical support for perceived organizational literature across communication disciplines including public relations, but it also propels an interdisciplinary approach to perceived organizational listening scale development.

Before answering our second research question, we checked if perceived organizational listening is affected by different communication tactics, in other words, the two experimental groups – media relations tactic (only news article condition) vs. media relations and social media tactic (news article and Instagram post condition). As a result of the t-test, there was no significant difference between the two conditions: $t(337) = -.035$, $p = .972$.

To answer our second research question, we divided our samples into groups depending on their sexual orientation (LGB = 165, non-LGB = 174), gender (gender diverse = 327, nongender diverse = 12), and race (white = 279, non-white = 60). We then compared the reported perceived organizational listening scores from the groups applying Mann-Whitney U, which is one of the nonparametric analyses since our sample distribution was not following normal distribution and the numbers of participants in the compared groups were different. According to the analyses, the group of sexual minorities (e.g., lesbian, gay, bisexual) perceived POL from the Skittles' campaign ($M = 4.83$, $SD = 1.25$) as similar to the group of non-LGB people ($M = 4.64$, $SD = 1.45$, $p = .298$). However, we found that gender minorities (e.g., transgender and queer) reported significantly higher POL ($M = 5.65$, $SD = 1.32$) than the group of people who are not gender minorities ($M = 4.70$, $SD = 1.35$, $p = .019$). Our result also demonstrated that non-white people felt a higher level of POL ($M = 4.65$, $SD = 1.35$) from the stimulus than white people ($M = 5.11$, $SD = 1.34$, $p = .015$).

According to our analyses, in the context of the Skittles' campaign, sexual minorities (e.g., lesbian, gay, bisexual) perceive organizational listening similarly to nonsexual minorities, suggesting sexual orientation does not play a substantial role in perceptions of organizational listening. However, we found that gender minorities (e.g., transgender and queer) reported significantly higher perceived organizational listening than cisgender participants, suggesting gender minorities perceive Skittles as organizational listening is important for gender minorities. Our results also demonstrated that non-white participants felt a higher level of organizational listening from the stimulus than white participants.

This study developed a perceived organizational listening scale in the context of LGBTQ communication. This study is innovative in developing a perceived organizational listening scale that can be used to measure the effectiveness of public relations and communication efforts, as well as perceived authenticity of LGBTQ communication. Although perceived organizational listening can measure the perception of organizational efforts to hear the voice of the individual, perceived organizational listening also can be utilized to understand the perception of an organization's efforts to communicate with a specific public, in this case, LGBTQ individuals. Therefore, we modified our scale to measure perceived organizational listening in terms of identity group level rather than individual level. The questions asked about organizational listening efforts regarding identity groups to which an individual belongs (e.g., specific sexual orientation, gender, or race).

One observation from our analyses is that participants who are experiencing multiple forms of marginalization (e.g., non-white LGBTQ participants) report a higher level of organizational listening, suggesting they may feel more listened to by the brand. Since the stimulus we shared with participants in this experiment centered the voice of a Black gay public figure, the campaign highlighted intersectionality and the experience of sexual/gender minorities and racial minorities.

As the validity check, this analysis was conducted to test a question: "Does our scale work as we intended?" not only to investigate the groups' perceptions of the campaign. We believe that the gap between the mainstream groups and minorities was not huge (less than one point) although the campaigns apparently talked about minority issues. It means that mainstream groups also can get feel of POL when brands/organizations make effort to advocate minority issues. We assume that the effort to hear the voice of minorities can make all kinds of social groups have expectations, "the campaign shows that the organization will listen to my voice when I need them although the campaign is not about my gender/race/sexuality." Of note is there were no significant results when we ran analyses to compare white LGBTQ and non-white LGBTQ participants.

Therefore, there is no notable interaction between sexuality/gender identity and race when it came to participants' evaluation of perceived organizational listening.

Implications

This study not only provides empirical support for perceived organizational literature across communication disciplines including public relation, but it also propels interdisciplinary arenas to perceived organizational listening scale development. Importantly, this example focused on perceptions of corporate listening, and there are several other organizational realms where perceived listening needs to be explored. For example, LGBTQ stakeholders and governmental relations, at local, state, and national levels, as well as non-governmental entities like hospitals and health care systems, educational institutions, and advocacy and activist organizations.

As the Disney case conveys, listening requires work (Bickford, 1996), and organizations need to do the work of listening "to create healthy democracy and social equity" (Macnamara, 2016, p. 14). Macnamara (2016) reminds us that an *architecture of listening* is needed that is equipped with tools and technologies to carry out large-scale listening. We add that an ethic of listening that moves beyond listening for the purposes of homocommodification (Place et al., 2021). In what follows, we adapt Macnamara's (2016) elements, features, and characteristics for effective, ethical organizational listening to LGBTQ publics.

An organization must create and cultivate a *culture* that is open to listening to historically marginalized voices. Public relations must work with leadership to construct and maintain an ethos that acknowledges LGBTQ people are organizational stakeholders, both internally and externally and pays attention to the lives and perspectives of sexual and gender minorities. Public relations needs to work with management to cultivate spaces where LGBTQ publics feel safe to express their perspectives as a first step in organizational listening. In a hostile political climate, organizations committed to ethical LGBTQ communication needs to acknowledge LGBTQ people's right to speak and to hold space for the views of LGBTQ people, especially if this leads to the critique of organizational practices.

In order to engage in ethical LGBTQ communication, an organization needs *policies* that articulate and require listening to LGBTQ stakeholders, including practices to identify and address power differentials (Dreher, 2009). Public relations have a responsibility to acknowledge the heteronormativity that undergirds organizational communication. Corporations, like Disney, are governed by a hegemonic system of norms and practices that fashion heterosexuality as natural and relegate sexual minorities to a marginal status. In 1996, Walt Disney Co. extended health coverage to the partners of gay and lesbian employees, an issue that had been the subject of lobbying efforts within the company that had once been viewed as so anti-gay that it prevented two men from dancing together at Disneyland, a case that resulted in a lawsuit and garnered a flurry of local press coverage.

An organization needs *systems* that are accessible and collaborative, such as in-person and online platforms that allow individuals to provide input and pose questions. There are several strategies that can aid with organizational listening, for example, organizational town halls, listening sessions, and focus groups with employee resource groups. Disney's LGBTQIA+ Business Employee Resource Group is part of a robust network of groups formed around shared identities to build relationships, gather insights, and provide career development opportunities. Formal spaces like employee resource groups are critical parts of infrastructures that build in spaces and mechanisms for organizational listening to take place. Organizations need to devote resources to LGBTQ communication, specifically financial investment in staff and tools. This includes creating LGBTQ forums and consultations, inviting comments from LGBTQ stakeholders, and monitoring, analyzing, and responding to comments and questions. Despite robust social listening tools and software, organizations are still missing key opportunities to engage authentically with LGBTQ stakeholders. Public relations professionals have access to tools that aid listening, such as social media monitoring services for tracking media and online comments. Practitioners can create alerts to follow public sentiment around issues in order to see what and how people are talking about LGBTQ issues online. Additionally, practitioners can create alerts to gather additional information about their messaging, exploring what wording is effective in public messaging. For example, terminology within LGBTQ communities varies by demographics. Gender and age groups within the LGBTQ community have different opinions about terminology, and market research shows that some LGBTQ consumers believe the word queer is offensive, while others strongly feel organizations should exclusively use the word queer as the new umbrella term for the entire community, pointing to the complex relationship sexual and gender minorities have with the term. A deep and complex attention to community verbiage is one articulation of honing listening skills with marginalized publics. Lastly, and importantly, the representation of LGTBQ voices to decision-makers and policy-makers is fundamental to ethical organizational LGBTQ listening.

As Macnamara (2016) reminds us, unless there is a link to policy-making and decision-making for consideration of what is said to an organization, LGBTQ voice has no value to an organization. As Disney's bungled response to the controversial Florida "Don't Say Gay" bill demonstrates, organizations are embroiled in contemporary culture wars and play an active role in politics and policy-making. While companies have courted LGBTQ consumers as a financially lucrative market over the past couple of decades, companies are now forced to take a stand on social issues, a context that will require organizational listening.

Conclusion

Our research shows that campaigns centering issues affecting historically marginalized groups can drive positive organizational effects from diverse stakeholder groups. However, as the Disney example reveals, taking an organizational stance in support of sexual and gender minorities is complex and requires more than lip service. Therefore, public relations practitioners and scholars need to monitor the broader responses of multiple stakeholder groups and the resulting social dynamics that ensue from a campaign, and not only about reactions from the targeted groups. However, as scholars and practitioners, we need to move one step beyond this and really attend to the perceptions of those whose voices are less dominant in these spaces, those whose perspectives have been historically excluded or silenced. We have to understand the impact of organizational decisions, policies, procedures, etc. on stakeholder perceptions of the organization. Practical implications from this architecture of listening to LGBTQ publics reveals that organizations need consistency in their actions and communication. Representation in advertising campaigns is insufficient for contemporary LGBTQ stakeholders. Sexual and gender minorities want a company like Disney to put its money where its mouth is, funding employee resource groups, adopting best practices for LGBTQ employees and customers, and taking a public stand on social issues that affect their lives.

References

Alwood, E. (2015). The role of public relations in the gay rights movement, 1950–1969. *Journalism History*, *41*(1), 11.

Aurier, P., & de Lanauze, G. S. (2012). Impacts of perceived brand relationship orientation on attitudinal loyalty: An application to strong brands in the packaged goods sector. *European Journal of Marketing*, *46*(11/12), 1602–1627.

Bickford, S. (1996). *The dissonance of democracy: Listening, conflict and citizenship*. Cornell University Press.

Chavez, C., & Place, K. (2013). Absolut Vodka: Defining, challenging, or reinforcing gay identity? In N. T. J. Tindall & R. D. Waters (Eds.), *Coming out of the closet: Exploring LGBT issues in strategic communication with theory and research* (pp. 151–164). Peter Lang.

Cheung, K. (2022, June 6). Corporations bring back the pride month cringe. *Jezebel.com*. https://jezebel.com/corporations-bring-back-the-pride-month-cringe-1849021983

Ciszek, E. (2017). Activist strategic communication for social change: A transnational case study of lesbian, gay, bisexual, and transgender activism. *Journal of Communication*, *67*(5), 702–718.

Ciszek, E. (2020). "We are people, not transactions": Trust as a precursor to dialogue with LGBTQ publics. *Public Relations Review, 46*(1), 101759.

Ciszek, E., & Pounders, K. (2020). The bones are the same: An exploratory analysis of authentic communication with LGBTQ publics. *Journal of Communication Management, 24*(2), 103–117. https://doi.org/10.1108/JCOM-10-2019-0131

Comeforo, K. (2013). Mis(sed) representations: LGBT imagery in mainstream advertising. In J. Tindall & R. D. Waters (Eds.), *Coming out of the closet: Exploring LGBT issues in strategic communication with theory and research* (pp. 90–107). Peter Lang.

Dreher, T. (2009). Listening across difference: Media and multiculturalism beyond the politics of voice. *Continuum: Journal of Media & Cultural Studies, 23*(4), 445–458. https://doi.org/10.1080/10304310903015712

Edwards, L., & L'Etang, C. E. (2013). Invisible and visible identities and sexualities in public relations. In N. T. J. Tindall & R. D. Waters (Eds.), *Coming out of the closet: Exploring LGBT issues in strategic communication with theory and research* (pp. 41–56). Peter Lang.

Grimes, C. (2022). How Disney lost Florida. *Financial Times.* https://www.ft.com/content/e4e84eac-8502-4a7f-b51b-c372752b4b38

Gudelunas, D. (2013). Sexual minorities as advertising gatekeepers. In N. T. J. Tindall & R. D. Waters (Eds.), *Coming out of the closet: Exploring LGBT issues in strategic communication with theory and research* (pp. 73–89). Peter Lang.

Halaschak, Z. (2022, Feb. 19). Disney forced into strategic gamble against Florida bill, brand experts say. https://www.washingtonexaminer.com/policy/disney-forced-into-strategic-gamble-against-florida-bill-brand-experts-say

Jones, J. (2021, Feb. 24). LGBT identification rises to 5.6% in latest U.S. estimate. https://news.gallup.com/poll/329708/lgbt-identification-rises-latest-estimate.aspx

Kaur, H. (2016). *The determinants of consumer responses in the LGBT community: An* exploratory study of LGBT marketing in the context of New Zealand and USA advertisements. Unpublished Student Thesis. University of Canterbury. https://ir.canterbury.ac.nz/bitstream/handle/10092/12877/Kaur_P_MCom_2016_thesis.pdf?sequence=3

Lewis, L. (2020). *The power of strategic listening.* Rowman & Littlefield.

Lim, H. S., Ciszek, E., & Moon, W.-K. (2022). Perceived organizational authenticity in LGBTQ communication: The scale development and initial empirical findings. *Journal of Communication Management, 26*(2), 187–206. https://doi.org/10.1108/JCOM-02-2021-0023

Lipetz, L., Kluger, A. N., & Bodie, G. D. (2020). Listening is listening is listening: Employees' perception of listening as a holistic phenomenon. *International Journal of Listening, 34*(2), 71–96.

Macnamara, J. (2016). Organizational listening: Addressing a major gap in public relations theory and practice. *Journal of Public Relations Research, 28*(3–4), 146–169.

Navarro, C., Moreno, A., & Zerfass, A. (2018). Mastering the dialogic tools: Social media use and perceptions of public relations practitioners in Latin America. *Journal of Communication Management, 22*(1), 28–45. https://doi.org/10.1108/JCOM-12-2016-0095

Owusu, K., & Mathenge, T. (2017). *Is gay advertising out of the closet? A look into how explicit and implicit marketing is perceived by consumers.* Unpublished master's thesis. https://lup.lub.lu.se/student-papers/record/8918587/file/8918588.pdf

Place, K. R. (2019). Moral dilemmas, trials, and gray areas: Exploring on-the-job moral development of public relations professionals. *Public Relations Review*, *45*(1), 24–34.

Place, K. R., Edwards, L., & Bowen, S. A. (2021). Dignity and respect or homo-commodification? Applying moral philosophy to LGBTQ public relations. *Public Relations Review*, 47. https://doi.org/10.1016/j.pubrev.2021.102085

Roper, J. (2005). Symmetrical communication: Excellent public relations or a strategy for hegemony? *Journal of Public Relations Research*, *17*(1), 69–86.

Sender, K. (2004). Neither Fish nor Fowl: Feminism, desire, and the Lesbian consumer market. *The Communication Review*, *7*(4), 407–432.

Tindall, N. T. J. (2013). Invisible in a visible profession: The social construction of workplace identity and roles among lesbian and bisexual public relations professionals. In N. T. J. Tindall & R. D. Waters (Eds.), *Coming Out of the Closet: Exploring LGBTQ Issues in Strategic Communication with Theory and Research* (pp. 24–40). Peter Lang.

Tindall, N. T. J., & Waters, R. D. (2012). Coming out to tell our stories: Using queer theory to understand the career experiences of gay men in public relations. *Journal of Public Relations Research*, *24*(5), 451–475.

Toledano, M. (2018). Dialogue, strategic communication, and ethical public relations: Lessons from Martin Buber's political activism. *Public Relations Review*, *44*(1), 131–141. https://doi.org/10.1016/j.pubrev.2017.09.009

Waters, R. D. (2013). Harassment in the workplace: Violence, ambivalence, and derision experienced by LGBTQ strategic communicators. In N. T. J. Tindall & R. D. Waters (Eds.), *Coming Out of the Closet: Exploring LGBTQ Issues in Strategic Communication with Theory and Research* (pp. 7–23). Peter Lang.

13 Organizational Listening and Empowered Women in the Workplace

A Cross-Cultural Comparison between the United States and South Korea

Yeunjai Lee, Yo-Jun Queenie Li, and Enzhu Dong

Introduction

Despite the ongoing advocacy to increase diversity and foster inclusive work environments and corporate cultures around the world, discrimination in the workplace remains pervasive, such as gender-related mistreatment. In the United States, four out of ten working women have encountered discrimination at work due to their gender, ranging from making less money than male colleagues for doing the same work to being passed over for a promotion (Parker & Funk, 2017). In addition to establishing appropriate systems and policies, the organizations' internal communication is critical to understand women's experiences and address gender-related issues at work effectively and ethically. As gender discrimination in the workplace has been recognized as a global issue, insights from a cross-cultural perspective are necessary for public relations and internal communication scholars and practitioners.

This chapter aims to explain the importance of organizational listening efforts, characterized by symmetrical and participative communication, in empowering women to voice their workplace discrimination concerns and address injustice issues to cultivate an organizational culture of inclusivity and equality. Focusing on the United States and South Korea, two representative western and non-western cultures, this chapter examines women's discrimination experiences and empowerment in the workplace from a cross-cultural perspective. This chapter will answer the following questions:(1) How do women in the United States and South Korea perceive and evaluate gender discrimination at work differently? and (2) How does organizational listening become effective in increasing women employees' empowerment to speak up about gender discrimination issues in two countries?

DOI: 10.4324/9781003273851-17

Literature

Workplace Gender Discrimination

Workplace discrimination refers to an employee's perception about the differential treatment at work because of individual characteristics, such as gender, age, race/ethnicity, disability, or cultural background (US Equal Employment Opportunity Commission, 2020). It has been a focal topic in organizational management research for decades, as employees often perceive selective, unfriendly, unfair, and negative treatment in the workplace (Chung, 2001; Sanchez & Brock, 1996). Such experiences have been demonstrated to threaten the organizations' competitiveness and innovation, leading to economic losses (Ensher et al., 2001; Triana et al., 2019). More importantly, It may directly impact employee outcomes, including job satisfaction (Herrbach, 2006), commitment (Sanchez & Brock, 1996), productivity (Triana et al., 2019), and mental health (Jones et al., 2016). With the bandwagon of investigating workplace discrimination across disciplines, the previous literature has considered it a multidimensional construct with formal and informal aspects (Dhanani et al., 2018).

Among numerous types of discrimination, gender inequality is one of the most pervasive problems in the work environment. From a broad perspective, gender discrimination refers to an individual's perception of being treated unequally in the workplace because of gender (Allport, 1954). While gender discrimination could happen to all genders, it usually manifests in the gender gap and unequal rights between males and females (Muyidi et al., 2022). Triana et al. (2019) distinguished sexual harassment from gender discrimination, emphasizing that gender discrimination does not require unwanted sexual content in the workplace. Thus we solely discuss gender discrimination regarding unfair job-related decisions (i.e., formal) and inappropriate verbal and nonverbal workplace interactions (i.e., informal) in this chapter.

Previous literature has illustrated reasons for gender discrimination. For instance, the gender difference in career opportunity is partly explained by women's expected responsibility to a family: they would devote more time than men to childcare and household chores (Moreno et al., 2021). Extensive research has documented various gender-related challenges across countries and industries (e.g., Moreno et al., 2021; Muyidi et al., 2022), demonstrating the detrimental consequences of gender discrimination and the importance of resolving gender issues in the workplace. Thus, understanding how women perceive and cope with workplace discrimination is fundamental toward creating effective intervention programs and providing institutional support to recruit and retain a gender-balanced workforce.

Communication Management of Workplace Gender Discrimination: Organizational Listening

Effective internal communication has vaulted to prominence as rich literature has demonstrated its positive impacts on employee outcomes, such as enhancing engagement, boosting trust, and facilitating job satisfaction with the organization (Men & Bowen, 2016). Scholars indicated that establishing a work environment that values healthy communication between organizations and their employees is an imperative approach to preventing and reducing unfairness perceptions among employees (Lee et al., 2021; Zhang & Agarwal, 2009). Organizational listening, a critical element/characteristic of effective internal communication (Kim, 2007), has been deemed essential to encourage employees to speak up and to ensure that their voices are heard in the organization. For example, Macnamara (2016, 2019) suggested organizations to build an architecture of listening as a corollary to effective dialogue and favorable relationships with employees.

As an integral part of the communication process (Lipari, 2010), *listening* is defined as a capacity to detect others' underlying habitual characters and attitudes to develop "a sense of shared experience and mutual understanding" (Bodie & Crick, 2014, p. 106). Not only does it exist in the interpersonal communication that involves conversation between speakers and listeners, public relations scholars suggested that listening can also be implemented in a large-scale setting (Barbour, 2017; Grunig, 2006; Men et al., 2022). Such a practice can "enable decision-makers and policymakers in organizations to actively and effectively access, acknowledge, understand, consider and appropriately respond to all those who wish to communicate with the organization or with whom the organization wishes to communicate interpersonally or through delegated, mediated meanings" (Macnamara, 2019, p. 14).

In internal communication research, scholars often describe organizational listening by using the terms of symmetry and participation. Communication that highlights two-way symmetrical dialogs between organizations and employees and values employee participation in decision-making serves as the foundation of effective organizational listening practices (Kang & Sung, 2017; Lee et al., 2021; Men, 2014). It is considered as an interactive process of establishing a beneficial relationship between organizations and employees (Grunig, 1989; Grunig et al., 2003). As an opposite concept of asymmetrical communication that emphasizes manipulation, control, and power (Grunig & White, 1992), symmetrical communication in the organizational context focuses on the needs of employees. It provides employees with "opportunities to speak out, become involved, be listened to, and actively participate" (Smidts et al., 2001, p. 1059). Such concept corresponds to the public relations theory of dialogic communication and organizational relationship management

(Claro, 2022; Grunig et al., 2003; Taylor & Kent, 2014), highlighting the importance of dialogical and employee-centric communication in encouraging employees to voice disagreements and opinions toward organizations' operations (Neill & Bowen, 2021).

In the context of addressing workplace gender discrimination, organizational listening plays an essential role in helping female employees cope with problems. As a communication strategy with the purpose of "developing and maintaining a bidirectional, symmetrical relationship" (Claro, 2022, as cited in Worthington & Fitch-Hauser, 2018; p. 224) through a dialogue process, organizational listening has been acknowledged to foster a sense of confidence among employees, which makes them feel safe to voice for themselves (Claro, 2022). This chapter aims to demonstrate the potential applicability of organizational listening in empowering female employees to seek justice and gender equality in the workplace, which encourages them to adopt proactive communicative behaviors to address the issue.

Role of Cultural Value

This chapter takes a step further by validating the effectiveness of organizational listening through a cross-cultural comparative approach. As culture plays an important role in forming social norms, as well as corporate cultures in relation to gender equality (Ansah & Louw, 2019; Neculaesei, 2015), tailored communication programs and strategic management efforts for assisting organizations in addressing workplace gender discrimination issues in various cultures are imperative. The consideration of cultural influences in gender roles will provide a meaningful, real-work scenario in which to test the proposition that cultural differences may affect the effectiveness of strategic internal communication on empowering female employees to cope with workplace discrimination. We discussed cross-cultural differences that may affect organizational communication management in addressing workplace gender discrimination problems.

Gender Equality

Although many countries are investing in various approaches that help eliminate gender inequality issues, some have failed due to traditional attitudes and cultural beliefs with regard to gender role (Spade & Valentine, 2011). A great amount of academic attention has thus been provided to this topic in understanding how cultural characteristics shape societies' traditional gender norms that become potential barriers to gender equality (Lee & Pratto, 2018). Scholars indicated that traditional beliefs in gender roles influenced by cultural values determine appropriate characters and behaviors for men and women, and thus create unequal power and gender-based hierarchy in society (Lee et al., 2020).

Cultural values provide a cognitive thinking framework for individuals to interpret the world. Members of a culture are more likely to accept certain ideas when the ideas are consistent with the mainstream norms and beliefs (Hofstede, 2001). This notion can also be applied to how individuals perceive gender roles and equality. The idea of gender equality seems consistent with Western cultural values (e.g., United States) as it emphasizes on individual interests, freedom, and equality as its core values, as well as the gender equality (Schwartz & Rubel-Lifschitz, 2009). By contrast, such an idea built on individualism may defy the collectivistic and group-oriented values in Eastern societies, and thus creates tension in how members of this culture grapple with gender equality issues (Hu & Scott, 2016).

South Korea

South Korea is known for its male-dominated corporate culture and deep-rooted patriarchal ideologies (Triana et al., 2019). The country has consistently been in the media spotlight due to workplace gender discrimination scandals, which comprise sexual harassment and assault, in various industries (Strother, 2019). Although the country has the highest education rate for women between the ages of 25 and 34 years, it ranks 30 out of 36 OECD members in terms of women employment rate (OECD, 2019) and 115 out of 149 countries in terms of wage equality between working men and women (Kim, 2018). The #MeToo movement has sparked antifeminist backlash among young men in South Korea (Kwon, 2019), thereby revealing the complexity and challenges in addressing workplace gender discrimination in the socially conservative country.

The country is known for its patriarchal and collectivistic culture, which is influenced and dominated by Confucianism (Kim & Park, 2018). Although rapid economic development and social changes over previous decades have facilitated South Koreans' endorsement of individualistic values (Kim & Park, 2018), traditional norms of gender roles that are strongly rooted in Confucianism still contribute to the prevalence of gender inequality across the nation.

Discrepancies in gender equality perceptions were found to be magnified in work settings (Kim et al., 2020). South Korea is known for its long history of male-dominant corporate culture in which women are often struggling in the workplace (Soh, 1993). This organizational culture is established and promoted by "the ideology of housewife and husband-provider and the gender division of labor" rooted in Confucian values (Moon, 2005, p. 66). Women in South Korea are expected to obey with the designated role of being housewives, subordinates, supportive, and docile under these traditional values in society (Kim, 2001), which lead to the deep-seated workplace gender discrimination issue in the country.

Moreover, the business masculinity culture in East Asian countries created a standard workplace norm of long working hours (Reid et al., 2018). The custom of long working hours has also contributed to the marginalization and exclusion of the female workforce (Nemoto, 2016). Due to these traditional gender norms and subsequent corporate culture in South Korea, we anticipate that working women in South Korea will report weaker perceptions of gender equality and more gender discrimination experiences than those in the United States.

Organizational Communication Management

Culture beliefs and values in a country have also been acknowledged to shape management, strategic planning, and operations in organizations in that country (Hofstede et al., 2005). Thus, the organizations' communication practices with their employees cannot be void of cultural impact (Sriramesh & Vercic, 2003). The two selected countries in this study represent distinct cultures. In consideration of Hofstede's cultural dimensions, at one end is the United States that holds low uncertainty avoidance and small power distance, whereas South Korea is a collective culture with strong uncertainty avoidance and large power distance (Kim & Kim, 2010). These two dimensions may influence the extent to which internal communication flows without restrictions within organizations (Leonard et al., 2009), as they are linked to the relationship between leadership and subordinates of organizations (Hofstede, 1980). In organizational culture contexts, the power distance dimension refers to the dependence level of subordinates on their superiors, while the uncertainty avoidance index implies a degree to which organizations tolerate ambiguity and uncertainty (Hofstede, 2001).

High value on power distance and uncertainty avoidance dimensions often reflect an organizational culture that adopts "authoritarian and paternalistic leadership, hierarchical structure, and a bureaucratic managerial style" (Bae & Lawler, 2000, p. 504). These leadership styles are considered as the traditional features of organizational management in South Korea (Bae & Lawler, 2000; Shin et al., 2011). By contrast, consistent with America's relatively low values on power distance and uncertainty avoidance, employees in the United States prefer leadership characteristics that coordinate communication, respond proactively, and advocate employees' interests, which emerge as a democratic style (Shin et al., 2011). The extent to which an organization adopts effective leadership plays an important role in how likely the organization practices effective internal communication (Jiang & Men, 2017; Men & Stacks, 2014). A growing line of research has found that authoritarian and bureaucratic leadership often leads to a poor quality of top-down communication, whereas democratic leadership encourages communication that values participation, openness, and shared responsibilities (Jiang & Men, 2017; Kelly &

MacDonald, 2019). A less powerful leadership often respects employees by attentively listening to their concerns (Roebuck et al., 2016).

Therefore, various organizational leadership styles endorsed in these two countries contributed by their opposite cultural values may constitute distinct internal communication practices. Moreover, such influence of leadership styles based on the national cultures of power distance may also affect the employees' perceptions of empowerment at work. Balanced power that allows equal opportunities to participate in decision-making at all hierarchical levels is closely relevant for effective implementation of empowerment in organizations (Sparrow & Hiltrop, 1997). By contrast, imbalance of power inhibits employees from accessing knowledge and power, thus reduces employees' perceived autonomy in the workplace and becomes less empowered (Wilson & Chaudhry, 2017). Following these reasonings, it is expected that employees in the United States, who are governed by relatively more democratic leadership affected by low power distance value, would perceive greater levels of listening in internal communication and a stronger sense of empowerment than those in South Korea.

Exposure to internal communication emphasizing listening by organizations may have the potential to boost the employees' perceived empowerment. Exposure to the opportunity to participate in the conversations within organizations with regard to gender discrimination problems likely enhances perceptions that employees have a sense of autonomy and control to tackle such issues in the workplace. However, varying effectiveness of internal communication practices depending upon the national culture indicates that the relationship between organizational listening and perceived empowerment can be moderated at the country level, such that it may be more likely in the United States, where organizations have effectively communicated with employees in a listening manner.

Employee Behaviors

To deal with gender discrimination experiences effectively, employees engage in diverse coping strategies. Public relations scholars have examined the employees' communicative behaviors (ECBs) as employees' major responses to organizations' communication management strategies (Kim, 2018; Kim & Rhee, 2011). Employees not only seek out information relevant to their organization but also share the information with members within an organization to help and see their company succeed. When employees encounter or observe problems or issues within their organizations, such as discriminatory acts, they engage in communicative behaviors to solve them (Lee & Li, 2021).

As cultural values significantly affect individuals' beliefs, attitudes, and behaviors, scholars have argued that "how people react to an upsetting event, experience and express emotion, and seek support may vary perhaps substantially across cultures" (Mortenson et al., 2009). For example, employees in lower power distance cultures are more likely to address a problem in a proactive manner, such as filing complaints or approaching their supervisors for help compared to those in higher power distance cultures (Offermann & Hellmann, 1997).

Another well-known cultural dimension, individualism/collectivism, was also found to determine individuals' behaviors. Individualism emphasizes independence, autonomy, and personal interests, whereas collectivism values group's needs and harmony (Chun et al., 2006; Triandis, 1988). To maintain group harmony and avoid conflicts, individuals in collectivistic cultures likely choose to internalize the stressful emotions rather than seek social support or disclose their struggles (Mojaverian & Kim, 2013). The high context characteristics in collectivistic cultures that focus on how messages are stated rather than what is actually communicated also inhibit individuals from explicit verbal communications of thoughts (Falconier et al., 2016). Thus, for the sake of group interests, avoidance coping becomes a common approach in which members of collectivistic values may use to manage problems (Yeh et al., 2006). By contrast, people in individualistic cultures often disclose stress and overtly ask for help because "a person is encouraged to explicitly signal personal needs and actively draw on social relationships for meeting them" (Taylor et al., 2007, p. 832). The low context features in individualistic cultures enable members in this group to be direct and overt in communication, motivating them to manage problems in an explicit way (Falconier et al., 2016).

Considering that the United States is an individualistic culture with small power distance while South Korea is a collectivistic culture with large power distance (Kim & Kim, 2010), we should expect that female employees in the United States are more likely to manage workplace gender discrimination in a proactive communicative approach than those in South Korea. Perceptions of empowerment have the potential to boost communicative behaviors, wherein such an effect size may vary depending upon the cultural context. The effect is more likely to be stronger in cultures in which perceived empowerment is adequately high (i.e., the United States) than in those in which it is relatively low (i.e., South Korea).

Method

To test the conceptual reasoning above, we conducted two online surveys with current female employees. Only employees who self-identified as a woman were recruited for this study. One was administered to 402 employees in the United States across industry sectors through Qualtrics panels in October 2020. The other survey was administered to 400 employees in South Korea across industry sectors. For the Korean survey, the English questionnaire was translated into South Korean. A back-translation approach was adopted to ensure both English and South Korean versions were comparable (Brislin et al., 1973). Two South Korean native speakers reviewed the translations for accuracy. The questionnaire was distributed through a research company, Embrain, which is located in Seoul, South Korea, during a one-week period in November 2020.

Participants were asked to answer a series of questions to measure their workplace discrimination experiences, perceptions of gender inequality, and organizational listening concerning the issue. The measures were adopted and adapted from previous literature. *Gender equality* was measured with five items adopted from Sharma (2010) (Cronbach's α = .93). Sample items are "Men and women can be equally aggressive" and "Women can be as ambitious as men." Workplace gender discrimination was examined with two aspects: formal and informal discrimination. *Formal discrimination* was measured with five items adopted from Sanchez and Brock (1996) and Shaffer et al. (2000) and adjusted to the current study's context (α = .87). Sample items are "At work, I do not get enough recognition because of my gender" and "Gender has negatively affected the way my career has progressed." *Informal discrimination* was measured with five items adopted from Cortina et al. (2001) and adjusted to the current study's context (α = .89). Sample items are "At work, people make jokes or negative commentaries about my gender." and "People at my work pay little attention to my statement or show little interest in my opinion because of my gender." *Organizational listening* was measured with eight items adopted from Dozier et al. (1995) and Men (2014). The scale included two aspects: symmetry (five items, α = .94, e.g., the purpose of communication in our company is to help managers be responsive to the problems of employees) and participation (three items, α = .92, e.g., the company asks for feedback from people like me about the quality of its information.). *Employees' perceived empowerment* was measured with five items adapted from Lee (2019) and adjusted to the current study's context (α = .93). Sample items are "I am not afraid to take actions to make changes for gender discrimination issues at my company" and "I feel comfortable taking action for gender discrimination issues at my company." *Communicative behavior* was measured with five items adopted from Clark (2002) and adapted to our research context (α = .91). Sample items are "I often ask any questions related to my company's working environment for women to my supervisor" and "I often talk about any issues or concerns about working environment for women with my supervisor."

Findings

Our first research question aims to explore how female employees in the United States and South Korea perceive and evaluate gender discrimination at work differently. According to the results of a *t*-test analysis, a significant difference across two countries was found ($t[800] = 5.11$, $p < .001$). Specifically, female employees in South Korea reported a lower level of gender equality perception ($M = 5.49$, $SD = 1.03$) compared to those in the United States ($M = 5.90$, $SD = 1.21$). Meanwhile, the ANOVA results indicated significant differences both in female employees' formal discrimination experiences ($t(800) = -8.89$, $p < .001$) and informal discrimination experiences ($t[800] = -4.65$, $p < .001$). South Korean female employees reported more formal gender discrimination experience ($M = 3.42$, $SD = 1.46$) than those in United States ($M = 2.73$, $SD = 1.34$). Such phenomenon was also found in informal discrimination, where female employees in South Korea reported more informal discrimination experience ($M = 2.45$, $SD = 1.62$) than female employees in the United States ($M = 2.24$, $SD = 1.61$).

Our second research question seeks to understand how organizational listening becomes effective in increasing women employees' empowerment to speak up about gender discrimination issues in two countries. According to a t-test analysis, female employees in the United States perceived greater levels of listening in organizational internal communication regarding gender equality than those in South Korea ($t[800] = 15.59$, $p < .001$). Female employees in the United States reported a significantly higher level of listening in organizational communication ($M = 4.97$, $SD = 1.47$) compared to those in South Korea ($M = 3.45$, $SD = 1.27$). This finding suggested a possible fact that, from the perspectives of female employees, South Korean companies may adopt fewer listening practices compared to US companies.

The findings also suggested that female employees in the United States perceived greater empowerment in addressing gender inequality issues than those in South Korea based on the results of a t-test analysis ($t[800] = 10.22$, $p < .001$). South Korean female employees reported a significantly lower level of perceived empowerment ($M = 3.72$, $SD = 1.26$) compared to female employees in the United States ($M = 4.72$, $SD = 1.51$) in terms of addressing gender inequality issues at workplace.

We also found that female employees in the United States were more likely to perform communicative behaviors than those in South Korea (t-test result: $t[800] = 5.40$, $p < .001$). Female employees in the United States reported a higher level of communicative behaviors ($M = 4.69$, $SD = 1.22$) compared to South Korean female employees ($M = 4.24$, $SD = .93$).

Next, we examined the effect of organizational listening practices on female employees' empowerment and communication behaviors in both countries. We conducted a two-group k-means cluster analysis process to classify American and South Korean employees based on their perceptions of organizational listening. The independent variable consisted of two levels: High degree of organizational listening (United States: $n = 284$; South Korea: $n = 124$) and low degree of organizational listening (United States: $n = 118$; South Korea: $n = 276$).

Table 13.1 *t*-Test comparison between perceptions of American and South Korean female employees

Variables	United States M	SD	South Korea M	SD	t	df
Perceived gender equality	5.90	1.21	5.49	1.03	5.11***	800
Perceived formal discrimination	2.73	1.34	3.42	1.46	−8.89***	800
Perceived informal discrimination	2.24	1.61	2.45	1.62	−4.65***	800
Organizational listening	4.97	1.47	3.45	1.27	15.59***	800
Empowerment	4.72	1.51	3.72	1.26	10.22***	800
Communicative behaviors	4.69	1.22	4.24	.93	5.40***	800

Note: Two-tailed significance levels ***$p < .001$.

According to a *t*-test analysis ($t[800] = 15.59, p < .001$), female employees in the United States who perceived greater levels of organizational listening reported a significantly higher level of perceived empowerment (high listening: $M = 5.19, SD = 1.36$; low listening: $M = 3.61, SD = 1.25$). The group also reported a significantly greater degree of communicative behaviors (high listening: $M = 4.05, SD = 1.19$; low listening: $M = 3.75, SD = 1.47$). Similar to the patterns in the United States, female employees in South Korea who perceived greater levels of organizational listening also reported a significantly higher level of perceived empowerment (high listening: $M = 4.54, SD = 1.15$; low listening: $M = 3.48, SD = 1.22$). The group also reported a significantly greater degree of communicative behaviors (high listening: $M = 3.46, SD = 1.98$; low listening: $M = 2.57, SD = 1.60$). The information is summarized in Table 13.1.

We further conducted a mediation analysis by using PROCESS macro (Model 4) to test the effects of organizational listening practices on both perceived empowerment and communication behaviors. With the sample of American employees, the results showed that organizational listening was approaching significance as a predictor of empowerment ($b = .61, SE = .04, p < .001$). Perceived empowerment was associated with an increase in communication behaviors ($b = .39, SE = .07, p < .001$). The indirect effect of organizational listening on communicative behaviors through perceived empowerment was tested using a bootstrap estimation approach with 5000 resamples. These results indicated that the indirect effect was significant ($b = .24, SE = .05, p < .001$, CI = [.14, .35]).

With the sample of South Korean employees, the results showed that organizational listening was approaching significance as a predictor of empowerment ($b = .41, SE = .04, p < .001$). Perceived empowerment was associated with an increase in communication behaviors ($b = .33, SE = .05, p < .001$). The indirect effect of organizational listening on communicative behaviors through perceived empowerment was tested using a bootstrap estimation approach with 5000 resamples. These results indicated that the indirect effect was significant ($b = .14$, $SE = .03$, $p < .001$, CI = [.08, .20]).

Discussion

The results highlighted the important role of organizational listening in the context of organizational diversity and inclusion management. It presents one of the earliest investigations on how strategic organizational listening can help empower female employees, who are a key group of internal publics, to speak up and combat gender discrimination in the workplace. Much theoretical deliberation on internal communication theories and practices has explicated the "speaking" (e.g., informing, educating, and persuading) aspect, organizational listening has received relatively less scholarly attention. Macnamara (2016) noted that public relations professionals interviewed in the Organizational Listening Project indicated that organizations typically have disparate engagement in speaking versus listening (80:20 ratio of attention). Crawford (2009) highlighted listening in the age of Web 2.0: Although the usage of media increased two-way communication, listening was still not a dominant metaphor for participating in online interactions compared to "speaking." Results demonstrated the effectiveness of organizational listening in facilitating diversity and inclusion in the workplace, informing organizations that the practice of listening is indispensable.

As culture plays an important role in influencing social norms as well as corporate cultures in relation to gender roles and perceptions, distinctive and tailored communication programs for helping global organizations address workplace gender discrimination issues in various nations are imperative. This critical global issue has yet to be sufficiently examined by cross-cultural comparative studies to understand cultural differences in how women cope with workplace discrimination, as well as the significance of internal communication for empowering female employees. Thus, this study focuses on South Korea, which is a developed economy that is culturally distinct from the United States, to provide much-needed cultural insights beyond the Western context. This study informs internal communication literature by proposing that cultural contexts and differences play an important role in helping determine the female employees' experiences of inequality and reactions to it. Consistent with literature on cross-cultural differences in organizational management (Ansah & Louw, 2019), organizations in Western and Asian countries may attribute various properties to gender equality, organizational listening practices, employee empowerment, and communicative behaviors because of their national cultures. The results of our cross-cultural surveys show that the proposed mechanism is significantly moderated by the country. With relatively fewer practices of organizational listening in their organizations, female employees in South Korea feel less empowered, which would ultimately result in lower readiness to perform communicative behaviors. Such patterns could be explained by the potential influences of national cultures, their dimensions of individualism/collectivism, and power distance. When a country is highly collectivistic-oriented with a large power distance value, the hierarchy of authority and imbalanced power distribution in organizations are common (Hannay, 2009) and may serve to explain less listening in organizational communication, as well as less empowerment perceptions among employees.

Such findings shed a novel cross-cultural understanding on how internal communication practices, employee empowerment, and communicative behaviors may vary between employees in Western and Asian countries that differ in these national cultures, particularly during responses to gender discrimination problems in the workplace. The findings provide insights particularly for organizations with the global market and community. Organizations should be aware that individuals' perceptions, attitudes, and behaviors regarding workplace gender discrimination can interact with national cultures and this influences employee reactions to such issues. For example, according to the results of this study, specific attention must be given to working women in South Korea, who appear to perceive greater gender inequality and recognize more gender discrimination problems at work but feel less empowered to voice out. Some evidence indicating that organizations that aim to tackle workplace gender discrimination among South Korean female employees should first overcome the negative effects of cultural characteristics in this specific context. The national cultures of collectivism and high-power distance in South Korea may lead to higher prevalence of workplace gender discrimination. However, such cultural values may also hinder the organizations' listening practices and thus reduce the employees' empowerment perceptions and readiness to speak up against the problems. These two characteristics in South Korean organizational settings may interrupt the employees' coping mechanism as it makes them concerned about others' reactions, as well as risks to their career development.

Thus, our study recommends organizations of collectivistic employees, particularly those of South Korean descent, to be mindful of the cultural impacts and provide them with a clear, open, and safe dialogue platform to voice out their experiences on gender discrimination. Particularly for organizations in high-power distance culture, the investment in such an environment is highly desired to empower employees, especially when they need to take actions that require a strong sense of autonomy and control. By considering possible influence of cultural backgrounds, organizations may be able to recognize the specific needs among the employees and thus design and implement culturally tailored communication programs that help empower female employees to fight against workplace gender discrimination.

References

Allport, G. (1954). *The nature of prejudice*. Beacon Press.
Ansah, M. O., & Louw, L. (2019). The influence of national culture on organizational culture of multinational companies. *Cogent Social Sciences, 5*(1), 1623648.
Bae, J., & Lawler, J. J. (2000). Organizational and HRM strategies in Korea: Impact on firm performance in an emerging economy. *Academy of Management Journal, 43*(3), 502–517.
Barbour, J. B. (2017). Listening and organizing. *The International Encyclopedia of Organizational Communication*, 1–5. https://doi.org/10.1002/9781118955567.wbieoc126
Bodie, G. D., & Crick, N. (2014). Listening, hearing, sensing: Three modes of being and the phenomenology of Charles Sanders Peirce. *Communication Theory, 24*(2), 105–123.
Brislin, R. W., Lonner, W. J., & Thorndike, R. M. (1973). *Cross-cultural research methods* (Vol. 11). J. Wiley.
Chun, C. A., Moos, R. H., & Cronkite, R. C. (2006). Culture: A fundamental context for the stress and coping paradigm. In *Handbook of multicultural perspectives on stress and coping* (pp. 29–53). Springer.
Chung, Y. B. (2001). Work discrimination and coping strategies: Conceptual frameworks for counseling lesbians, gay and bisexual clients. *Career Development Quarterly, 50*(1), 33–44.
Clark, S. C. (2002). Communicating across the work/home border. *Community, Work & Family, 5*(1), 23–48.
Claro M, C. (2022). Organizational listening and its implementation in the Chilean multi-store sector. *Public Relations Inquiry, 11*(2), 221–239. https://doi.org/10.1177/2046147X221081173
Cortina, L. M., Magley, V. J., Williams, J. H., & Langhout, R. D. (2001). Incivility in the workplace: Incidence and impact. *Journal of Occupational Health Psychology, 6*(1), 64–80.
Crawford, K. (2009). Following you: Disciplines of listening in social media. *Continuum: Journal of Media & Cultural Studies, 23*(4), 525–535.
Dhanani, L. Y., Beus, J. M., & Joseph, D. L. (2018). Workplace discrimination: A meta-analytic extension, critique, and future research agenda. *Personnel Psychology, 71*(2), 147–179.
Dozier, D. M., Grunig, L. A., & Grunig, J. E. (1995). *Manager's guide to excellence in public relations and communication management*. Lawrence Erlbaum Associates.
Ensher, E. A., Grant Vallone, E. J., & Donaldson, S. I. (2001). Effects of perceived discrimination on job satisfaction, organizational commitment, organizational citizenship behavior, and grievances. *Human Resource Development Quarterly, 12*(1), 53–72.
Falconier, M. K., Randall, A. K., & Bodenmann, G. (Eds.). (2016). *Couples coping with stress: A cross-cultural perspective*. Routledge.
Grunig, J. E. (1989). Publics, audiences and market segments: Segmentation principles for campaigns. *Information Campaigns: Balancing Social Values and Social Change*, (18), 199–228. Sage Publications.
Grunig, J. E. (2006). Furnishing the edifice: Ongoing research on public relations as a strategic management function. *Journal of Public Relations Research, 18*(2), 151–176.

Grunig, L. A., Grunig, J. E., & Dozier, D. M. (2003). *Excellent public relations and effective organizations: A study of communication management in three countries.* Routledge.

Grunig, J. E., & White, J. (1992). *Excellence in public relations and communication management.* Lawrence Erlbaum.

Hannay, M. (2009). The cross-cultural leader: The application of servant leadership theory in the international context. *Journal of International Business and Cultural Studies, 1,* 1–12.

Herrbach, O. (2006). A matter of feeling? The affective tone of organizational commitment and identification. *Journal of Organizational Behavior, 27*(5), 629–643.

Hofstede, G. (1980). *Culture's consequences: International differences in work-related values* (Vol. 5). Sage Publications.

Hofstede, G. (2001). *Culture's consequences: Comparing values, behaviors, Institutions and organizations across nations.* Sage Publications.

Hofstede, G., Hofstede, G. J., & Minkov, M. (2005). *Cultures and organizations: Software of the mind* (Vol. 2). New York: McGraw-Hill.

Hu, Y., & Scott, J. (2016). Family and gender values in China: Generational, geographic, and gender differences. *Journal of Family Issues, 37*(9), 1267–1293.

Jiang, H., & Men, R. L. (2017). Creating an engaged workforce: The impact of authentic leadership, transparent organizational communication, and work-life enrichment. *Communication Research, 44*(2), 225–243.

Jones, K. P., Peddie, C. I., Gilrane, V. L., King, E. B., & Gray, A. L. (2016). Not so subtle: A meta-analytic investigation of the correlates of subtle and overt discrimination. *Journal of Management, 42*(6), 1588–1613.

Kang, M., & Sung M. (2017). How symmetrical employee communication leads to employee engagement and positive employee communication behaviors: The mediation of employee-organization relationships. *Journal of Communication Management, 21*(1), 82–102.

Kelly, S., & MacDonald, P. (2019). A look at leadership styles and workplace solidarity communication. *International Journal of Business Communication, 56*(3), 432–448.

Kim, H. M. (2001). Work, nation and hypermasculinity: The "woman" question in the economic miracle and crisis in South Korea. *Inter-Asia Cultural Studies, 2*(1), 53–68.

Kim, H. S. (2007). A multilevel study of antecedents and a mediator of employee-organization relationships. *Journal of Public Relations Research, 19*(2), 167–197.

Kim, S. (2018, December 18). *Korea ranks 115th in gender parity report by WEF.* The Korea Herald. http://www.koreaherald.com/view.php?ud=20181218000472

Kim, Y. (2018). Enhancing employee communication behaviors for sensemaking and sensegiving in crisis situations: Strategic management approach for effective internal crisis communication. *Journal of Communication Management, 22*(4), 451–475.

Kim, Y., & Kim, S. Y. (2010). The influence of cultural values on perceptions of corporate social responsibility: Application of Hofstede's dimensions to Korean public relations practitioners. *Journal of Business Ethics, 91*(4), 485–500.

Kim, G., Kim, J., Lee, S. K., Sim, J., Kim, Y., Yun, B. Y., & Yoon, J. H. (2020). Multidimensional gender discrimination in workplace and depressive symptoms. *Plos One, 15*(7), e0234415.

Kim, E., & Park, H. (2018). Perceived gender discrimination, belief in a just world, self-esteem, and depression in Korean working women: A moderated mediation model. *Women's Studies International Forum, 69,* 143–150.

Kim, J. N., & Rhee, Y. (2011). Strategic thinking about employee communication behavior (ECB) in public relations: Testing the models of megaphoning and scouting effects in Korea. *Journal of Public Relations Research, 23*(3), 243–268.

Kwon, J. (2019, September 23). *South Korea's young men are fighting against feminism.* CNN. https://www.cnn.com/2019/09/21/asia/korea-angry-young-men-intl-hnk/index.html

Lee, Y. (2019). An examination of the effects of employee words in organizational crisis: Public forgiveness and behavioral intentions. *International Journal of Business Communication, 59*(4), 589–620. https://doi.org/10.1177/2329488419877

Lee, I. C., Hu, F., & Li, W. Q. (2020). Cultural factors facilitating or inhibiting the support for traditional household gender roles. *Journal of Cross-Cultural Psychology, 51*(5), 333–352.

Lee, Y., & Li, J. Y. (2021). Discriminated against but engaged: The role of communicative actions of racial minority employees. *Communication Monographs, 89*(4), 1–25. https://doi.org/10.1080/03637751.2021.2021432

Lee, Y., Li, J. Y., & Tsai, W. S. (2021). Diversity oriented leadership, internal communication, and employee outcomes: A perspective of racial minority employees. *Journal of Public Relations Research, 33*(5), 314–334.

Lee, I. C., & Pratto, F. (2018). Gendered power: Insights from power basis theory. In N. Dess, J. Marecek, D. Best, & L. Bell (Eds.), *Gender, sex, and sexualities: Psychological perspectives* (pp. 149–170). Oxford University Press.

Leonard, K. M., Van Scotter, J. R., & Pakdil, F. (2009). Culture and communication: Cultural variations and media effectiveness. *Administration & Society, 41*(7), 850–877.

Lipari, L. (2010). Listening, thinking, being. *Communication Theory, 20*(3), 348–362.

Macnamara, J. (2016). Organizational listening: Addressing a major gap in public relations theory and practice. *Journal of Public Relations Research, 28*(3–4), 146–169.

Macnamara, J. (2019). Explicating listening in organization-public communication: Theory, practices, technologies. *International Journal of Communication, 13,* 5183–5204.

Men, L. R. (2014). Strategic internal communication: Transformational leadership, communication channels, and employee satisfaction. *Management Communication Quarterly, 28*(2), 264–284.

Men, L. R., & Bowen, S. A. (2016). *Excellence in internal communication management.* Business Expert Press.

Men, L. R., & Stacks, D. (2014). The effects of authentic leadership on strategic internal communication and employee-organization relationships. *Journal of Public Relations Research, 26*(4), 301–324.

Men, L. R., Zhou, A., & Tsai, W. S. (2022). Harnessing the power of chatbot social conversation for organizational listening: The impact on perceived transparency and organization-public relationships. *Journal of Public Relations Research, 34*(1–2), 20–44.

Mojaverian, T., & Kim, H. S. (2013). Interpreting a helping hand: Cultural variation in the effectiveness of solicited and unsolicited social support. *Personality and Social Psychology Bulletin, 39*(1), 88–99.

Moon, S. (2005). *Militarized modernity and gendered citizenship in South Korea*. Duke University Press.

Moreno, Á, Khalil, N., & Tench, R. (2021). Enemy at the (house) gates: Permanence of gender discrimination in public relations career promotion in Latin America. *Communication & Society, 34*(3), 169–183.

Mortenson, S. T., Burleson, B. R., Feng, B., & Liu, M. (2009). Cultural similarities and differences in seeking social support as a means of coping: A comparison of European Americans and Chinese and an evaluation of the mediating effects of self-construal. *Journal of International and Intercultural Communication, 2*(3), 208–239.

Muyidi, A., Zhang, Y. B., & Gist-Mackey, A. (2022). The influence of gender discrimination, supervisor support, and government support on Saudi female Journalists' job stress and satisfaction. *Management Communication Quarterly*, 08933189221103623.

Neculaesei, A. N. (2015). Culture and gender role differences. *Cross-Cultural Management Journal, 17*(01), 31–35.

Neill, M. S., & Bowen, S. A. (2021). Employee perceptions of ethical listening in US organizations. *Public Relations Review, 47*(5), 102123.

Nemoto, K. (2016). *Too few women at the top: The persistence of inequality in Japan*. Cornell University Press.

OECD (2019). *Employment rate* (indicator) [Data set]. https://doi.org/10.1787/1de68a9b-en

Offermann, L. R., & Hellmann, P. S. (1997). Culture's consequences for leadership behavior: National values in action. *Journal of Cross-Cultural Psychology, 28*(3), 342–351.

Parker, K., & Funk, C. (2017, December 14). *Gender discrimination comes in many forms for today's working women*. Pew Research Center. https://www.pewresearch.org/fact-tank/2017/12/14/gender-discrimination-comes-in-many-forms-for-todays-working-women/

Reid, E. M., O'Neill, O. A., & Blair Loy, M. (2018). Masculinity in male-dominated occupations: How teams, time, and tasks shape masculinity contests. *Journal of Social Issues, 74*(3), 579–606.

Roebuck, D. B., Bell, R. L., Raina, R., & Lee, C. E. (2016). Comparing perceived listening behavior differences between managers and nonmanagers living in the United States, India, and Malaysia. *International Journal of Business Communication, 53*(4), 485–518.

Sanchez, J. I., & Brock, P. (1996). Outcomes of perceived discrimination among Hispanic employees: Is diversity management a luxury or a necessity? *Academy of Management Journal, 39*(3), 704–719.

Schwartz, S. H., & Rubel-Lifschitz, T. (2009). Cross-national variation in the size of sex differences in values: Effects of gender equality. *Journal of Personality and Social Psychology, 97*(1), 171.

Shaffer, M. A., Joplin, J. R., Bell, M. P., Lau, T., & Oguz, C. (2000). Gender discrimination and job related outcomes: A cross-cultural comparison of working women in the United States and China. *Journal of Vocational Behavior, 57*(3), 395–427.

Sharma, P. (2010). Measuring personal cultural orientations: Scale development and validation. *Journal of the Academy of Marketing Science, 38*(6), 787–806.

Shin, J. H., Heath, R. L., & Lee, J. (2011). A contingency explanation of public relations practitioner leadership styles: Situation and culture. *Journal of Public Relations Research, 23*(2), 167–190.

Smidts, A., Pruyn, A. T. H., & Van Riel, C. B. (2001). The impact of employee communication and perceived external prestige on organizational identification. *Academy of Management Journal, 44*(5), 1051–1062.

Soh, C. H. S. (1993). Sexual equality, male superiority, and Korean women in politics: Changing gender relations in a "patriarchal democracy." *Sex Roles, 28*(1), 73–90.

Spade, J. Z., & Valentine, C. G. (2011). *The kaleidoscope of gender: Prisms, patterns, and possibilities*. Sage Publications.

Sparrow, P. R., & Hiltrop, J. M. (1997). Redefining the field of European human resource management: A battle between national mindsets and forces of business transition? *Human Resource Management, 36*(2), 201–219.

Sriramesh, K., & Vercic, D. (Eds.). (2003). *The global public relations handbook: Theory, research, and practice*. Routledge.

Strother, J. (2019, November 11). *South Korea's #MeToo movement challenges workplace sexual harassment*. Voice of America. https://www.voanews.com/east-asia-pacific/south-koreas-metoo-movement-challenges-workplace-sexual-harassment

Taylor, M., & Kent, M. L. (2014). Dialogic engagement: Clarifying foundational concepts. *Journal of Public Relations Research, 26*(5), 384–398.

Taylor, S. E., Welch, W. T., Kim, H. S., & Sherman, D. K. (2007). Cultural differences in the impact of social support on psychological and biological stress responses. *Psychological Science, 18*(9), 831–837.

Triana, M. D. C., Jayasinghe, M., Pieper, J. R., Delgado, D. M., & Li, M. (2019). Perceived workplace gender discrimination and employee consequences: A meta-analysis and complementary studies considering country context. *Journal of Management, 45*(6), 2419–2447.

Triandis, H. (1988). Collectivism v. Individualism: A reconceptualisation of a basic concept in cross-cultural social psychology. In G. K. Verma, & C. Bagley (Eds.), *Cross-cultural studies of personality, attitudes and cognition* (pp. 60–95). Palgrave Macmillan.

US Equal Employment Opportunity Commission. (2020). *Race/color discrimination*. https://www.eeoc.gov/racecolor-discrimination

Wilson, M. S., & Chaudhry, A. (2017). Can empowerment and organizational support for development stem turnover? It depends on power distance. *South Asian Journal of Human Resources Management, 4*(1), 72–95.

Worthington, D., & Fitch-Hauser, M. (2018). *Listening process, functions, and competency*. Routledge.

Yeh, C. J., Arora, A. K., & Wu, K. A. (2006). A new theoretical model of collectivistic coping. In P. T. P. Wong, & L. C. J. Wong (Eds.), *Handbook of multicultural perspectives on stress and coping* (pp. 55–72). Springer.

Zhang, H., & Agarwal, N. C. (2009). The mediating roles of organizational justice on the relationships between HR practices and workplace outcomes: An investigation in China. *The International Journal of Human Resource Management, 20*(3), 676–693.

Unit 4
Cultural and Global Considerations for Organizational Listening

14 The Local and the Global in Organizational Listening Amid an Evolving Media Landscape

Ingrid Bachman and Claudia Labarca

Introduction

In recent years, organizations worldwide – regardless of their scope – have had to face and deal with the complexities of globalization and the new aspects of publics in such scenario (see Lee, 2005). In an increasingly transnational context, matters of globalization, digital transformation, the empowerment of historically less-considered non-state actors, new stakeholders, and the power to engage global audiences have added new demands and challenges to organizations and communication professionals (Fitzpatrick et al., 2013; Melissen, 2011; see also Gregory, 2015).

Indeed, the world and its citizens have become more connected and interdependent, making challenges spill across borders as well, to the extent that what once were national, regional, or local issues have become global interests and concerns, including affairs regarding trade, health, energy, organized crime, the environment, and migration (Fitzpatrick, 2017, p. 82). More so, digital media have favored extraordinary opportunities for expressing one's voice. This in turn has opened up new chances for speaking and listening, and therefore, for participation in decision-making – at least in theory (Dreher et al., 2016; Joyce, 2020).

It has been argued that organizational listening is a necessary step to truly engage with any organization's public (Macnamara, 2015, 2016, 2022) in order to "achieve two-way communication, dialogue, and relationships" (Macnamara, 2016, p. 153). As such, organizational listening (as a corollary of the act of speaking) would be critical to engage with audiences and stakeholders to fulfill the core function of public relations, even though Macnamara's own research shows that organization-public communication is greatly comprised of organizational *speaking,* and that listening is very rare in contemporary post-industrial societies (2015, 2022).

Drawing on the theoretical approaches that have pervaded Western thought in the field of public relations (excellence theory; relationship management, rhetorical, dialogic, and sociocultural theories, as well as the concepts of engagement and strategic communication), Macnamara's

DOI: 10.4324/9781003273851-19

formulations include components of modern conceptualizations of public relations shared by all these theoretical approaches. In Macnamara's perspective, organizational listening is built upon the concepts of two-way communication, relationships, dialogue, engagement, and co-orientation. The latter is understood as the convergence among the organization and the interests of its stakeholders, therefore placing the accent in a dyadic approach, leaving aside contextual variables that may shape these interactions.

In this chapter, we argue that such concepts may work in Global North settings, but are not necessarily suitable in other contexts, and that distinct features of different cultures need to be considered when trying to successfully establish relationships with publics (see Valentini, 2007; Wakefield, 2010). More so, we posit that practice and analysis of organizational listening in Latin America in particular must be understood within the sociopolitical framework in which organizations develop, grow and maintain relationships, dialogue, and engagement with their publics. After all, relationships, and therefore, dialogue, do not occur in a vacuum (Labarca & Mujica, 2022). Instead, they are inserted into a sociopolitical system that shapes communicative and listening processes. In Latin America, colonialism, political instability, human right violations, and social inequalities – among others – have historically defined the configuration of different publics and organizational communication practices, making distrust a prominent feature in organization-public interactions.

Thus, following the steps of Macnamara (2022), we argue that trust – or rather *distrust* – heavily influences how organizations listen to their publics in the Latin American continent and highlights the growing distrust toward institutions and news media.[1] Using Chile as a case study, we posit that besides the main points addressed by the literature, the theoretical argumentation on organizational listening needs to consider regional key sociopolitical issues to fully comprehend organization-public relationships in non-Western contexts. In so doing, we stress the role of local insights to a global theoretical perspective in an ever-changing world, since communication practices of all kinds would benefit from indigenous approaches that take into consideration the realities of specific cultures and nation-states (Bachmann & Proust, 2020).

Global Publics, Global Media?

There is no denying that development in digital and network technologies have dramatically changed communication practices and media flows in the last few decades, with the internet as the dominant platform. The mostly centralized, national (and even local), limited mass media systems of the 20th century have given way to much more varied, multi-channel systems embracing a wide range of platforms reaching across traditional geopolitical borders (Price, 2008). In other words, contents and audiences are increasingly globalized (Sriramesh, 2007). Globalization, after all, has thrust public relations and organizational communication into the limelight, providing new opportunities while posing immense challenges as well (Sriramesh, 2007).

Indeed, digital transformation has helped to create widely dispersed and decentralized systems of communication that are nonetheless thoroughly interconnected and that easily cross national and continental borders (Price, 2008; see also Joyce, 2020). In the current media environment, mostly digital media shape the way we see, comprehend and respond to reality in our increasingly globalized world. This has favored the existence of so-called global publics, which Lee (2005) defined as "groups of individuals or organizations whose primary interests and concerns are pursuing the world as a whole beyond their own national and cultural boundaries" (p. 15). In other words, global publics share similar values and norms as world citizens, and have a somewhat ephemeral nature since they are a function of widespread discussions and interactions favored by digitalization (Price, 2008; see also Fitzpatrick et al., 2013).

This is an ongoing process. In a world of globalized economy and communications, several structural changes keep reconfiguring the media ecosystem, the outlook of organizations, and communication practices. For instance, the so-called high-choice media environments (see Prior, 2007), where users have multiple options to consume information and entertainment have been consolidated worldwide (e.g., De Albuquerque, 2018; van Aelst et al., 2017), and organizations are no longer able to clearly segment stakeholders as they did, since they need to respond to new needs and expectations even faster than before (e.g., Harrison & Bosse, 2013; Mostaghel et al., 2022).

The rise of social networks has made them become the center of dissemination of all types of content and has resulted in the platforming of media consumption habits and social mediatization (van Zoonen & van de Meer, 2015; Gil de Zúñiga et al., 2017). In addition, the way in which citizens access information has changed, which has ousted the once hegemonic filter of professional journalists, communication professionals, and clearly defined outlets to determine the content that is disseminated. As a result, not only has the information offer been decentralized but also media and other organizations have lost the centrality they used to have in the social life of communities (García-Perdomo et al., 2018; Kunelius & Reunanen, 2016; Masip et al., 2019).

Information is one of the main resources to function in society and for both people and organizations to make decisions. However, we are currently in a scenario of over-information and communicative complexity due to the concurrence of social networks and other forms of mediated communication to which public and organizations have access (van Aelst et al., 2017; Sanders, 2019). Thus, extreme connectivity, as well as the access to a hyperabundance of information, drive people's expectations and, arguably, lead to greater demands for transparency, participation, and responsiveness (Sanders, 2019; see also Fitzpatrick et al., 2013). Digital technologies also define current public communication forms, which makes social media literacy, data analytical skills, and knowledge about stakeholder engagement and as key competences needed by organizational communicators amid settings defined by volatility, uncertainty, complexity, and ambiguity (Sanders, 2019).

This makes for a major challenge. Information and communication technologies have reconfigured networks, power structures, information transmission, economies, and public life. While social media has created the possibility for all kinds of new publics and even global spaces to emerge – see, for instance, feminist activists' use of digital media to mainstream their concerns in Argentina (Bedrosian, 2022) or emerging digital cultures among Indigenous people to influence government policy in Australia (Dreher et al., 2016) – those that do emerge still tend to endure more disadvantages that benefits from embracing digital media (see Lupien, 2020). How do two-way communication, engagement, and dialogue work in an increasingly cacophonic and polarized environment, legitimacy and trust crises, multiple voices, and contesting viewpoints? How can public spaces be defined and approached when multiple groups are battling for those spaces? As Macnamara (2015, p. 62) warned, "[t]oday we have the skills and technologies to listen to the universe. But often we don't listen to people around us."

The Need for a Latin American Perspective on Listening

Previous literature has already pointed out the prevalence of grand theories on public relations based on the Global North conceptualizations (e.g., Culbertson & Chen, 2013; L'Etang, 2008; Labarca & Mujica, 2022) that have driven the study of the field and inspired hundreds of academic studies worldwide. Since the 1980s, the excellence theory, for example, has emerged as the most influential theoretical paradigm in public relations that helped "to explain the value of public relations to an organization and to identify the characteristics of a public relations function that increase its value" (Grunig & Grunig, 2008, p. 327). Excellence theory has been applied and contextualized to different settings such as Asia or Europe (see, for example, Grunig et al., 1995; Rhee, 2002), and it has also deeply influenced the practice of the profession and the prevalence of a functional perspective of public relations.

As the excellence theory, the dialogic conceptualization of the public relations' function proposed by Kent and Taylor (2002) has influenced the field, placing the accent on an "open, honest, ethical, and respectful communication oriented towards genuine dialogue with the public" therefore, a more normative perspective on the field, which nonetheless has found an empirical application to social media interactions with the public (Liu et al., 2020). This theoretical conceptualization has also echoed important academic research outside the Global North (e.g., Capriotti et al., 2021; Gálvez-Rodríguez et al., 2019; Ngai et al., 2020; to name a few). Another important perspective is given by Ledingham (2003, 2006, 2015), who, based on the idea of Ferguson (1984) on the relational aspect of public relations, understood the field as the study of organization–public relationship management.

However, these models seem to operate in a contextual vacuum without considering cultural and sociopolitical variables – the local dimension (Labarca & Ampuero Ruiz, 2020; Labarca & Mujica, 2022). At most, they somewhat adapt to local phenomena such as the excellence model that incorporates the personal influence model (Labarca & Ruiz, 2020) in Asian contexts. Despite this, there are existing claims that globalization has pushed public relations to consider multiculturality and local issues when defining and conceptualizing the field (Sriramesh, 2007; see also Wakefield, 2010) since public relations are complex, conceptually rich and, furthermore, fluid (Curtin, 2012; Kenny, 2016).

Latin America has not been exempted from these theoretical influences. These grand theories – particularly the prevalence of functionalism – have somehow shaped academic work, teaching in communication schools, as well as public relations practice (Kaplún, 2013). Ferrari (2013), for example, highlights how excellence theory has dominated PR practice within the continent. Some authors argue that this may stem from the foreign approach that has prevailed in the last decades in many communication schools in Latin America. Sadi and Ferrari (2022), for instance, underscore the prevalence of functionalism – derived from Global North conceptualizations, primarily the excellence theory – in Argentinian higher education. Others have contended that this was born out of multinationals that arrived on the continent (e.g., Ferrari & França, 2011) that dominated the field and allowed public relations practices to respond to standard approaches (Mellado & Barría, 2012; Molleda et al., 2018).

Arguably, native Latin American theoretical proposals have not been able to influence the practice of public relations or trespass their own geographical sphere, despite the existence of a Latin American school of thought attached to academic associations and particular scholars (Molleda, 2001; Molleda et al., 2018). Brazil, Argentina, and Mexico have led the development of a Latin American school of thought in the region with some particular characteristics (Suárez-Monsalve, 2022), such as entangling the practice of public relations to the political context, as in the work of Porto Simões (1993, 2001a, 2001b). But as we have explained elsewhere (Labarca & Mujica, 2022), the foreign impact cannot be denied. Vásquez and Marroquín Velásquez (2016) emphasize North American positivism and European critical thinking as the main determinants of public relations theoretical proposals in Latin America. In this respect, one of the most systematic overviews belongs to Kaplún (2013), who offered a typology of four perspectives influencing Latin American communication studies and public relations theoretical development. He proposed four main theoretical influences that have lived in the region since the 1950s: (a) *critical*, (b) *cultural*, (c) *alternativist* (to mainstream and hegemonic communication theories), and (d) functionalism. Three of these are rooted in Europe or North America, and are mixed with local theoretical development, in line with the idea that scientific work in communications in Latin America points out to theoretical hybridism, a kind of "mestizo" (mixed) research Latin American-rooted (Martín-Barbero, 1999).

Another important element in these formulations is the very definition of "public." Most of the time, they imply the notion of stakeholders or publics characterized by the interest and power they have concerning an organization, always stressing the relational aspects and considered as a group, but ignoring their context. Furthermore, as we pointed out above, there is the notion of a global public engrained in the public relations literature (see Lee, 2005), also criticized because it leaves aside cultural nuances and socio-political settings that may interfere with the relationship between the organization and its publics (Labarca & Ampuero Ruiz, 2020).

Therefore, we posit that the Latin American perspective on public relations needs to address, both in theory and in practice, that there are certain specificities of the Latin American context shaping the relationship between the organization and its publics, heavily determined by trust – or actually, *distrust*. The region past and present has been marked by human rights abuses, corruption, violence, colonialism, disenfranchisement, structural inequalities, and segmented access to civil, political, and social rights (Cárdenas, 2011; Coatsworth, 2008; Munck & Luna, 2022). We argue that organizational listening may help to understand and engage with these specificities through active organizational listening. Specifically, we posit that three contextual elements that need to be considered to understand organizational listening: political and economic instability, social unrest, and institutional weakness, particularly weak institutional trust in the continent.

Social and Political Trust in Latin America

Abundant literature has tackled the importance of social trust for the well-being of society, whether it is considered a social lubricant that allows economic exchange (Arrow, 1974) or because of its role in diminishing systems' complexity (Luhmann, 1979). Trust has been associated with growth and economic development (Bjørnskov, 2012, 2017; Fukuyama, 1995), social capital (Putnam, 1993, 2000), and general social cooperation.

On the other hand, political trust (or trust toward political institutions) is related to healthy and stable democracies (Newton & Norris,

2000; Wences & Güemes, 2016) and it is especially needed in developing countries and newborn democracies (Letki, 2018). There is evidence that shows political trust has a causal effect on generalized social trust (Dinesen et al., 2022) and thus "on the creation of trusting publics and, ultimately, well-functioning societies, good government lays the foundation for political trust, which then, in turn, stimulates trust between citizens with positive downstream consequences for the cooperation between citizens" (Dinesen et al., 2022, p. 12). This goes in line with the role attached to public relations as an engine that may "strengthen system interactions through the creation of trust among systems" (Valentini & Kruckeberg, 2011, p. 91)

Still a contended and multidimensional concept, trust has, nevertheless, captured growing academic interest in the public relations field (Valentini, 2021), although largely constrained to the role of trust as either a consequence or by-product of an excellent public relations performance (Labarca & Mujica, 2022). Along these lines, we believe the notion of trust should be addressed in a more comprehensive way and in line with Gambetta's (1988) definition: "trust (or, symmetrically, distrust) is a particular level of the subjective probability with which an agent assesses that another agent or group of agents will perform a particular action, both before he can monitor such action (or independently of his capacity ever to be able to monitor it) and in a context in which it affects his own action" (p. 217).

As it has been argued in previous studies, Latin America, as a region, has very weak levels of social trust (Labarca et al., 2022). Social trust – understood as that directed toward those we do not know personally (Uslaner, 2018) – fosters cooperation between groups, economic development, and social well-being (Putnam, 1993, 2000). To some, the relatively low levels of social trust exhibited by Latin Americans – *universal distrust*, according to Mattes and Moreno (2018) – would be consistent with low levels of satisfaction with democracy and high distrust towards political institutions (Zmerli & Newton, 2008). Nevertheless, high social mistrust has been a constant in Latin America since at least the 1990s (Mattes & Moreno, 2018). This comes as no surprise, since social trust develops through processes of sociability, and is relatively immune to short- or medium-term phenomena (Uslaner, 2018).

Political trust has also been sharply declining in recent years in Latin America (Mattes & Moreno, 2018) and social and political instability resurfaces in the region (Labarca et al., 2022). Current scholarship shows a direct relationship between political trust and democratic governance (Levi & Stoker, 2000; Warren, 2018), to the extent that political trust has been deemed a prerequisite for democratic maturity (Levi & Stoker, 2000). Further, trust in institutions expands the scope of collective self-regulation (Warren, 2018), while favoring governance as it cements the social contract between citizens and governments (Dalton, 2017). Also, trust allows both legitimacy and governability, and is therefore key to democracy and social life (Mani & Echeverría, 2019). Yet, as Álvarez-Nobell and colleagues (2022) assert, the "Latin American region has some of the most notable political and ideological contrasts and antagonisms and fluctuating dynamics and cycles that continually reconfigure dissimilar and contradictory contexts and scenarios" (p. 1).

There is also evidence that media play an important role in shaping both social and political trust, but media themselves have been enduring a trust crisis in recent years. Latin America is no exception. This is not surprising given the levels of political parallelism in the continent. While some saw in social media the promise of the disruption of concentrated corporate models of media organization and the growth of citizen media, evidence shows that new forms of digital media power and monopoly have also manifested (Joyce, 2020; see also Labarca et al., 2022). More importantly, the growth of social media has gone in hand with major critiques to mainstream media, and the rise of alternative outlets, populist discourses, and the proliferation of disinformation, often exploited for political advantage (Joyce, 2020; Santos & Valenzuela, 2022). Several authors have argued that misinformation ends up undermining trust in institutions, discrediting the diversity of opinions and even affecting interpersonal trust (e.g., Ognyanova et al., 2020). In this context, organizations have to face the challenges of getting the attention of stakeholders and gaining a reputation for reliable and truthful communication in a context of clickbait and so-called fake news and alternative facts (Sanders, 2019).

States in Latin America have not often been responsive to informal public pressure, which may explain a surge of protests and growing political discontent in the continent in the last few years. Street rallies, roadblocks, riots, and massive demonstrations have threatened democratic governance in places like Brazil, Chile, Colombia, Costa Rica, Ecuador, and Perú, with demonstrators often complaining that their grievances and voices were not being heard not addressed by governments, corporations, and institutions at large – that is, a failure to listen.

A Cautionary Tale: The Case of Chile

Such a failure was evident in October 2019 in Chile. Over the years, the broad sense that the system benefited a few members of the elite resulted in increasing social discontent with the far-reaching vulnerability, income inequality, and financial debt that clashed with the (unfulfilled) social mobility promises of the "Chilean model" (Bachmann et al., 2021; Gonzalez & Mouran 2020; Somma et al., 2021). On October 18, 2019, after weeks of subway fare evasions in Santiago, the capital, in rejection of a fare increase of 30 Chilean pesos (about four US cents), massive protests turned into riots, arson, and looting that by the following day expanded to most cities in Chile. President Sebastián Piñera then decreed a state of emergency, placed most of the country under curfew for the first time since the return to democracy in 1990, and had the Army taking charge of security (Gonzalez & Mouran, 2020; Somma et al., 2021). However, the unrest continued amid multiple reports of human right violations by the police and the military. Labeled "estallido social" (social outbreak), it was the start of a major socio-political crisis that was forced to the sidelines the COVID-19 pandemic reached Chile in March 2020 (Bachmann et al., 2021).

The crisis was seemingly unforeseen by the country's political and social elites, who even said multiple times that they "did not see it coming." Indeed, only a few days before, President Piñera had called Chile an "oasis" within Latin America (Bachmann et al., 2022; Somma et al., 2021). Yet the crisis was long in the making given the glaring inequalities in the nation as shown by two of the most popular slogans of protesters: "Chile awoke" and "It's not 30 pesos, it's 30 years" (Bachmann et al., 2021, 2022). Growing inequalities and a sense of being abused not only by political institutions but also by a neoliberal economic system that allowed the existence of private companies in critical areas have been deemed as one of the causes of the Chilean 2019 protests. As explained by Somma and colleagues (2021, p. 496), "this [neoliberal model] privileges the private sector in welfare provision, resulting in a highly criticized, privatized pension system, and segmented education and healthcare, with lower-quality public services for the majority and expensive private ones for the well-off. Market-based inequalities have been politicized since the return to democracy." Protests, then, were related to both public and private sectors, which were accused by demonstrators of having "discriminatory behavior and an overall sense of unfair advantages that benefited the few against the many" (Gonzalez & Mouran, 2020, p. 231).

There were also several signs of growing and widespread discontent, as well as a sharp decline in institutional trust, for at least a decade leading to the *estallido*. This went in hand with highly covered corruption scandals involving the Army, the police, and congressional campaigns (Bargsted et al., 2022). Distrust extended to other organizations as well, including companies and corporations: a 2018 report showed that almost 60% of Chileans did not trust big businesses (Flores, 2019). Several collusion scandals may have accelerated this discontent and, indeed, they were syndicated as an important issue during the 2019 protests (Tagle Montt & Claro, 2021; see also Bargsted et al., 2022).

Although the subject of organizational listening is new to academia in Latin America, and particularly in Chile (Claro, 2022; Tagle Montt & Claro, 2021), the few studies on the matter that companies indeed do not engage in dialogue or active listening in Chile. In a study on the retail sector, Claro (2022) found that Chilean companies "do not have the concept of listening internalized as an element of management, or that the intense competition in Chilean retail prevents those who work there from stopping to listen properly." Not surprisingly, Claro concludes that "a culture of monologue prevails" in these companies (p. 23).

Beyond speculation, it is impossible to say whether the *estallido* would have occurred had there been active organizational listening occurring in Chile. But it is clear that organizations that are at the core of Chilean society were not only not engaging at all with their publics, but also sent a consistent message that they did not care about them – there was no such as dialogue and no two-way communication. Paraphrasing Macnamara (2022), since these organizations were not listening, they could not understand their stakeholders and publics. In order to create a fairer and more just society, organizations need to start acknowledging and paying more attention to *all* their stakeholders, but rebuilding trust when distrust is already widespread will not be an easy task. Bring it on.

Recommendations for Practice

In this chapter, we make a call for addressing the very specific and concrete contexts in organizational communication practices as well as avoiding universalizing approaches in organizational listening. In that sense, we strongly recommend that organizational communicators never forget the local when listening, since the particularities may be more insightful and telling. We also propose checking out the levels of (dis)trust at the societal level, as this will influence the effectiveness of organization-publics interactions. It is important to always listen and pay attention, not only to stakeholders but also to social trends. And finally, when engaging in organizational listening is necessary, one should keep in mind that (dis)trust is a transitive concept – if one's publics and stakeholders do not like something, any related category to that may start from a distrust point.

The practice and analysis of organizational listening must consider the many factors shaping communicative and listening processes, and that includes the particularities of specific cultures and nation-states. Political, social, and institutional antecedents heavily determine organization-public interactions, and when distrust and disaffection are the norm, as it is the case in Latin America, large-scale and active listening becomes particularly challenging.

Note

1 This work was supported by a grant from ANID-National Fund for Science and Technology Program (Fondecyt 1201316).

References

Álvarez-Nobell, A., Oliveira, A., Athaydes, A., & Barroso, B. (2022). Strategic communication and political ideologies in South America. COVID-19 crisis management in the cases of the populist governments of Argentina and Brazil. *International Journal of Strategic Communication*, *16*(3), 403–425. https://doi.org/10.1080/1553118X.2022.2056040

Arrow, K. J. (1974). *The limits of organization*. W.W. Norton and Company.
Bachmann, I., Grassau, D., & Labarca, C. (2022). Aliens, spies, and staged vandalism. In H. Wasserman, & D. Madrid-Morales (Eds.), *Disinformation in the global South* (pp. 74–87). Routledge.
Bachmann, I., & Proust, V. (2020). Old concerns, renewed focus and novel problems: Feminist communication theory and the global South. *Annals of the International Communication Association, 44*(1), 67–80. https://doi.org/10.1080/23808985.2019.1647445
Bachmann, I., Valenzuela, S., & Figueroa-Bustos, A. (2021). COVID-19 in Chile: A health crisis amidst a political crisis amidst a social crisis. In P. van Aelst, & J. Blumler (Eds.), *Political communication in the time of Coronavirus* (pp. 48–68). Routledge.
Bargsted, M., Bachmann, I., & Valenzuela, S. (2022). Corruption and political knowledge erosion: A cautionary tale from Latin America. *International Journal of Public Opinion Research, 34*(2). https://doi.org/10.1093/ijpor/edac015
Bedrosian, A. (2022). How# NiUnaMenos used discourse and digital media to reach the masses in Argentina. *Latin American Research Review, 57*(1), 100–116.
Bjørnskov, C. (2012). How does social trust affect economic growth? *Southern Economic Journal, 78*(4), 1346–1368. https://doi.org/10.4284/0038-4038-78.4.1346
Bjørnskov, C. (2017). Social trust and economic growth. In E. M. Uslaner (Ed.), *Oxford handbook of social and political trust* (pp. 535–555). Oxford University Press.
Capriotti, P., Zeler, I., & Oliveira, A. (2021). Assessing dialogic features of corporate pages on Facebook in Latin American companies. *Corporate Communications: An International Journal, 26*(5), 16–30.
Cárdenas, S. (2011). *Human rights in Latin America: A politics of terror and hope*. University of Pennsylvania Press.
Claro, M. C. (2022). Organizational listening and its implementation in the Chilean multi-store sector. *Public Relations Inquiry, 11*(2), 221–239. https://doi.org/10.1177/2046147X221081173
Coatsworth, J. H. (2008). Inequality, institutions and economic growth in Latin America. *Journal of Latin American Studies, 40*(3), 545–569.
Culbertson, H., & Chen, N. (2013). *International public relations: A comparative analysis*. Routledge.
Curtin, P. A. (2012). Public relations and philosophy: Parsing paradigms. *Public Relations Inquiry, 1*(1), 31–47. https://doi.org/10.1177/2046147X11422150
Dalton, R. (2017). Political trust in North America. In S. Zmerli, & T. van der Meer (Eds.), *Handbook of political trust* (pp. 375–394). Edward Elgar.
De Albuquerque, A. (2018). Political parallelism. In *Oxford research encyclopedia of communication*. https://doi.org/10.1093/acrefore/9780190228613.013.860
Dinesen, P., Sønderskov, K., Sohlberg, S., & Esaiasson, P. (2022). Close (causally connected) cousins? Evidence on the causal relationship between political trust and social trust. *Public Opinion Quarterly*. https://doi.org/10.1093/poq/nfac027
Dreher, T., McCallum, K., & Waller, L. (2016). Indigenous voices and mediatized policy-making in the digital age. *Information, Communication & Society, 19*(1), 23–39. https://doi.org/10.1080/1369118X.2015.1093534

Ferguson, M. A. (1984, August). Building theory in public relations: Inter-organizational relationships. *Paper presented at the annual meeting of AEJMC*, Gainesville, FL.

Ferrari, M. A. (2013). The Grunig legacy to academic studies and professional practice in Latin America. In K. Sriramesh, A. Zerfass, & J.-N. Kim (Eds.), *Public relations and communication management* (pp. 364–375). Routledge.

Ferrari, M. A., & França, F. (2011). *Relaciones públicas. Naturaleza, función y gestión en las organizaciones contemporáneas* [Public relations. Nature, role and management in contemporary organizations]. La Crujía.

Fitzpatrick, K. (2017). Public diplomacy in the public interest. *Journal of Public Interest Communications*, *1*(1), 78–93. https://doi.org/10.32473/jpic.v1.i1.p78

Fitzpatrick, K., Fullerton, J., & Kendrick, A. (2013). Public relations and public diplomacy: Conceptual and practical connections. *Public Relations Journal*, *7*(4), 36.

Flores, R. (2019, March 20). ¿Qué tanto confían los chilenos en las grandes empresas? [How much do Chileans trust in big companies?]. *La Tercera*. https://www.latercera.com/que-pasa/noticia/tanto-confian-los-chilenos-las-grandes-empresas/

Fukuyama, F. (1995). *Trust: The social virtues and the creation of prosperity*. The Free Press.

Gálvez-Rodríguez, M. M., Haro-de-Rosario, A., García-Tabuyo, M., & Caba-Pérez, C. (2019). Building online citizen engagement for enhancing emergency management in local European government: The case of the November 2015 Paris attacks. *Online Information Review*, *43*(2), 219–238. https://doi.org/10.1108/OIR-09-2016-0286

Gambetta, D. (1988). Can we trust trust? In D. Gambetta (Ed.), *Trust making and breaking cooperative relations* (pp. 213–237). Blackwell.

García-Perdomo, V., Salaverría, R., Brown, D. K., & Harlow, S. (2018). To share or not to share: The influence of news values and topics on popular social media content in the United States, Brazil, and Argentina. *Journalism Studies*, *19*, 1180–1201. https://doi.org/10.1080/1461670X.2016.1265896

Gil de Zúñiga, H., Weeks, B., & Ardèvol-Abreu, A. (2017). Effects of the news-finds-me perception in communication: Social media use implications for news seeking and learning about politics. *Journal of Computer-Mediated Communication*, *22*, 105–123. https://doi.org/10.1111/jcc4.12185

Gonzalez, R., & Mouran, C. (2020). The 2019–2020 Chilean protests: A first look at their causes and participants. *International Journal of Sociology*, *50*(3), 227–235. https://doi.org/10.1080/00207659.2020.1752499

Gregory, B. (2015). Mapping boundaries in diplomacy's public dimension. *The Hague Journal of Diplomacy*, *11*(1), 1–25. https://doi.org/10.1163/1871191X-12341317

Grunig, J. E., & Grunig, L. A. (2008). Excellence theory in public relations: Past, present, and future. In A. Zerfass, B. van Ruler, & K. Sriramesh (Eds.), *Public relations research* (pp. 327–347). VS Verlag für Sozialwissenschaften.

Grunig, J., Grunig, L. A., Sriramesh, K., Huang, K., & Lyra, A. (1995). Models of public relations in an international setting. *Journal of Public Relations Research*, *7*, 163–186. https://doi.org/10.1207/s1532754xjprr0703_01

Harrison, J. S., & Bosse, D. A. (2013). How much is too much? The limits to generous treatment of stakeholders. *Business Horizons*, *56*(3), 313–322. https://doi.org/10.1016/j.bushor.2013.01.014

Joyce, D. (2020). *Informed publics, media and international law*. Bloomsbury.
Kaplún, G. (2013). Viejas y nuevas tradiciones en la comunicación latinoamericana [Old and new traditions in Latin America communication]. *Revista Latinoamericana De Ciencias De La Comunicación, 10*(18), 66–76.
Kenny, J. (2016). Excellence theory and its critics: A literature review critiquing Grunig's strategic management of public relations paradigm. *Asia Pacific Public Relations Journal, 17*(2), 78–91.
Kent, M. L., & Taylor, M. (2002). Toward a dialogic theory of public relations. *Public Relations Review, 28*(1), 21–37.
Kunelius, R., & Reunanen, E. (2016). Changing power of journalism: The two phases of mediatization. *Communication Theory, 26*, 369–388. https://doi.org/10.1111/comt.12098
L'Etang, J. (2008). *Public relations concepts, practice and critique*. Sage.
Labarca, C., & Ampuero Ruiz, P. (2020). Cultural and global perspectives to relationship management in international public relations: The Sino-Chilean case study. *International Communication Gazette, 83*(8), 776–798. https://doi.org/10.1177/1748048520929817
Labarca, C., & Mujica, C. (2022). Trust as a contextual variable for public relations: Reflections from Latin America. *Public Relations Inquiry, 11*(2), 315–330. https://doi.org/10.1177/2046147X221081172
Labarca, C., Valenzuela, S., Bachmann, I., & Grassau, D. (2022). *Medios de comunicación y confianza política en América Latina: Análisis individual y contextual del rol de las noticias en la confianza en el gobierno y el estado* [Media and political trust in Latin America: Individual and contextual analysis of the role of news in trust in government and the state]. Revista Internacional de Sociología.
Ledingham, J. A. (2003). Explicating relationship management as a general theory of public relations. *Journal of Public Relations Research, 15*(2), 181–198. https://doi.org/10.1207/1532754XJPRR1502_4
Ledingham, J. A. (2006). Relationship management: A general theory of public relations. In C. H. Botan, & V. Hazleton (Eds.), *Public relations theory II* (pp. 465–483). Lawrence Erlbaum Associates.
Ledingham, J. A. (2015). Managing relationship management: A holistic approach. In E.-J. Ki, J.-N. Kim, & J. A. Ledingham (Eds.), *Public relations as relationship management* (pp. 78–92). Routledge.
Lee, S. (2005). The emergence of global public and international public relations. *Public Relations Quarterly, 50*(2), 14–16.
Letki, N. (2018). Trust in newly democratic regimes. In E. M. Uslaner (Ed.), *Oxford handbook of social and political trust* (pp. 335–356). Oxford University Press.
Levi, M., & Stoker, L. (2000). Political trust and trustworthiness. *Annual Review of Political Science, 3*(1), 475–507. https://doi.org/10.1146/annurev.polisci.3.1.475
Liu, W., Xu, W., & Tsai, J.-Y. (2020). Developing a multi-level organization-public dialogic communication framework to assess social media-mediated disaster communication and engagement outcomes. *Public Relations Review, 46*(4). https://doi.org/10.1016/j.pubrev.2020.101949
Luhmann, N. (1979). *Trust and power*. Wiley.
Lupien, P. (2020). Indigenous movements, collective action, and social media: New opportunities or new threats? *Social Media + Society, 6*(2). https://doi.org/10.1177/2056305120926487

Macnamara, J. (2015). *Creating an "architecture of listening" in organizations. The basis of engagement, trust, healthy democracy, social equity, and business sustainability*. University of Technology Sydney.

Macnamara, J. (2016). Organizational listening: Addressing a major gap in public relations theory and practice. *Journal of Public Relations Research, 28*(3–4), 146–169. https://doi.org/10.1080/1062726X.2016.1228064

Macnamara, J. (2022). *Organizational listening in public communication: Emerging theory and practice*. University of Technology Sydney.

Mani, E., & Echeverría, M. (2019). Confianza política y medios de comunicación. Teoría, hallazgos y metodologías [Political trust and media. Theory, findings and methodologies]. *Revista De Comunicación Política, 1*, 53–74. https://doi.org/10.29105/rcp1-3

Martín-Barbero, J. (1999). Aventuras de un cartógrafo mestizo en el campo de la comunicación [Adventures of a mestizo cartographer in the field of communication]. *Revista Latina De Comunicación Social, 19*(1). www.ull.es/publicaciones/latina/a1999fjl/64jmb.htm

Masip, P., Ruiz-Caballero, C., & Suau, J. (2019). Active audiences and social discussion on the digital public sphere. *El Profesional De La Información, 28*, https://doi.org/10.3145/epi.2019.mar.04

Mattes, R., & Moreno, A. (2018). Social and political trust in developing countries: Sub-Saharan Africa and Latin America. In E. M. Uslaner (Ed.), *Oxford Handbook of social and political trust* (pp. 357–382). Oxford University Press.

Melissen, J. (2011). *Beyond the new public diplomacy*. Clingendael Papers N° 3. Netherlands Institute of International Relations.

Mellado, C., & Barría, S. (2012). Development of professional roles in the practice of public relations in Chile. *Public Relations Review, 38*(3), 446–453. https://doi.org/10.1016/j.pubrev.2012.04.001

Molleda, J. C. (2001). International paradigms: The Latin American school of public relations. *Journalism Studies, 2*(4), 513–530. https://doi.org/10.1080/14616700120098915

Molleda, J. C., María, S. M. A., & Andréia, S. A., Said, G., Elim, H., Ricardo, V. 2018). Influences of postcolonialism over the understanding and evolution of public relations in Latin America. In E. Bridgen, & D. Vercic (Eds.), *Experiencing public relations: International voices* (pp. 152–164). Routledge.

Mostaghel, R., Oghazi, P., Parida, V., & Sohrabpour, V. (2022). Digitalization driven retail business model innovation: Evaluation of past and avenues for future research trends. *Journal of Business Research, 146*, 134–145. https://doi.org/10.1016/j.jbusres.2022.03.072

Munck, G. L., & Luna, J. P. (2022). *Latin American politics and society: A comparative and historical analysis*. Cambridge University Press.

Newton, K., & Norris, P. (2000). Confidence in public institutions: Faith, culture, or performance? In S. J. Pharr, & R. D. Putnam (Eds.), *Disaffected democracies. What's troubling the trilateral countries?* (pp. 52–73). Princeton University Press.

Ngai, C. S. B., Einwiller, S., & Singh, R. G. (2020). An exploratory study on content and style as driving factors facilitating dialogic communication between corporations and publics on social media in China. *Public Relations Review, 46*(1), https://doi.org/10.1016/j.pubrev.2019.101813

Ognyanova, K., Lazer, D., Robertson, R. E., & Wilson, C. (2020, June 2). Misinformation in action: Fake news exposure is linked to lower trust in media, higher trust in government when your side is in power. *Harvard Kennedy School (HSK) Misinformation Review*, 1(4). https://misinforeview.hks.harvard.edu/article/misinformation-in-action-fake-news-exposure-is-linked-to-lower-trust-in-media-higher-trust-in-government-when-your-side-is-in-power/

Porto Simões, R. (1993). *Relaciones públicas: función política en la empresa y en la institución pública* [Public relations: political function in the company and in the public institution]. Consejo Superior de Comunicación y Relaciones Públicas de España.

Porto Simões, R. (2001a) *Informação, inteligecia e Utopia. Contribuições â teoria de relações públicas* [Information, intelligence and Utopia. Contributions to public relations theory]. Summus.

Porto Simões, R. (2001b). *Relações Publicas e Micropolítica* [Public relations and micro-politics]. Summus.

Price, V. (2008). Democracy, global publics and world opinion. In M. Albrow, H. K. Anheier, M. Glasius, M. E. Price, & M. Kaldor (Eds.), *Global civil society 2007/8: Communicative power and democracy* (pp. 20–33). Sage.

Prior, M. (2007). *Post-broadcast democracy. How media choice increases inequality in political involvement and polarizes elections.* Cambridge University Press.

Putnam, R. D. (1993). *Making democracy work: Civic traditions in modern Italy.* Princeton University Press.

Putnam, R. D. (2000). *Bowling alone: The collapse and revival of American community.* Simon & Schuster.

Rhee, Y. (2002). Global public relations: A cross-cultural study of the excellence theory in South Korea. *Journal of Public Relations Research*, *14*(3), 159–184. https://doi.org/10.1207/S1532754XJPRR1403_1

Sadi, G., & Ferrari, M. A. (2022). Disciplinary approaches and theories in Argentinian public relations undergraduate programmes. *Public Relations Inquiry*, *11*(2), 275–291. https://doi.org/10.1177/2046147X221081177

Sanders, K. (2019). Government communication and political public relations. In J. Strömback, & S. Kousis (Eds.), *Political public relations* (pp. 165–186). Routledge.

Santos, M., & Valenzuela, S. (2022). Changing media landscapes and political participation. In M. Giugni and M. Grasso (Eds.), *The Oxford handbook of political participation*, https://doi.org/10.1093/oxfordhb/9780198861126.013.50

Somma, N. M., Bargsted, M., Disi, R., & Medel, R. R. (2021). No water in the oasis: The Chilean spring of 2019-2020. *Social Movement Studies*, *20*(4). https://doi.org/10.1080/14742837.2020.1727737

Sriramesh, K. (2007). The relationship between culture and public relations. In E. L. Toth (Ed.), *The future of excellence in public relations and communication management: Challenges for the next generation* (pp. 507–526). Routledge.

Suárez-Monsalve, A. M. (2022). Evolution of the public relations profession in Latin America: A brief review of the development of public relations in Latin American countries. *Public Relations Inquiry*, *11*(2), 257–274. https://doi.org/10.1177/2046147X221081175

Tagle Montt, F. J., & Claro, M. C. (2021). Escándalos de corrupción mediática y escucha empresarial: Caso papel tissue en Chile [Corruption scandals on the media and corporate listening: the Tissue paper case in Chile]. *Quorum Académico*, *18*(2), 59–78.

Uslaner, E. (2018). The study of trust. In E. M. Uslaner (Ed.), *Oxford handbook of social and political trust* (pp. 3–14). Oxford University Press.

Valentini, C. (2007). Global versus cultural approaches in public relationship management. The case of the European Union. *Journal of Communication Management*, *11*(2), 117–133.

Valentini, C. (2021). Trust research in public relations: An assessment of its conceptual, theoretical and methodological foundations. *Corporate Communications: An International Journal*, *26*(1), 84–106. https://doi.org/10.1108/CCIJ-01-2020-0030

Valentini, C., & Kruckeberg, D. (2011). Public relations and trust in contemporary society: A Luhmannian perspective of the role of public relations in enhancing trust among social systems. *Central European Journal of Communication*, *4*(1(6)), 89–107.

van Aelst, P., Strömbäck, J., Aalberg, T., Esser, F., & de Vreese, C., Matthes, J., Hopmann, D., Salgado, S., Hubé, N., Stepinska, A., Papathanassopoulos, S., Berganza, R., Legnante, G., Reinemann, C., Sheafer, T., & Stanyer, J. (2017). Political communication in a high-choice media environment: A challenge for democracy? *Annals of the International Communication Association*, *41*, 3–27. https://doi.org/10.1080/23808985.2017.1288551

van Zoonen, W., & van der Meer, T. (2015). The importance of source and credibility perception in times of crisis: Crisis communication in a socially mediated era. *Journal of Public Relations Research*, *27*, 371–388. https://doi.org/10.1080/1062726X.2015.1062382

Vásquez, C., & Marroquín Velásquez, L. (2016). Forum introduction: Organizational communication in Spanish-speaking Latin American countries. *Management Communication Quarterly*, *30*(2), 245–248. https://doi.org/10.1177/0893318915620456.

Wakefield, R. (2010). Why culture is still essential in discussions about public relations. In R. L. Heath (Ed.), *The Sage handbook of public relations* (pp. 659–670). Sage.

Warren, M. (2018). Trust and democracy. In E. M. Uslaner (Ed.), *Oxford handbook of social and political trust* (pp. 75–94). Oxford University Press.

Wences, I., & Güemes, C. (2016). Democracia republicana y confianza en América Latina: La esperanza que no llega, que no alcanza [Republican democracy and confidence in Latin America: The hope that does not arrive, that is not enough]. *Andamios*, *13*(30), 13–37.

Zmerli, S., & Newton, K. (2008). Social trust and attitudes toward democracy. *Public Opinion Quarterly*, *72*(4), 706–724. https://doi.org/10.1093/poq/nfn054

15 Listening across Borders

Global Considerations for Listening and Public Diplomacy

Leysan Storie and Sarah Marschlich

Introduction

Communication scholarship has been criticized for the lack of research on listening, despite continued focus on engagement, integration of ideas, and relationship management. Public diplomacy has suffered from the same criticism, although some recent studies have attempted to conceptualize listening from the public diplomacy perspective (see Di Martino, 2020b). In this chapter, we first introduce public diplomacy as an academic field. We then suggest the range of purposes for listening in public diplomacy, and a range of actors that participants in public diplomacy should listen to. We also identify how public diplomacy actors can listen, focusing on digital media as an increasingly popular way to communicate with foreign publics. Our assumption is that depending on the goals and purposes of a public diplomacy program, actors decide who to listen to and how (see Figure 15.1). Lastly, we offer critical reflections on listening in public diplomacy, questioning the dominant Western approach to listening in public diplomacy scholarship. We conclude the chapter with a few recommendations for public diplomacy practitioners who want to implement listening practices.

Public Diplomacy and Listening

Approaches to Public Diplomacy

Public diplomacy is often described as a government's communication activities directed at foreign publics "in an attempt to bring about understanding for its nation's ideas and ideals, its institutions and culture, as well as its national goals and policies (Tuch, 1990, p. 3.) Traditionally public diplomacy was seen as government communication, with the purpose of explaining one country's policy and culture to strategically important foreign audiences. This approach to public diplomacy emphasizes influence as an important aspect of diplomacy at large: Governments are seen

DOI: 10.4324/9781003273851-20

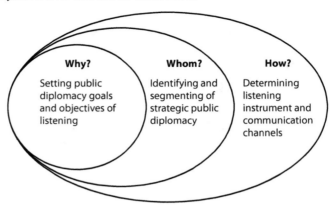

Figure 15.1 Listening process model in public diplomacy (own presentation)

to influence not only foreign public opinion but also the norms and rules of the environment in which they operate (see Pamment, 2020).

Previous studies looked at different ways that governments exerted influence. Prior to social media, governments primarily used mass media to influence foreign publics' perceptions, trying to control when and how their countries were framed in foreign media (e.g., Entman, 2008; Sheafer et al., 2014). With social media, public diplomats could reach foreign publics directly and persuade them, often using emotions to do so (see Duncombe, 2019.) The widespread access to the internet prompted new ways of influencing foreign environments, such as disinformation campaigns. These new competitive environments prompted some scholars to use the term *information war* alongside public diplomacy (see Szostek, 2020), thus reinforcing the focus on influence and control in public diplomacy.

Other scholars defined public diplomacy as engagement not only between governments and foreign citizens but also other international actors, such as non-governmental organizations, international corporations, grassroot citizen groups, etc. (see Marschlich & Storie, 2022). In this approach, the purpose of public diplomacy may shift from persuading and explaining one country, to a mutual understanding and relationship building (see Fitzpatrick, 2007). This approach highlights trust, long-term focus, listening, and dialogue, as integral elements of relational public diplomacy (see Fitzpatrick, 2009; Storie, 2017). A related concept of *collaborative* public diplomacy describes initiatives that involve various international actors (e.g., governments, NGO's, advocacy groups, publics) who engage in dialogue and negotiation to look for innovative solutions to complex global problems (Fisher, 2013; Zaharna, 2013). Global problems that public diplomacy actors strive to resolve may relate to health (e.g., pandemics), environment (e.g., global warming), and turbulent financial systems (Zhang & Swartz, 2009), to name a few. As

Fitzpatrick (2017) argued, collaborative and relational approaches may define public diplomacy in the 21st century and would require innovative approaches to involve global publics.

Listening in Public Diplomacy

Although the different approaches emphasize different public diplomacy goals, they all include listening as an integral part of the practice. Historically, public diplomacy listening occurred when rulers traveled around their territories and abroad to listen to people (see example of Scandinavian rulers in Cull, 2016). In modern times, listening was often carried out by embassies, who monitored mass media in countries to which they were assigned (e.g., Khakimova, 2013). Monitoring mass media provided governments with the understanding about the issues of concern, and how their country was presented in mass media outlets abroad. More sophisticated public diplomacy programs included polling and follow-up surveys (see example of Switzerland in Cull, 2008). In the digital era, public diplomacy actors acquired new tools to listen to foreign publics. Social media presented opportunities to engage in dialogue on governmental and organizational social media accounts, as well as scrape data from the internet at large. Digital platforms allowed different groups to communicate with national and foreign audiences. As a consequence, the opportunity to find and listen to all, including previously marginalized voices became "a key strategic advantage of digital platforms" for public diplomacy actors (Bjola et al., 2019, p. 100).

Yet, although scholars agree that listening is important in public diplomacy (e.g., Cull 2008, 2019; Di Martino, 2020a, 2020b), there is little research on public diplomacy listening. In one of the earliest attempts to conceptualize public diplomacy listening, Cull (2008) placed it as the first of five dimensions of public diplomacy. In a later article, Cull (2019, pp. 21–29) again placed listening ("systematically collecting and analyzing the opinions of foreign publics") as the first of seven core principles of conducting public diplomacy. In the following discussions, we attempt to synthesize previous research on listening in public diplomacy, focusing on why public diplomacy actors listen, to who, and how. Because research about listening and publics is limited in public diplomacy (see Di Martino, 2020b; Tam & Kim, 2018), the following discussion draws from both public diplomacy and public relations research, the two disciplines that share common functions (see Fitzpatrick et al., 2013; L'Etang, 2009).

Public Diplomacy Listening Purposes

The first purpose for listening in public diplomacy is to understand target publics and use that understanding to craft successful public diplomacy campaigns, what Di Martino (2020b) called *tactical* listening. Public diplomacy actors may listen to publics and stakeholders at different points of a public diplomacy program to prove effectiveness as well as make necessary changes to increase effectiveness in the future (see Cortes & Jamieson, 2020). For example, listening can occur at the start of a public diplomacy campaign to understand target public's opinions and in the middle of a campaign to test its effectiveness. When a public diplomacy program has several stages, listening can occur at the end of every stage, and insights can be incorporated in planning or modifying later stages. This type of listening is almost synonymous with monitoring, with publics being seen and treated as targets and sources of information (Di Martino, 2020b). Governments use tactical listening when they want to ensure that their messages achieve the intended goal (see Ingenhoff & Chariatte, 2020).

The second purpose for listening is for image purposes, what Macnamara (2018) called "fake listening" or "pseudo listening." As listening to publics is expected in the democratic systems, actors may feel compelled and obligated to show that they listen to publics. It may happen less in international contexts than national contexts, due to differences in political and social systems in countries involved. A study of a community project in Spain, where a provincial government provided several opportunities for senior policy members to listen to citizens, showed that those senior policy makers initially felt that they were listening to find support for their own initiatives rather than to understand different points of view and incorporate them in their decisions (Canel et al., 2022). In this case, the goal of listening is to build a perception of a dialogue and an image of a government that listens.

The third purpose for listening in public diplomacy is to identify risks and prevent crises. Social media may play a particularly useful role, as social media platforms allow to monitor issues related to a particular country, and listen to public's concerns, views, and arguments. One example is the issue of child protection in Sweden. In late 2021 and the beginning of 2022, several videos about children being taken away from Muslim families in Sweden became viral on social media (see TRT world, 2022). The Swedish child protection agency was accused of kidnapping children from Muslim families in Sweden. The issue was not new: In 2019, there were media reports of a Russian father who had lived in Sweden but left with his children when child protection agency placed his children with another immigrant family and limited his visiting rights (Metsel, 2019). In 2022, the issue received increased attention in the Middle East as well as in Sweden, leading to protests (Altuntas, 2022). Eventually, the Swedish Ministry for Foreign Affairs issued a statement framing online and offline activities as a disinformation campaign and describing it as misleading and aimed "to create tensions and spread mistrust" (Swedish Ministry for Foreign Affairs, 2022). Timely listening and strategic responses may prevent such crises from occurring, and even provide opportunities for communicating about country's values and policies.

The fourth purpose for listening in public diplomacy is to foster international understanding and to collaborate in addressing global issues. This type of listening is congruent with the understanding of public diplomacy as "co-constructed discourses of engagement: a dynamic dialogic process" that includes participation, interaction, and co-creation (Dolea, 2018, p. 331). From this stance, listening is seen as a form of participation, and as a "communication enabler" (Di Martino, 2020b, p. 135). Listening becomes an integral part of dialogue, where participants show a genuine interest in others' views and perspectives.

The approach to listening as part of dialogue, a way to create understanding rather than persuade or influence, is congruent with the collaborative and network approaches to public diplomacy, where governments, international and non-profit organizations, as well as grassroots establishments, work together to resolve regional or global issues (see Marschlich & Storie, 2022). Collaborative initiatives can involve different actors, and can include, for example, collaboration between governments and private actors (Marschlich & Ingenhoff, 2021b). Listening becomes a reciprocal and co-creational process that enhances the capacity for cognitive exchange and creates a mutual understanding of goals and issues (see Zaharna, 2018).

Di Martino (2020b) argued that listening as part of dialogue was a normative approach as it assumed that actors were not concerned with foreign policy goals. We argue that even this approach, which Di Martino (2020b) described as ethical and genuine, may contribute to foreign policy in indirect ways. When public diplomacy actors engage in dialogue and collaborations, their reputation may improve as an outcome of collaborative work. Ultimately and over time, engaging listening can help public diplomacy actors to build their legitimacy and earn publics' trust, provided that the process is open to different opinions and values and has a long-term orientation (see Marschlich & Ingenhoff, 2021a). Besides, listening for the purpose of resolving global issues is particularly relevant for non-state public diplomacy actors such as non-profit organizations, activist groups, and corporations, to name a few.

Who: Identifying and Segmenting Publics

The next step after identifying the purpose of listening is to choose relevant stakeholders and publics. In public relations, organizations listen to stakeholders and publics. Stakeholders can be defined as "any group or individual who can affect or is affected by the achievement of the firm's objectives" (Freeman, 2010, p. 25). Publics are those groups that "constrain or enhance an organization's ability to reach its goals" (Kim et al., 2008, p. 52). The main difference between "stakeholders" and "publics" is that the organization mostly defines stakeholders, whereas publics appear on their own, mainly around issues (see Grunig, 2005).

We can differentiate between a *general* public, closely linked to the term public opinion, and a *strategic* public reflecting a collection of individuals that are related based on some characteristic or relation to a specific issue. In public diplomacy, Fitzpatrick (2012) defined *strategic* publics as those "individual[s] or group[s] that ha[ve] the ability to enhance or constrain a nation's ability to accomplish its mission," further suggesting that "a nation should focus its limited resources on those publics that are most important or essential to the accomplishment of national goals and objectives" (p. 424). Internationally, public diplomacy stakeholders and publics may include foreign governments, international NGOs and social movements, multinational corporations, civil citizens, and international (news) media. Domestic stakeholders and publics are national citizens and residents, local companies, NGOs, to name a few.

To understand different types of publics and how governments choose them, Pacher (2018) developed a typology based on two dimensions: public's strategic importance in relation to the actor's objectives, and public's perceived power position. The typology rests on the assumption that public diplomacy is part of diplomacy, and target publics are chosen to achieve public diplomacy objectives.

Pacher (2018) proposed six types of publics along the two dimensions. The first type is *traditional diplomatic actors*, who are perceived to have most power, often represented by heads of state and diplomats. The second type is *imminent* strategic publics, i.e., powerful individuals or groups who may represent a government, an economically influential corporation, or international organization. The third type is *protocollary* strategic publics, represented by individuals (e.g., celebrities, influencers) or groups that do not have political or economic power and are themselves strategically unimportant for a public diplomacy actor, but they have soft power to influence strategically important publics. The fourth type is *salient* publics, who do not have power but are strategically important for public diplomacy actor's objectives (e.g., students in international exchanges). The fifth type is *remote* strategic publics, i.e., representatives of political entities that are not strategically important and have little perceived power. The sixth type is *global* mass publics, i.e., diverse individuals that are not connected to each other in any way and are affiliated with different political entities that may or may not be strategically important for a public diplomacy actor.

Another typology was proposed by Tam and Kim (2018) is based on publics' experiences with another country. Thus, their typology does not include publics that do not have any relationship with the actor. In Tam and Kim's model, four types of publics emerge at the intersection between behavioral experiences (first-hand experience with a foreign country, for example, in a cultural exchange or interpersonal interaction with an individual from another country) and symbolic environment (messages that publics receive about other countries through mass media, social media, or hearsay.). The assumption behind Tam and Kim's typology (2018) is that public diplomacy actors should invest in publics that already have some relationship with a foreign country, whether it is based on personal experience, on messages from media and organizational entities, or, as is often the case, a combination of sources.

Depending on behavioral experiences and symbolic environment, Tam and Kim (2018) suggested that publics could be found in four segments. *Ambassadorial* publics are a country's ambassadors that hold positive beliefs about a given country, are part of the positive symbolic environment and may share positive messages. *Advocational* publics may have had positive beliefs about the country but are exposed to a negative symbolic environment, e.g., through reading negative news about the country. With their positive beliefs about the country, they may become advocates for the country. *Accusational* publics hold negative views regarding the country due to negative experiences but are exposed to a positive symbolic environment (e.g., social media posts showing the country in a positive light). They may cause damage to the country's image by spreading negative word-of-mouth. Thus, they are highly relevant to listen to by public diplomacy actors. Finally, *adversarial* publics are the most critical publics due to their negative experiences with a country and a negative symbolic environment.

The presented approaches to understanding publics in public diplomacy share a gap: Publics are seen apart from other groups, and interactions *between* publics are neglected. Thus, another approach suggested by Fitzpatrick (2012) may be valuable in looking at publics as a part of a network. Social network analysis (see Granovetter, 1973; Rowley, 1997) may help to identify relevant publics and their position. Although social network analysis can also help identify group offline, social media provided increased opportunities for social network analysis, as digital publics can be active participants and communicate with individual and collective actors, including governments.

A network perspective becomes especially relevant as non-state actors are recognized as public possible diplomacy actors. In conducting social network analysis, the structures between individual actors or publics (e.g., around hashtags or keywords) can be analyzed to determine which actors are well-connected to others and have a high reach, or are particularly close to a central point in a network (Hanneman & Riddle, 2014). Consequently, social network analysis allows identifying opinion leaders, alternative or counter-publics, and/or protest movements.

How: Approaches to Listening

Public diplomacy listening approaches vary depending on public diplomacy purposes and goals as well as the target publics. Previously, we identified four purposes of public diplomacy. In the following discussion, we discuss how public diplomacy actors achieve their listening objectives, as suggested in previous research. To understand target publics, to prove effectiveness of public diplomacy efforts, and to maintain image, public diplomacy actors increasingly use digital media, thus we start this section by looking at studies that explored digital media use for tactical listening. To identify risks and prevent crises, issue management and social media monitoring are valuable instruments. To foster international understanding and to collaborate in addressing global issues, previous research suggested dialogic and engagement approaches. The discussion below elaborates on the instruments used for those public diplomacy purposes.

Digital Media Use for Tactical Listening in Public Diplomacy

Tactical listening was and can still be conducted with research tools such as surveys and polls, especially to listen to publics that are not online. Those quantitative measures can ask foreign audiences about their perceptions and feelings about a country, its politics, culture, and values (see Buhmann & Ingenhoff, 2015.) Yet increasingly, governments communicate on Twitter, Facebook, and other web-based platforms to amplify their policies, share their perspectives, and promote events (Collins et al., 2019). In doing so, governments and their diplomatic institutions use their official accounts to engage with foreign publics (Manor, 2016; Strauss et al., 2015). Likewise, citizens and organizations use social media platforms to express their opinion on issues, policies, or state actors' actions by creating, commenting, and sharing posts. This wide volume of information provides valuable insights about conversations that happen naturally, and that may help governments understand their target publics, their concerns, and perceptions.

One of the common ways for diplomats to use social media platforms for listening is to assess the impact of their programs, with likes and shares as measures of reach and influence (e.g., Bjola et al., 2020). It is important, however, to understand the limits of social media metrics and how they are be interpreted. Bjola et al. (2020) argued, there was an increasing awareness about the complexity of social media metrics, where a retweet could suggest the reach of a message but not how the tweet was perceived. To address this issue, Bjola et al. (2020) made several suggestions as to what social media can offer in terms of public diplomacy listening. First, a mix of qualitative and quantitative measurements can be used to explore public opinion and attitudes, which can be done through sentiment analysis. Second, public diplomacy actors can explore how messages travel in their networks and whether they have any influence over the discussions in the networks. Third, public diplomacy actors can use hashtag correlations to understand if there is a relationship between different issues discussed in a country.

Yet research suggested that governments' use of digital media for listening was limited. For example, the analysis of several countries' embassies' Twitter accounts showed listening was the least likely approach, while advocacy and cultural diplomacy were the most frequent (Dodd & Collins, 2017). Another study investigating Swedish, US-American, and Indian digital diplomacy efforts on Twitter and Facebook showed that almost one-fifth of the efforts reflected listening opportunities (Mazumdar, 2021). While the results appeared promising, listening opportunities were limited to a rather limited strategy of posing questions and largely ignored other more meaningful strategies, such as asking for input, requesting user-generated content, and polls. Thus, Mazumdar (2021) concluded that "digital diplomacy actors appear unwilling to utilize the affordances of SNSs [Social Networking Sites] for dialogic communication with publics [...] [although] listening is a requisite for dialogue."

Issues Management and (Social) media Monitoring

Issues management is a common approach in public relations to identify risks and to respond to them (see Heath & Palenchar, 2009). Issues can be positive and add value if they are recognized and strategically used in communication. On the other hand, issues can also involve risks, for example, when a topic and/or associated organizations are discussed critically in the mass media or social media. An issue becomes relevant for an organizational entity if it can influence organizational decisions, if it is associated with concrete expectations of the stakeholders toward organizational efforts, or if it is of public concern (see Heath & Palenchar, 2009; Ingenhoff et al., 2020a).

Similar to public relations, issues management in public diplomacy begins with observing, identifying, and analyzing relevant issues. By identifying and addressing relevant issues, public diplomacy actors can strengthen or at least safeguard their reputations and ensure their actions' legitimacy (Di Martino, 2020b). Identifying and then listening to understand the issues is essential, in large part because "a nuanced understanding of the issue leads to appropriately designed programs and more effective foreign policy outcomes" (Cortes & Jamieson, 2020, p. 1215). Wu and Yang (2017) also argued that issue management should not only happen in the first stages of public diplomacy initiatives but should be a continuous process and take place at different stages (i.e., strategic planning, long-term planning, media relations/public opinion monitoring, relational advocacy, and relationship building).

Social media use is particularly useful to issue management. In the study of two public diplomacy cases, Zhang (2013) argued that online public diplomacy efforts should start with strategic issue management and follow four phases. During the first phase, "*the issues ferments and goes viral"* when "signs of an issue emerge on social media" and a triggering even may make the issue go viral (Zhang, 2013, p. 1325). During the second *proactive* phase, public diplomacy actors investigate the issue and use various communication channels to influence public opinion. During the third *reactive* phase, publics respond and those responses may lead to a conflict. During the fourth phase, *"the issue recedes and a new issue ferments"* (Zhang, 2013, p. 1325), and public diplomacy actors may use social media to continue cultivating relationships with publics. Zhang (2013) argued that among the four phases, social media is a strategic tool in the proactive and reactive phases, and a tactical tool in the other two.

Digital tools that can be used to listen to publics are constantly changing. It is clear that to monitor societal issues, public diplomacy actors must go beyond monitoring their own social media channels and even their networks. For instance, the tool Google Trends allows one to analyze terms that were searched in combination with a country or government officials over a certain period and thus identify trends in topics and issues, both negative and positive, and their significance for public diplomacy efforts (Ingenhoff et al., 2020b). Artificial intelligence can also be useful in digital listening. For example, in public relations research, chatbots that embodied social presence and conversational voice, contributed to publics' perceptions of organizational listening and even organizational transparency (Men et al., 2022). Moreover, those chatbots that were perceived as good listening agents, together with organizational listening, impacted publics' relationships with organizations (Men et al., 2022). In other words, chatbots can be valuable listening agents if and when they are designed well.

Dialogic and Engagement Approaches to Listening

When the aim is to gain mutual understanding and, ultimately, to participate in a collaborative decision-making process, listening is part of a dialogue. At the core of engagement and dialogue are exchange, interaction, and mutual listening, with multiple opportunities for feedback from all actors involved. Engagement can be described "as a relational process that facilitates understanding and evaluation, involvement, exchange of information and opinions, about a concept, issue or project," enhancing social outcomes (Johnston et al., 2018, p. 173), such as legitimacy and positive relationships (Marschlich & Ingenhoff, 2021a). Some previous studies suggested the role of listening in collaborative and network public diplomacy and suggested how public diplomacy actors should and should not listen in collaborative initiatives.

For example, analysis of China's projects on addressing the Ebola epidemic in West Africa, showed that Chinese agencies and organizations provided engagement opportunities in their public diplomacy initiatives (Wu & Yang, 2017). It is not clear if local stakeholders could influence how the projects were managed, but the Chinese agencies did create opportunities for different organizations, both local and international, to meet and discuss solutions to the Ebola crisis (Wu & Yang, 2017). In other words, public diplomacy actors provided *dialogic opportunities* for other actors to meet and engage, to listen to each other, and to work together for disease prevention.

Indeed, listening is what distinguishes true dialogue and engagement from other forms of communication. Yet research in international development communication showed even initiatives that claimed to be based on dialogue and listening to local publics, were in fact using listening as a tactic to sell their own ideas and projects (e.g., Dutta & Thaker, 2020; Paquette et al., 2015).

A study of USAID's initiatives in Bolivia showed that although USAID – the leading US government's development agency – claimed that their projects were based on dialogue with local stakeholders, there was little evidence of listening to the stakeholders' concerns and suggestions (Paquette et al., 2015). Although a casual look at the project may suggest that the agency listened to the publics, a closer examination showed that it primarily relied on interpersonal dialogue and was rather used an ad hoc tool implemented to achieve the project's goals (Paquette et al., 2015). The study's authors concluded that the organization-claimed participation and dialogue, could be described as "passive collaboration" or "manipulative consultation" (see Huesca, 2008), rather than a true dialogue, that "would have involved meeting with the farmers and giving them a voice on systematic problems" and an opportunity to influence the project's plans "rather than selling them ready made plans" (Paquette et al., 2015, p. 36). They concluded that dialogue, involving listening, should be a *long-term commitment* woven into the very structure of an initiative.

Some other considerations for listening as part of dialogue in public diplomacy include the following. Firstly, different publics should be considered in the listening process, even if this might become challenging due to conflicting interests. Zaharna (2018) argued that engagement in public diplomacy is about engaging publics globally, which would require listening to different publics simultaneously. Secondly, a dialogic approach to listening must be culture-specific and consider the values and norms of involved parties. Previous research pointed to language and sociopolitical context playing a role in how publics engage with foreign actors (see Storie, 2015). Particular attention should be given to understanding local listening practices. For example, in the United Arab Emirates, it is common for government agencies and organizations to hold so-called Majlis meetings, a traditional way to talk about business and partnerships, and which often start with personal conversations (Marschlich & Ingenhoff, 2021a). We further elaborate on the value of expanding the understanding of listening as a global practice in the following section.

Critical Reflections on Public Diplomacy Listening

As we continue to explore the role of listening in public diplomacy, it is important to question our assumptions about the nature and practice of listening. The following discussions seek to contribute to a critical view on current public diplomacy research by looking at listening as a global practice and questioning assumptions about who to listen to.

In public diplomacy research, listening is largely explored in the Western contexts often using Western theories and models (e.g., Fitzpatrick, 2007; Khakimova, 2013; Yun, 2006). The understanding of listening has been based on the Western models of communication, which, in fact, predominantly focused on speaking rather than listening. As Macnamara (2018) pointed out, in North America, human communication scholarship has until recently been labeled as *speech* communication. In other words, the emphasis was on speaking rather than on listening. Yet, we know little about listening in communication in non-Western contexts, and even less so in the context of public diplomacy.

What we do know is that culture influences communication. From the known works of Hofstede (1991) about cultural differences and impacts on communication, to more recent research on cultural influences on public diplomacy (Anagondahali & Zhu, 2016), it is clear that culture matters. In terms of listening, culture was found to influence listening processes in interpersonal business settings (Roebuck et al., 2016). Thus, research on how governments in non-Western contexts listen, and who they listen to, may reveal radically different methods and approaches.

Anthropological, inductive approaches would be most appropriate to explore global models of listening in public diplomacy. Yet, as L'Etang argued in 2012 about the use of anthropological approaches, "ethnographic work is almost entirely absent from the genre of international/global/cultural public relations literature" (p. 172). Unfortunately, ten years later, this is still the case. It is the long-term ethnographic projects that could help understand how listening between governments, organizations, and publics occurs in a nation and how it might inform international communication, including public diplomacy.

Another important aspect of studying listening in public diplomacy is reflecting on the assumptions about who should have a voice and who should be listened to. The culture-centered approach to communication pays particular attention to subaltern publics – groups that previously did not have the resources, the infrastructure, and the power to communicate (e.g., Dutta & Thaker, 2020). Subaltern studies in communication reject colonial hegemony and point to the role of the "other" (see Dutta & Pal, 2010). At the foundation of the culture-centered approach is the creation of "communication infrastructures of listening" (Dutta, 2018, p. 240). The culture-centered approach interrogates the hegemonic practices, acknowledging the subaltern voices and working, possibly changing, the structures that limit the agency of local communities (Sastry & Dutta, 2017). This approach to the study of public diplomacy would question the legitimacy of many public diplomacy initiatives in imposing meaning and values in countries abroad, particularly among populations that had little power.

Protesters and activists are other groups that are often neglected by public diplomacy practitioners and researchers. Protesters are often seen as a threat, with negative implications for country's image. Yet, Jimenez-Martinez (2022) called for a different approach, where protests are not seen as a distraction from governments' public diplomacy messages, but rather as part of a country's public diplomacy. Such a view has implications for listening: Protesters and activists then would be seen as actors that need to be engaged with. Yet, "despite claims of listening to or engaging with the public, diplomats, politicians and communication strategists have historically considered the people either as a problem – particularly during the conduct of negotiations or in situations of conflict – or as a resource to be exploited in order to benefit those in power" (Jimenez-Martinez, 2022, p. 34).

Indeed, there are some examples of activist movements that successfully communicated with publics abroad and rallied their support, including support from government officials (see the example of the Saudi movement for the right to drive in Khalil & Storie, 2021). But where these publics are located and in which context may also play a role in how they are perceived. For example, there is a tendency to view activists and protesters from non-Western countries, as "true" representatives of their states and "emerging signs of democracy" while local protesters are perceived as "unrepresentative deviances of who "we" really are" (Jimenez-Martinez, 2022, p. 35), which ultimately influences how if and how they are listened to and engaged in dialogue.

Recommendations for Practice

Based on the discussion in this chapter, the following recommendations may help communication professionals working with public diplomacy to incorporate listening in public diplomacy initiatives.

Firstly, governments and organizations should identify the purpose of listening for a given public diplomacy program. The purpose of the public diplomacy program and the campaign will dictate who should be engaged in listening and how. For example, governments may be interested in changing foreign perceptions and/or building a positive image. In that case, it is useful to identify the target publics for the program. It may be useful to focus on accusational and adversarial publics (Tam & Kim, 2018) to change their attitudes. In that case, tactical listening will help a public diplomacy actor to understand what those publics believe and why and use appropriate arguments to change those perceptions and opinions. Digital media may be particularly useful for tactical listening, as digital media platforms provide insights into naturally occurring conversations. Tactical listening is particularly important before starting a public diplomacy program, but also important throughout a program to ensure that messages are indeed interpreted the way they were intended.

For preventing risks and crisis, listening is likely to focus on societal conversations, rather than specific publics. It is important to remember that issues have several stages in their development (Zhang, 2013). If public diplomacy actors identify an issue at the first stage, where an issue ferments, they may prevent it from going viral. Once the issue goes viral, the goal is to investigate and listen, and use that knowledge in responding to the issue. After that, public diplomacy actors continue to listen to the response of the public. Ideally, then the issue recedes.

If and when public diplomacy actors seek to address a global issue, the goal of listening may be to understand different perspectives, initiatives, challenges, and to create collaborative projects. In this case, dialogue and listening would need to be woven into the very structure of a public diplomacy program, and the outcomes would largely depend on the conversations with stakeholders and publics. In other words, listening in collaborative public diplomacy is one of the goals rather than a means to achieve predetermined public diplomacy goals. Public diplomacy actors trying to address a problem or an issue, must reflect on the publics that must be engaged in those processes, and how they should be engaged. Foreign publics, including subaltern publics, that have never been engaged in public diplomacy projects, may become useful partners in addressing issues that affect them as well. In engaging with traditionally disempowered groups, public diplomacy actors should be cautious against co-opting local knowledge and using tactical listening in disguise.

Conclusion

In this chapter, we attempted to synthesize research related to listening in public diplomacy, attempting to show that how listening is understood and practiced can be different for various public diplomacy actors. Although studies are limited, they suggest several ways that public diplomacy actors may conduct their listening activities, depending on the purpose of a specific public diplomacy program. In that process, actors choose who to communicate with, depending on publics' strategic importance, their perceived power (Pacher, 2018), their experience and attitudes toward a country (Tam & Kim, 2018), or their position in a network (Fitzpatrick, 2012). Yet it is important to keep in mind that how we understand listening is largely based on theories and models developed from research on public diplomacy initiatives of Western governments. Future anthropological and inductive research on public diplomacy by actors in Asia, Africa, Middle East, and Latin America, may address this gap and offer new approaches to listening.

As the world grapples with various global issues related to environment, security, and health, to name a few, future public diplomacy efforts may benefit from dialogic approaches to listening, engaging new publics (subaltern, protesters, activists, etc.) in dialogue, and when appropriate, collaborative initiates. In that process, public diplomacy actors should keep in mind the critique of previous so-called collaborative efforts, in which listening was often used as a manipulation tool. Instead, future collaborative practice should carefully interrogate power differentials, and provide a listening infrastructure, that would ensure that various voices are not only heard but also considered in proposed solutions.

References

Altuntas, A. (Feb. 14, 2022). *Muslim immigrant families protest against Swedish agency for taking their children.* Anadolu Agency. https://www.aa.com.tr/en/europe/muslim-immigrant-families-protest-against-swedish-agency-for-taking-their-children/2501850

Anagondahali, D., & Zhu, L. (2016). Culture's role in public diplomacy: Predicting and preventing crises. *The Journal of International Communication, 22*(1), 64–81.

Bjola, C., Cassidy, J., & Manor, I. (2019). Public diplomacy in the digital age. *The Hague Journal of Diplomacy, 14*, 83–101.

Bjola, C., Cassidy, J. A., & Manor, I. (2020). In N. Snow, & N. J. Cull (Eds.), *Routledge handbook of public diplomacy* (2nd ed.) (pp. 405–412). Routledge.

Buhmann, A., & Ingenhoff, D. (2015). Advancing the country image construct from a public relations perspective: From model to measurement. *Journal of Communication Management, 19*(1), 62–80. https://doi.org/10.1108/JCOM-11-2013-0083

Canel, M. J., Barandiaran, X., & Murphy, A. (2022). What does learning by listening bring to citizen engagement? Lessons from a government program. *Public Relations Review, 48*, 1–8.

Collins, S. D., DeWitt, J. R., & LeFebvre, R. K. (2019). Hashtag diplomacy: Twitter as a tool for engaging in public diplomacy and promoting US foreign policy. *Place Branding and Public Diplomacy, 15*(2), 78–96. https://doi.org/10.1057/s41254-019-00119-5

Cortes, J. J., & Jamieson, T. (2020). Incorporating research design in public diplomacy: The role of listening to foreign publics. *International Journal of Communication, 14*, 1214–1231.

Cull, N. J. (2008). Public diplomacy: Taxonomies and histories. *The ANNALS of the American Academy of Political and Social Science, 616*, 31–54.

Cull, N. J. (2019). The tightrope to tomorrow reputational security, collective vision and the future of public diplomacy. *The Hague Journal of Diplomacy, 14*, 21–35.

Cull, N. J. (2016). A region speaks: Nordic public diplomacy in historical context. *Place Branding and Public Diplomacy, 12*, 152–159.

Di Martino, L. (2020a). The spectrum of listening. In N. Snow, & N. J. Cull (Eds.), *Routledge handbook of public diplomacy* (2nd ed.) (pp. 21–29). Routledge.

Di Martino, L. (2020b). Conceptualizing public diplomacy listening on social media. *Place Branding and Public Diplomacy, 16*(2), 131–42. https://doi.org/10.1057/s41254-019-00135-5

Dodd, M. D., & Collins, S. J. (2017). Public relations message strategies and public diplomacy 2.0: An empirical analysis using Central-Eastern European and Western embassy Twitter accounts. *Public Relations Review, 43*(2), 417–425. https://doi.org/10.1016/j.pubrev.2017.02.004

Dolea, A. (2018). Public diplomacy as co-constructed discourses of engagement. In K. A. Johnston, & M. Taylor (Eds.), *The handbook of communication engagement* (pp. 331–346). John Wiley & Sons.

Duncombe, C. (2019). Digital diplomacy: Emotion and identity in the public realm. *The Hague Journal of Diplomacy, 14*, 102–116.

Dutta, M. J. (2018). Culture-centered approach in addressing health disparities: Communication infrastructures for subaltern voices. *Communication Methods and Measures, 12*(4), 239–259. https://doi.org/10.1080/19312458.2018.1453057

Dutta, M. J., & Pal, M. (2010). Dialog theory in marginalized settings: A subaltern studies approach. *Communication Theory, 20*, 363–386.

Dutta, M. J., & Thaker, J. (2020). Sustainability, ecology, and agriculture in women Farmers' voices: Culture-centering gender and development. *Communication Theory, 30*, 126–148.

Entman, R. M. (2008). Theorizing mediated public diplomacy: The US Case. *The International Journal of Press/Politics, 13*(2), 87–102. https://doi.org/10.1177/1940161208314657

Fisher, A. (2013). *Collaborative public diplomacy: How trans-national networks influenced American studies in Europe.* Palgrave Macmillan.

Fitzpatrick, K. R. (2007). Advancing the new public diplomacy: A public relations perspective. *The Hague Journal of Diplomacy, 2*, 187–211.

Fitzpatrick, K. R. (2009). *The future of US Public diplomacy: An uncertain fate.* Koninklijke Brill.

Fitzpatrick, K. R. (2012). Defining strategic publics in a networked world: Public diplomacy's challenge at home and abroad. *The Hague Journal of Diplomacy, 7*(4), 421–440. https://doi.org/10.1163/1871191X-12341236

Fitzpatrick, K. R. (2017). Public diplomacy in the public interest. *Journal of Public Interest Communications, 1*, 78–92.

Fitzpatrick, K. R., Fullerton, J., & Kendrick, A. (2013). Public relations and public diplomacy: Conceptual and practical connections. *Public Relations Journal, 7*(4), 1–21.

Freeman, R. E. (2010). *Strategic management: A stakeholder approach.* Cambridge University Press.

Granovetter, M. S. (1973). The strength of weak ties. *American Journal of Sociology, 78*(6), 1360–1380. https://doi.org/10.1086/225469

Grunig, J. E. (2005). Situational theory of publics. In R. L. Heath (Ed.), *Encyclopedia of public relations* (Vol. 2; pp. 778–780). Sage.

Hanneman, R. A., & Riddle, M. (2014). Concepts and measures for basic network analysis. In J. Scott, & P. Carrington (Eds.), *The SAGE handbook of social network analysis* (pp. 340–69). Sage. https://doi.org/10.4135/9781446294413.n24

Heath, R. L., & Palenchar, M. J. (2009). *Strategic issues management: Organizations and public policy challenges* (2nd ed.). Sage.

Huesca, R. (2008). Tracing the history of participatory communication approaches to development: A critical appraisal. In J. Servaes (Ed.), *Communication for development and social change* (pp. 180–198). Sage.

Hofstede, G. (1991). Empirical models of cultural differences. In N. Bleichrodt, & P. J. D. Drenth (Eds.), *Contemporary issues in cross-cultural psychology* (pp. 4–20). Swets & Zeitlinger Publishers.

Ingenhoff, D., Borner, M., & Zerfass, A. (2020a). Corporate listening und issues management in der unternehmenskommunikation. In A. Zerfass, M. Piwinger, & U. Röttger (Eds.), *Handbuch unternehmenskommunikation*. Springer. https://doi.org/10.1007/978-3-658-03894-6_26-1

Ingenhoff, D., & Chariatte, J. (2020). *Solving the public diplomacy puzzle—Developing a 360-degree listening and evaluation approach to assess country images. CPD perspectives.* https://uscpublicdiplomacy.org/sites/default/files/useruploads/u47441/Solving%20the%20Public%20Diplomacy%20Puzzle_1.9.21.pdf

Ingenhoff, D., Segev, E., & Chariatte, J. (2020b). The construction of country images and stereotypes: From public views to google searches. *International Journal of Communication, 14*, 92–113.

Jimenez-Martinez, C. (2022). The public as a problem: Protest, public diplomacy, and the pandemic. *Place Branding and Public Diplomacy, 18*, 33–36.

Johnston, K., Lane, A. B., Hurst, B., & Beatson, A. (2018). Episodic and relational community engagement: Implications for social impact and social license. In K. A. Johnston, & M. Taylor (Eds.), *The handbook of communication engagement* (pp. 169–185). John Wiley & Sons. https://doi.org/10.1002/9781119167600.ch12

Khakimova, L. (2013). Public diplomacy at Arab embassies: Fighting an uphill battle. *International Journal of Strategic Communication, 7*, 21–42.

Khalil, A., & Storie, L. K. (2021). Social media and connective action: The case of the Saudi women campaign for the right to drive. *New Media and Society.* https://doi:10.1177/1461444820943849

Kim, J.-N., Ni, L., & Sha, B.-L. (2008). Breaking down the stakeholder environment: Explicating approaches to the segmentation of publics for public relations research. *Journalism and Mass Communication Quarterly, 85*(4), 751–768.

L'Etang, J. L. (2009). Public relations and diplomacy in a globalized world. *American Behavioral Scientist, 53*(4), 607–626.

L'Etang, J. L. (2012). Public relations, culture and anthropology—Towards an ethnographic research agenda. *Journal of Public Relations Research, 24*, 165–183.

Macnamara, J. (2018). Toward a theory and practice of organizational listening. *The International Journal of Listening, 32*(1), 1–23.

Manor, I. (2016). *Are we there yet: Have MFAs realized the potential of digital diplomacy?* Brill.

Marschlich, S., & Ingenhoff, D. (2021a). Stakeholder engagement in a multicultural context: The contribution of (personal) relationship cultivation to social capital. *Public Relations Review, 47*(4), 102091. https://doi.org/10.1016/j.pubrev.2021.102091

Marschlich, S., & Ingenhoff, D. (2021b). The pole of public relations in corporate diplomacy: How relationship cultivation increases organizational legitimacy. *Journal of Public Relations Research, 33*(2), 86–105. https://doi.org/10.1080/1062726X.2021.1981332

Marschlich, S., & Storie, L. (2022). The past, the present, and the future of public diplomacy research. In J. Falkheimer, & M. Heide (Eds.), *Research handbook of strategic communication*. Edward Elgar Publishing.

Mazumdar, B. T. (2021). Digital diplomacy: Internet-based public diplomacy activities or novel forms of public engagement? *Place Branding and Public Diplomacy*. https://doi.org/10.1057/s41254-021-00208-4

Men, L. R., Zhou, A., & Tsai, W.-H.S. (2022). Harnessing the power of chatbot social conversation for organizational listening: The impact on perceived transparency and organization-public relationships. *Journal of Public Relations Research, 34*(1–2), 20–44.

Metsel, M. (2019). *Russian immigrant who smuggled his daughters away from their Muslim foster family in Sweden returns to Russia*. Meduza. https://meduza.io/en/feature/2019/11/06/russian-immigrant-who-smuggled-his-daughters-away-from-their-muslim-foster-family-in-sweden-returns-to-russia

Pacher, A. (2018). Strategic publics in public diplomacy: A typology and a heuristic device for multiple publics. *The Hague Journal of Diplomacy, 13*(3), 272–296. https://doi.org/10.1163/1871191X-13020004

Pamment, J. (2020). Public diplomacy and development communication: Two sides of the same coin? In N. Snow, & N. J. Cull (Eds.), *Routledge handbook of public diplomacy* (2nd ed.) (pp. 430–437). Routledge.

Paquette, M., Sommerfeldt, E. J., & Kent, M. L. (2015). Do the ends justify the means? Dialogue, development, communication, and deontological ethics. *Public Relations Review, 41*, 30–39.

Roebuck, D. B., Bell, R. L., Raina, R., & Lee, C. E. (2016). Comparing perceived listening behavior differences between managers and nonmanagers living in the United States, India, and Malaysia. *International Journal of Business Communication, 53*(4), 485–518.

Rowley, T. J. (1997). Moving beyond dyadic ties: A network theory of stakeholder influences. *The Academy of Management Review, 22*(4), 887–910.

Sastry, S., & Dutta, M. J. (2017). Health communication in the time of Ebola: A culture-centered interrogation. *Journal of Health Communication, 22*, 10–14. https://doi.org/10.1080/10810730.2016.1216205

Sheafer, T., Shehnav, S. R., Takens, J., & van Atteveldt, W. (2014). Relative political and value proximity in mediated public diplomacy: The effect of state-level homophily on international frame building. *Political Communication, 31*, 149–167.

Storie, L. K. (2015). Lost publics in public diplomacy: Antecedents for online relationship management. *Public Relations Review, 41*, 315–317.

Storie, L. K. (2017). Relationship cultivation in public diplomacy: A qualitative study of relational antecedents and cultivation strategies. *Journal of Public Relations Research, 29*(6), 295–310.

Strauss, N., Kruikemeier, S., Meulen, H., & van Noort, G. (2015). Digital diplomacy in GCC countries: Strategic communication of Western embassies on Twitter. *Government Information Quarterly, 32*(4), 369–379.

Swedish Ministry for Foreign Affairs (Feb. 11, 2022). *A disinformation campaign is currently under way on various social media—both in Sweden and abroad.* https://twitter.com/SweMFA/status/1492120646104629248?ref_src=twsrc%5Etfw%7Ctwcamp%5Etweetembed%7Ctwterm%5E1492120646104629248%7Ctwgr%5E%7Ctwcon%5Es1_&ref_url=https%3A%2F%2Fwww.trtworld.com%2Fmagazine%2Fwhy-do-sweden-s-authorities-stand-accused-of-kidnapping-muslim-children-55050

Szostek, J. (2020). What happens to public diplomacy during information war? Critical reflections on the conceptual framing of international communication. *International Journal of Communication, 14*, 2728–2748.

Tam, L., & Kim, J.-N. (2018). Who are publics in public diplomacy? Proposing a taxonomy of foreign publics as an intersection between symbolic environment and behavioral experiences. *Place Branding and Public Diplomacy, 15*(1), 28–37. https://doi.org/10.1057/s41254-018-0104-z

TRT World (Feb 23, 2022). *Why do Sweden's authorities stand accused of kidnapping Muslim children?* https://www.trtworld.com/magazine/why-do-sweden-s-authorities-stand-accused-of-kidnapping-muslim-children-55050

Tuch, H. N. (1990). *Communicating with the world: US Public diplomacy overseas.* St. Martin's.

Wu, D., & Yang, A. (2017). China's public diplomatic networks on the Ebola issue in West Africa: Issues management in a network society. *Public Relations Review, 43*, 345–357.

Yun, S.-H. (2006). Toward public relations theory-based study of public diplomacy: Testing the applicability of the excellence study. *Journal of Public Relations Research, 18*(4), 287–312. https://doi.org/10.1207/s1532754xjprr1804_1

Zaharna, R. S. (2013). Network purpose, network design: Dimensions of network and collaborative public diplomacy. In R. S. Zaharna, A. Arsenault, & A. Fisher (Eds.), *Relational, networked, and collaborative approaches to public diplomacy: The connective mindshift* (pp. 173–191). Routledge.

Zaharna, R. S. (2018). Global engagement: Culture and communication insights from public diplomacy. In K. A. Johnston, & M. Taylor (Eds.), *The handbook of communication engagement* (pp. 313–330). John Wiley & Sons.

Zhang, J. (2013). A strategic issue management (SIM) approach to social media use in public diplomacy. *American Behavioral Scientist, 57*(9), 1312–1331.

Zhang, J., & Swartz, B. C. (2009). Public diplomacy to promote global public goods (GPG): Conceptual expansion, ethical grounds, and rhetoric. *Public Relations Review, 35*(4), 382–287.

Conclusion

Directions for Future Research of Organizational Listening and Strategic Communication

Katie R. Place and Debashish Munshi

This edited volume showcased the eclectic range of research that is building organizational listening theory and practice for an evolving public relations and strategic communication discipline. Chapters offered insights to guide the development of more robust organizational listening competencies, policies, practices, and tools to foster more comprehensive, ethical, equitable, and culturally relevant listening methods.

The development of organizational listening scholarship and practice must be guided by a mindfulness of why we are listening, how we are listening, and to whom. Organizational listening structures, tools, and techniques must be grounded in concepts of dialogue, plurality, ethics, and social justice – particularly to foster listening to those who have historically been marginalized or silenced. Combined insights from this volume suggest that future research, specifically, should concentrate on how organizational listening may foster organization-public relationships, "close the loop" in the dialogic process, and promote equity and sustainability.

Several chapters called for future research in strategic communication to explore how organizational listening may best foster mutually beneficial organization-stakeholder relationships in both small- and large-scale contexts. Kang and Moon (Chapter 3), for example, suggest that future scholarship addresses the utilization of dialogic practices to foster more participatory organizational environments and climates of mutual orientation. Approaches to organizational listening that apply interpersonal values and practices, such as openness, transparency, genuineness, and receptiveness may build employee trust. As digital and social media evolve, organizations must also consider methods to listen to and forge relationships with vast and scattered publics. Worthington and Bodie (Chapter 1), as well as Zhou et al. (Chapter 4), recommend that organizations continue to develop digital listening tools (such as video content and artificial intelligence functions) that model dialogic engagement, rather than simply surveil. Listening via such tools should be developed by professionals with appropriate listening and communications training and respond to publics in ways that are authentic, engaging, and friendly.

DOI: 10.4324/9781003273851-21

As organizational listening on an increasingly technological and global scale evolves, listening practices must still be tailored to local cultures and trends and acknowledge historical context, Bachman and Labarca (Chapter 14) recommend. Ultimately, as Neill and Bowen (Chapter 6) suggest, future research should center on organizations' responsibility to cultivate proactive and ethical listening relationships with stakeholders.

Likewise, several chapters referenced the need for organizations to "close the loop" in the listening process, guided by commitments to articulate what they have heard and how they will change. English et al., (Chapter 8) for example, recommend that organizational listening research, particularly with Black stakeholders, address how listening can be employed to shift balances of power and disrupt systems of inequity across municipalities. Coman and Vasquez (Chapter 9), likewise, call for research to "close the listening loop" with internal employee activist publics. Organizational listening structures and techniques must employ feedback mechanisms, guided by dialogic principles, authenticity, and a commitment to employee engagement. "Closing the loop" means that organizations must dedicate resources, personnel, and time to effectively evaluate their listening with internal and external publics. Future research must explore how organizations can evaluate organizational listening practices to ensure they avoid ethical misconduct, whitewashing, or misrepresentation (Place, 2015; Volk & Buhmann, 2019), as Volk (Chapter 5) recommends. Organizations must also avoid utilization of organizational listening programs or practices as a façade for blatant instrumental or manipulative objectives.

Most importantly, however, is the call for future research regarding organizational listening in strategic communication to blaze a path for more equitable, authentic, and sustainable engagement among organizations and publics. Organizational leaders must critically examine why they remain averse to listening to stakeholder groups, particularly those who are marginalized or historically excluded from civic dialogue. Lim et al., (Chapter 12) studying LGBTQ+ publics, for example, urged for organizational listening to be "more than lip service." They call for future research to explore how organizations may better listen and respond to nondominant publics in an authentic and consistent manner. Similarly, Place (Chapter 10) suggests that scholarship further applies intersectional and critical race-informed perspectives (i.e., Logan, 2021) to understand how organizational listening may promote social justice and equity. More insight is needed to understand how dedicated personnel, organizational groups, community partnerships, and formal listening techniques may be best utilized to support such goals. Organizational listening, centering on the concept of plurality, offers additional fruitful paths for future research. Capizzo (Chapter 11), for example, urges for research to focus on the development of organizational listening practices guided by an orientation to community, an intentional presence, and engagement of stakeholders and publics as equals.

Growing efforts to acknowledge the importance of organizational listening to ethical public relations emphasize a shift in according primacy to listening over speaking. This is certainly a good step but to do this, it is useful to problematize the notion of voice. In many ways, voice represents agency. Following Anthony Giddens's (1984) structuration theory, Iverson et al. (2018) say that "agency basically entails knowledgeably intervening in or changing the course of events," as agents "draw on, and may either transform or just maintain structures (i.e., rules and resources)" (p. 44). Postcolonial scholarship in communication studies has in fact highlighted the agency of communities marginalized by mainstream discourses of communication to structures of oppressive power (see e.g., Cruz & Sodeke, 2021; Dutta & Pal, 2010; 2011; Munshi & Kurian, 2005; Munshi & Pal, 2018; Shome & Hegde, 2002). As Dutta and Pal (2010) say, it "is in these spaces of resistive practices that alternative imaginations of public relations" can emerge (p. 205). One such alternative imagination of public relations is Munshi and Kurian's (2021) conceptualization of public relations as sustainable citizenship in which alliances of marginalized publics build networks of resistance "to challenge the exercise of unjust power by elite, dominant publics (often elite, dominant actors)" (p. 4).

From a postcolonial perspective, agency is "constantly negotiated and changing, depending on who is narrating the action, as well as actively exploring silences and absences present in narrative accounts" (Broadfoot et al., 2018, p. 137). Similarly, voice too is dynamic and conceptions of voice need to factor in listening and incorporate silences as well to constitute a "process of engagement between larger social or institutional discourses and localized, personal narratives performed verbally and non-verbally by culturally produced subjects in social interaction" (Broadfoot et al., 2018, p. 124).

Culture is the keyword here. Listening can help locate the cultural aspects of public relations and resist the stridency of the material-obsessed voice of dominant public relations. It can also expose the self-congratulatory messages of dominant publics, so characteristic of mainstream public relations. The radical postcolonial thinker Frantz Fanon drew on cultural resistance to colonial oppression in his works as he exhorted colonized people to shun the proclaimed supremacy of European thought. In his celebrated book *Wretched of the Earth*, Fanon (1961/2004) uncovered the hypocritical accounts of enlightenment and progress of colonialist empires and showed how colonization had led to impoverishment, misery, and trauma in the colonized world. Fanon's argument has been extended by the postcolonial historian Dipesh Chakrabarty (2000/2008) who negates the primacy given to Western accounts of history by "provincializing" Europe and focusing instead on alternative histories of marginalized social groups, embodied, for example, in the works of the Subaltern Studies collective (Guha, 1982; see also, McKie & Munshi, 2007).

Although the colonial era has passed in temporal terms, oppressive economic and political regimes in contemporary times are not that different. As Dutta and Pal (2020) point out, "Continuous with the capitalist impulse that has historically formed the backbone of the colonial project, the spaces of livelihoods, material and symbolic creations, collective knowledge, and the bodies of communities in these extractive zones are the targets of global capital as it seeks ever-new frontiers of profiteering" (p. 349). What the articulations of subaltern publics reveal are alternative voices that remain unheard in dominant organizational theoretical formulations. Recognizing, acknowledging, and listening to these voices are part of alternative communication practices. As Cheney and Munshi (2017) say, alternative communication practices "function as alternative organizing itself, as when experimentation with different forms of *dialogue* – as genuinely interactive communication aimed at intersubjective understanding – and *participation,* become institutionalized in a new organization." Yet another aspect of alternative communication practices is the consideration of silence as an integral part of resistive communication: Such practices help "facilitate listening to the ways in which silence works in organizational settings, both as an expression of vulnerability in the face of exploitative power of dominant groups as well as an act of resistance against such power" (Cheney & Munshi, 2017). Indeed, Covarrubias and Windchief (2009) provide a deep account of how Native American groups use silence to not only express their identities but also to resist onslaughts against their cultural survival. In such a context, silence is also a way of resisting speech that expresses colonial ideologies.

Any future theorizing of organizational listening as a key feature of sustainable, equitable strategic communication must continue to address listening to silence. This is one aspect of reframing listening to foster a sense of reflexivity among communication practitioners so that they can review the dynamics of power embedded in communication practices they take for granted. Only then can public relations move away from its narrow vision of serving key or privileged stakeholders to becoming a process that fosters equity and diversity in organizational listening relationships, shifting the emphasis from the material to the cultural.

References

Broadfoot, K., Munshi, D., & Cruz, J. (2018). Releasing/translating agency: A postcolonial disruption/engagement of the master's voice among Liberian market women. In B. Brummans (Ed.), *The agency of organizing: Perspectives and case studies* (pp. 123–141). Routledge.

Chakrabarty, D. (2000/2008). *Provincializing Europe: Postcolonial thought and historical difference*. Princeton University Press.

Cheney, G., & Munshi, D. (2017). Alternative forms of organization and organizing. In C. R. Scott, & L. Lewis (Eds.), *The international encyclopedia of organizational communication* (pp. 59–68). Wiley-Blackwell.

Covarrubias, P., & Windchief, S. (2009). Silences in stewardship: Some American Indian college students examples. *The Howard Journal of Communications*, *20*(4), 333–352.

Cruz, J., & Sodeke, C. (2021). Debunking eurocentrism in organizational communication theory: Marginality and liquidities in postcolonial contexts. *Communication Theory*, *31*(3), 528–548.

Dutta, M., & Pal, M. (2011). Public relations and marginalization in a global context: A postcolonial critique. In N. Bardhan, & C. K. Weaver (Eds.), *Public relations in global cultural contexts: Multiparadigmatic perspectives* (pp. 195–225). Routledge.

Dutta, M., & Pal, M. (2020). Theorizing from the global South: Dismantling, resisting, and transforming communication theory. *Communication Theory*, *30*, 349–369.

Dutta, M. J., & Pal, M. (2010). Dialog theory in marginalized settings. A subaltern studies approach. *Communication Theory*, *20*, 363–386.

Fanon, F. (1961/2004). *Wretched of the Earth* (R. Philcox, trans.). Grove Press.

Giddens, A. (1984). *The constitution of society: Outline of the theory of structuration*. University of California Press.

Guha, R. (1982). *Subaltern studies I*. Oxford University Press.

Iverson, J., McPhee, R., & Spaulding, C. (2018). Being able to act otherwise: The role of agency in the four flows at 2-1-1 and beyond. In B. Brummans (Ed.), *The agency of organizing: Cases and perspectives*. Routledge.

Logan, N. (2021). A theory of corporate responsibility to race (CRR): Communication and racial justice in public relations. *Journal of Public Relations Research*, *33*(1), 6–22. https://doi.org/10.1080/1062726X.2021.1881898

McKie, D., & Munshi, D. (2007). *Reconfiguring public relations: Ecology, equity, and enterprise*. Routledge.

Munshi, D., & Kurian, P. (2005). Imperializing spin cycles: A postcolonial look at public relations, greenwashing, and the separation of publics. *Public Relations Review*, *31*(4), 513–520.

Munshi, D., & Kurian, P. (2021). *Public relations and sustainable citizenship*. Routledge.

Munshi, D., & Pal, M. (2018). Colonialism/postcolonialism. In R. L. Heath, & W. Johansen (Eds.), *The international encyclopedia of strategic communication*. John Wiley & Sons.

Place, K. R. (2015). Exploring the role of ethics in public relations program evaluation. *Journal of Public Relations Research*, *27*(2), 118–135.

Shome, R., & Hegde, R. (2002). Postcolonial approaches to communication: Charting the terrain, engaging the intersections. *Communication Theory*, *12*(3), 249–270.

Volk, S. C., & Buhmann, A. (2019). New avenues in communication evaluation and measurement (E&M): Towards a research agenda for the 2020s. *Journal of Communication Management*, *23*(3), 162–178. https://doi.org/10.1108/JCOM-08-2019-147

Index

Note: Page references in *italics* denote figures and in **bold** tables.

Accessibility to Voice (AV) 52, 56
accusational publics 275
active-empathic listening (AEL) 25, 36; example matrix of *28*; in interpersonal communication 29; responses 31; in social media 27–29; *see also* listening
actualized plurality 206–207; architecture of listening 200–201; and deliberative society 201–202; Hannah Arendt 204–209; literature 200–204; and organizational listening 201–202; organizational listening in public relations 200; pluralism in public relations 202–203; practical implications 209–212; presence in listening 203–204; propinquity and presence in public relations 203; theoretical implications 209–212; *see also* plurality
adversarial publics 275, 281
advocacy: corporate climate 157–174; corporate social 157–158; LGBTQ 219–229
advocational publics 275
affective dimension 105, 222
algorithmic filtering xxvi
Álvarez-Nobell, A. 260
Amazon 161–162; climate change and customer service 168–169; The Climate Pledge 161–162, 167, 173; climate-related posts **163**; positioning, as hero/leader 167–168; sweeping aside criticism and AECJ 170–173; as villain 170
Amazon.com 26

Amazon Employees for Climate Justice (AECJ) 4, 161–162; and criticism 170–173; posts **164**
ambassadorial publics 275
American South 142
appearance 206–207, 211
appreciative inquiry xxv
appreciative listening 105
architecture of listening xxii–xxiv, 38, 44, 46, 81, 83–84, 183, 200–201
Arendt, Hannah 4, 204–209; and plurality 204–205; plurality in organizational listening 209–212; plurality in public relations 209–212
Aristotle xviii
Arnold, C. L. 16
Arthur W. Page Society 2, 108
articulation xxiv, 291
artificial intelligence (AI) xxv, 63, 278, 288; communication systems 74–75; and organizational listening 63–65
attributes: defined 11; listening 11
audience 89–90; external 159; foreign 269, 271, 276; global 253; globalized 255; internal 159, 173; public 25, 204; target 90–91
authenticity 106, 148; and organizational listening 289; perceived, of LGBTQ communication 226; perceived organizational 71, 225
automated messages 33
automatic speech recognition (ASR) 64
Autozone 33

Back, L. xix
baked-in bias xxvi
Barclay, L. 50

Bardhan, N. R. 184, 196
Bartlett, J. 203
behavioral activation system 48
behavioral dimension 105
behavioral inhibition systems 48
behavioral insights xxv
Best Buy 26, 28
Bezos, Jeff 161
Bieber, M. 104
big data analytics 83
Bjola, C. 276
Black community: and churches 149; Fort Worth's policing issues in 143–147; and trust 152
Black Lives Matter 140, 189
Black residents: as minoritized publics 141; and municipalities 142–143, 148; OPRs between local government and 151; perceptions among 147–150
Bodie, G. D. 64
Boeing 737 Max 8 catastrophe 9
borders, listening across 269–283
Borner, M. 83, 159, 173
Botan, C. 43
Bowen, S. A. 106, 142, 183
Brandt, D. R. 125
British Government Communication Service (GCS) 89
Brock, P. 240
Brooks, Christina 147, 150
Broom, G. 105
Brose, Anna 18
Brown, K. A. 127
Brownell, J. 64
Buhmann, A. 89
Burger King 219
Burger King Austria 219
Burnside-Lawry, J. xxi–xxii, 11, 44, 46
Burris, E. R. 49

Cambridge Analytica scandal 9
Carey, James xvii
Carr, Ashley 150
Cathcart, R. 24
Chakrabarty, Dipesh 290
Chapek, Bob 219–220
chatbots xxv, 3, 278; AI-enabled social 65, 65–66; as organizational social listening tool 63–75; overview 63; perceived corporate character 71–72; perceived listening 69–70; perceived organizational transparency 70–71; social conversation 66–73; stakeholder communication 66
Chen, Z. F. 67
Cheney, G. 291
Chile 254, 260–262
Chun, R. 71
Cicero xviii
City Manager Mutual Accountability Group 147
Clark, S. C. 240
Claro, M. C. 182, 261
climate change 157–158, 168–169
Coakley, C. G. 46
cognitive dimension 104–105
collaborative public diplomacy 5, 270, 282
collectivistic culture 236–237, 239
commitment 222, 233; affective 173; defined 72; to LGBTQ communities 219; long-term 279; vs. trust 72
commtech xxvi, 75
communicare xviii
commūnicātiō xviii
communication: crisis 135; and culture 280; defined xvii; dialogical 158–161; employee (*see* employee communication); participatory employee (*see* participatory employee communication); post-discipline of xviii; speech xix; value of 85
Communication Ethics in Dark Times: Hannah Arendt's Rhetoric of Warning and Hope (Arnett) 204
communication management: and evaluation 85; organizational 237–238; teams 74; of workplace gender discrimination 234–235
communicative behavior 45, 122–123, 133, 235, 238–244
communis xviii
competency: organizational listening 25, 32, 46, 56–57; organizational response 30–32
complex societies xix
comprehensive listening 105, 117
computer vision (CV) 64
Confucianism 236
contemporary agonism 202
conversational human voice (CHV) 66–69, 71
Cooper, L. O. 45, 46

corporate character 71–72
corporate climate advocacy 157–158; and climate change 157–158; and corporate social advocacy 157–158; organizational social listening and 157–174
corporate culture 11, 232, 235–237, 243
corporate social advocacy 157–158
corporate social responsibility (CSR) 157–158
Cortina, L. M. 240
Costa, Maren 161
Couldry, Nick xix
Covarrubias, P. 291
COVID-19 pandemic 81, 124, 146, 150, 158, 191
Craig, Jacqueline 144–145
Craig, Robert xix
Crawford, K. 243
Crick, N. 64
crisis: climate 157–158, 161, 174; communication 135; of democracy xxvi; Ebola 279; of listening 103; social media 81; socio-political, in Chile 261; trust 260
critical listening 105, 117
cross-cultural: differences in organizational management 235, 243; perspective 232; surveys 243
Cull, N. J. 271
cultural values 236; role of 235; Western 236
culture(s) 142–143, 227, 290; business masculinity 237; collectivistic 236–237, 239; and communication 280; corporate 11, 232, 235–237, 243; ethical 182; gay 222; and gender equality 235; higher power distance 239, 244; individualistic 239; lower power distance 239; organizational xxiv, 42, 89, 125, 182, 227, 237; patriarchal 236; and social norms 235, 243
Cunningham, Emily 161
customer journey mapping xxv
Cutlip, S. M. 89

Das, G. 35
data analytics xxv
dataveillance xxvi
Davidson, S. 202
Dean, Aaron 146, 150
deliberative democracy 202

deliberative polling xxv
deliberative society, and organizational listening 201–202
democracy 259–261; crisis of xxvi; deliberative 202
DeSantis, Ron 220
designated organizational listeners 190–191
Detert, J. R. 49
Deutsche Public Relations Gesellschaft/International Controller Association (DPRG/ICV) framework 89
Dewey, John xvii
Dhanesh, G. S. 203
dialogical communication 158–161
dialogical listening 278–279
dialogic employee communication 42–44
dialogue xviii, 160; and external stakeholders 16; with stakeholders 37; technical 31
digital diplomacy 277
digitalization 81, 83, 255
digital media 253, 255; and feminist activists 256; and foreign publics 269; governments' use of 277; platforms 282; and tactical listening in public diplomacy 276–277
digital technologies 256
Di Martino, L. 272–273
discrimination: formal 240; informal 240; workplace 232, 233, 235, 240, 243; workplace gender 234–235
discriminative listening 105
Disney 220, 227; LGBTQIA+ Business Employee Resource Group 228
Disney World 220
distrust 254, 258; universal 259
diversity 4, 183–185; defined 184; in public relations 184; racial 193–194
diversity, equity, and inclusion (DE&I) 4, 183–185; analysis 186–187; designated organizational listeners 190–191; employee resource groups (ERGs) 189–190; formal surveys and meetings 187–189; grassroots organizing lens 191–192; listening futility 192–194; organizational listening for 181–196; procedure 186; sampling and recruitment 186
Dobson, Andrew xx

"Don't Say Gay" bill (Florida) 220, 228
Dozier, D. M. 240
Dutta, M. 290–291

Ebola crisis 278–279
echo chambers xxvi
efficacy, and employee silence 48
Embrain 240
emojis 33, **34**, 34–35, 37
empathy 28–31, 43, 71, 105–106, 148–149, 187
employee activism 160–161
employee communication: defined 42; dialogic 42–44; participatory (*see* participatory employee communication)
employee-organization relationships (EORs) 41, 47
employee resource groups (ERGs) 189–190
employees: behaviors 238–239; empowerment of 173, 232, 238–244; LGBTQ 189, 220, 221, 229
employee silence: causes of 48–50; *vs.* employee voice 48; participatory employee communication 47–50; understanding 47–48
empowerment: of employees 173, 232, 238–244; perceived 238–242
engagement approach to listening 278–279
Engstrom, C. L. 184, 196
environmental scanning 3, 106, 124
equity 91, 183–185; racial 194–195; social 185, 227; *see also* diversity, equity, and inclusion (DE&I)
ESPN 220
ethical listening 103–119; effective 112–115; findings 109–116; method 107–109; overview 103; theoretical bases of listening 103–107
ethics: and limits of plurality 207–209; of listening xxvi
The Ethics of Listening: Creating Space for Sustainable Dialogue (Parks) 204
evaluation: defined 85; formative 87; foundations of 85–88; methods, of organizational listening 91–92; of organizational listening 88–91; process 87; relevance, for organizational listening 83–85; summative 87
evaluation model 88–91; impacts 91; inputs 90; outcomes 90–91; outputs 90
excellence theory 159, 256–257
Explanation of Voice Procedure and Outcomes (EVPO) 55, 56
external listening: channels for 106–107; theory and strategy for 106
external stakeholders: building relationships 17–18; conceptualizations of organizational listening 9–19; and dialogue 16; and ethical listening 103–119; use of social media 17; *see also* stakeholders

Facebook 9, 32, 33, 162, 167, 277
Fair Procedure to Voice (FPV) 55, 56
fake listening 83, 272
feedback 9, 11, 25–26; from community members 141; customer 125; external stakeholders 64, 107, 123; internal stakeholders 64, 123; loops 92, 118; mechanism 50, 174, 183, 289; from the public 159; from VOC 104
Ferguson, M. A. 257
Ferrari, M. A. 257
filter bubbles xxvi
Financial Times 220
Fitzgerald, Joel 145
Fitzpatrick, K. R. 271, 274–275
Floyd, George 140, 150, 189
Flynn, J. 44
formal discrimination 240
formal surveys and meetings 187–189
formative evaluation 87
Fort Worth, Texas: Atatiana Jefferson, killing of 145–147; background 144; Black community, policing issues in 143–147; communication efforts 145–147; Jacqueline Craig's arrest and activist community 144–145; Task Force on Race and Culture 145
Fort Worth Police Department 146–147, 150–151
functionalism 257–258

Gambetta, D. 259
gay culture 222
Gearhart, C. C. 11, 15

gender 184–185; identity 4, 186, 221; inequality 233, 240–241, 244; minorities 221–229; workplace discrimination 234–235; *see also* LGBTQ
gender equality 5, 235–236, 240; and culture 235; and workplace gender discrimination 235–236
Giddens, Anthony 290
GIFs 33, 34, **34**, 37
GLAAD (LGBTQ American NGO) 223
Glenn, E. xxi
Global Climate Strike 161
globalization 253, 255, 257
global listening 219–220
global mass publics 274
global media 254–256
Global North 254, 256, 257
global publics 254–256
Google Trends 278
government listening 127, 142–143, 153, 272–282
grassroots organizing lens 191–192
Gregory, A. 24, 89
Gretry, A. 68
Grimes, Christopher 220
Grunig, J. E. 126
Gumpert, G. 24

Hall, Todrick 223
Han, S. 67
hearing *vs.* listening xx–xxi, 64, 66, 133
historically marginalized publics 219–229
Hobbes, Thomas xviii
Hofstede, G. 237, 280
Honneth, A. xxiv
The Human Condition (Arnett) 205
Husband, C. xxiv, 204

imminent strategic publics 274
Imperfect Foods 32
implicit theory of organizational listening 11–12
inclusion 4, 183–185; barriers for 210; defined 184; *see also* diversity, equity, and inclusion (DE&I)
individualistic culture 239
inequality: gender 233, 240–241, 244; income 260
informal discrimination 240
information acquisition 12

information war 270
Institute for Public Relations 181
intelligence: artificial 63–65, 278, 288; emotional 74; listening 85, 91, 93
intentionality 206
intentional listening 35
interactive communicator 45
International Association for the Measurement and Evaluation of Communication (AMEC) 89
International Journal of Listening xxi, 24
International Listening Association (ILA) 159
interpersonal factors, and employee silence 49
interpersonal listening: mediated listening responses 33–35; and organizations 25–27; overview 24–25; practices in social media 24–38; *see also* listening
intersectionality 125, 185, 226
issues management 83; effective 116–117; external listening 106; and (social) media monitoring 277–278

James, William xxi
Janusik, L. A. 45
Jefferson, Atatiana 3, 140, 141, 144; and Fort Worth's communication efforts 145–147; killing of 145–147
Ji, Y. G. 72
Jim Crow 142
Jimenez-Martinez, C. 281
Jimmy Choo 27
Jung von Matt Donau 219

Kaplún, G. 258
Kelleher, T. 68, 141
Kent, M. L. 31, 123, 203, 256
Ki, E. J. 127
Kim, J.-N. 126, 274–275
Kraus, Ed 146
Kurian, P. 290

Laclau, Ernesto 208
Lane, A. 31, 203
"Language of Diversity" report 181
Latin America 260; perspective on listening 256–258; social and political trust in 258–260
Lawrence, K. 141
Ledingham, J. A. 257

Lee, E.-J. 66
Lee, S. 255
Lee, Y. 184, 240
Legitimacy of Employee Voice and Perspective (LEVP) 55, 56
Lerbinger, O. 106
L'Etang, J. L. 280
Lewis, Laurie 9, 103, 222
Lexis-Nexis 144
LGBTQ: community 191; employees 189, 220, 221, 229; media and representation 221–222; Pride campaign 223; publics 4, 221–222, 227, 229, 289
LGBTQ advocacy: implications 227–229; perceived organizational listening in 219–229
LGBTQ public relations 221–224; LGBTQ employees 221; LGBTQ media and representation 221–222; organizational listening 222; research 223–224
Liebrecht, C. 68
The Life of the Mind (Arnett) 205
Likely, F. 89
Lindenmann, W. 89
listening: across borders 269–283; approaches to 275–279; architecture of 183, 200–201; attributes 11; benefits and necessity of xxvi; defined 1, 63–64, 234; dialogic and engagement approaches to 278–279; dimensions 104–105; ethics of xxvi; futility 192–194; government 127, 142–143, 153, 272–282; *vs.* hearing xx–xxi, 64, 66, 133; to historically marginalized publics 219–229; Latin American perspective on 256–258; organizational social 157–174; and participatory employee communication 45; in polarized times 199–212; politics of xxiv, 143, 152, 183; presence in 203–204; in public diplomacy 269–271, *270*, *271*; and structural racism 141–143; systems xxiv–xxv; and systems theory 105–106; theoretical bases of 103–107; training 36; and trust 141–143
listening agents/trainers 35–36
listening competency: defined 45–46; organizational 25, 32, 46, 56–57
Listening Concepts Inventory (LCI) 11–12, 15

Logan, N. 184
logos xviii
Loidolt, S. 204, 206–208
Lowe's 26
Lu, B. 67
Luhmann, N. 105

Maben, S. K. 11, 15
Macnamara, J. 4, 10, 17–19, 24, 38, 44, 46, 64, 66, 69, 83, 89, 103, 105, 106–107, 142, 173, 182, 183, 185, 200, 205, 210, 223, 227, 243, 253–254, 256, 262, 272, 280; definition of organizational listening 122–123; organization-centric motivations for listening 134
management cycle 86, *87*
Managerial Listening Survey (MLS) 46
manipulative consultation 279
Marroquín Velásquez, L. 257
masspersonal communication model (MPCM) 24–26
Mattes, R. 259
Mazumdar, B. T. 277
measurement 86; qualitative 276; quantitative 276; reliability 52
media: digital (*see* digital media); global 254–256; social (*see* social media)
(social) media monitoring 277–278
media richness theory 34
mediated listening responses 33–35; emojis 33, **34**, 34–35; GIFs 33, 34, **34**; memes 33, 34, **34**
Meesters, M. 134
memes 33, 34, **34**
Men, L. R. 67, 68, 69, 72, 73, 240
meta-evaluations 87–88
#MeToo movement 236
Milliken, F. J. 49
Moon, B. B. 126
Moreno, A. 259
Morrison, E. W. 48, 49
Mouffe, Chantal 208
Munshi, D. 290, 291

National Black Trans Advocacy Coalition 223
natural language processing (NLP) 64
Neal, Kim 147, 150
Neill, M. S. 183
neo-pluralism 202
Newberry, C. 16

Noakes, Neil 150
"No Label" campaign (Absolut) 222
non-LGBTQ publics 221
Nordstrom 26

Old Navy 26
organizational communication management 237–238
organizational culture xxiv, xxiv, 42, 89, 125, 182, 227, 237
Organizational Employee Listening Competency (OELC) model 3, 41–42, 47; components of 50–51; diagnostic scale development 51–56, **53–54**; dimensions of 52–55, 56; and employee silence motives 55–56; steps for assessing 57
organizational factors, and employee silence 49–50
organizational justice 49–50
organizational listening xix, 158–161, 182, 234–235; and artificial intelligence 63–65; challenges of xx; characteristics of xx; definitions of xxi–xxii, 83; and deliberative society 201–202; for diversity, equity, and inclusion 181–196; effectiveness **110**, 110–112, *111–112*; and empowered women in workplace 232–244; evaluation of 88–91; examples of effective 112–115; external stakeholders conceptualizations of 9–19; future research of 288–291; goals and motivations for 130–131; implicit theory of 11–12; LGBTQ public relations 222; overview 10–11; from perspectives of stakeholders 122–124; and plurality in public relations 209–212; and practitioners 124–125; in public relations 200; relevance of evaluating 83–85; stakeholders expectations for 29–30; technology tools utilized for 115–116; *see also* listening
organizational listening competency 25, 32, 46, 56–57
Organizational Listening Project xxii–xxiv, **xxiii,** 200, 243
Organizational Listening: The Missing Essential in Public Communication (Macnamara) 200
Organizational Listening: The Missing Link in Public Communication (Macnamara) xxii

organizational response competency 30–32
organizational silence 47–48
organizational social listening 157–174
organizational social media listening 26–27
organizational speaking 253
organizational transparency: components of 70; perceived 70–71
organization-public dialogic communication (OPDC) 43–44
organization-public relationships (OPRs) 72–73

Pacher, A. 274
Pal, M. 290–291
Parker, Mattie 150
Parks, E. S. 185, 204
participatory action research (PAR) xxv
participatory employee communication 41; challenges for 44–50; dialogic employee communication 42–44; employee silence 47–50; organizational listening competency 45–47; understanding listening 45
parvenu 204, 210
passive collaboration 279
patriarchal culture 236
Peoples, Deborah 145
perceived corporate character 71–72
perceived empowerment 238–242
perceived listening 69–70
perceived organizational listening 65–66, 69–70, 72, *74*, **224**; in LGBTQ advocacy 219–229
perceived organizational transparency 70–71
perceptions among Black residents 147–150
Phenomenology of Plurality: Hannah Arendt on Political Intersubjectivity (Loidolt) 204
Piñera, Sebastián 260–261
Pixar 220
Place, K. R. 125, 183, 184, 185, 210, 222
Plato xviii
pluralism 199, 202; and plurality 207; power-aware 202; in public relations 202–203; pure 202; radical 202
plurality 199; ethics and limits of 207–209; and Hannah Arendt

204–205; in organizational listening 209–212; and pluralism 207; in public relations 209–212
policies xxiv, 1–2, 18, 46–47; and climate of silence 50; government-sanctioned 141; and LGBTQ communication 227; listening 182–183; racist 148; social media 36
policing 140–143, 145, 149–150
political trust 258–260
Politics (Aristotle) xviii
politics of listening xxiv, 143, 152, 183; *see also* listening
Pompper, D. 202
post-discipline of communication xviii
power-aware pluralism 202
The Power of Strategic Listening (Lewis) 9
practitioners: interviews 129–133; and organizational listening 124–125; surveys 125–130
presence: in listening 203–204; in public relations 203
Price, Betsy 146–147, 150
Pride campaigns 219
Pride Whopper 219
process evaluation 87
The Promise of Politics (Arnett) 205
propinquity in public relations 203
protocollary strategic publics 274
pseudo listening 143, 272
psychological safety, and employee silence 48
public diplomacy: approaches to 269–271; digital media use for tactical listening in 276–277; and listening 269–271; listening process model in *270*
public diplomacy listening: approaches 275–279; critical reflections on 280–281; purposes 271–273; recommendations for practice 281–282
public information model 35
public relations: dialogic principles of 42; LGBTQ 221–224; listening-informed 4; organizational listening in 200; pluralism in 202–203; plurality in 209–212; professionals 121; propinquity and presence in 203; *see also* organization-public relationships (OPRs)

Public Relations Society of America (PRSA) 108
publics 1, 3–5, 42–44, 63, 66–67, 72–74; accusational 275; adversarial 275, 281; advocational 275; ambassadorial 275; global 254–256; global mass 274; identifying and segmenting 273–275; imminent strategic 274; LGBTQ 4, 221–222, 227, 229, 289; non-LGBTQ 221; protocollary strategic 274; remote strategic 274; salient 274
pure pluralism 202

RACE formula 86
racial equity 194–195
racism, structural 141–143, 151–152
radical pluralism 202
Rainbow campaigns 219
relationship building 12
relationship management 5, 106, 253, 257, 269
remote strategic publics 274
resources xxiv, 1, 10, 41, 46, 122, 125, 142, 173, 201–202; external 65; fair distribution of 184; monetary 72
rhetoric xviii
ROPE formula 86

Sadi, G. 257
Sahay, S. 125, 182
salient publics 274
Sanchez, J. I. 240
satisfaction 73; affective 73; job 233–234; of listening insights 91; stakeholder 19
sense making methodology xxv
sexual orientation 4, 219, 221, 223, 225–226
Sha, B. 105
Shaffer, M. A. 240
Shannon, C. xvii
Sharma, P. 240
Shin, S. Y. 66
skills/competencies xxiv; *see also* competency
Skittles 223, 226
Smith, James 140
social chatbots *65*, 65–66
social equity 185, 227
social media 2, 158–161; active-empathic listening in 27–29; analytics 37; automated messages

33; and external stakeholders 17; interpersonal listening practices in 24–38; listening agents/trainers 35–36; policies 36; response 36–37
social presence 66–69
social trust 258–260
society, deliberative 201–202
Somma, N. M. 261
source, message, channel, receiver (SMCR) model xvii
South Korea 236–237; workplace gender discrimination 236–237, 244
speech communication xix
stakeholders: centric goals **131**; co-orientating with 132–133; defined 273; dialogue with 37; engagement 18, 256; external, conceptualizations of organizational listening 9–19; interviews 129–133; listening to 2; mapping and choice of channels 131–132; and organizational listening 29–30, 122–124; surveys 125–130; surveys on use of social media 32–33
Stewart, M. C. 16
strategic communication 85–86; CHV 67–69; future research of 288–291
strategic listening 103, 104
structural racism 151–152; and listening 141–143; and trust 141–143
structured listening 84
subjectivity 206
summative evaluation 87
Sung, Y. 72
Sweetser, K. D. 68
systematic listening 83–84
systems xxiv, 228; behavioral activation 48; behavioral inhibition 48; cultural 5; democratic 272; political/social 272; sociopolitical 5
systems theory 3; and listening 105–106

tactical listening 272, 276–277, 282
Tam, L. 274–275
Taylor, M. 123, 203, 256
technical dialogue 31
technologies xxiv, 37–38, 46, 55, 122, 173–174; AI-powered communication 64–65, 74–75; digital and network 254, 256; tools 115–116; video conferencing 182
Tindall, N. T. J. 221
Toledano, M. 221
toxic tech xxvi
traditional diplomatic actors 274
Transparent Communication Manner (TCM) 52, 56
Triana, M. D. C. 233
trust: and Black community 152; *vs.* commitment 72; defined 72; and listening 141–143; political 258–260; social 258–260; and structural racism 141–143
Twitter 277

uncertainty 237, 256
universal distrust 259
unstructured/explorative listening 84
USAID 279

value of communication 85
van Hooijdonk, C. 68
van Noort, G. 68
Vardeman-Winter, J. 184
Vásquez, C. 257
Viertmann, C. 85
voice: conversational human 66–69, 71; defined xix; employee 48
voice of the consumer (VOC) 104
voice to text (VTT) software programs 104
Volk, S. C. 89
vox populi (voice of the people) xix

Waisbord, S. xviii
The Wakeman Agency 181
Walt Disney Co. 220, 227
Ward, S. J. A. 103
Wasserman, H. 103
Waters, R. D. 221
Waymer, D. 142
Weaver, W. xvii
Web 2.0 70, 75, 243
Weimar Germany 208
Western, Educated, Industrialized, Rich, and Democratic (WEIRD) societies 19
Western cultural values 236
Whiteside, D. B. 50
Willemsen, L. M. 68
Williams, Raymond xvii
Windchief, S. 291
Wolvin, A. D. 46
Women's March 208
Working Memory model 45
workplace: discrimination 232, 233, 235, 240, 243; empowered women in

232–244; and organizational listening 232–244
workplace gender discrimination 5, 233; communication management of 234–235; employee behaviors 238–239; and gender equality 235–236; organizational communication management 237–238; and organizational listening 234–235; South Korea 236–237, 244

Wretched of the Earth (Fanon) 290
Wrigley 223
Wu, D. 277

Yang, A. 277
Yang, S. U. 43–44, 126

Zaharna, R. S. 279
Zerfass, A. 83, 85, 159, 173
Zhang, J. 277–278
Zhao, X. 124